Lyndon B. Johnson School of Public Affairs
Policy Research Project Report
Number 89

Financing Community Care for the Chronically Mentally Ill in Texas

Sponsored by the
Hogg Foundation for Mental Health
and the
Commission on the Community
Care of the Mentally Ill

A report by the
Policy Research Project
on Financing Care for the
Chronically Mentally Ill in Texas
1990

Library of Congress Number: 90-63816
ISBN: 0-89940-697-1

© 1990 by the Board of Regents
The University of Texas

Printed in the U.S.A.

Project Participants

Students

Jana S. Blasi, B.A. (Political Science), North Texas State University

Charles Blissett, Ph.D. (Pharmacy/Microbiology), University of Florida at Gainsville

Hugh F. Crean, B.A. (Psychology), St. Michaels College

Pamela M. Diamond, M.A. (Psychology), Texas Women's University

Kathleen A. Fahey, A.B. (Psychology), Occidental College

Minh Ly Griffin, B.A. (Plan II), The University of Texas at Austin

Joellen M. Harper, B.A. (Economics and Government), Skidmore College

Nicholas L. Hoover, B.A. (Sociology), Trinity University

Ronnie G. Jung, B.B.A. (Accounting), The University of Texas at Austin

Carolina L. Martinez, B.A. (Political Science, Psychology), Pan American University

Lynn Parish, B.A., University of Pennsylvania

Janice Rienstra, B.A., (Chemistry), The University of Texas at Austin

Norma Rodriguez, B.A. (Psychology), The University of Texas at Austin

Timothy J. Tompkins, B.A. (Spanish, Business), Appalachian State University and The University of Madrid, Spain

Rudolfo R. Vega, B.A. (Psychology), San Jose State University

Project Directors
David Warner, Ph.D., Professor, Lyndon B. Johnson School of Public Affairs

L. Connie Harris, Ph.D., Participating Faculty, Hogg Foundation for Mental Health (Fall 1988)

Scott Kier, Ph.D., Participating Faculty, Hogg Foundation for Mental Health (Spring 1989)

Reymundo Rodriguez, M.Ed., M.P.A., Participating Faculty, Hogg Foundation for Mental Health

Contents

Foreword xix

Preface xxi

Acknowledgments xxiii

Chapter 1. The Evolution of Texas Public Mental Health Policy:
            The Past as Prologue 1

            Introduction 1
            Origins of Public Responsibility for Persons
               with Mental Illness 2
            Public Mental Health Care in Texas: 1856-1963 3
            Public Mental Health Care in Texas: 1963-1988 7
            The Organization of Texas Public Mental Health Services ... 11
            Report Overview 13
            References 15

SECTION ONE: CLIENTS 19

Chapter 2. The Texas Public Mental Health System: Patterns of Use from
            Fiscal Years 1984 through 1988 21
            The Inpatient System 21
            The Community-Based System 23
            Policy and Procedural Issues Affecting the Entire System ... 23
            Client Assignment and Registration (CARE) 29
            Overview of the Inpatient Public Mental Health System
               in Texas from FY 1984 to FY 1988 30
                  Facility-Based Data 30
                  Client-Based Data 38
            The Population of the Public Inpatient System
               on August 31, 1988 38
            Recidivism in the Texas Mental Health System 43
            Clients Using the Inpatient Mental Health System From September
               1, 1983, through August 31, 1988 47
            A Closer Look at Some of the High Users of the System 51
                  Old-Timers 51
                  High-Users 52
            An Overview of the Community-Based Mental Health
               System in Texas 53
            Further Considerations 58
            Conclusions 60
            Appendix 2.1. Admissions to Inpatient Facilities -
               FY 1984 through FY 1988 64
            References 72

Chapter 3. Minority Populations 75
            Overview of the Literature for Mexican-Americans 75
                  Utilization Rates Have Not Been Age-Adusted ... 76
                  Lower Frequency and Severity of Mental Illness ... 77
                  Alternate Sources of Treatment 77

Barriers Which Inhibit Utilization of
        Mental Health Services 78
    Sources of Data 80
        Procedures 80
        Utilization of Mental Health Services by Hispanics . . . 80
        Utilization of Mental Health Services by Blacks
            in Texas 82
        Black Clients at TDMHMR Facilities 83
        Black Clients at TDMHMR Community Mental Health
            Facilities 84
    Demographics 85
        Population Projections 85
    Conclusions 87
    Appendix 3.1. Definition of Terms (Data Books,
        1982-1986). 88
    References 89

Chapter 4.   The Criminal Justice System and Its Impact on the Mentally Ill 93
    Recent History 93
    Local Systems 95
        Mental Health Deputies Units 96
    County Jails 102
    Vernon State Hospital's Maximum Security Unit 104
    Texas Adult Probation Commission 105
    Texas Board of Pardons and Paroles 107
    Texas Department of Corrections 111
    Interagency Council on Mentally Retarded, Developmentally
        Disabled, and Mentally Ill Offenders 122
    The 71st Legislature's Impact on the Mentally Ill Offender . . 126
    Conclusions 127
    References 129

SECTION TWO: SERVICES 133

Chapter 5.   Crisis Response Services 135
    24-Hour Emergency Screening and Assessment 136
        Crisis Hot Line 136
        Crisis Intervention Team 137
        Multidisciplinary Assessment 137
    Structured Crisis Residential Services 138
    Other Approaches to Crisis Residential Services 142
        Individual Approach 142
        Group Approach 145
    References 151

Chapter 6.   Psychosocial Rehabilitation 153
    Social Support Activities 153
    Independent Living Skills 154
    Vocational Skills Development 154
        Prevocational Training 155
        Vocational Training 155
        Sheltered Employment 155
        Stations in Industry 156
        Transitional Employment 156
    Availability of Psychosocial Rehabilitation 156
    Conclusions 157

References 159

Chapter 7. Case Management 161
            Case Management in Texas 162
                Structural Organization of Case Management 164
                Funding for Case Management 165
                Who Receives Case Management? 171
                Case Management in Action 175
                Effectiveness of the Case Management Program 175
                Future Changes in Texas Case Management 177
            Expansion of the Texas Medicaid Plan to Include
                Case Management 178
                Limitations to Reimbursement 178
                State Medicaid Plan Amendment Process 179
                Potential Benefits for Case Management 181
            Conclusions 182
            Appendix 7.1. Case Management Assessment Form 183
            References 187

Chapter 8. Family Support Services 189
            The Economic Burden on Families 189
            Legislative Mandate for Family Support Services 189
            Family Support: A Model Program 190
            Respite Care 191
            Conclusions 192
            References 193

Chapter 9. Medication-Related Services 195
            Community Mental Health and Mental Retardation Centers .. 195
                Medication Clinic 195
                Laboratory Monitoring and Physical Examinations 195
                Medication Education 195
                Mental Health Maintenance, Education, and Counseling 196
                Medication Provision 196
            State Mental Hospitals 196
            Provider Recommendations 197

Chapter 10. Continuity of Care 199
            Coordination Between Hospital and Community Services 199
            Coordination Within and Among Community Services 201
            References 202

Chapter 11. Residential Services and Other Community Housing Alternatives
            for Persons with Chronic Mental Illness 203
            Types of Residential Services 204
            Funding for Residential Services and Other Housing 205
            Community-Based Residential Programs in Texas 206
            Conclusions 211
            References 212

Chapter 12. Income Support Programs 213
            SSDI and SSI Programs 213
                Disability Determination 213
                Eligibility for SSI 215
                Eligibility for SSDI 216
                Benefit Levels 218

vii

How Many Persons with Mental Illness
    Use SSI and SSDI? 219
Problems with SSI and SSDI for the CMI 220
SSI Supplementation 221
The Food Stamp Program in Texas: Implications for the
    Chronically Mentally Ill 223
Eligibility and Benefits 223
Food Stamps and the CMI 225
The In-Home and Family Support Program 226
Use of 1154 232
Future Directions of 1154 233
Potential Problems 233
Conclusions 234
References 236

SECTION THREE: FINANCING TRENDS AND ARRANGEMENTS 239

Chapter 13.   Texas Department of Mental Health and Mental Retardation 243
Operations 244
Action of the 71st Texas Legislature 245
Reaction of the Court-Appointed Monitor 246
Funding Process 246
The Class Action Suit 246
The $35.50 Program 247
The Incentive Diversion Program 249
    Has the $35.50 Program Been a Success? 250
    New Funds for the Community Programs 253
Conclusions 253
References 257

Chapter 14.   Community Mental Health and Mental Retardation Centers 259
Purpose 259
Contracting 259
Administration 263
Operations 263
Total Revenues for Mental Health and Mental Retardation . . 266
Local Tax Effort 266
Bonding Authority 268
Other State Agency Revenue 269
Mental Health Revenues 272
Financial Condition of the Community Centers 272
    Liquidy 273
    Debt 273
    Investments in Fixed Assets 273
Conclusions 273
Appendix 14.1. Explanation of the Derivation of
    Financial Data 276
Appendix 14.2. List of Audited Financial Reports of
    the CMHMRCs and TDMHMR, and Unaudited Reports
    of TDMHMR-Operated Facilities Used in the
    Compilation of Financial Data 285
References 289

Chapter 15.   Federal Revenue Sources 291
Federal Block Grants 291

Alcohol Drug Abuse and Mental Health
    Block Grant 291
Stewart B. McKinney Homeless Assistance Act
    Block Grant 297
Medicaid Expansion: Implication for the CMI in Texas 298
    Expansion Options for Texas 299
    Areas of Possible Expansion 302
    Proposals to Amend the Texas State
        Medicaid Plan 306
    State Medicaid Plan Amendment Process 308
    Control of Private Sector Participation 310
    Potential Problems if Amendments Are Approved 312
Conclusions 313
References 314

Chapter 16. The Role of Voluntary Organizations in Financing Care for
the Chronically Mentally Ill 317
Direct Volunteerism 317
Major Voluntary Organizations 318
    National Foundations: The Robert Wood
        Johnson Foundation 319
    Hogg Foundation for Mental Health 321
    The United Way 321
    The Mental Health Association 323
    The Texas Alliance for the Mentally Ill 324
    The Salvation Army 324
    The Disciple Outreach for the Mentally Ill 326
Conclusions 327
References 328

Chapter 17. Conclusions and Recommendations 331
Increase Funding 333
Long-Term Community-Based Care 335
Organize the System to Provide Long-Term
    Community-Based Services 335
Financing Mechanism to Support Long-Term
    Community Care 336
System-Wide Accountability Standards and
    Performance Incentives 338
References 340

List of Tables

Table 1.1.   State Lunatic Asylum of Texas: 1878 Admissions
              Report of Supposed Cause of Insanity of
              Admissions Since September 1, 1877 3

Table 1.2.   Diagnoses of All Mental Patients in State
              Hospitals as of August 31, 1952 6

Table 1.3.   Daily Census, Admissions to, and Costs Per Client in Texas
              State Hospitals in 1973 and 1975 9

Table 2.1.   Geographic Area and Population Density for the
              35 Community Mental Health Centers in Texas 25

Table 2.2.   Geographic Area and Population Density for the State
              Hospital and State Center Community
              Outreach Regions 28

Table 2.3.   Admissions to Inpatient Facilities from
              September 1, 1983, through August
              31, 1988 31

Table 2.4.   Clients in Residence at a State Inpatient
              Facility on August 31, 1988, Who Had Been
              Admitted for That Episode During the Past
              Five Years 39

Table 2.5.   Clients in Residence at TDMHMR Inpatient
              Facilities as of August 31, 1988, with
              Admission after September 1, 1983, and
              a Community Center Assignment: Agreement
              between Inpatient and Community Center
              Diagnoses 41

Table 2.6.   Clients in Residence at a State Inpatient
              Facility on August 31, 1988, with a
              Record of Residence for at least Five
              Consecutive Years 42

Table 2.7.   A Comparison of Admission Data from the
              Period FY 1977 through 1982 with That
              from FY 1983 through 1988 45

Table 2.8.   A Comparison of Bed Day Usage Patterns for the
              Period FY 1977 through FY 1982 with FY 1984
              through FY 1988 46

Table 2.9.   A Comparison of Average Lengths of Stay for Clients
              Admitted during FY 1977-1982 and FY 1983-1988 48

Table 2.10.   Demographics for Clients Admitted into the Public
              System from FY 1984 through FY 1988 49

Table 2.11. Demographic Information on Active Community Center
Clients 55

Table 2.12. Survey Information from a Representative Sample of Mental
Health Clients from Community Facilities 56

Table 3.1 Unduplicated Total Number of Clients Served at
TDMHMR Inpatient Facilities by Ethnicity During
FY 1984-1988 81

Table 4.1. Behavioral Elements Attracting Police Attention
(n=337) 94

Table 4.2. Source of Contacts for the Galveston County Mental
Health Deputies Unit 97

Table 4.3. Reasons for Referral to the Galveston County Mental
Health Deputies Unit 98

Table 4.4. Disposition of Contacts for the Galveston County
Mental Health Deputies Unit 99

Table 4.5. Summary Statistics for Travis County Mental
Health Deputies Unit, January through
July 1989 99

Table 4.6. Legislative Appropriations to the Texas Adult
Probation Commission for FY 1988 105

Table 4.7. Texas Adult Probation Commission Average Cost
per Day per Client (FY 1988) 106

Table 4.8. Estimated Numbers of Those Paroled with a Moderate
to Severe Emotional Problem and Recidivism
Rates for Those with an Emotional Problem
versus Those without Emotional Problem (FY 1988) . . 108

Table 4.9. Texas Board of Pardons and Paroles Release
Population by Levels of Supervision and
Recidivism Rates for Those Classifications
during FY 1988 109

Table 4.10. Average FY 1988 Cost per Day per Client of the Texas
Board of Pardons and Paroles 110

Table 4.11. Texas Board of Pardons and Paroles Agency Expenditures
for FY 1988 110

Table 4.12. Capacity, Location, and Average Daily Population
of TDC's Four Inpatient Programs 112

Table 4.13. Special-Needs Offender Frequency Distribution for
Major Texas Counties 113

Table 4.14.   Sampling Procedure Utilized in Special-Needs Offender
                Study 113

Table 4.15.   Projected Number of Initial Transfer Recommendations
                Based on a Total July 1988 TDC Population
                of 38,000 115

Table 4.16.   Projected Number of Initial Transfer Recomendations
                Based on a Total TDC Population of 49,412 118

Table 4.17.   Projected Number of Annual Transfer Recommendations
                Based on a Total July 1988 TDC Population
                of 38,000 118

Table 4.18.   Projected Number of Annual Transfer Recommendations
                Based on a Total TDC Population of 49,412 119

Table 4.19.   Report on Inpatient Services at Ellis II (TDC) 121

Table 4.20.   Texas Department of Corrections Total Appropriations
                and Funds Appropriated for Serving the
                CMI for FY 1988 121

Table 4.21.   Agencies Comprising the Interagency Council on
                Mentally Retarded, Developmentally Disabled,
                and Mentally Ill Offenders 123

Table 4.22.   Specified Biennium Funding for Agencies Associated
                with the Interagency Council on Mentally
                Retarded, Developmentally Disabled, and
                Mentally Ill Offenders 123

Table 5.1.   Characteristics of Residential Programs Based on
                Services Definitions FY 1988 Structured
                Residential Programs 139

Table 5.2.   Structured Crisis Residential and Respite
                Beds, FY 1988 141

Table 5.3.   Alternative Home Program of the Southwest Denver
                Mental Health Center, Denver, Colorado 143

Table 5.4.   Alternative Home Program of Crossing Place,
                Wooley House, Washington, D.C. 146

Table 5.5.   PATH (Positive Alternatives to Hospitalization)
                Apalachee Center for Human Services,
                Tallahassee, Florida 147

Table 5.6.   Comparison of Alternative Programs and Hospitals 148

Table 5.7.   Residential Services--Capacity and Cost
                per Day, FY 1988 149

Table 6.1   Texas CMHMRC Total and Per Capita
                Psychosocial Funding 158

Table 7.1.   Case Management: Departmental Requirements 163

Table 7.2.   FY 1988 Statistics for the Texas Case Management
                  Program 166

Table 7.3.   CMHMRC Mental Health Case Management
                  FY 1988 Amounts Budgeted 167

Table 7.4.   FY 1988 Budgets for State Hospitals and State
                  Centers for Mental Health Case Management 168

Table 7.5.   Case Management Provider Data for the First and
                  Second Quarters of FY 1988 169

Table 7.6.   Mental Health Eligibility Criteria for Case
                  Management Services 172

Table 11.1.   Structured Crisis Residential Programs 207

Table 11.2.   Structured Noncrisis Residential Programs 208

Table 11.3.   Intermediate Residential Programs 209

Table 11.4.   Semi-Independent Residential Programs 210

Table 12.1.   Work Credits Needed for SSDI Eligibility 217

Table 12.2.   Approximate Monthly Disability Benefits If
                  the Worker Became Disabled in 1988 and
                  Had Steady Earnings 218

Table 12.3.   SSI and SSDI Recipients in Texas in December
                  of 1987 219

Table 12.4.   Number and Percentage of the National Distribution
                  of SSDI Recipients with Schizophrenia by Year 220

Table 12.5.   Texas Mental Health Case-Managed Patients Receiving
                  Federal Support during FY 1988 220

Table 12.6.   SSI Maximum Allowable Income Limits for Individuals
                  for Selected States in January of 1988 222

Table 12.7.   Food Stamps Monthly Allotment by Monthly Countable
                  Income and Household Size as of May 1988 224

Table 12.8.   Example of the Calculation of Monthly Food
                  Stamp Benefit 225

Table 12.9.   Texas Food Stamp Client Profile State Totals,
                  December 1987 227

Table 12.10.   Median Family Income for Participation in the 1154
                  Program with No Copayment Required 229

xiv

Table 12.11.   Maximum Copayment Range by Percentage
                of Median Income 229

Table 12.12.   H.B. 1154 Obligation for Mental Health Services
                for FY 1988 and 1989 230

Table 13.1.   Expenditures for Mental Health Services Through
                TDMHMR, FY 1984 to 1988 244

Table 13.2.   TDMHMR General Revenue Fund Legislative
                Appropriation Biennial Funding for
                FY 1988-1989 and 1990-1991 245

Table 13.3.   Texas Local Mental Health Authorities' Adjusted
                FY 1983 Baseline and Incentive Diversion
                Program Baseline 251

Table 13.4.   Total $35.50 Program Earnings 255

Table 14.1.   Local Mental Health Authorities Total and Per Capita
                TDMHMR Funding for FY 1987 and FY 1988 261

Table 14.2.   Listing of CMHMRCs and Location 262

Table 14.3.   Expenditures by Texas CMHMRCs for Mental Health
                Services FY 1984 through FY 1988 263

Table 14.4.   CMHMRC Mental Health Expenditures by
                Object for FY 1988 264

Table 14.5.   CMHMRC Mental Health Expenditures by Program
                for FY 1988 265

Table 14.6.   Total CMHMRC Revenue by Source, Summary of FY 1984
                through FY 1988 266

Table 14.7.   CMHMRC Mental Health Revenue by Source for FY 1988 . . 267

Table 14.8.   Local Tax Effort of the CMHMRCs and Percentage
                of Total CMHMRC Budgets 268

Table 14.9.   CMHMRCs Participating in the CMHMRC Acquisition
                Program 269

Table 14.10.   CMHMRC Revenue from Other State Agencies
                for FY 1988 270

Table 14.11.   CMHMRC Mental Health Expenditures for FY 1984
                through FY 1988 271

Table 14.12.   Overall Liquidity of the CMHMRCs 272

Table 14.13.   CMHMRC Financial Condition as of August 31, 1988 274

Table 15.1.   ADMBG Mental Health Allocations for
                FY 1983 through 1988 294

Table 15.2.   CMHMRCs Receiving TCADA Portions of ADMBG
                   During FY 1988 296

Table 15.3.   Sites Receiving McKinney Act Funds: Amount Allocated
                   and Local Match for FY 1988 and 1989 298

Table 15.4.   Medicaid Mental Health Outpatient Options by State 300

Table 15.5.   Medicaid Mental Health Inpatient Options by State 303

Table 15.6   Examples of Controls on the Optional Medicaid
                   Programs in Other States 310

Table 16.1.   Volunteer Hours and Dollars Contributed to Texas
                   State Hospitals in 1987 and 1988 318

Table 16.2.   Selected Foundation Grants to Texas Mental Health
                   Agencies, 1988 319

Table 16.3.   Robert Wood Johnson Foundation Funding
                   for ATCMHMRC 320

Table 16.4.   Hogg Foundation Grants to CMI-Related Projects,
                   1986 and 1987 321

Table 16.5.   United Way of Texas Sources of Giving 322

Table 16.6.   United Way Funding Areas to CMI in Texas:
                   Five-Year Trend 322

Table 16.7.   Salvation Army Services Provided in Texas in 1987 325

Table 16.8.   Salvation Army Service Unit Welfare Programs for 1987 . . . 325

List of Figures

Figure 1.1.   Adult Psychiatric Beds in Texas by Type of
Provider 14

Figure 2.1.   TDMHMR Inpatient Facilities and Catchment
Areas for State Hospitals 22

Figure 2.2.   Location of the 35 Community Mental Health and Mental
Retardation Centers in Texas 24

Figure 2.3.   Areas Covered by State Hospital Outreach Centers
and Locations of State Hospital Associated
with Each Outreach Area 27

Figure 2.4.   Total Number of Admissions to State Inpatient
Facilities from FY 1984 to FY 1988 32

Figure 2.5.   Percentages of Total Admissions That Were
Involuntary from FY 1984 to FY 1988 34

Figure 2.6.   Number of First Admissions Annually for Serious
Mental Illness and Substance Abuse among
Young Adults at the Eight State Hospitals,
1983 to 1987 35

Figure 2.7.   Inpatient Stays of Less than One Week in Duration
by Ethnicity during FY 1987 and FY 1988 59

Figure 2.8.   Discharge Status for Clients Discharged for the Eight Texas
State Hospitals from 1981 until 1988 61

Figure 2.9.   Percentage of Clients Discharged with No Reassignment,
Hospital and Year 62

Figure 4.1.   Comparison of Ethnicity in TDC's Psychiatric Inpatient
Special-Needs Offender Sample versus TDC's
Total Population 114

Figure 4.2.   Comparison of Types of Crimes Committed by TDC's
Psychiatric Inpatient Special-Needs Offender
Sample versus TDC's Total Population 116

Figure 4.3.   Comparison of Lengths of Stay by TDC's Psychiatric
Inpatient Special-Needs Offender Sample versus
TDC's Total Population 117

Figure 7.1.   Diagnoses of FY 1988 Mental Health Case Management
Clients with a Diagnosis Report on CARE 174

Figure 13.1.   R. A. J. Average Daily Census, June 1983 to
March 1989 254

FOREWORD

The Lyndon B. Johnson School of Public Affairs has established interdisciplinary research on policy problems as the core of its educational program. A major part of this program is the nine-month policy research project, in the course of which two or three faculty members from different disciplines direct the research of ten to twenty graduate students of diverse backgrounds on a policy issue of concern to a government agency. This "client orientation" brings the students face to face with administrators, legislators, and other officials active in the policy process and demonstrates that research in a policy environment demands special talents. It also illuminates the occasional difficulties of relating research findings to the world of political realities.

This report on financing care for the chronically mentally ill in Texas is the result of a policy research project conducted during the 1988-89 academic year. The project was sponsored and primarily funded by the Hogg Foundation for Mental Health as a parallel activity to their Commission on the Chronically Mentally Ill in Texas. This report examines the public mental health system in Texas and how it identifies and finances care for the chronically mentally ill. This volume also discusses the public services and resources available to the chronically mentally ill in Texas. The findings of this report are intended to provide information and insights that will aid mental health professionals, advocates, and legislators in addressing the plight of the mentally ill in Texas.

The curriculum of the LBJ School is intended not only to develop effective public servants but also to produce research that will enlighten and inform those already engaged in the policy process. The project that resulted in this report has helped to accomplish the first task; it is our hope and expectation that the report itself will contribute to the second.

Finally, it should be noted that neither the LBJ School nor The University of Texas at Austin necessarily endorses the views or findings of this study.

Max Sherman
Dean

PREFACE

This volume is the outcome of a Policy Research Project on financing care for the chronically mentally ill in Texas, which was conducted during the 1988-89 academic year at the LBJ School of Public Affairs at the University of Texas at Austin. In the fall of 1987 Reymondo Rodriquez and Wayne Holtzman encouraged me to develop this project to be a parallel activity to the Commission on the Chronically Mentally Ill in Texas which the Hogg Foundation had formed earlier in the year. In addition to this volume we published a companion volume of four case studies of community mental health centers and one state outreach center and their delivery of mental health care. The primary sources of funding for the entire project were the Hogg Foundation and the University of Texas. Other funding has been provided by the John Sharpe Fellowship, the Mike Hogg Endowment, and the Wilbur Cohen Professorship at the LBJ School of Public Affairs.

In this study we have attempted to pull together information from a variety of sources in order to better describe and analyze the public mental health system in Texas. In particular we have analyzed data from the CARE data system as well as annual reports and other studies in the section of the report concerning clients, minorities, and the criminal justice system. In the section on services we used data from annual reports, budgets, special studies and other sources. Finally in the section on financing we analyzed the annual financial reports of the CMHMRCs and TDMHMR-operated facilities, as well as state and federal budgetary and expenditure data and annual reports of foundations.

We hope that this volume will provide the overview of the public institutions involved in mental health care in Texas which is needed for informed policy making.

David C. Warner
November 1990

Acknowledgments

This research was enhanced and made possible by a large number of persons at the community centers, in state government, and elsewhere who graciously answered questions, reviewed drafts, and provided guidance at each point of the project.

Although many of the students worked hard throughout the project, several should be mentioned for their continuing and outstanding contributions. Jan Rienstra was in many ways the de facto director of this project. She contributed her experience, her insights, and her hard work to making sure that we treated this project seriously and completely. Pam Diamond, and Hugh Crean also continued to work on the project over the summer and beyond. Nicholas Hoover who worked on it as a student, a volunteer, and as a research associate ultimately assisted in pulling everything together and was crucial in making sure that it got to the publication stage. He was a continuing source of strength. None of them should be held unduly accountable for errors or omissions, for all of us involved in the project stand jointly responsible. Melanie Padgett selflessly produced many drafts of this text and contributed in many ways to the final product.

During the spring of 1988, Gary Watts, M.D., worked with Connie Harris, Ph.D., Reymundo Rodriguez, and David Warner to develop bibliographic material as well as a taxonomy of issues that provided resources and structure to the project. Laurie Crumpton worked during the summer of 1988 to further refine this information, and participated in the class during the fall semester. Scott Kier, Ph.D, joined the project in March 1989, replacing Connie Harris as a participating faculty member on the project, and as the research director for three Hogg Foundation commissions.

Persons who addressed the class in the course of the year and shared their expertise and insights included Karen Hale, Mental Health Association of Texas; David Pharis, special monitor for the R. A. J. v. Jones settlement agreement; Spencer McClure, Executive Director of the Texas Council of Community Mental Health and Mental Retardation Centers; John Brubaker, Executive Director, Mildred Vuris, Director, Mental Health Services, Scott Kier, Director of Evaluation, Alan McCoy, Executive Assistant, and Michael Figer, Director of Finance, all at Austin-Travis County MHMR; Genevieve Hearon, President of the Texas Alliance for the Mentally Ill; Don Green, Legislative Budget Board; George Fairweather, Ph.D., Michigan State University; Ira Iscoe, Ph.D., Professor of Psychology, Hogg Foundation, University of Texas; Robert Campbell, Touche Ross; Rush Russell, Revenue Officer, Linda Logan, SQA, and Cathy Collier, Assistant Deputy Commissioner of Mental Health Services, all of the Texas Department of Mental Health and Mental Retardation; and Charles Holzer and Fernando Trevino of the University of Texas Medical Branch at Galveston.

Persons at the Texas Department of Mental Health and Mental Retardation who have helped in this project include Dennis Jones, Commissioner; Tom Suehs, former Deputy Commissioner for Management and Support; Sally Anderson and Julie Bonner of Information Services; Leilani Rose, Clyde Allen, Debra Watson, and Virginia Leininger of Budget and Fiscal Services; Tom Martinec of Internal Audit; Jim Dalton and Dan Kern of Claims; Mike Laritz of Contracts; Don Vaughn, Assistant Deputy Commissioner; Bruce Nunn, Chuck Roberts, and Gary Anderson, Management Analysis and Reporting Unit (MARU); Cathy Collier, Carolee Moore, and Phyllis Gipson, Assistant Deputy Commissioners for Mental Health Services; Nancy Ditmar, Ph.D., Director of Special Programs, Mental Health Services; Ann Denton, Coordinator, Adult Residential Services; Linda Logan, SQA; Rush Russell, Revenue Officer; Vijay Ganju, Ph.D., and Carol Bouchard of the Office of Strategic Planning; Janet Collins, of Case Management Services; G. F. "Jeff" England, Resource Development; Edwina Milton, Program

Consultant; and Marion Norris, Vernon State Hospital.

Other people who aided in the compilation of this volume included William Burke, and Michael Eisenberg of the Texas Department of Pardons and Paroles; J. Crump of the Texas Commission on Jail Standards; Matthew Ferrara, Ph.D., and Steve Gilliland of the Texas Department of Corrections; Dee Kifowit of the Texas Council on Offenders with Mental Impairments; Lieutenant P. Martinez of the Travis County Sheriff's Department; G. Rodriguez of the Travis County Adult Probation Department; W. Simmons of the Travis County Jail; Demetria Pope of the Texas Adult Probation Commission; Deborah Reyna of the City of Austin Police Department; Larry Cotten and John Gill of Dallas County MHMR Center; Cheryl Petty and Paul Ferris of the Austin-Travis County MHMR Center; Angelina Ramos of the U.S. Department of Housing and Urban Development; Jack Schmulowitz and John Smith of the Social Security Administration; Dot Young of Tri County MHMR Services; Susan Berliner of the United Way of Austin; Rod Coleman of Disciples Outreach for the Mentally Ill; Wayne Ewen of the Mental Health Association in Austin; Genevieve Hearon and George Peterson of the Texas Alliance for the Mentally Ill; Karen Hale of the Mental Health Association in Texas; and Ron Kingsbury of the Salvation Army.

In addition there were certainly dozens of other perons who were extremely helpful and contributed to this project. We are greatful to all of them and hope that they find this volume has repaid their help and will serve to advance care for the chronically mentally ill in Texas.

We hope that this volume will give readers a greater understanding of the complexity of providing and financing care for the chronically mentally ill at the federal, state, and community level in Texas and that through a better understanding of the configuration and organization of the public mental health system in Texas, as citizens we will all be more effective at improving the conditions faced by persons served by this system.

Chapter 1. The Evolution of Texas Public Mental Health Policy: The Past as Prologue*

This Policy Research Project took on the task of examining community-based care of the chronically mentally ill in the public mental health system in Texas. By way of introduction to subsequent chapters, this chapter looks at the mental health system in Texas from a historical perspective, by discussing the evolution of the treatment of the mentally ill and the organization of the public mental health services in Texas.

INTRODUCTION

Although federal, state, and local governments spent $17 billion in 1987 for public mental health services for the chronically mentally ill, most states still have very inadequate services (NIMH, 1987, p. 144; Torrey and Wolfe, 1988, p. iii). The costs per person served continue to rise along with the numbers of those in need. Measures of effectiveness continue to be elusive, and virtually all ways of delivering assistance to those in need resist change (Vallance and Sabre, 1982, p. 125). The respective roles and responsibilities of federal, state, and local governments for public mental health services are vague, having been defined more by default than by design. Most federal expenditures, about 60 percent of the total, are for indirect benefits, primarily Supplemental Security Income, Social Security Disability Income, Food Stamps, Medicare, and Medicaid. Of state expenditures, 38 percent of the total, two-thirds are appropriated to support aging state mental hospitals. Local governments contribute only about 2 percent of the total costs (Rubin, 1987, p. 111).

That the quality of state mental health systems depends upon an adequate level of resources is basic. Even more important to high-quality systems, however, is the structure of their financing and of their organization (Mechanic, 1987, p. 8). A systems approach to improving the adequacy and availability of public mental health services should encompass three basic, interrelated elements: the definition of the persons to be served, the services to be provided, and the financing mechanisms to fund those services (NIMH, 1986, p. I-3). Ideally, decisions about these elements should be sequentially related: first, who is to be served; second, what services they need; and, third, how the needed services are to be financed.

However, in virtually every state, the converse is true. Decisions about which services are provided and who receives those services have been determined by the financing mechanisms available. Even though all states have made dramatic reductions in the size of their public mental hospital census in the past ten years, the state hospitals still demand the greatest proportion of state funds. Moreover, most states now are defining only those persons with serious, chronic mental illness as their target population. The impetus for both of these phenomena was not good systems design but retrenchment in an era of shrinking funds.

New public mental health policy directions may have to come, not from new funds, but from redirection and better management of existing programs (Rochefort, 1987, p. 101). Changing the way existing dollars are spent is different from changing the numbers of people who are eligible for services or the amounts they are eligible to receive (Rubin, 1987, p. 113).

In Texas, as in many other states, the provision of public care for persons with severe, chronic mental illness is seriously deficient. Most of these persons depend

---

*This chapter was written by Janice Rienstra.

1

exclusively on underfinanced, fragmented, and often inaccessible public services (Mechanic and Aiken, 1987, p. 1634). Compared with other states, Texas traditionally has been parsimonious in its support of human services; mental health services are no exception. Texas ranks near the bottom among the states in total per capita funding for public mental health services. In 1983 Texas ranked 48th in state mental health expenditures, with per capita spending of $12.58; the national average was $24.82 (NASMHPD, July 1987, p. 40). In 1985, Texas ranked 49th, above only Idaho and Arizona, among the 50 states and the District of Columbia in its per capita expenditures for public mental health services. That year, while Texas ranked 22nd in the nation in per capita income (at $13,500), it spent $18.70 per capita for mental health services. The average state per capita expenditure, at $38.40, was more than twice that of Texas (Torrey and Wolfe, 1988, p. 109). Moreover, in 1985, Texas spent 68.8 percent ($11.92 per capita) of its mental health dollars for state hospitals and 25.5 percent ($4.42 per capita) for community-based programs (NIMH, 1987, p. 165). The Texas Department of Mental Health and Mental Retardation has been criticized by some for excessive expenditures on its rapidly depopulating state hospitals. However, when compared with other states, Texas provides a low number of inpatient beds for persons with serious mental illness. During 1985 in Texas there were approximately 35 state hospital inpatients per 100,000 population; the average inpatient rate among all states was 49 per 100,000 (Torrey and Wolfe, 1988, p. 108).

In addition to the extraordinary low level of state support, other indicators of the inadequacy of Texas mental health services include R. A. J. v. Jones, a 16-year-old major federal class action lawsuit and settlement, significant legislative activity, and increasingly vocal consumer and advocacy groups. The historical development of public mental health policy and practice in Texas generally has tracked that of other states and the federal government, at least in form. A number of state hospitals, established over the years, experienced a rapid decline in census following years of deplorable, overcrowded conditions. The federal Community Mental Health Center (CMHC) initiative took root in Texas soon after its passage. However, Texas public mental health policy is and has been substantively unlike that in all other populous states because of the long-standing inadequacy of public funds. Texas has been and continues to be a poor provider of mental health services; history clearly shows that mental health problems and issues simply have not been of great importance in Texas politics (McCleskey, 1968, p. 138).

ORIGINS OF PUBLIC RESPONSIBILITY FOR PERSONS WITH MENTAL ILLNESS

In a pluralistic society, the process of defining health and human services policies is more a political, rather than a rational, process. The degree to which interest groups can organize and mobilize frequently influences the allocation of resources (Wagenfeld, Lemkau, and Justice, 1982, p. 311). And mental health care is as much influenced by general social policy and culture as it is by policy decisions within the mental health system (Mechanic, 1987, p. 1).

Institutional decision-making does not occur in a historical vacuum; usually an issue becomes policy as a result of the melding of long-term social, intellectual, scientific, and professional trends (Rochefort, 1987, p. 96). A look at the history of mental health services provides valuable information and perspective about the origins of present attitudes which linger on and continue to shape the nature of services (Vallance and Sabre, 1982, p. 17). Therefore, the first step in an analysis of public mental health services is an assessment of the social and institutional processes of mental health care and the ways that they have been shaped by historical factors and by systems of government, law, health, and public benefits (Mechanic, 1987, p. 1).

It is clear that society has decided that certain activities are legitimately performed by governments (Steiner, 1977, p. 27). Medicine and government have been mutually associated with the care of mentally ill persons since early recorded history (Lemkau, 1982, p. 16). In *The Republic*, Plato (c. 428-348 B.C.) wrote that government has the responsibility to enforce care of persons who are mentally ill. Earlier, Hippocrates (c. 460-371 B.C.) concluded that mental illness was a medical responsibility, since he believed it had natural, as opposed to supernatural, causes. The subsequent evolution of public mental health care manifests fundamental advances in psychiatric technology and more precise definitions of the role of government. However, these modern changes occurred within and were tempered by the contexts of far more pervasive ideological, social, and political changes.

PUBLIC MENTAL HEALTH CARE IN TEXAS: 1856-1963

In 1856, eleven years after attaining statehood, Texas established its first State Lunatic Asylum, now Austin State Hospital, on a plot of land north of Austin. The building was constructed according to the so-called Kirkbride model, which was used for a number of state hospitals built in the late 1800s. According to Dr. Thomas Kirkbride, the basic goal of state hospital construction was to provide accommodations for as many patients as possible at the lowest cost of construction. The Kirkbride model dictated one long building; the administrative section was in the middle, with male wards on one side and female wards on the other. Additional wards could be built onto the ends. Although Kirkbride had insisted that there should not be more than 200 patients in any one hospital, most hospitals were far larger. One New York mental hospital building extended one-half mile from the middle administrative section to the end of each lateral wing (Evans, 1964, p. 10). The new asylum admitted its first patients in 1861 and was quickly filled to capacity. When the census reached 54 patients in 1866, the superintendent wrote: "The asylum at present seems crowded to its limit of accommodation" (Evans, 1964, p. 17).

Although by the late 1800s few people thought that the mentally ill were demonically possessed, very little was known about the nature of mental illness. Table 1.1 illustrates the variety of diagnoses subsumed under the label of "insane" in 1878.

Table 1.1. State Lunatic Asylum of Texas: 1878 Admissions Report of Supposed Cause of Insanity of Admissions Since September 1, 1877

Cause	Number	Cause	Number
Religious Excitement	14	Hepatic Derangement	1
Solitary Habit	19	Pubescence	4
Bad Health	2	Disappointed Affections	4
General Dissipation	1	Intemperance	8
Syphilis	3	Desertion	1
Traumatic	3	Uterine Trouble	3
Malicious Report	1	Fright	3
Pecuniary Trouble	3	Neglect	5
Predisposing Cause/ Hereditary	8	Measles	1
Senility	4	Suppressed Menses	2
Epilepsy	17	Change of Scene	1
Insolation	3	Irregular Habits	3
Brain Fever	3	Pregnancy	1
Domestic Bereavement	8	Spiritualism	2
Opium Habit	2	Unknown	12
		Total	**142**

Source: TDMHMR, 1975.

3

Other state hospitals were eventually opened: Terrell State Hospital, 1885; San Antonio State Hospital, 1892; Abilene State Hospital (later converted to a state school), 1904; Rusk State Hospital (converted from a state prison), 1918; Wichita Falls State Hospital (WFSH), 1922; Vernon State Hospital (first created as a branch of WFSH), 1950; Big Spring State Hospital, 1939; Mexia State School and Home (a former prisoner of war camp acquired to relieve overcrowding of other institutions), 1946; and Kerrville State Hospital (a former tuberculosis sanatorium), 1949 (Guthrie, 1950).

The first extensive survey of Texas state hospitals was conducted in 1916. Until this time, each of the asylums operated under its own board of managers, who in turn reported directly to the governor (TDMHMR, 1975, p. 5). The survey's major conclusion was that all the state's eleemosynary institutions should be placed under a central board of control in order to get more mental patients out of the jails and almshouses (Evans, 1964, p. 27).

The legislature subsequently consolidated 21 separate agencies under a new State Board of Control in 1920. The board's major functions included purchasing and management for all the state asylums and other institutions, which included the tuberculosis hospitals, the institutions for the blind and the deaf, and the Alabama-Coushatta Indian Reservation in east Texas (Evans, 1964, p. 28). In 1924, the legislature renamed the asylums by replacing the words "lunatic," "insane," and "asylum" with "state hospital" (Evans, 1964, p. 29).

Few funds were spent for Texas state hospitals during the Great Depression. In 1931, the legislature requested a study of the state hospitals in order to curtail expenses through "better organization and operation" (Evans, 1964, p. 30). In 1934, the State Board of Control asked the legislature for a Texas sterilization law which would be applicable to persons in the state institutions; it asked again in 1936 and in 1938. At that time, 29 states had such laws. To its credit, the Texas legislature did not pass such a law (Evans, 1964, p. 31).

By the end of World War II, Texas and Mississippi were the only two states which still required that a person be declared insane by a jury in order to receive treatment at a state hospital; there were no provisions for voluntary admission. Soon thereafter, Mississippi changed its law to waive the jury trial requirement (Evans, 1964, p. 51). The Texas mental health code was amended in 1935 to allow a person to be temporarily (up to 90 days) committed to a hospital with the testimony of two physicians in lieu of a jury trial. Commitment for more than 90 days still required a jury trial; medical or psychiatric testimony was not required (Evans, 1964, p. 52). By 1942, despite the highly restrictive commitment law, Texas state hospitals' waiting list included 1,400 persons who had been declared insane but were held in county jails because there was no room in the hospitals. Hospital staffs made some efforts to relieve the problem by putting beds closer together and placing pallets in hallways and on porches (Evans, 1964, p. 36).

Texas not only has traditionally ranked low among the states in appropriations for mental health care, but has seen its already low ranking drop in the past 50 years. In 1939 Texas ranked 28th with an average annual per patient expenditure of $228.92. By 1949, Texas had dropped to 38th, with an annual per patient expenditure of $516.14, even though total state mental health appropriations had increased by 125 percent during the decade (BTSHSS, 1950).

In 1949 the legislature created the Board for Texas State Hospitals and Special Schools, with jurisdiction over the state's institutions for the mentally disabled, TB hospitals, and several other institutions. Later in 1949, Governor Allan Shivers asked the federal Public Health Service (PHS) to conduct a survey of the state hospitals. The 1950 PHS preliminary report to the Governor concluded that although no state met all the requirements of the American Psychiatric Association, no other state fell so far below the standards as did Texas (Evans, 1964, p. 42). The PHS report contained numerous findings and recommendations:

> Patients are segregated according to color, the tuberculous, seniles, the infirm, continued treatment cases, the dangerous and elopers, the disturbed and noisy, the convalescent, and the receiving service . . . Electric-shock therapy is the chief method of treatment, and is used on most of the wards . . . During the past fiscal year at the Austin State Hospital, 2,563 patients received 12,452 electric-shock treatments . . . Very little aftercare or follow-up of patients in the community is undertaken. (Guthrie, 1950, pp. 30-51)

Most of the PHS report's recommendations addressed increasing community care:

> The treatment of the mentally ill does not properly begin at the level of commitment to the mental hospital; nor should it end with discharge . . . Study should be made of the possibilities of deflecting admissions through early diagnosis and preventive work in community mental hygiene clinics, and the patient should be able to receive follow-up care for at least a year after discharge . . . It is strongly recommended that the State of Texas study community resources available for a comprehensive mental hygiene program, and also study the experience of other states in setting up and operating such programs. (Guthrie, 1950, p. 20)

The state's response to the PHS report was to embark on a massive building program to shore up the state institutions; little attention was given to the recommended community care component. Governor Shivers called a special session of the legislature to address the problems of the state's mental institutions. Shivers urged the legislature to take immediate action:

> Texas, the proud Lone Star state--first in oil--48th in mental hospitals. First in cotton--worst in tuberculosis. First in raising goats--last in caring for its state wards. We have 24,000 people crowded into space that properly should house only 14,000. I do not know how many of these unfortunate people are being held in jails or elsewhere, awaiting the time when a cubicle of space may be open for them in a state hospital. For an example of the personnel problem, look no farther than the Austin State Hospital, a mere stone's throw from the Capitol. It has ten doctors and four registered nurses for 3200 mental patients. (Evans, 1964, p. 45)

The legislature passed an omnibus tax increase to allocate $5 million per year for the next seven years to a state hospital building fund (Evans, 1964, p. 47). Historically, governors have exercised very little positive leadership--administratively, politically, or legislatively--in Texas mental health policy. Most Texas governors took very little interest in the lives of mentally ill persons in the institutions. An exception was James Hogg (1891-1895), an avid reader on the subject who made numerous personal visits to the institutions. As governor, he did much to bring about some needed improvements (Evans, 1964, p. 21). No Texas governor has carried the banner for improved mental health services to the public in the same way that issues of education, water resources, or tourist development have been promoted. McCleskey credits Shivers, through his 1951 special legislative session for hospital building funds, as another exception to the general rule (McCleskey, 1968, p. 140).

By 1957 the condition of state hospital buildings had improved, but overcrowding was still a critical problem. The standard used in Texas for measuring hospital capacity was 60 square feet per patient; the minimum federal standard at the time was 70 square feet per patient (BTSHSS, 1951, p. 15).

The Board for Texas State Hospitals and Special Schools, which had become accustomed to a sizable building fund, requested additional funds to build a large state hospital in Houston. However, the legislature responded that too much emphasis had been on bricks and not enough on treatment and restoration. The legislature then asked the Texas Medical Association to sponsor a study of the state's mental health services. The association employed a consultant from Illinois; his report emphasized the need for community-based care and research. The recommended community-based component lost out a second time, this time to research. The Houston State Psychiatric Institute, a research facility, was funded instead of the state hospital proposed by the board (McCleskey, 1968, p. 145).

Although psychiatry had progressed significantly since the 19th century, theory and practice in the early 1950s were still primitive by today's standards. Table 1.2 illustrates the diagnostic categories used in Texas state hospitals in 1952.

Table 1.2. Diagnoses of All Mental Patients in State Hospitals as of August 31, 1952

Diagnosis	Number	Diagnosis	Number
General Paresis	911	Manic-Depressive	1,853
Other Cerebral Syphilis	135	Schizophrenia	6,269
Alcoholic	85	Paranoia/Paranoid	134
Traumatic	60	Psychopathic Personality	54
Cerebral Arteriosclerosis	678	With Mental Deficiency	1,139
Epilepsy	210	Undiagnosed Psychoses	62
Senile	710	Psychoneuroses	77
Involutional	305	Without Psychosis	485
Other Metabolic Disease	144	Miscellaneous	97
Organic Change	148	Undiagnosed	811
		Total	**142**

Source: TDMHMR, 1975.

In 1956 a constitutional amendment to provide for a waiver of the jury trial requirement and require psychiatric or medical testimony in lieu thereof for all state hospital commitments was approved by Texas voters. This amendment led to a new Texas Mental Health Code, enacted in 1957, which provided for voluntary admissions well as involuntary commitments. The new code provided for three types of involuntary commitment: (1) emergency (up to 96 hours); (2) temporary (up to 90 days); and (3) indefinite (Evans, 1964, p. 66). The impact of the new code was immediate. Of 10,230 total admissions to the state hospitals in 1960, 34 percent were voluntary admissions (Evans, 1964, p. 147).

In 1963, more than a decade after the PHS report recommending community care, the board established community clinics affiliated with four state hospitals in Austin, Big Spring, Terrell, and Wichita Falls. These clinics served nearly 9,000 clients in FY 1963. Other state clinics, independent of a hospital, were established in San Antonio and Dallas in 1958, and in Fort Worth and Harlingen in 1962. The independent clinics served 20,000 persons in FY 1963 (McCleskey, 1968, p. 97). The board also initiated separate contracts for community-based mental health services with hospitals and clinics in El Paso, Beaumont, and Lubbock in 1964 and later with Houston's Ben Taub Hospital (McCleskey, 1968, pp. 13, 98).

PUBLIC MENTAL HEALTH CARE IN TEXAS: 1963-1988

Because of the stipulations of the 1946 federal law, Texas' "mental health authority" in the early 1960s was the state health department, not the Board for Texas State Hospitals and Special Schools. As an example of the lack of interagency coordination, parallel planning was begun by both the health department's Division of Mental Health and the Board for Texas State Hospitals and Special Schools for clinic services in the same geographic area, neither knowing of the other's plans (McCleskey, 1968, p. 102).

Two unrelated planning processes were the ultimate roots of the Texas response to the federal CMHC initiative before Congress officially passed the 1963 CMHC act. One planning process was initiated by a committee of representatives from the Texas Medical Association (TMA), the Texas Neurological Association (TNA), and the Texas Association for Mental Health (TAMH). This committee began work on a state plan for mental health services under the pending new federal requirements.

The second planning process was started by the state health department. The health department's Division of Mental Health was small. It was one of five divisions in its Preventive Medical Services branch, which in turn was one of seven major branches in the health department. The division subsisted only on NIMH grants; in 1964 it had a staff of eight professionals (McCleskey, 1968, p. 99). The two groups did eventually converge, since the health department's commissioner happened to be a member of the first group. Interestingly, it was the TMA that approved the final Texas grant application to NIMH for state mental health planning funds under the 1963 CMHC act. The legislature was not involved (McCleskey, 1968, p. 146).

The state health department then played the leading role in implementing the plan, since as the state mental health authority, it received the NIMH planning grant. Several committees, involving 110 persons plus a 17-member steering committee, were appointed. Almost 60 percent of the committees' membership consisted of mental health professionals. Other state agencies, including the Board for Texas State Hospitals and Special Schools, were considered relatively insignificant in the planning process (McCleskey, 1964, pp. 147-150).

One result of the planning committee's negotiations for a new administrative structure for mental health services was an agreement between the board and the health department for administrative rationalization of both mental health and tuberculosis services. The health department would turn over the Division of Mental Health to the board and the board would cede jurisdiction of the tuberculosis hospitals to the health department (McCleskey, 1964, p. 150).

The product of the planning committee's work was proposed legislation for a complete reorganization of the state's mental health (and mental retardation) services. The bill, House Bill 3, was intended to be a draft for further action, not a finished proposal. Although there were some compromises, particularly over the number of physicians to be appointed to the new agency's board, there was general legislative support for reorganizing the hospitals and schools and establishing authority for Community Mental Health and Mental Retardation Centers (CMHMRC) (McCleskey, 1968, p. 155). The legislature passed HB 3, the 1965 Texas Mental Health and Mental Retardation Act.

The statute, which is still called HB 3, abolished the old Board for Texas State Hospitals and Special Schools and created the Texas Department of Mental Health and Mental Retardation (TDMHMR) as the state authority for mental health and mental retardation. TDMHMR was to have a nine-member board appointed by the governor; the commissioner had to be psychiatrist. HB 3 also authorized the establishment of nonprofit community mental health and/or mental retardation centers by local sponsoring agencies, which could be a city, a county, a hospital district, a school district, or a combination of these. The sponsoring agencies were to appoint persons to the center's board of trustees, who were granted administrative authority over the center. New Community Mental Health and Mental Retardation Centers could apply for the federal grants available under PL 88-164 and for grants-in-aid from TDMHMR. It could be inferred from the language of HB 3 that local sponsoring agencies could also provide funds to a community center. The CMHMRCs were required by both federal and state legislation to provide free services to indigent persons. For the FY 1966-1967 biennium, the total state appropriation for new Texas CMHMRCs was $600,000 (Frazier, 1978, p. 79).

At the time, there was a state constitutional limitation on state assistance to local governments, which directly affected the HB 3 provision for grants-in-aid to local CMHMRCs. Article XVI, Section 54, of the Texas Constitution provided that the state was responsible for custody and maintenance of indigent lunatics (McCleskey, 1964, p. 162). This problem was eliminated in 1966 when voters approved a constitutional amendment to Section 6 of Article XVI, which now reads "This . . . does not prohibit state agencies authorized to render services to the handicapped from contracting with privately-owned or local facilities for necessary and essential services . . . ." Section 54 was deleted by constitutional amendment in 1969 (Dallas Morning News, 1985, p. 520).

For Texas, the vision encompassed by HB 3 was a revolutionary advance. However, the state's funding pattern for mental health services remained regressive. In 1961, 1.78 percent of the state budget was spent on mental health services; by 1964, spending dropped to 1.53 percent of the state budget. Similarly, in FY 1960-1961, mental health appropriations comprised 41 percent of all state health expenditures; this had decreased to 36 percent by FY 1966-1967. Despite real growth in the size of the state's coffers, mental health funding continued to lose ground. Between 1960 and 1966, when the total state budget increased by 50 percent, mental health appropriations increased by only 30 percent. By the FY 1966-1967 biennium, state per capita mental health expenditures were $2.52, placing Texas 49th in the country (McCleskey, 1968, p. 156).

In addition to the state hospitals, the new TDMHMR inherited three types of community-based service entities and three methods of state support for them: (1) state-operated outpatient clinics; (2) contracts with local agencies for services to indigent persons; and (3) grants-in-aid to new CMHMRCs. In FY 1966-1967, state funds for all these community services were budgeted in one $1,350,000 line item for the biennium. The TDMHMR board had to decide how to allocate the funds among the competing entities. Each method had different consequences and implications (McCleskey, 1968, p. 157).

Within 18 months of the passage of HB 3, 24 CMHMRCs had been established in Texas (DeMoll, 1978, p. 62). The federal grant funds, which most of these CMHMRCs received, came with regulations, including minimum (75,000) and maximum (200,000) limits on the population size or catchment area of a CMHMRC. As a result, CMHMRCs were established in virtually all urban areas of the state, but very few were created in the large, sparsely populated areas of west and south Texas.

HB 3, echoing PL 88-164, established the CMHMRC as a new entity, separate and distinct from TDMHMR and its state institutions. In the late 1960s and early 1970s, most Texas CMHMRCs operated almost wholly independently of the state and of each other. Those with federal grants received their federal funds directly. The amount of state grants-in-aid available to the CMHMRCs through TDMHMR was $4 million in 1969

(TDMHMR, 1975). If this amount had been divided equally among the 24 existing CMHMRCs, each would have received an annual allocation of a little less than $167,000.

This era of rapid growth of the new CMHMRCs came at a time when the new TDMHMR was undergoing substantial changes. In TDMHMR's first nine years it was headed by eight individuals as interim, acting, or official commissioner (TDMHMR, 1975). Dramatic changes were also taking place within the state hospital system. The state hospitals had housed more than 16,000 persons in 1951. The average daily census of those hospitals was 8,850 by FY 1974 following the rapid deinstitutionalization of the 1960s and 1970s.

The deinstituionalization during this period could also be seen as a "reinstitutionalization" movement. Usually, the first patients to leave the state hospitals were the elderly; in many cases, they were placed in Medicaid-funded nursing homes. Thus the burden of paying for their care was taken on by the federal government rather than the state (Farabee, 1978, p. 72).

Although the hospitals' 1974 census had dropped to half its size in 1951, the number of hospital admissions remained relatively static. Table 1.3 illustrates this point by showing that although the daily census decreased 25 percent, the number of admissions increased only 2 percent.

Table 1.3. Daily Census, Admissions to, and Costs Per Client in Texas State Hospitals in 1973 and 1975

Texas	1973	1975	Percent Change
Average Daily Census	9,937	7,467	-24.9
Admissions	25,610	26,061	1.8
Per day $	15.42	26.56	65.8
Nat'l Ave $	25.20	37.54	49.0

Source: CSG, 1976, p. 7.

During this period the legislature also established "state centers." The state centers were to be operated by TDMHMR as an experimental alternative to locally operated CMHMRCs in the unserved areas of the state. The state hospitals also opened community outreach programs to serve nearby rural areas.

In the late 1970s and early 1980s, a series of significant events occurred which moved TDMHMR and the CMHMRCs closer together, in both the policy and operational spheres. The federal staffing grants to CMHMRCs began to expire, so the CMHMRCs looked increasingly to the state for continuation funds. As the state's costs increased, a cluster of legislative committees and independent research groups were asked to conduct studies of the mental health system.

Three major events occurred in 1981 which were to have long-lasting impact on state mental health policy. For the first time in Texas law, some of the respective responsibilities of the state institutions and the CMHMRCs in providing a continuum of care for persons with mental illness were defined (SB 791). Second, the 1981 federal Omnibus Reconciliation Act (PL 97-35) consolidated all the CMHMRCs' individual federal staffing grants into a block grant directly to the state. The funds were to be disbursed and administered by TDMHMR.

The third major event of 1981 was the resolution and settlement reached in the major federal class action lawsuit, originally styled Jenkins v. Cowley and now known as R. A. J. v. Jones. The suit was filed in 1974 against all Texas state hospitals on behalf of all past, current, and future patients of the hospitals. The plaintiffs had charged that the hospitals failed to provide adequate treatment in the least restrictive environment, were understaffed, overmedicated their patients, and provided living conditions that were oppressive and unhealthy (TDMHMR, 1985, p. 5). The 1981 settlement mandated many improvements to the hospitals, including stringent staff-to-patient ratios. The federal judge in the case established a court-appointed monitor made up of a three-member panel to monitor TDMHMR compliance with the requirements of the settlement. Since that time, the three-member panel has been has been pared down to one court-appointed monitor who still oversees TDMHMR's compliance with the settlement of the case.

Compliance with the court settlement would prove to be costly. TDMHMR considered two alternate ways to meet the staff ratio requirement: (1) hire a large number of new staff for the persons already in the hospitals, or (2) reduce the total number of people in the hospitals by paying CMHMRCs to take care of those discharged. In either event, more money would be necessary. TDMHMR chose to do some of both. At that time, the TDMHMR appropriations structure was more restrictive than it is now. Line-item appropriations were made to individual state hospitals; another line item was for all CMHMRC grants-in-aid. The state board had only limited authority to transfer funds between line items.

In 1983 TDMHMR requested and received legislative approval for unprecedented authority to transfer funds between line items. Under the agreement reached, a new line item, Staff-to-Patient Ratios, was created. TDMHMR could allocate funds from this line-item either to the CMHMRCs to help fund services for discharged hospital patients or allocate funds to the state hospitals for additional staff to meet the required staffing ratios. Determination of the amount to be paid to CMHMRCs was based on available resources and not on the costs of services or the needs of the discharged persons. The $16 million available was divided by the number of hospital bed days to be reduced per year (estimated at 450,000) in order to meet the staffing requirement; the arithmetic result was $35.50. The CMHMRCs and state-operated community services were to be reimbursed $35.50 for each bed day reduction under a predetermined baseline, attributed to residents of their respective service areas who were part of the class named in the R. A. J. v. Jones lawsuit. Originally called the "$35.50 incentive program," this mechanism has been refined several times and is now known as the mental health incentive diversion program (TDMHMR, 1989).

There is little question that compliance with the R. A. J. v. Jones resolution and settlement has resulted in additional funds for TDMHMR. It has been estimated that TDMHMR received $150.3 million for compliance from 1983 to 1989 (Pharis, 1989). However, the court monitor still considers the system grossly underfunded, especially the community-based mental health services (Pharis, 1989, p. 22).

In 1983 the legislature overhauled the 1957 Mental Health Code. As a result of federal court decisions in the 1970s and early 1980s regarding the civil rights of persons with mental illness, many provisions of the 1957 code had to be changed. For example, in 1979 the U.S. Supreme Court decided in Addington v. Texas that the substantive due process standard used in civil commitments, preponderance of the evidence, was not sufficient. The next higher standard, clear and convincing evidence, was to be applied. Other changes included a stricter definition of mental illness required for commitment,

10

replacement of "indefinite" with "extended" (up to one year) commitments, and new authorization for peace officers to take persons to a hospital for emergency evaluation without a warrant (Churgin, 1988, p. 5).

Despite the stricter commitment law and the $35.50 incentive payments to CMHMRCs and state community services for hospital bed day reduction, the costs of compliance with the court settlement continued to mount. In response to the growing economic pressure, the lieutenant governor and the speaker of the Texas House of Representatives established a Legislative Oversight Committee (LOC) to study TDMHMR in June 1984. The LOC was to develop recommendations for allocating available resources to meet the mandate of the settlement, and recommendations for the future directions of public mental health services in Texas. The LOC's three-volume 1985 report to the 69th Legislature listed 93 recommendations for TDMHMR; most of these were enacted in Senate Bill 633 several months later (LOCMHMR, February 1985). The major provisions of SB 633 included requirements that TDMHMR define its priority population for mental health services, replace the CMHMRCs' grants-in-aid mechanism with performance contracts, and ensure the provision of five core services in all 63 local service areas.

The most recent major legislative initiative was the first formal review of TDMHMR by the Sunset Advisory Commission in 1985. The resulting TDMHMR Sunset legislation, SB 257, which amended HB 3, is replete with privatization initiatives for current state hospital services, with strong emphasis on community services. SB 257 also added two more core services and removed the requirement that the commissioner be a psychiatrist.

Another factor in the evolution of Texas mental health policy has been the increasingly vocal consumer and advocacy groups which have lobbied both TDMHMR and the legislature for improvements in services and funding. The Mental Health Association of Texas (MHAT, formerly TAMH) has chapters in major Texas cities. The Texas Alliance for the Mentally Ill (TEXAMI) is a relatively new organization whose membership is primarily parents of mentally ill persons, but also includes other family members, former mental patients, and some mental health professionals. Both MHAT and TEXAMI advocate for increased funds for community-based services but remain committed to quality services in the state hospitals. Other consumer-oriented groups include Advocacy, Inc., a federally mandated and funded agency established as the clients' rights protection and advocacy entity required in all states, and the Texas Network of Mental Health Consumers, comprised of persons who are receiving or have received services from the public system.

Of the provider and professional interest groups which influence TDMHMR activities, the most vocal is the Texas Council of Community Mental Health and Mental Retardation Centers, established in 1976 as an association of boards of trustees of CMHMRCs; 31 of the 35 CMHMRCs are members. Other influential interest groups include the Texas Medical Association, the Texas Society of Psychiatric Physicians, and the Texas County Judges' Association.

THE ORGANIZATION OF TEXAS PUBLIC MENTAL HEALTH SERVICES

TDMHMR is the state's largest agency, with over 29,000 employees. During the FY 1988-1989 biennium it had a budget of $1.54 billion for mental health and mental retardation services. Agency policy and annual budgets are approved by the nine-member board appointed by the governor. The commissioner is responsible for the administration of TDMHMR and is designated as the state mental health authority (TDMHMR, 1988a, p. 13). TDMHMR directly administers the inpatient and community outreach operations of seven state hospitals, which are located in Austin, San Antonio, Big Spring, Wichita Falls, Terrell, Rusk, and Kerrville. Three of the five state centers provide mental health inpatient and community outreach services; these three are located in El Paso, Laredo, and Harlingen. Vernon State Hospital provides only forensic inpatient services and services for youth with serious substance abuse problems. The Waco Center for Youth provides inpatient services for children and adolescents with emotional problems.

TDMHMR administers two systems of community-based public mental health services. One system is locally operated by the 35 CMHMRCs under performance contracts with TDMHMR. The second system is directly operated by TDMHMR through its hospital and state center outreach programs. Both CMHMRCs and state facilities are designated by TDMHMR as local mental health authorities (LMHA).

Following a recommendation of the 1978 report of the President's Commission on Mental Health, TDMHMR divided the state into 63 geographic service areas (LSAs) in 1982 (USDHEW, pp. B-6, B-12). TDMHMR designated a "core service agency" or local mental health authority in each LSA as responsible for community services to persons with serious mental illness in its respective LSA. Each of the 35 CMHMRCs is the designated authority for its service area; in the 28 LSAs not served by CMHMRCs, the state hospital or state center closest to the area is the designated LMHA.

The LSAs were aggregated into seven mental health regions in 1987. Before 1987, the service area boundaries of some CMHMRCs serving more than one county were not contiguous with the state hospitals' service area boundaries. The result was that people in the CMHMRC's area were served by one of two hospitals, depending on their county of residence. The service areas of some of the hospitals were realigned, over the protests of many of the affected county judges, in order to be contiguous with those of the CMHMRCs in their area.

The assignment of responsibility for services to persons with mental illness on a geographic basis may have its advantages. However, in a state the size of Texas, sheer distance is perhaps the greatest impediment to mental health service continuity. For state hospital treatment, an El Paso resident must travel 650 miles round trip to the region's state hospital in Big Spring. People who live in the Lower Rio Grande Valley must travel almost as far to their region's state hospital in San Antonio. Compounding the great distances between LMHAs and the state hospital in their region, many of the LMHAs themselves serve vast geographic areas. The service area of the Amarillo CMHMRC covers 21,400 square miles; the CMHMRCs in San Angelo and Lufkin each serve nearly 10,000 square miles. The areas served by the state LMHAs are also large; for example, Wichita Falls State Hospital serves 17,700 square miles; San Antonio State Hospital, 15,700 square miles.

The second major characteristic of the state which greatly influences mental health service delivery is the extraordinary variation in population density across the state. The population density of 2,057 persons per square mile in Dallas County, served by the Dallas CMHMRC, is 158 times that of the San Angelo CMHMRC's service area. Harris, Dallas, Bexar, and Tarrant counties each have a population greater than that of many states. At the other end of the spectrum, three CMHMRC LSAs and 12 state LSAs serve areas with fewer than 20 people per square mile. Even without regard to the level of funding, the geographic size and the population density of a service area inevitably dictate the types and modes of mental health service delivery which are locally most effective.

The final comment on the organization of Texas public mental health services system is a perspective on its role relative to all public and private mental health services provided in the state. TDMHMR provides, both directly and through CMHMRC contract, less than one-quarter of the estimated total of 16,000 adult psychiatric beds available in the state. The other public and private providers include private psychiatric hospitals, psychiatric wards in general hospitals, nursing homes, and veterans' hospitals (Figure 1.1.).

REPORT OVERVIEW

This Policy Research Project report presents a thorough examination of the mental health system in Texas as it affects the chronically mentally ill. Section One examines the client population served by the public mental health system. Chapter 2 presents a detailed examination of the population served by TDMHMR. Chapter 3 looks at the special needs of the minority populations in Texas. Chapter 4 examines the problems experienced by the interaction between the criminal justice system and the public mental health system.

Section Two examines the services provided by the Texas public mental health system, particularly the "core" and "noncore" services which the CMHMRCs provide, as well as other services which the chronically mentally ill need when trying to cope with life outside of the institution. These services include crisis response services, psychosocial rehabilitation, case management, family support services, medication-related services, continuity of care, residential services, and other community housing alternatives. The section ends with a discussion of federal and state income support programs.

Section Three discusses the financing trends and arrangements for the provision of public mental health services in Texas. The section begins with an examination of the role and structure of TDMHMR in financing care for the CMI. The next chapter looks at the financial structure of the local CMHMRCs and how they are contracted to provide community-based services for the CMI. The subsequent chapters in this section examine the role of the federal government in financing care for the CMI through block grants and through Medicaid. The possibilities for the expansion of Medicaid to cover more mental health services and the role of voluntary organizations in the provision of ental health care are also discussed.

The last chapter of this report offers conclusions and recommendations regarding the financing of mental health care in Texas and the provision of services to the client population. It is hoped that this report will not only be of aid to those in the field of mental health but also inform those who wish to become familiar with the intricacies of this complicated system.

**Figure 1.1. Adult Psychiatric Beds in
Texas by Type of Provider**

Total Beds = 16,133

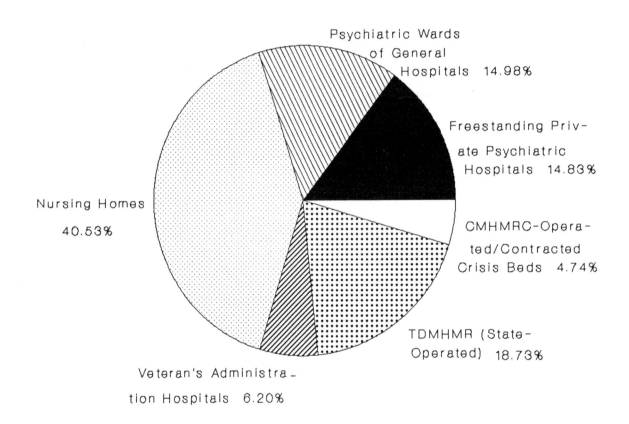

Psychiatric Wards
of General
Hospitals   14.98%

Freestanding Priv-
ate Psychiatric
Hospitals   14.83%

CMHMRC-Opera-
ted/Contracted
Crisis Beds   4.74%

TDMHMR (State-
Operated) 18.73%

Nursing Homes

40.53%

Veteran's Administra-
tion Hospitals   6.20%

Sources: TDMHMR, 1988a; TDMHMR, 1988c; TDH/THA, 1987.

14

References

Board for Texas State Hospitals and Special Schools (BTSHSS). 1950. "Report of the Board: Annual Report of the Board for Texas State Hospitals and Special Schools for the Fiscal Yeath Ending August 31, 1950." Austin, Texas.

_____. 1951. "Report of the Board: Annual Report of the Board for Texas State Hospitals and Special Schools for the Fiscal Year Ending August 31, 1951." Austin, Texas.

_____. 1952. "Report of the Board: Annual Report of the Board for Texas State Hospitals and Special Schools for the Fiscal Year Ending August 31, 1952." Austin, Texas.

Churgin, M. 1988. An Analysis of the Texas Mental Health Code. Austin, Texas: Hogg Foundation for Mental Health, The University of Texas at Austin.

Council of State Governments (CSG). 1976. State Responsibilities to the Mentally Disabled. Lexington, Ky.

Dallas Morning News. 1985. 1986-1987 Texas Almanac. Dallas, Texas.

DeMoll, Louis E., ed. 1978. Mental Health for the People of Texas. Austin: Hogg Foundation for Mental Health, The University of Texas at Austin.

Evans, J. L. 1964. "The Care of the Mentally Ill in Texas." Master's Thesis. The University of Texas at Austin.

Farabee, Helen. 1978. "Taking the Next Steps for Community Mental Health." In Mental Health for the People of Texas, ed. L. E. DeMoll. Austin, Texas: Hogg Foundation for Mental Health, The University of Texas at Austin.

Frazier, S. 1978. "From a Decade Ago Toward the Decades Ahead." In Mental Health for the People of Texas, ed. L. E. DeMoll. Austin, Texas: Hogg Foundation for Mental Health, The University of Texas at Austin.

Guthrie, Riley H. 1950. A Survey of Mental Institutions of the State of Texas: Final Report. Rockville, Maryland: National Institute of Mental Health.

Legislative Oversight Committee on Mental Health and Mental Retardation (LOCMHMR). February 1985. Report to the Texas Legislature, February, 1985: Volume I: Mental Health. Austin Texas. February.

Lemkau, P. 1982. "Historical Background." In Public Mental Health: Perspectives and Prospects, ed. M. Wagenfeld, P. Lemkau, and B. Justice. Volume 5. Sage Studies in Community Mental Health. Beverly Hills, Calif.: Sage Publications.

McCleskey, C. 1968. "Houston." In The Politics of Mental Health: Organizing Community Mental Health in Urban Areas, ed. R. H. Connery. New York, NY: Columbia University Press.

Mechanic, David, and L. Aiken. 1987. "Improving the Care of Patients with Chronic Mental Illness." Hospital and Community Psychiatry, vol. 37, no. 26 (December 24).

Mechanic, David, ed. 1987. _Improving Mental Health Services: What the Social Sciences Can Tell Us_, San Francisco, Calif.: Jossey-Bass, Inc.

National Association of State Mental Health Program Directors (NASMHPD). July 1987. _Final Report: Funding Sources and Expenditures of State Mental Health Agencies: Revenue/ Expenditure Results Fiscal Year 1985_. Alexandria, Va.

National Institute of Mental Health (NIMH). 1986. _Financing Mental Health Services: Perspectives for the 1980s_. USDHHS Pub. No. (ADM)86-1438. Washington, D.C.: U.S. Government Printing Office.

_____. 1987. _Mental Health, United States, 1987_. Ed. R. W. Manderscheid and S. A. Barrett. USDHHS Pub. No. (ADM)87-1518. Washington, D.C.: U.S. Government Printing Office.

Pharis, David B. 1989. "State Hospital Reform in Texas: A History of the _R. A. J._ Class Action Lawsuit." In _Community Care of the Chronically Mentally Ill_, ed. C. M. Bonjean, M. T. Coleman, and Ira Iscoe. Proceedings of the Sixth Robert Lee Sutherland Seminar in Mental Health, Austin Texas: Hogg Foundation for Mental Health, The University of Texas at Austin.

Rochefort, D. 1987. "The Political Context of Mental Health Care." In _Improving Mental Health Services: What the Social Sciences Can Tell Us_, ed. David Mechanic. San Francisco Calif.: Jossey-Bass, Inc.

Rubin, J. 1987. "Financing Care for the Seriously Mentally Ill." In _Improving Mental Health Services: What the Social Sciences Can Tell Us_, ed. David Mechanic. San Francisco, Calif.: Jossey-Bass, Inc.

Steiner, P. 1977. "The Public Sector and the Public Interest." In _Public Expenditure and Policy Analysis_, ed. R. H. Haveman and J. Margolis. 2nd ed. Chicago, Ill: Rand McNally.

Texas Department of Health/Texas Hospital Association (TDH/THA). 1987. "Texas Department of Health/Texas Hospital Association Hospital Survey." Austin, Texas.

Texas Department of Mental Health and Mental Retardation (TDMHMR). 1975. _Mental Illness and Mental Retardation: A History of State Care in Texas_. Austin, Texas.

_____. 1985. _Self-Evaluation Report to the Sunset Advisory Commission: Part I_. Austin, Texas.

_____. 1988a. FY 1988 Budget Data. Austin, Texas. (Computer printout.)

_____. 1988b. "Future Directions for Community Mental Health Services. Working Draft." Austin, Texas. (November 18.)

_____. 1988c. "Private Mental Hospitals Licensed by TDMHMR." Austin, Texas. (December 23.)

_____. 1989. Staff Memorandum for Estimates under the Omnibus Budget Reconciliations Act of 1987. Austin, Texas.

Texas Mental Health and Mental Retardation Act. 1965. Art. 5547-201, sec. 1.01 (a)-(e). V.T.C.S. 1966. Austin, Texas.

Texas S. B. 791. 1981. 67th Leg. Regular Session. Austin, Texas: Texas State Legislature.

Torrey, E., and S. Wolfe. 1988. Care of the Seriously Mentally Ill: A Rating of State Programs. Washington. D.C.: Health Research Group.

U.S. Comptroller General. 1976. Returning the Mentally Disabled to the Community: Government Needs To Do More. HRD-76-152. Washington, D.C.: U.S. Government Printing Office.

U.S. Department of Health, Education and Welfare (USDHEW). 1979. Report of the HEW Task Force on Implementation of the Report to the President from the President's Commission on Mental Health. Pub. No. (ADM)79-848. Rockville, Md.: U.S. Government Printing Office.

U.S. Department of Health and Human Services (USDHHS). December 1980. Toward a National Plan for the Mentally Ill. Washington, D.C.: U.S. Government Printing Office.

Vallance, T. R., and R. M. Sabre. 1982. Mental Health Services in Transition: A Policy Sourcebook. New York, N.Y.: Human Sciences Press.

Wagenfeld, M., P. Lemkau, and B. Justice, eds. 1982. Public Mental Health: Perspectives and Prospects. Volume 5. Sage Studies in Community Mental Health. Beverly Hills, Calif.: Sage Publications.

Warner, David C. 1988. Financial Costs of Caring for the Chronically Mentally Ill in Texas. Background Paper. Sixth Robert Sutherland Seminar, Hogg Foundation for Mental Health. Austin, Texas. Sept. 30-Oct. 1, 1988.

Warner, David C., Laurie Crumpton, and Gary Watts. 1989. "Financial Costs of Caring for the Chronically Mentally Ill in Texas." In Community Care of the Chronically Mentally Ill, ed. C. Bonjean, M. T. Coleman, and Ira Iscoe. Austin, Texas.: Hogg Foundation for Mental Health, The University of Texas at Austin.

Section One. Clients

The chronically mentally ill in Texas are not a homogenous group. Mental illness strikes across all demographic lines with equally dramatic effect. The commonality with most of these persons is that they will at some time find themselves using the public mental health system.

This section attempts to examine the client population of the Texas public mental health system. Chapter 2 will discuss at some length the usage patterns within this system in Texas over the five fiscal-year periods from September 1, 1983, through August 31, 1988. Initially, the discussion will be system based, providing information on the facilities that are available and the patterns of client flow through those systems of care. Following that overview of the system as a whole, the discussion will shift to an analysis of client usage patterns over the same period. The following fundamental questions will be addressed and discussed. Which clients are using the system the most? Are these patterns changing over time? What is the relationship between the community-based system and the hospital-based system? Are the links between these two vital parts of the system strong or are there gaps? These are just some of the issues this chapter will address in examining the clients and organizations which make up the public mental health system in Texas.

Chapter 3 examines the availability, utilization, and adequacy of mental health services for members of minority groups who are chronically mentally ill in Texas. The chapter begins with an overview of the literature on services for the minority chronically mentally ill. Second, a brief description of the demographic characteristics of this population is outlined. Then, demographic characteristics and projections for the general population are provided, followed by a set of recommendations to improve mental health service delivery to the minority chronically mentally ill. Finally, an assessment of the resources available in Texas which can help address the needs of minority groups will be offered.

Chapter 4 paints a broad picture of the levels and types of programming which have recently been developed to better serve those mentally ill persons also involved in the criminal justice system. The chapter begins with a recent history of the problem of the mentally ill impacting the criminal justice system, then describes local programming designed to divert mentally ill offenders from entering the criminal justice system. The role of TDMHMR's Maximum Security Unit at Vernon State Hospital is explained, followed by a discussion of services provided by three main state agencies directly responsible for the treatment and supervision of the state's offenders. The chapter ends with a summary of the functions and goals of the recently established Interagency Council on Mentally Retarded, Developmentally Disabled, and Mentally Ill Offenders.

Chapter 2. The Texas Public Mental Health System: Patterns of Use from Fiscal Years 1984 through 1988[*]

Most seriously mentally ill people find themselves using the services of the public mental health system at some time during their illness. The episodic, chronic nature of most serious mental illnesses generally leads to long-term needs for service from mental health providers. These service needs usually exceed the coverage provided by even the best health insurance or support systems, requiring those clients who were able to initiate treatment in the private sector to resort to the public sector as their illness progresses. Others begin their treatment in the public system, perhaps because they have no mental health insurance coverage, or because the public system is the only provider available in their location, or because the services provided in the public mental health system are the most appropriate.

THE INPATIENT SYSTEM

There are 14 state-administered inpatient mental health facilities currently functioning in Texas. Eight are state hospitals, five are state centers, and one (Waco Center for Youth) is a specialized treatment center for youth between the ages of 10 and 17. During the early part of the period 1983-1988, there was an additional inpatient facility in Houston (TRIMS) which doubled as a research center. This facility, however, was closed at the end of FY 1984. The state also currently operates two county-based psychiatric inpatient facilities in Harris and Tarrant counties. However, because data are not available from these hospitals, they will not be discussed in this chapter.

In addition to the specialized mental health facilities listed above, the state operates eight state schools for the mentally retarded. There is an occasional mental health admission to one of these facilities when a client is dually diagnosed with mental illness and mental retardation; however, this appears to be an uncommon occurrence.

Figure 2.1 shows the locations of the state hospitals, state centers, and currently operating specialized facilities. The shaded areas represent the service districts for each of the state hospitals. As can be seen from the map, the geographic areas covered by most of the state hospital facilities are quite large, making access difficult at best for many of the clients within each catchment area.

While most of the state hospitals admit any client with a mental health diagnosis considered serious enough to warrant inpatient treatment, some of these facilities offer services to special populations either in addition to their regular population or exclusively. Until the spring of 1988, Rusk State Hospital served as the forensic facility for the State of Texas. Clients who were too dangerous to be cared for in the less secure facilities were placed there, as were those individuals determined by the court to be "criminally insane."   In the spring of 1988, however, all Rusk maximum security patients were transferred to Vernon State Hospital, which is now the maximum security facility for the state. Rusk currently has dual functions. Half of the facility serves as a general-purpose state hospital while the other half is used by the Texas Department of Corrections as a psychiatric treatment center for offenders. Vernon, on the other hand, is a totally specialized facility, having eliminated its general psychiatric services in March 1988 when the Rusk patients were transferred there. In addition to its maximum security patients, which are housed at its North Campus, Vernon has a program for drug-dependent youth between the ages of 13 and 21 at its South Campus. This program has been in operation since November of 1977. In order to close out its general psychiatric

---

[*]This chapter was written by Pamela M. Diamond.

Figure 2.1. TDMHMR Inpatient Facilities and Catchment Areas for State Hospitals

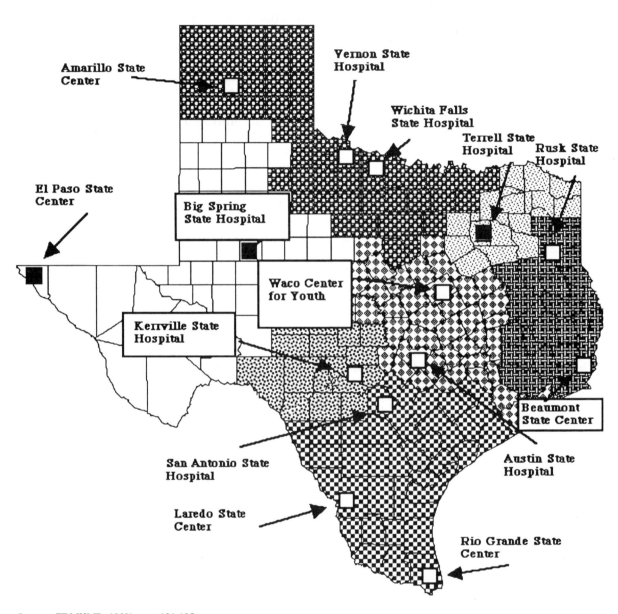

Amarillo State Center

Vernon State Hospital

Wichita Falls State Hospital

Terrell State Hospital

Rusk State Hospital

El Paso State Center

Big Spring State Hospital

Waco Center for Youth

Kerrville State Hospital

Beaumont State Center

San Antonio State Hospital

Austin State Hospital

Laredo State Center

Rio Grande State Center

Source: TDMHMR, 1989b, pp. 131-135.

services, Vernon transferred its general psychiatric clients to Wichita Falls State Hospital in the spring of 1988 (Bonner, Interview, November 6, 1989).

Kerrville State Hospital houses many geriatric mentally ill clients in addition to its general population. Many of these older patients have been in the system for quite a long time. The other state hospitals--San Antonio, Austin, Terrell, Big Spring, and Wichita Falls--all provide general psychiatric services.

The five state centers are in many ways hybrids within the system. Two of these centers--Amarillo and Beaumont--offer few inpatient services. In fact, Amarillo closed all inpatient units in April of 1987, and Beaumont only has one inpatient unit open currently, and it is for the mentally retarded. El Paso State Center currently has two units for the mentally retarded, two for the mentally ill, and one for substance abusers. The mental health and substance abuse units opened in 1984. Rio Grande State Center operates predominantly mental health units; however, a transitional living unit and a substance abuse unit were added in 1988. Laredo State Center has one mental health unit and one mental retardation unit. Although the centers vary in the amount and types of inpatient services which they offer, most do offer outpatient services to both mentally ill and mentally retarded clients (Bonner, Interview, November 6, 1989).

THE COMMUNITY-BASED SYSTEM

There are 35 community-based mental health centers which are administered by local boards. Figure 2.2 shows the locations of the service areas covered by these centers, while Table 2.1 provides detailed information on the area covered by each. The numbers on the map correspond to the numbers of the centers in the table. These centers cover areas that range from densely populated urban areas to areas which have been called "frontier" because of their sparse population and vastness (Leff, 1989). All of these centers provide a wide range of services to their communities in the areas of both mental health and mental retardation. Although their emphasis is on outpatient services, these centers also are mandated to provide community-based crisis residential services as well.

In the areas of Texas not covered by a CMHMRC, the state hospitals and state centers provide outpatient services through their outreach clinics. The outreach clinics are generally small operations, located within the outlying communities and connected administratively to the state hospital or state center. Over the past five years, these territories have varied considerably as TDMHMR has attempted to equalize responsibilities and maximize services to the outlying areas. Figure 2.3 shows the current configuration of outreach responsibility for the various state hospitals and state centers. As seen in Figure 2.2, the service areas covered by each of the state hospitals and state centers are quite large. Table 2.2 provides more detailed information on each of the state hospital and state center outreach areas. As noted in the table, Big Spring State Hospital's outreach services, in West Texas, cover the largest area, and the San Antonio State Hospital's outreach services are responsible for the largest population base.

POLICY AND PROCEDURAL ISSUES AFFECTING THE ENTIRE SYSTEM

In September of 1984, during the fourth quarter of FY 1984, some important changes took place within TDMHMR. The $35.50 plan, which is described in more detail in Section Three, was put in place at that time. This plan provided community mental health providers with financial incentives to reduce their bed days in the state hospitals. The plan was initiated to help the inpatient facilities to reduce their census to comply with the R. A. J. v. Jones settlement mandates regarding staff-to-patient ratios.

Figure 2.2. Locations of the 35 Community Mental Health and Mental Retardation Centers in Texas

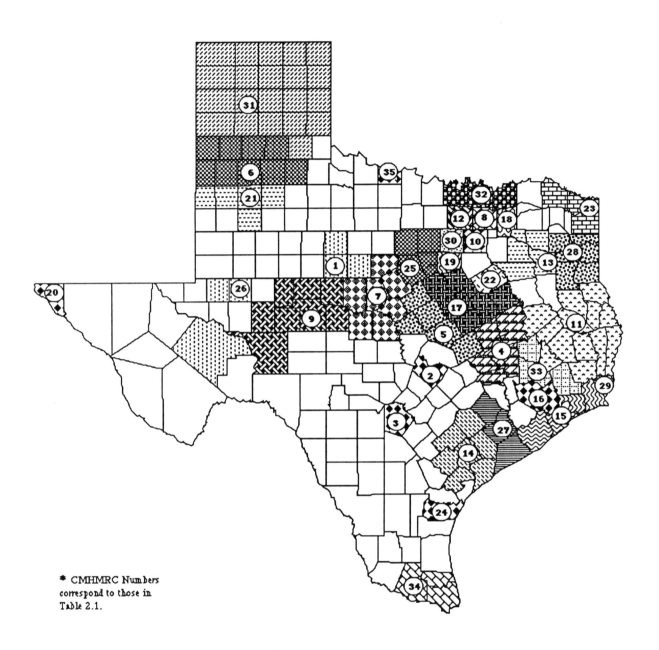

* CMHMRC Numbers
correspond to those in
Table 2.1.

Source: TDMHMR, 1989b, pp. 131-135.

Table 2.1. Geographic Area and Population Density for the 35 Community Mental Health Centers in Texas

	Mental Health Center	Primary Location	Number of Counties	Square Miles in Area	Population of Area	Population Density
1.	Abilene Regional MHMR	Abilene	3	2,747	167,127	60.8
2.	Austin Travis County MHMR	Austin	1	989	545,587	551.7
3.	Bexar County MHMR	San Antonio	1	1,248	1,169,911	937.4
4.	MHMRA of Brazos County	Bryan	7	5,080	252,754	49.8
5.	Central Counties Center for MHMR Services	Temple	5	4,681	302,308	64.6
6.	Central Plains Comprehensive Community MHMR	Plainview	9	8,369	105,183	12.6
7.	Central Texas MHMR	Brownwood	7	9,369	125,863	13.4
8.	Collin County MHMR	McKinney	1	851	214,514	252.1
9.	Concho Valley Center for Human Advancement	San Angelo	7	9,369	125,863	13.4
10.	Dallas County MHMR	Dallas	1	880	1,827,414	2076.6
11.	Deep East Texas Regional MHMR Services	Lufkin	13	10,782	379,136	35.2
12.	Denton County MHMR	Denton	1	911	195,708	214.8
13.	MHMR Regional Center of East Texas	Tyler	5	3,607	295,765	82.0
14.	Gulf Bend MHMR	Victoria	7	5,782	172,963	29.9
15.	Gulf Coast Regional MHMR	Galveston	2	1,806	431,989	239.2
16.	MHMRA of Harris County	Houston	1	1,734	3,044,916	1756.0
17.	Heart of Texas Region MHMR Center	Waco	6	5,577	294,650	52.8
18.	Hunt County Family Services	Greenville	1	840	67,896	80.9
19.	ohnson County MHMR	Cleburne	1	731	89,927	123.0
20.	Life Management Center	El Paso	1	1,014	584,094	576.0
21.	Lubbock Regional MHMR	Lubbock	5	4,369	280,952	64.3

(Continued Next Page)

25

Table 2.1 (Continued). Geographic Area and Population Density for the 35 Community Mental Health Centers in Texas

Mental Health Center	Primary Location	Number of Counties	Square Miles in Area	Population of Area	Population Density
22. Navarro County MHMR	Corsicana	1	1,068	40,304	37.7
23. Northeast Texas MHMR	Texarkana	3	2,882	131,613	45.7
24. Nueces County MHMR Community Center	Corpus Christi	1	847	321,599	379.7
25. Pecan Valley MHMR Region	Stephenville	5	3,544	147,436	41.6
26. Permian Basin Community Centers for MHMR	Midland	3	6,581	289,650	44.0
27. Riceland Regional MHA	Wharton	4	4,053	331,379	81.8
28. Sabine Valley Center	Longview	6	3,897	308,516	79.2
29. MHMR of Southeast Texas	Beaumont	3	1,915	381,920	199.4
30. Tarrant County MHMR	Fort Worth	1	868	1,092,242	1258.3
31. Texas Panhandle MHA	Amarillo	21	21,432	381,432	17.8
32. MHMR Services of Texoma	Denison	3	2,722	152,596	56.1
33. Tri-County MHMR Services	Conroe	3	3,007	333,159	110.8
34. Tropical Texas Center for MHMR	Edinburg	3	3,063	667,003	217.8
35. Wichita Falls Community MHMR Center	Wichita Falls	1	606	133,108	219.7

Sources: TDMHMR, 1989b; TDMHMR, 1989c.

Figure 2.3. Areas Covered by State Hospital Outreach Centers and Locations of State Hospital Associated with Each Outreach Area

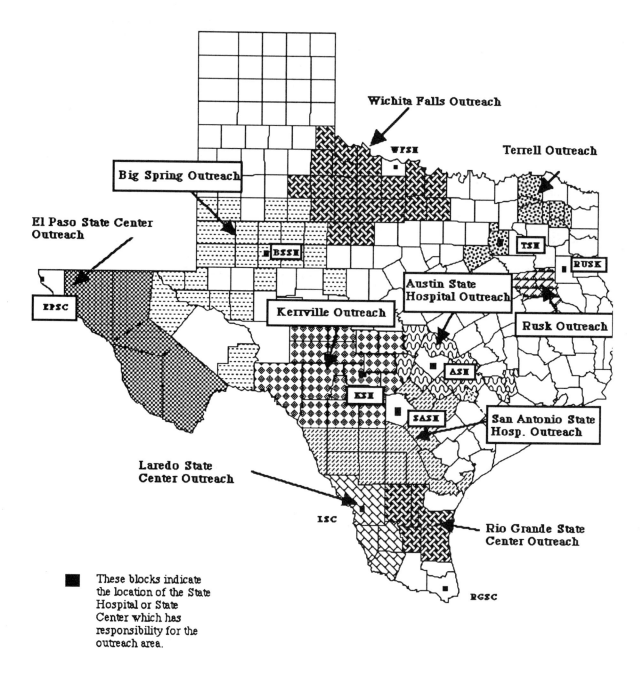

Wichita Falls Outreach

Terrell Outreach

Big Spring Outreach

El Paso State Center Outreach

Austin State Hospital Outreach

Kerrville Outreach

Rusk Outreach

San Antonio State Hosp. Outreach

Laredo State Center Outreach

Rio Grande State Center Outreach

These blocks indicate the location of the State Hospital or State Center which has responsibility for the outreach area.

Source: TDMHMR, 1989b, pp. 131-135.

Table 2.2. Geographic Area and Population Density for the State Hospital and State Center Community Outreach Regions

State Hospital/Center	Number of Counties	Square Miles in Area	Population of Area	Population Density
Big Spring State Hospital	23	25,017	250,349	10.0
Wichita Falls State Hospital	20	17,676	177,466	10.0
Austin State Hospital	10	7,715	356,200	46.2
San Antonio State Hospital	16	15,729	405,366	25.8
Kerrville State Hospital	16	20,634	215,202	10.4
Terrell State Hospital	10	5,006	289,451	57.8
Rusk State Hospital	2	2,129	97,625	45.9
El Paso State Center	5	20,665	23,425	1.1
Laredo State Center	4	6,724	185,548	27.6
Rio Grande State Center	5	5,846	104,614	17.9

Source: TDMHMR, 1989b, pp. 131-135.

Theoretically, the additional monies, which were to go to the communities, would allow them to provide a wider, more adequate, and more accessible array of services within the community. It was hoped that a circular process would be initiated in which the primary locus of psychiatric care would be transferred into the community, hospitals would be used less, more funds would thus be generated for the community, and community services would continue to grow as hospital usage decreased (Miller and Rago, 1987).

This policy change was expected to impact usage patterns throughout the public mental health system. State hospitals were to be used only as a last resort, for individuals who occasionally needed long-term care, or for those people who were judged to be too dangerous or suicidal in the community to be cared for adequately there. Acute care was to be shifted into the community and provided, in most instances, at local hospitals with psychiatric beds operated by the community mental health centers. Ongoing care and follow-up was also to be the responsibility of the centers.

Given that this was to happen, it can be postulated that not only would fewer individuals be admitted to the inpatient facilities overall, but also that recidivism to the state inpatient facilities would decrease as communities assumed the ongoing care of seriously mentally ill persons. One might also assume that, with an increase in the availability of community-based crisis stabilization units, very short-term admissions to the state hospitals would also decrease, thus enabling the state hospitals to better focus their energies on the clients requiring longer-term care and rehabilitation. Applying the same logic, one would also expect that, again with better community treatment and after-care, patients could be discharged from the state hospitals after more moderate lengths of stay. Taken together, these arguments point to a change in state hospital usage patterns in which the more common length of stay is moderate rather than very long or short.

CLIENT ASSIGNMENT AND REGISTRATION (CARE)

A second important change was implemented at about the same time as the $35.50 plan, which in many ways made this current chapter possible. A management information system called Client Assignment and Registration (CARE) was developed, and all TDMHMR clients were assigned unique case numbers within the system. The data available on CARE includes diagnostic information, commitment history, and demographics for each inpatient stay or community assignment. CARE numbers were assigned to all clients entering the system after it went on line, and efforts were made to ascertain, from demographic information, if they had been in the system previously. If so, their old records were appended to the new ones. There were some difficulties with the transition from one system to the other. Not all facilities and centers began consistently reporting to CARE at the same time, and the data from the communities have, from the start, been less reliable than that from the facilities. At present, there are reasonably complete computerized records with unique case numbers for all clients who have entered the system since October 1, 1984.

Computer tapes from the CARE system were used as a basis for the present chapter. These tapes contained both inpatient and outpatient data for all clients who were active in the system at any time from October 1, 1984, to September 30, 1988. A separate record was available for each inpatient admission and each community assignment. If the client had been admitted prior to the 1984 date, those records were also available. Records for individuals who entered the system prior to the 1984 date but who did not have any contact during these more recent years were not available.

OVERVIEW OF THE INPATIENT PUBLIC MENTAL HEATH SYSTEM IN TEXAS FROM FY 1984 TO FY 1988

Facility-Based Data

Table 2.3 shows the number of admissions to inpatient facilities during the time period of interest by facility type. Data for individual facilities are included in Appendix 2.1. In Table 2.3, admissions are broken down by diagnosis,[1] commitment type, average length of stay, sex, and ethnicity of the clients who were admitted. These admission data are aggregate, however, and do not reflect individual clients, nor do they provide information on any client admitted prior to the study period. They do, however, represent the flow of people through each of the facilities during the past five years, excluding those few clients who entered prior to the five-year period and remained throughout that time.

Figure 2.4 presents an overview of the total number of inpatient admissions to the eight state hospital facilities during the study period. Several of these facilities have experienced moderate decreases in their yearly admissions over this time period; however, Kerrville, Big Spring, and Vernon were fairly stable, while Austin showed the largest decrease in admissions--about 2,200 fewer in 1988 than in 1984. Terrell and San Antonio state hospitals both decreased admissions by about 400 per year over the same period.

The large decrease in admissions at Austin State Hospital is likely due to a combination of two factors. It was during this period that the 250-bed Harris County psychiatric facility was opened in Houston, providing local care for many Houston residents who might otherwise have been sent to Austin State Hospital. In addition, the responsibility for Harris County clients requiring inpatient care in a state hospital was shifted from the Austin State Hospital to Rusk State Hospital during this time.

---

[1]Diagnosis, in this chapter, is based on the 2-digit diagnostic code which is used in the CARE system database. This code is computed from DSM III diagnoses and has been further consolidated into four categories for this discussion. The 2-digit codes which define the four categories used in this paper are listed below.

    01 Schizophrenia and related disorders
    02 Depressive disorders
    03 Other nonorganic psychoses
    04 Alcohol-related
    05 Drug-related
    06 Other organic disorders
    07 Autism/pervasive disorders
    08 Other developmental disorders
    09 Anxiety/somatoform/dissociative
    10 Personality/factitious/impulse
    11 Mental retardation
    12 Adjustment/other nonpsychotic
    13 No mental disorder
    14 Undiagnosed

An individual with a diagnosis of 01, 02, or 03 is considered SMI (seriously mentally ill). If the diagnosis is 04 or 05 the individual is categorized as SA (substance abuse). If the code is 13 or 14, the individual is considered to have no diagnosis (NO DIAG). Anyone not already categorized is considered to be OTHER, which includes both minor mental illness, developmental disorders, and organic illnesses.

Table 2.3. Admissions to Inpatient Facilities from September 1, 1983, through August 31, 1988

All State Hospitals

	1984		1985		1986		1987		1988	
Total Admissions	18,664		17,640		15,973		15,291		14,613	
Commitment Type										
Voluntary	8,024	43%	6,936	39%	5,820	36%	5,403	35%	4,969	34%
Involuntary	10,619	57%	10,685	61%	10,130	63%	9,564	63%	9,149	63%
Respite	0	0%	0	0%	0	0%	4	0%	0	0%
Ethnicity										
Black	3,259	17%	3,178	18%	2,642	17%	2,625	17%	2,799	19%
Hispanic	2,751	15%	2,579	15%	2,747	17%	2,747	18%	2,570	18%
White	12,505	67%	11,735	67%	10,420	65%	9,801	64%	9,141	63%
Other	149	1%	148	1%	164	1%	118	1%	103	1%
Sex										
Female	6,286	34%	5,840	33%	5,245	33%	5,105	33%	4,991	34%
Male	12,378	66%	11,800	67%	10,728	67%	10,186	67%	9,622	66%
Diagnosis										
Serious Mental Illness	8,877	48%	8,148	46%	6,883	43%	6,136	40%	6,066	42%
Substance Abuse	6,389	34%	6,162	35%	6,174	39%	6,208	41%	5,429	37%
Other	2,725	15%	2,603	15%	1,964	12%	1,968	13%	1,888	13%
No Diagnosis	673	4%	727	4%	947	6%	979	6%	1,231	8%
Admissions With Lengths of Stay That Were										
One Week or Less	2,659	14%	2,579	15%	2,381	15%	2,192	14%	2,063	14%
Over 60 Days	5,674	30%	5,143	29%	4,807	30%	4,697	31%	4,034	28%

All State Centers, Specialty Facilities and State Schools

	1984		1985		1986		1987		1988	
Total Admissions	1,361		2,221		1,884		1,898		2,010	
Commitment Type										
Voluntary	827	61%	1,247	56%	985	52%	946	50%	1,094	54%
Involuntary	533	39%	971	44%	896	48%	876	46%	782	39%
Respite	0	0%	1	0%	1	0%	1	0%	2	0%
Ethnicity										
Black	107	8%	167	8%	70	4%	55	3%	62	3%
Hispanic	672	49%	1,218	55%	1,223	65%	1,258	66%	1,390	69%
White	568	42%	808	36%	579	31%	557	29%	521	26%
Other	14	1%	28	1%	12	1%	28	1%	37	2%
Sex										
Female	533	39%	813	37%	634	34%	621	33%	685	34%
Male	828	61%	1,408	63%	1,250	66%	1,277	67%	1,324	66%
Diagnosis										
Serious Mental Illness	707	52%	1,117	50%	867	46%	891	47%	872	43%
Substance Abuse	334	25%	498	22%	471	25%	526	28%	576	29%
Other	229	17%	316	14%	325	17%	351	18%	377	19%
No Diagnosis	91	7%	290	13%	221	12%	130	7%	184	9%
Admissions With Lengths of Stay That Were										
One Week or Less	311	23%	516	23%	490	26%	470	25%	551	27%
Over 60 Days	195	14%	273	12%	285	15%	300	16%	218	11%

Source: TDMHMR, 1988a.

31

Figure 2.4. Total Number of Admissions to State Inpatient Facilities from FY 1984 to FY 1988

Source: TDMHMR, 1988a.

Differences in the ratio of voluntary to involuntary commitments were notable at four of the facilities, as shown in Figure 2.5. Austin has shown a consistent trend toward more involuntary commitments; however, San Antonio, Kerrville, and Terrell state hospitals have varied a great deal over the years of the study, showing no consistent pattern. Changes in the proportions of voluntary to involuntary commitments were also noted at Rusk, Vernon, and Wichita Falls; however, these were most notable during 1988 and are consistent with the system changes made during that year when Rusk transferred its maximum security patients to Vernon, Vernon sent its overflow to Wichita Falls, and Houston began sending its clients to Rusk.

The ethnic and gender distributions for these facilities remained, for the most part, constant over the five years of the study. It is notable that Rusk, which served as the maximum security facility during most of this time, had the highest proportion of blacks in the system. However, when its maximum security clients were transferred to Vernon, the proportion of blacks at Vernon went up. The proportion of blacks at Rusk did not decrease correspondingly, however, probably because of the higher proportion of blacks in the Harris County area who are now assigned to Rusk for care. Rusk also shows a surprisingly small proportion of Hispanics over the entire study period, given that it accepted clients from all over the state to its maximum security units. The proportion of Hispanics seen at Rusk more nearly represents that found in northern Texas than the state as a whole.

Four of the facilities, San Antonio, Austin, Wichita Falls, and Terrell, showed a decrease in admissions for serious mental illness over the study period, with a concomitant increase in admissions for substance abuse. The reverse of this trend is seen at Big Spring and Vernon. A rather gross measure of incidence for substance abuse (at least substance abuse serious enough to warrant inpatient care) can be obtained by looking at first admissions to state facilities for individuals between the ages of 15 and 24, the age range when substance abuse is most likely to appear as a problem. As shown in Figure 2.6, when these first admissions are compared with first admissions within the same age range for serious mental illness, which also generally makes its first appearance between the ages of 15 and 24, it can be seen that the incidence of substance abuse is not only increasing at most of the facilities, but it has been consistently higher than the incidence of serious mental illness at many of these facilities over time. These admissions represent entry into the system of individuals who may continue to require services over time, either in the inpatient system or from the community-based system. Given that substance abuse seems to be a growing phenomenon, showing increases over time in both incidence and overall admissions, it will be of interest to see whether this trend continues at these major state hospitals and, if so, what it means for the care of those seriously mentally ill who may be competing for the limited bed space.

At San Antonio State Hospital, Austin State Hospital, and Kerrville State Hospital, about 20 percent of the admissions each year are for stays of less than one week, while at the same facilities, there was a slightly higher percentage of stays of over 60 days. It would seem from these numbers that these hospitals are being used a great deal as crisis facilities, while at the same time providing relatively long-term care to many of their residents. Overall, for the state hospitals, the percentage of short-term admissions has remained rather constant at 14 percent. The percentage of long-term admissions has also remained constant over time at about 30 percent.

The state centers are somewhat more variable in their admission patterns than the state hospitals. As mentioned before, some of the state centers did not begin to report their inpatient data into CARE at the beginning of this study period. El Paso and Laredo began reporting during FY 1984, but it is doubtful that the numbers for that year are complete. Laredo and Rio Grande have mostly patients committed on a voluntary basis, while for El Paso the opposite is true. The ethnic distribution for each

33

Figure 2.5. Percentages of Total Admissions That Were Involuntary from FY 1984 to FY 1988

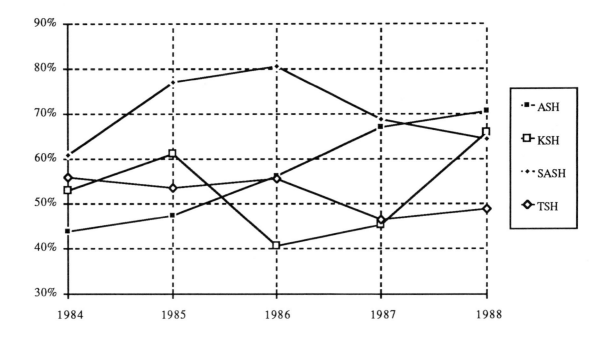

Source: TDMHMR, 1988a.

Figure 2.6. Number of First Admissions Annually for Serious Mental Illness and Substance Abuse among Young Adults at the Eight State Hospitals, 1983 to 1987

FIRST ADMISSIONS FOR CLIENTS AGES 15-24 TO AUSTIN STATE HOSPITAL

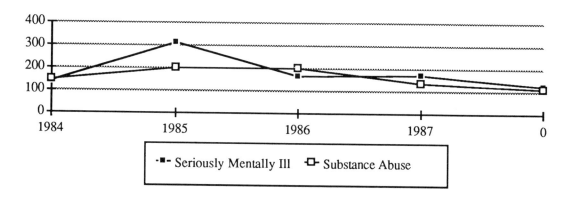

FIRST ADMISSIONS FOR CLIENTS AGES 15-24 TO BIG SPRING STATE HOSPITAL

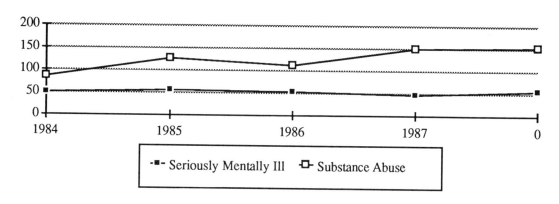

FIRST ADMISSIONS FOR CLIENTS AGES 15-24 TO KERRVILLE STATE HOSPITAL

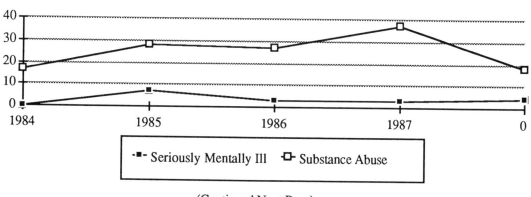

(Continued Next Page)

FIRST ADMISSIONS FOR CLIENTS AGES 15-24 TO RUSK STATE HOSPITAL

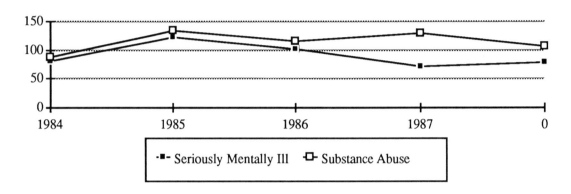

FIRST ADMISSIONS FOR CLIENTS AGES 15-24 TO SAN ANTONIO STATE HOSPITAL

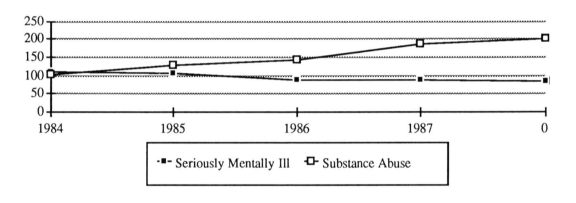

FIRST ADMISSIONS FOR CLIENTS AGES 15-24 TO TERRELL STATE HOSPITAL

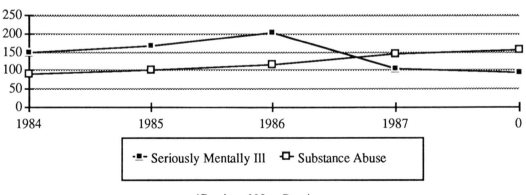

(Continued Next Page)

FIRST ADMISSIONS FOR CLIENTS AGES 15-24 TO VERNON STATE HOSPITAL

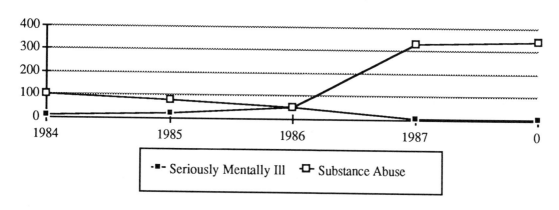

FIRST ADMISSIONS FOR CLIENTS AGES 15-24 TO WICHITA FALLS STATE HOSPITAL

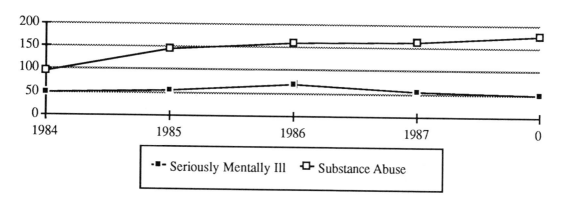

Source: TDMHMR, 1988a.

of the centers is consistent with their locations in predominantly Hispanic areas of the state. The gender distribution is fairly stable at 30-35 percent female to 65-70 percent male. Serious Mental Illness (SMI) is consistently the most frequent diagnosis, followed closely by Substance Abuse (SA) in all but the Laredo State Center. Laredo and Rio Grande both have high percentages of short-term admissions.

Of the specialized facilities, only the Waco Center for Youth has continued to operate throughout the study period. Its admissions are mostly voluntary, male, white individuals who stay over 60 days, and half of the beds at Waco are reserved for youth who are wards of the Texas Department of Human Services. The most common diagnoses are under the category of "other," which includes the adjustment reactions common to adolescence. The number of admissions to Waco has increased over the years, but seems to have stabilized at around 170 a year. The closing of the locked unit at Waco in the spring of 1989 due to budgetary constraints means that in the future many seriously mentally ill youth cannot be accommodated at Waco.

Client-Based Data

The data in the sections which follow are based on individual admissions, linked to unique identifiers for each client. Whereas the facility-based information tells us about the overall flow, characteristics, and hospital use of patients through the hospital over the study period, the client-based information is more useful for determining how the system is being used and by whom. Facility-based information contains duplicate counts of clients. We know that a given number of admissions occurs and where; but we don't know whether 1 or 20 different clients were served by that facility. Client-based information allows us to investigate the amount of recidivism and to trace an individual's course throughout the public mental health system. In this way, it can be much more useful to planners and policy makers who are interested in how the system is working as a unit for the benefit of specific groups of clients.

THE POPULATION OF THE PUBLIC INPATIENT SYSTEM ON AUGUST 31, 1988

Two distinct groups of clients made up the population of the public inpatient mental health system on August 31, 1988. The admission date for one group of clients (n=2,455) was comparatively recent (during the five-year span of the current study); however, the other group (n=586) represents a minority of clients who have been continuously in residence throughout the study period and who were admitted into the system prior to September 1, 1983. Taken together, these 3,041 clients represent a point prevalence of known individuals in the state hospitals and state centers as of August 31, 1988.

Table 2.4 provides some basic information on those individuals who were admitted within the study period and were also in residence at one of the state facilities at the time the data tapes were made. For 25.9 percent of these 2,455 individuals, the current admission was their first. Almost half of this in-residence group (45.5 percent), however, had admission histories predating the study period, with the date of first admission ranging back to 1925. The number of admissions which these individuals have had since the beginning of FY 1984 ranges from 1 to 29, with half having at least 2 admissions during this time. Most (79 percent) of these people have had 3 or fewer admissions during the study period. The average age at first admission for this group was 30.75 years with a median age of 25. In order to compare ages among groups at a given point in time, each client's age in 1986 was calculated. The members of this group had an average age of 36.28 in 1986 and a median age of 32.

Table 2.4. Clients in Residence at a State Inpatient Facility on August 31, 1988, Who Had Been Admitted for That Episode during the Past Five Years

Ethnicity		Marital Status		Sex	
20.0 %	Black	11.6 %	Married	38.1 %	Female
18.2 %	Hispanic	84.6 %	Not Married	61.9 %	Male
60.7 %	White	3.8 %	Unknown		
1.1 %	Other				

Diagnosis		
	First	Most Frequent
SMI	61.4 %	65.6 %
SA	9.7 %	4.9 %
Other	21.8 %	23.9 %
No Diag	7.1 %	5.6 %

(n=2,455)

Source: TDMHMR, 1988a.

Although this group appears to have fewer Hispanics than might be expected from the proportion in the population, and more blacks, when tested against the population projections for 1985 (Marshall and Bouvier, 1986) using a Chi Square Goodness of Fit Test, the difference is not statistically significant. Some age differences were noted among the ethnic groups, with the "other" groups being younger (average age in 1986= 29.12) and the whites being older (average age in 1986=37.53). The average age in 1986 for the Hispanics was 33.63 and for blacks, 35.26. The only significant difference was between the whites and the "other" category. The distribution of males to females is rather consistent with national inpatient psychiatric norms (Rosenstein et al., 1987). Women, who had an average age of 41 in 1986, were also significantly older than the men in this group, who had an average age of 33.36. Of the unmarried group of people, 56.9 percent had never been married. As is consistent with the mandate of the state facilities, the majority of these people are suffering from severe mental illnesses. As might be expected, the substance abusers were the youngest of this group of clients (average age in 1986=29.37), and those with various organic disorders were the oldest (average age in 1986=43.9). The first and most frequent commitment status of this group of 2,455 clients was involuntary (63-67 percent), which parallels the most frequent diagnosis of severe mental illness. That many of this group also had lengths of stay of over 60 days is also consistent with the frequent diagnosis of severe mental illness.

Of these 2,455 individuals in residence at the end of FY 1988, 68.3 percent have had assignments to community centers for outpatient treatment.[2] Of those with community center assignments, however, it is interesting to note that 31.7 percent were given no diagnosis by that center, 31.1 percent were diagnosed with a severe mental illness, 0.4 percent were diagnosed as substance abusers, and 34.5 percent were in the "other" category. This distribution clearly differs from that of the inpatient facilities, and agreement between the last diagnosis as an inpatient and the community center diagnosis is consistently poor for all clients regardless of whether they had one inpatient stay or many. As shown in Table 2.5, only 37.5 percent of the diagnoses given in the community centers agree with those given in the most recent inpatient facility. It is also notable from the table that the majority of clients undiagnosed in the community centers were considered severely mentally ill in the inpatient facilities.

In summary, a person who was in residence at a state facility at the end of FY 1988 and who had been admitted during the study period was likely to be a white, unmarried male in his mid-thirties. He was probably involuntarily committed to the facility for a serious mental illness. He also may well have had prior admissions during which he stayed in residence for over 60 days. Although he may have had some contact with the community-based system of care, it is very likely that he was not given a diagnosis by that community center.

Table 2.6 provides similar information on those individuals who were in residence at the time the data tapes were made but who were admitted prior to the study period. There were 586 clients in this group, and many (41.5 percent) were in Kerrville State Hospital. To date, these individuals have stayed on the average 5,104 days in residence-- about 14 years. Most (67.7 percent) were involuntarily admitted, and the average age at first admission was 44.8 years. The maximum length of stay among this group was about

---

[2]Community assignment was determined by matching unique CARE numbers for clients who had inpatient (campus) assignments with their corresponding CARE number in the community database. If an individual had a recorded community assignment on CARE in that database, whether it was currently open or closed, he or she was coded as having had a community assignment. If, on the other hand, a number was not found in the community database, he or she was coded as not having a recorded community assignment.

Table 2.5. Clients in Residence at TDMHMR Inpatient Facilities as of August 31, 1988, with Admission after September 1, 1983, and a Community Center Assignment: Agreement between Inpatient and Community Center Diagnoses

Community Center Diagnosis

		SMI	SA	Other	None	
	SMI	561	4	13	559	1,137
Inpatient	SA	21	0	31	68	120
Diagnosis	Other	137	2	5	158	302
	None	45	3	7	63	118
		764	9	56	848	1,677

Source: TDMHMR, 1988a.

Note: SMI = Serious Mental Illness
SA = Substance Abuse

41

Table 2.6. Clients in Residence at a State Inpatient Facility on August 31, 1988, with a Record of Residence for at least Five Consecutive Years

Ethnicity		Sex		Principal Diagnosis	
12.3 %	Black	48.5 %	Female	SMI	64.5 %
15.7 %	Hispanic	51.5 %	Male	SA	2.2 %
71.3 %	White			Other	30.9 %
.7 %	Other			No Diag.	2.4 %

Source: TDMHMR, 1988a.

Note: SMI = Serious Mental Illness
               SA = Substance Abuse

56 years. By definition, then, these individuals are going to be quite different from the prior group since they have been inpatients for five or more years continuously and represent those clients for whom community care has not been at all successful.

The ethnic distribution is somewhat different from that of the other group, with more whites and fewer Hispanics and blacks. It still does not differ from the population distribution by more than would be expected by chance. The gender distribution is also a bit different from the more recently admitted group, since there is almost an equal number of males and females. However, this difference may be a function of age. This group had an average age in 1986 of 56.5, which is somewhat older than the group with more recent admissions, and since women are somewhat more highly represented in the general population in this age group than are men (TEC, 1989, p. 8), this may explain the evening out of the male-female proportions. In fact, the women in this group were found to be significantly older than the men, who were on the average 53 years old, compared to the women, who were 60. The diagnostic pattern is quite similar, however, to the other in-residence group, with the majority being in the severe mental illness category.

It is interesting that when age in 1986 is broken down by diagnostic category, those individuals in the substance abuse category are significantly older (average age in 1986= 66.76) than those few in the "no diagnosis" category (average age in 1986=45.21), but not significantly different from the SMI group (average age in 1986=55.53) or the "other" group (average age in 1986=58.76). A finer breakdown of the "other" category reveals some differences. In the first group of in-residence individuals--those who have not been in the hospital continuously since prior to 1984--the "other" category contains a lower percentage of organic diagnoses (about 17 percent of the total) than the group with continuous stays (about 22 percent). The fact that 2.4 percent of these people who have been continuously in residence for over five years have no diagnosis is a bit puzzling, however.

Thus, the long-term resident of the inpatient facilities is likely to be a white male or female with serious mental illness who was committed to the facility a long time ago. Unlike the more recently admitted person, however, this resident is likely to be in his or her middle fifties and to have lived at the state hospital for about 14 years.

The above sections provide a snapshot into the system at a given point in time, but they give little information about the flow of clients through the system. The next several sections will focus on this client flow during the five years from September 1, 1983, through August 31, 1988.

RECIDIVISM IN THE TEXAS MENTAL HEALTH SYSTEM

In 1983, Virginia Mickel, a planner with TDMHMR, investigated recidivism within the Texas public mental health system. She looked at the population data for admissions to inpatient facilities for the period from October 1, 1977, through September 30, 1982--five fiscal years. In her study, she found that 26.1 percent of the clients were responsible for 50.1 percent of the admissions to state facilities over the study period. These were the clients with two or more admissions to facilities during the period (Mickel, 1983). The conclusions of the Mickel study regarding recidivism were thought to be conservative, however, because at that time, TDMHMR had no system of assigning unique case numbers to the clients. This meant that a client who was admitted to two state facilities showed up as a single admission twice rather than as a multiple admission. In the study which follows, unique case numbers were available, and the data should be more accurate.

The following section is an attempt to parallel as closely as possible the Mickel study in order to provide a rough comparison of the data from the most recent five-year period to that covered in the prior study.[3] During the period of time between September 1, 1983, and August 31, 1988 (FY 84 to FY 88), there were 91,624 admissions to TDMHMR inpatient facilities, and there were 61,599 different clients admitted. Of these clients, 59.3 percent had one admission only during the study period and none prior to that time. Another 14.7 percent (9,078) had only one admission during the study period but also one or more admissions prior to that time. The 45,618 individuals who experienced only one inpatient admission during the study period were responsible for 49.8 percent of the admissions. The remaining clients (15,981), those with two or more admissions during the study period, were therefore responsible for the other 50.2 percent of the admissions. Of the 61,599 clients admitted during this period, 58,401 had been discharged by the date the tape was made, 419 had died, 2,455 were still in residence, and the remainder were either absent on leave or on unauthorized departure.

As shown in Table 2.7, a comparison of findings from the recent analysis with those of Mickel's study reveals several things. First, there were fewer clients admitted overall during the more recent five-year period. Second, there were fewer admissions during the current five-year period than during the previous five years. Third, in the current study the actual recidivism rate (the proportion of individuals with a history of more than one inpatient admission during the five-year period studied) is about the same when compared to that of the prior study. As the data from the Mickel study are not directly comparable to the current data because of the lack of unique case numbers in the earlier study, it is difficult to draw any hard conclusions from these data. However, it does appear from the current study that once a client has been admitted into the system, he or she is just about as likely to have more than one additional admission to the system now as in the prior five-year period. Given the many recent system changes and additions that were supposed to improve community care and thereby reduce the need for inpatient care, this is a little surprising.

Another interesting comparison involves the total number of bed days used by the various client groups over the time of the study. As shown in Table 2.8, the 61,599 clients admitted to state facilities during the study period stayed a total of 5,691,409 days in the various hospitals during that time. Over half (54.9 percent) of those days were spent by individuals with histories of two or more admissions during the study period. In other words, those individuals with two or more admissions to the facilities (25.9 percent of the clients) were responsible for over half of the total bed days used during the study period, excluding the days used by those 586 individuals who were continuously in residence. When the days spent by those individuals continuously in residence are added, the distribution changes somewhat. The total number of days in residence increases to 6,760,859, with the continuous-use group being responsible for 16 percent of that total. Those individuals who had multiple admissions during the study period account for 46 percent of the days, and those with a single admission during the five years account for 38 percent of the days. Therefore the multi-admission group continues to account for almost half of the bed days, even when the days for those very long-term clients are added to the total.

Using the ratio of clients to days from the Mickel study, we would predict that 25.9 percent of the clients (those with two or more admissions during the study period) would be responsible for 46.4 percent of the total bed days rather than the 54.9 percent

[3]Only clients with at least one admission during the study period (FY 1983-FY 1988) are included in the following analyses. Any client who was continuously in residence throughout the study period is therefore not considered in this particular database.

Table 2.7. A Comparison of Admission Data from the Period FY 1977 through 1982 with That from FY 1983 through 1988

	Mickel Study - FY 1977--FY 1982	Current Study - FY 1984--FY 1988
Number of admission events	96,263	91,624
Number of clients	65,054	61,599
Number of clients with one admission only during the study period	48,083	45,618
Number of clients with two or more admissions during the study period	16,971	15,981
Percentage of clients with two or more admissions during the study period	26.1 %	25.9%
Percentage of admission events used by those with two or more admissions	50.1 %	50.2%

Sources: Mickel, 1983; TDMHMR, 1988a.

Table 2.8. A Comparison of Bed Day Usage Patterns for the Period FY 1977 through FY 1982 with FY 1984 through FY 1988

	Mickel Study - FY 1977-FY 1982	Current Study - FY 1984-FY 1988
Number of clients	65,054	61,599
Total number of bed days used during the five-year period	6,199,538	5,691,409
Number of bed days used by clients with only one admission during the study period	3,295,270	2,566,844
Percentage of total bed days used by clients with only one admission during the study period	53.2 %	45.1 %
Number of bed days used by clients with more than one admission during the study period	2,904,268	3,124,668
Percentage of bed days used by clients with more than one admission during the study period	46.8 %	54.9%

Sources: Mickel, 1983; TDMHMR, 1988a.

which was actually obtained. Therefore, the clients with multiple admissions were responsible for a higher percentage of total time in the hospital than we would expect using the earlier ratio. It seems that the clients with one admission only are using fewer of the days than would be expected, while the repeat admissions are using more days than in the prior study.

When average lengths of stay[4] are compared for the various groups, however, as shown in Table 2.9, it does appear that, although the average overall length of stay per client is decreasing, this is primarily due to the marked decrease in length of stay for those clients with only one admission. Those clients with two or more admissions during the current study period actually have a longer average length of stay than the comparable group in the Mickel study. When this recidivistic group is further broken down into two groups, however, one with all admissions during the five-year period and the other with longer histories, it is the latter group of longer-term clients who have the longest average lengths of stay during the study period (83.97 days for the long-term clients versus 56.12 days for the more recent clients). Therefore it seems that this second group of clients continues to stay in the hospital for fairly long periods of time when admitted.

CLIENTS USING THE INPATIENT MENTAL HEALTH SYSTEM FROM SEPTEMBER 1, 1983, THROUGH AUGUST 31, 1988

In order to look more closely at the characteristics of the individuals who were admitted to the inpatient system during the study period it is helpful to divide them into four groups. The first group contains those individuals who had only one admission during the study period and no prior admissions to the system. The second and third groups both have had multiple admissions to the inpatient system during the five years of the study. Members of group two had their first admission and all subsequent admissions during the five-year period covered by this study. Members of group three had their first admission, and often several other admissions, prior to the study period and at least two admissions during the study period. While members of group four had only one admission during the study period, they had also had one or more admissions prior to that time. Groups one and two represent relative newcomers into the system, while groups three and four contain individuals with longer histories of system use, having entered the inpatient system before September of 1983. Those clients who were continuously in residence in an inpatient facility during the study period have been excluded from these analyses, since they were described in an earlier section.

A comparison of the four groups, outlined in Table 2.10, shows many similarities. White unmarried males are most highly represented in all groups. For the two groups with admission histories predating the study period, over half of the people are categorized as seriously mentally ill, and this proportion is even higher for the group with multiple admissions throughout the study period. In the groups of individuals who more recently entered the inpatient system, substance abuse is almost as likely a diagnosis as serious mental illness for those with multiple admissions and even more likely for those individuals with one admission only. Age varies in the expected way, with about a ten-year difference between the average age of the individuals with histories predating the study and that of more recent entrants into the system.

Those individuals who entered the system during the most recent five-year period have consistently shorter average stays as inpatients. Several reasons might be postulated

---

[4]Those clients still in residence at the time the tape was made are not included in any of the calculations of average length of stay.

Table 2.9. A Comparison of Average Lengths of Stay for Clients Admitted during FY 1977 through FY 1982 and FY 1983 through FY 1988

	Mickel Study - FY 1977--FY 1982	Current Study - FY 1984--FY 1988
Average length of stay per admission for total population	64 days	59 days
Average length of stay per admission for clients with only one admission during the study period	68 days	56 days
Average length of stay per admission for clients with two or more admissions during the study period	60 days	69 days

Sources: Mickel, 1983; TDMHMR, 1988a.

Table 2.10. Demographics for Clients Admitted into the Public System
From FY 1984-1988

		Multiple Admissions		
	Only One Admission	All in Study Period	At Least One Prior to Study Period	Only One During Study Period
Number of Clients	36,540	8,537	7,444	9,078
Number of Admissions (during study period)				
Minimum--Maximum (prior to study period)	1--1	2--17	2 -- 29	1--1
Minimum--Maximum	0--0	0--0	1--76	1--37
Average Length of Stay (during study period)	49 Days	42 Days	84 Days	85 Days
Average Age in 1986	33	32	38	43
Ethnicity				
Black	13%	15%	21%	19%
Hispanic	19%	23%	21%	16%
White	67%	61%	58%	64%
Other	1%	1%	6%	5%
Marital Status				
Married	25%	19%	16%	21%
Not Married	72%	78%	80%	76%
Unknown	3%	4%	4%	3%
Gender				
Female	33%	33%	35%	36%
Male	67%	67%	65%	64%
Diagnosis				
SMI	28%	36%	69%	53%
SA	48%	34%	23%	34%
Other	18%	18%	6%	7%
No Diagnosis	6%	12%	2%	6%

(Continued Next Page)

	Only One Admission	All in Study Period	Multiple Admissions	
			At Least One Prior to Study Period	Only One During Study Period
Commitment Status				
Voluntary	43%	28%	35%	41%
Involuntary	57%	72%	65%	59%
Length of Stay				
< 3 Days	6%	6%	4%	3%
3-7 Days	12%	15%	9%	8%
8-14 Days	12%	19%	13%	12%
15-30 Days	26%	30%	21%	22%
31-60 Days	23%	30%	23%	22%
> 60 Days	21%	37%	45%	33%
Length of Stay for Seriously Mentally Ill				
< 3 Days	18%	26%	32%	26%
3-7 Days	22%	28%	35%	28%
8-14 Days	27%	35%	48%	36%
15-30 Days	19%	33%	51%	39%
31-60 Days	27%	40%	63%	50%
> 60 Days	46%	58%	81%	74%

Source: TDMHMR, 1988a.

to explain this. First, the increase in the proportion of admissions for substance abuse during the past five years may be a major factor, since substance abuse treatment has generally been associated with shorter stays than the treatment for serious mental illnesses. Another possibility is that those individuals who began treatment prior to the study period and who continue to require periodic inpatient care may represent a cohort of more seriously ill individuals whose care cannot be provided exclusively or primarily in the community and who typically require a longer time while in the hospital to stabilize their condition. The fact that serious mental illness represents the largest proportion of admissions in these two groups would support this argument as well.

A CLOSER LOOK AT SOME OF THE HIGH USERS OF THE SYSTEM

It seemed from the data that there might be more than one homogeneous group of individuals who were responsible for much of the hospital bed use in the state. The one thing which underlies these groups is their recurrent use of the system. Beyond that similarity, it is possible that there are many differences. To ascertain the existence of different client groups, usage patterns among those clients with multiple admissions or unusually long stays as inpatients were investigated more closely.

Old-Timers

The obvious group that surfaced first were the "old-timers." These were the individuals who had a history of cumulative lengths of stay in excess of 20 years. (The longest length of stay for a client who is still periodically using the system is a little over 23,000 days--about 63 years). In spite of deinstitutionalization, there are still a few people (185) with this type of history who are being hospitalized periodically, and most (63.8 percent) continue to be hospitalized for over 60 days at a time when they come in. Only 8 of them have been in for mostly short-term (less than 3 days) stays during the more recent years.

The total number of admissions for this group ranges from 2 to 21 with 77 percent having 6 or fewer admissions over their lifetime. Although 41 percent have had one consistent diagnosis throughout their history in the system, 59 percent have been assigned two to five different diagnoses over time. Many (43.2 percent) have used only one hospital, while 40.5 percent have been in two and 16 percent have used three to five different hospitals. The most frequently used hospitals are Austin State Hospital (21.6 percent), San Antonio State Hospital (20 percent), and Wichita Falls State Hospital (16.2 percent). A similar usage pattern holds for county of residence with the major urban counties being most highly represented (Bexar 11 percent; Harris 9.7 percent; Dallas 7.8 percent; Tarrant 5.2 percent; Travis 4.5 percent).

The most frequent diagnosis among this group is schizophrenia (78.7 percent), and 73.2 percent were admitted under court order most of the time. The ethnic breakdown is rather consistent for Texas--68.6 percent white, 17.8 percent Hispanic, and 13.5 percent black. The average age at first admission was 25 years old, and in 1986 the average person in this group was 58 years old. About half (47.6 percent) are female, and the other half (52.4 percent) are male. Most (63.8 percent) have never married.

These individuals averaged three to four admissions prior to FY 1984. Most (56.2 percent) had one or two admissions prior to this time, and only a small percentage (8 percent) had eight or more admissions prior to the study period. The year of first admission ranged back to 1925 and continued into the early 1960s, peaking in the middle 1950s. The time of last admission during the study period covers the range of the five years, indicating that these people are still, for the most part, alive (actually six of them have died) and using the hospitals periodically. In fact, 40 percent of these particular clients were still in residence at the time the tapes were made.

The obvious comparison group for these clients are those people who have been continuously in residence throughout the five years of the study. Although both groups are primarily seriously mentally ill and currently about 58 years old, the individuals with continuous recent residence entered the hospital in their middle forties and stayed. The group described above, with histories of 20 years or more in residence, entered the hospital first when they were about 25, came out occasionally, but frequently returned for long periods of time. A finer breakdown on diagnosis than the one used in the current study would probably help to explain some of these differences.

It is interesting that, despite their extensive history of long-term hospitalization, 28.6 percent of these persons with histories of 20 years or more as inpatients have no reported history of actually attending a community center for continuing care. This situation cannot be attributed to the fact that they are still in the hospital and have no need of community treatment because, of the discharged clients in this group, 24 percent have no reported community assignment.[5]

High-Users

Another group of interest to this study are the "high-users." This group is defined as individuals who have had four or more admissions during the five-year study period, an average of about one a year. These clients make up about 6 percent of the people who were active during this period. These individuals seem to have histories of moderate lengths of stay. Only 1.7 percent have had very short-term stays (less than 3 days), and 5.7 percent have had stays of primarily over 60 days. Most had admissions prior to the study period (ranging from 1 to 76), but 31.4 percent have had all of their admissions during the five-year period under study. Their admission rate (calculated as number of admissions per year within the five-year period) ranges from 0.80 to 5.8, with 53.5 percent of them having at least one admission per year during this period. These people have used 1,149,043 bed days during the study period, and in their lifetime, they have used 2,430,725 days total.

Individuals in this group have had from 1 to 11 different diagnoses during their stay in the system, and 44.2 percent have had 3 or more different diagnoses. They have stayed in from one to nine different hospitals, with 22.1 percent having stayed in three or more. They have lived in from 1 to 13 different counties (15.3 percent had 3 or more counties of residence), and when the most consistent diagnosis is checked, 71.7 percent of them are in the category of seriously mentally ill (Schizophrenia, Severe Depression, and Nonorganic Psychoses), 19.6 percent are substance abusers, and only 8.7 percent are in the other less severe categories. The majority of these clients (69 percent) are admitted involuntarily most of the time.

The hospitals of choice are, as to be expected, on the basis of population density, Austin State Hospital (26.6 percent), San Antonio State Hospital (21.8 percent), and Terrell State Hospital (12.1 percent); and the counties of residence are primarily the urban areas, Bexar (13.6 percent), Travis (10.5 percent), Harris (9.5 percent), and Dallas (8.5 percent). Whites account for 53.3 percent of this group, with 19.8 percent black and 26.2 percent Hispanic. There are more males (67.3 percent) than females (32.7 percent). Only 13.3 percent of these individuals report being married, and 47.8 percent have never

---

[5]As before, community assignment refers to the individual's actually having been recorded on CARE at any time as an active client at a community center or outreach facility.

been married. The average age at first admission was 25 years old, and in 1986 the average member of this group was 35 years old. Based on the final status listed, 81.4 percent have been discharged, 20 percent are dead, and 16 percent are in residential assignments.

The average time in the hospital for these individuals during the five-year period was 357 days--a little over two months a year. In their lifetime, they have averaged 755 days and have been active in the system for an average of about eight years. Interestingly enough, given their extensive history of inpatient system use, 13.3 percent of these clients have not been seen in the community centers or outreach facilities. Of those seen in the community, only 20.2 percent are assigned to case management. When seen in the community, 43.8 percent were given no diagnosis, 42 percent were seen as SMI, and 8.4 percent as substance abusers. These people are, on the whole, chronically and severely ill, relatively mobile, fairly young, and using up a lot of resources.

As a group, these individuals share much with the "old-timers." They differ primarily in the fact that they entered the mental health system after deinstitutionalization policies were in effect, thereby limiting the likelihood that they might ever spend 20 years of their lives in a hospital setting. Their needs are likely to be just as continuous as those earlier entrants into the system; however, the community is supposed to be the primary locus of care for all but the most severe exacerbations of illness. For that reason, it is rather disturbing that even 13 percent of these severely ill individuals have not yet made the connection to a known community-based service.

A subgroup of the high-users that is of interest is the 10 percent who have had mostly short-term hospital stays (one week or less). Unlike the larger group, only 40 percent of these people are SMI (compared to 75 percent in the larger group) while 44 percent (compared to 17 percent) are substance abusers. Many (56 percent) are involuntarily committed, but not as many as in the larger group, of which 70.6 percent are committed. Of these individuals, 25 percent have no community assignment.

In summary, this investigation reveals two issues concerning the various high-use groups. One is that there are many individuals who would seem to benefit from community center involvement, given their history of inpatient use, but who are not receiving it. And another is that there are some individuals who seem to be using the state hospitals as short-term crisis units, a mandated core service to be provided by the community centers. Yet many of these people have had no contact with community centers.

Of the total population of individuals admitted to state inpatient facilities during this study period, in contrast to the high-users described above, only 56.3 percent have a recorded community assignment on the CARE system. Of those with community assignments, only 11.3 percent have been assigned to case management services. The majority (56 percent) of clients who have been in a state hospital and who have community assignments are listed as undiagnosed in that community center, while 25.1 percent are considered SMI and 12.1 percent are substance abusers.

AN OVERVIEW OF THE COMMUNITY-BASED MENTAL HEALTH SYSTEM IN TEXAS

The preceding discussion of the hospital-based system in Texas raises some interesting questions about the adequacy of the linkages between inpatient and outpatient care in Texas. It also raises the question of just who the community centers are serving if, in fact, they are providing services for only 56 percent of the discharged hospital clients.

This section will provide some information on the active clients in the community centers as of August 31, 1988. It is necessary to preface this section with a caution, however. The data from the community centers are not felt to be as reliable as those from the facilities. Cases are often left open on the CARE system when, in fact, they have been closed (Bonner, Interview, November 6, 1989). There is currently an effort to remedy this situation, but the tapes used for this study were made prior to some of these efforts. Thus, the information provided in this part of the study should be considered only an approximation of the situation as it exists in the community centers.

Individuals were included in the community center database if they had an open mental health assignment at the time the tapes were made (September 30, 1988). Aggregate data per client were then tabulated to provide some basic demographics on this group as well as some information on the services which were provided by the centers.

Table 2.11 provides some basic demographic information on the 113,120 clients who had an open community center assignment as of September 30, 1988. The ethnic distribution found in the community centers does not differ from what one would expect by chance alone, given the population projections for Texas. The gender distribution is close to an even split, and marital status is notable only in that it is unknown for so many clients.

It is especially interesting, given the mandate for the community centers to provide services to those individuals considered most seriously ill, that only 18.3 percent of their clients are considered seriously mentally ill, while 64.29 percent have no known/recorded diagnosis. Along the same line, only 6.8 percent of the clients in community centers are receiving case management services. It is heartening, however, that within the case-managed group, 44 percent are in the seriously mentally ill category.

Only about 20 percent of the active community center clients have been admitted to an inpatient facility during the study period. Most receive one primary service while assigned to the center--client and family support--which is a sort of catchall for any service not considered residential or case management. A little over 2,000 clients, however, receive case management as their only service within the center. This is a little odd in that, if a client needs case management, one would assume that he or she would also need some of the other services offered under client and family support.

The average age for a client in the community center is about 34 years old. This does not vary much by ethnicity, but it does vary quite a bit by diagnosis. Those individuals considered SMI are considerably older than the average community center client, indicating either that these clients stay in the system longer or that, if they stay in long enough, they will indeed be given a diagnosis. The age distribution for case-managed versus non-case-managed clients is consistent with the finding that the more seriously mentally ill clients, which make up almost half of the case-managed group, are older.

To augment these data and provide a little more information on the clients receiving services from the community centers, some additional information was taken from TDMHMR's Client Profile Survey. This survey was designed by TDMHMR to provide information on the functional levels, demographics, services used, and so forth of a regionally representative sample of mental health clients using either inpatient or community services (TDMHMR, 1989a). Table 2.12 summarizes some of the information from this survey for the community-based facilities.

In contrast to the information which was available from CARE, this survey shows that 74 percent of these clients would fall into the category of serious mental illness.

54

Table 2.11. Demographic Information on Active Community Center Clients

Ethnicity		Marital Status		Sex	
Black	18.3 %	Married	8.9 %	Female	55.5 %
Hispanic	17.4 %	Not Married	37.5 %	Male	44.3 %
White	63.3 %	Unknown	53.6 %		
Other	1.0 %				

Diagnosis		Inpatient History		In Case Management	
SMI	18.3 %	Yes	19.6 %	Yes	6.8 %
SA	3.7 %	No	80.4 %	No	93.2 %
Other	13.72 %				
None	64.29 %				

Age by Diagnosis		Age by Ethnicity		Age by C.M. Services	
SMI	42.26	Black	32.54	Yes	40.62
SA	37.44	Hispanic	35.02	No	34.64
Other	29.76	Anglo	33.66		
None	33.95	Other	35.47		

Type of Services Received	
Residential Only	1.7 %
Case Management Only	2.0 %
Client and Family Support Only	89.2 %
Residential and client and Family Support	2.0 %
Case Management and Client and Family Support	4.5 %
Case Management and Residential	.2 %
All Three Services Active	.1 %

Source: TDMHMR, 1988b.

**Table 2.12. Survey Information from a Representative Sample of
Mental Health Clients from Community Facilities**

Diagnosis	Community n=1217	Dual Diagnosis/ Serious Mental Illness and Substance Abuse	Community n=1217
Schizophrenia	43%		
Depression	28%		
Non-organic Psychoses	3%	Yes	8%
Other organic	3%	No	92%
Autism	0%		
Other developmental/ behavioral	0%		
Anxiety related	5%	Ethnicity	
Personality disorders	4%		
Mental Retardation	7%	Black	17%
Ajustment reactions	1%	Hispanic	28%
Undiagnosed	7%	White	55%

Most Recent Occupation		Gender	
Professional/technical	4%	Male	46%
Managerial	0%	Female	54%
Clerical	4%		
Sales	3%		
Skilled Labor	5%	Months Employed in Past Year	
Semi-Skilled Labor	9%		
Unskilled Labor	24%	None	49%
Homemaker	11%	1--6	8%
Student	2%	7--12	17%
Retired	4%	Unknown	26%
Never Worked	14%		
Other	6%		
Unknown or Missing	14%	Current Employment Status	

Highest Level of Education		Fulltime Work	13%
		Part time/irregular	11%
8th Grade or less	20%	Retired/housewife/ student	17%
9-12-no diploma	24%		
High School Graduate	24%	Unemployed/not able to work	38%
Some College	17%		
Undergraduate Degree	4%	Unemployed/able to work	12%
Graduate School	2%		
Information Unavailable	11%	Information Unavailable	10%

(Continued Next Page)

56

**Table 2.12 (continued). Survey Information from a Representative Sample of
Mental Health Clients from Community Facilities**

	Community		Community
	n=1217		n=1217

Referral Source		Current Living Situation	
Self	20%		
Family/friend	15%	Alone/no support services	13%
Court/police	7%	Alone/with support	8%
Private Psychiatrist	2%	With parents or family	46%
Physician	5%	With others/no	10%
State Hospital/Center	18%	supervision	
campus program		With others/some	5%
Private hospital	2%	supervision	
Public hospital	5%	With others/continuous	4%
State Hospital/Center	7%	supervision	
community program		State facility	2%
Community MHMR Center	7%	Homeless	0%
Other Community Social	4%	Other	5%
Service Agency		Information Unavailable	5%
Clergy	0%		
Other	3%		
Information Unavailable	3%		

Source: TDMHMR, 1989a

Since the data only provide information on "mental health" clients, substance abuse is not included as a primary diagnosis. However, 8 percent of the clients in the survey are considered dually diagnosed with a serious mental illness and substance abuse. Only 7 percent of the clients from the survey are considered undiagnosed as compared with the 64 percent in the CARE data. This seems to lend some credibility to the explanation that the lack of diagnosis noted in the CARE data is more a problem of recording the diagnosis than being assigned a diagnosis at the center.

The ethnic distributions for community clients noted on the survey and from the CARE data are somewhat different, while the gender distribution is very similar. The survey respondents consisted of 28 percent Hispanics and 55 percent whites, compared with the 17 percent Hispanics and 63 percent whites in the CARE data. The fact that the sample was drawn to be regionally representative probably accounts for these differences.

Perhaps of more interest is the information on education level, occupational status, and employment, since these data are not available from the CARE system. From Table 2.12 it can be seen that the majority of the community center clients sampled have a high school diploma or less, have worked very little during the past year, and are currently unemployed. This is in many ways consistent with the high percentage of seriously mentally ill clients in the sample, but it also points rather powerfully to the need in the community for ongoing rehabilitation and training for these individuals if they are to return to productive lives in their respective communities.

Referral source for community services varies quite a lot, with family, friends, and self-referrals the most common, accounting for 35 percent of the referral sources. In their living situations clients vary from being highly supervised to alone, but almost half of them live with their parents or families.

FURTHER CONSIDERATIONS

For 17 percent of the clients with inpatient experiences in the state facilities, the majority of their hospitalizations have been less than one week in duration. Of those clients with these short-term admissions, 58.5 percent have no history of community assignment. While most of these short-term clients have had only one admission to a state facility (72.9 percent) during the past five years, 21.2 percent have had two admissions, and 5.9 percent have had three or more. It seems that many individuals are using the state hospitals as short-term crisis units, sometimes more than once, and many of these people have no known contact with community mental health resources. These short-term clients are primarily substance abusers (43.7 percent), but there are some in the SMI category (23.9 percent) and a good number undiagnosed (11.8 percent). While most are involuntarily committed (55.5 percent), the rest are voluntary.

Figure 2.7 shows the patterns of short-term state hospital admissions over a two-year period, broken down by quarter. There are distinct increases in these admissions during the third and fourth quarter of the fiscal year. This graph provides some clue as to the possible explanation for the large number of short-term admissions to state inpatient facilities, when this service is supposed to be available in the communities. Funding is tight in the entire MHMR system. The community centers are mandated to provide several core services, but the dollar amounts provided for them to accomplish this are often inadequate. Crisis stabilization facilities within the community are core services, but funds for these services may be depleted before the end of the fiscal year in which they were to be used. For example, the Concho Valley Center for Human Advancement, which covers San Angelo and eight surrounding counties, has funding available to provide one crisis bed per day in the community. The center contracts with

Figure 2.7. Inpatient Stays of Less Than One Week in Duration by Ethnicity during FY 1987 and FY 1988

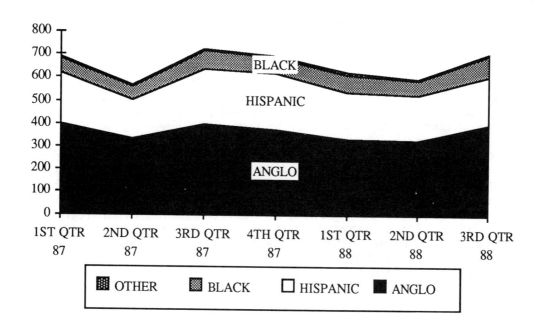

Source: TDMHMR, 1988a.

a local hospital for this service. More often than not the funds for the crisis bed are used up far before the end of the fiscal year, making it necessary to rely more heavily on the state hospital for crisis care (Crean, Rodriquez, and Vega, 1990). The graph in Figure 2.7 provides evidence that this may not be an isolated example.

It is difficult to determine exactly why so many individuals are not making the vital connection between the inpatient facilities and the community-based system of care. In many cases, it may simply be a recording problem. Many of the centers did not begin recording their client data on the CARE system when it first became available. Some still question the utility of the state-wide system and prefer to use their local computer systems for recording client data. Clients who are seen at the local centers only a few times may never make it onto the CARE system, and those who are seen only once are even less likely to be noted on CARE. Therefore, the percentages of discharged clients with community assignments on CARE may be artificially low.

Other difficulties in these linkages between the inpatient and community system may be more problematic. Until 1987 most clients (about 86 percent), as shown in Figures 2.8 and 2.9, were discharged from state facilities with "no more services" as their discharge status. A mandate from the R. A. J. v. Jones review panel initiated a statewide effort to ensure the links between inpatient care and community-based treatment. As can be seen in Figure 2.8, the change, at least on paper, was dramatic. Currently most clients leaving a state inpatient facility are given the discharge status of "with reassignment" and provided with a referral to the appropriate community facility for continuing care. This change is too recent in procedure to determine from this database whether this will make a difference in the number of clients making the connection between inpatient and community care, but it is certainly a step in the right direction.

CONCLUSIONS

Several questions were raised at the beginning of this chapter specifically relating to changes in system usage over time and in response to the many changes that have been implemented by TDMHMR as it seeks to provide more adequate community and inpatient care for Texans with mental illness. Is the inpatient system being used less frequently since the advent of the $35.50 plan? It would seem that this is so. There are fewer clients using these services, fewer bed days being used, and a declining total number of admissions to facilities. On the other hand, the recidivism rate has remained fairly constant, and those clients with multiple admissions are staying longer in the hospital when they are admitted than those who use the system less frequently.

Although the state inpatient facilities have reduced their overall censuses over the past five years, the absolute number of admissions to these facilities has not decreased nearly as dramatically. In 1984 the average daily census for the eight state hospital facilities was about 5,000 people. This census had dropped to about 3,500 by 1988, a reduction of about 30 percent over the earlier level (Nunn, 1990). Admissions to state hospitals, however, dropped from 18,664 in 1984 to 14,613 in 1988, which is a reduction of only about 22 percent. Given this information and the numbers of clients who are being readmitted to these facilities, it is clear that although the hospitals do not currently have as many available beds full on a daily basis, they continue to serve large numbers of clients repeatedly and these clients are using large numbers of bed days.

Recidivism in and of itself should not be seen as a sign of system failure. Seriously mentally ill clients experience episodic and recurring symptoms which often require rehospitalization for adequate treatment. Although most of the clients with multiple admissions stay for about 70 days per episode, the large number of repeat admissions to the state facilities that are short term in nature is quite surprising.

Figure 2.8. Discharge Status for Clients Discharged for the Eight Texas State Hospitals from 1981 until 1988

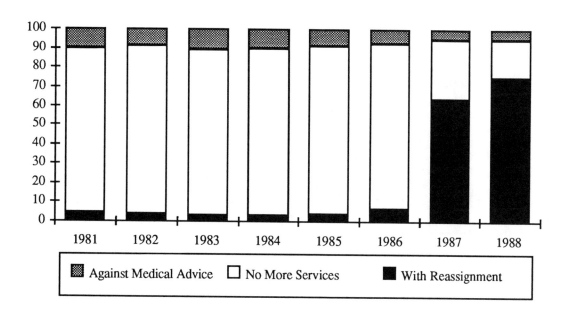

Source: TDMHMR, 1988a.

Figure 2.9. Percentage of Clients Discharged with No Reassignment, by Hospital and Year

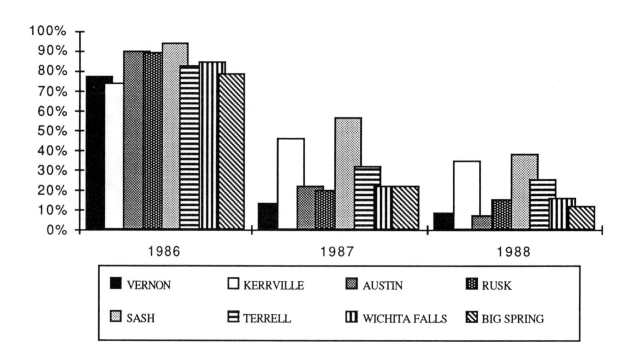

Source: TDMHMR, 1988a.

Theoretically, the community centers should be providing care for individuals requiring only short-term care. This is seen as less disruptive to the client's life and allows for a reasonable level of specialization within the inpatient facilities. The state hospitals could better meet the needs of their longer-term clients, who require highly structured rehabilitation, if they did not have to spilt their focus to meet the needs of the many emergency/crisis admissions which they receive.

Substance abusers are highly represented among those clients who have primarily short-term stays in the state inpatient facilities. They also make up over 40 percent of the group of highly recidivistic clients who have primarily short stays. It is possible, given these short lengths of stay and the primary diagnosis of substance abuse, that the state hospitals are being called upon to serve as temporary detoxification centers for these individuals. Again, the problem is not that these services are not needed, but that they may not be best provided by the state inpatient hospitals. It makes little sense, financially or clinically, to transport someone 100 miles to a hospital for detoxification when he or she will most likely stay for only one or two days and be released to return home, where he or she may or may not receive any further treatment. It would seem that the community would be a better locus for this type of care.

Perhaps most disturbing of all the findings in this study are those regarding continuity of care. The community centers are mandated to provide services to those individuals in the priority population--individuals with serious mental illness, dual diagnoses, histories of multiple inpatient admissions, etc. The hospitals are also required to refer discharged clients to the appropriate community services. However, large numbers of these clients are being discharged from the hospitals and not finding their way into the community-based system of care. It is possible that some of the problem is recording error. The CARE system is not as reliable for the community centers. However, it is doubtful that recording error can explain the large percentages of individuals with inpatient histories who have no community-based assignment.

The most seriously mentally ill people require the most help in obtaining needed services. They do not keep appointments well. They forget to take their medications and relapse. Their motivation is often poor. These are known facts about the nature of the illness. The community centers and state hospitals are directed to provide workers to facilitate this process, but, because of inadequate funding, there are too few of them to adequately follow the large numbers of clients requiring these intensive services (Reinstra, 1990). The linkages, therefore, are not always made, and individuals are lost to the system until the next crisis which requires hospital care.

Another disturbing fact that comes out of these data is that many individuals are not being assigned diagnoses within their community centers, even with extensive histories of hospitalization in which they did receive diagnoses. A diagnosis, in many ways, provides an efficient framework for treatment. It gives valuable information about history, prognosis, types of medications that are likely to be effective, and behavioral problems to be anticipated. Clearly, a diagnosis can change and should not be seen as unalterable. It provides, however, a working conceptual framework for clinicians to use as they attempt to alleviate symptoms and remedy problems. Not having an adequately thought-out diagnosis often means wasted time, misspent energies, and in general inefficient care. As in many other fields of endeavor, it is difficult to solve a problem which has not been clearly defined. For 56 percent of the clients coming into community centers from state hospitals, there is no diagnosis assigned at the community level, no problem defined in such a way that all who work with that client have access to the information. Clearly, this is a gap in continuity of care that should be addressed, whether it is a gap in recording or in understanding.

Appendix 2.1. Admissions to Inpatient Facilities - FY 1984 through FY 1988

Austin State Hospital

	1984		1985		1986		1987		1988	
Total Admissions	4,655		4,348		3,393		2,530		2,370	
Commitment Type										
Voluntary	2,619	56%	2,292	53%	1,491	44%	819	32%	667	28%
Involuntary	2,035	44%	2,055	47%	1,901	56%	1,696	67%	1,673	71%
Respite	0	0%	0	0%	0	0%	0	0%	0	0%
Ethnicity										
Black	1,045	22%	1,037	24%	803	24%	624	25%	517	22%
Hispanic	480	10%	426	10%	405	12%	289	11%	264	11%
White	3,068	66%	2,830	65%	2,134	63%	1,585	63%	1,557	66%
Other	62	1%	55	1%	51	2%	32	1%	32	1%
Sex										
Female	1,705	37%	1,527	35%	1,215	36%	945	37%	884	37%
Male	2,950	63%	2,821	65%	2,178	64%	1,585	63%	1,486	63%
Unknown	0	0%	0	0%	0	0%	0	0%	0	0%
Diagnosis										
Serious Mental Illness	2,664	57%	2,357	54%	1,938	57%	1,427	56%	1,197	51%
Substance Abuse	1,250	27%	1,261	29%	908	27%	671	27%	717	30%
Other	541	12%	505	12%	416	12%	339	13%	345	15%
No Diagnosis	200	4%	225	5%	131	4%	93	4%	111	5%
Admissions With Lengths of Stay That Were										
One Week or Less	1,013	22%	977	22%	701	21%	433	17%	458	19%
Over 60 Days	1,014	22%	850	20%	804	24%	648	26%	615	26%

Big Spring State Hospital

	1984		1985		1986		1987		1988	
Total Admissions	1,698		1,681		1,583		1,718		1,706	
Commitment Type										
Voluntary	882	52%	872	52%	844	53%	932	54%	897	53%
Involuntary	814	48%	805	48%	738	47%	739	43%	719	42%
Respite	0	0%	0	0%	0	0%	0	0%	0	0%
Ethnicity										
Black	154	9%	151	9%	137	9%	158	9%	149	9%
Hispanic	327	19%	335	20%	335	21%	396	23%	408	24%
White	1,205	71%	1,186	71%	1,101	70%	1,156	67%	1,140	67%
Other	12	1%	9	1%	10	1%	8	0%	9	1%
Sex										
Female	505	30%	564	34%	507	32%	562	33%	579	34%
Male	1,193	70%	1,117	66%	1,076	68%	1,156	67%	1,127	66%
Unknown	0	0%	0	0%	0	0%	0	0%	0	0%
Diagnosis										
Serious Mental Illness	653	38%	652	39%	582	37%	689	40%	725	42%
Substance Abuse	782	46%	745	44%	674	43%	777	45%	718	42%
Other	236	14%	263	16%	217	14%	227	13%	223	13%
No Diagnosis	27	2%	21	1%	110	7%	25	1%	40	2%
Admissions With Lengths of Stay That Were										
One Week or Less	177	10%	193	11%	247	16%	235	14%	228	13%
Over 60 Days	522	31%	455	27%	455	29%	469	27%	410	24%

Appendix 2.1 (Continued). Admissions to Inpatient Facilities - FY 1984 through FY 1988

Rusk State Hospital

	1984		1985		1986		1987		1988	
Total Admissions	2,817		2,648		2,093		2,541		1,999	
Commitment Type										
Voluntary	112	4%	111	4%	40	2%	49	2%	76	4%
Involuntary	2,700	96%	2,531	96%	2,051	98%	2,438	96%	1,882	94%
Respite	0	0%	0	0%	0	0%	3	0%	0	0%
Ethnicity										
Black	764	27%	782	30%	595	28%	783	31%	761	38%
Hispanic	144	5%	129	5%	114	5%	166	7%	140	7%
White	1,896	67%	1,724	65%	1,374	66%	1,574	62%	1,084	54%
Other	13	0%	13	0%	10	0%	18	1%	14	1%
Sex										
Female	830	29%	685	26%	496	24%	690	27%	561	28%
Male	1,987	71%	1,963	74%	1,597	76%	1,851	73%	1,438	72%
Unknown	0	0%	0	0%	0	0%	0	0%	0	0%
Diagnosis										
Serious Mental Illness	1,484	53%	1,381	52%	975	47%	1,114	44%	896	45%
Substance Abuse	816	29%	756	29%	715	34%	749	29%	521	26%
Other	469	17%	421	16%	229	11%	440	17%	294	15%
No Diagnosis	48	2%	90	3%	174	8%	238	9%	288	14%
Admissions With Lengths of Stay That Were										
One Week or Less	192	7%	241	9%	153	7%	195	8%	122	6%
Over 60 Days	1,262	45%	1,215	46%	929	44%	1,153	45%	791	40%

Kerrville State Hospital

	1984		1985		1986		1987		1988	
Total Admissions	422		438		424		393		566	
Commitment Type										
Voluntary	199	47%	170	39%	252	59%	209	53%	162	29%
Involuntary	223	53%	268	61%	172	41%	178	45%	373	66%
Respite	0	0%	0	0%	0	0%	0	0%	0	0%
Ethnicity										
Black	10	2%	5	1%	8	2%	13	3%	9	2%
Hispanic	38	9%	56	13%	45	11%	50	13%	130	23%
White	374	89%	377	86%	368	87%	328	83%	426	75%
Other	0	0%	0	0%	3	1%	2	1%	1	0%
Sex										
Female	153	36%	156	36%	174	41%	162	41%	195	34%
Male	269	64%	282	64%	250	59%	231	59%	371	66%
Unknown	0	0%	0	0%	0	0%	0	0%	0	0%
Diagnosis										
Serious Mental Illness	97	23%	94	21%	78	18%	80	20%	147	26%
Substance Abuse	228	54%	230	53%	232	55%	197	50%	251	44%
Other	85	20%	94	21%	82	19%	92	23%	136	24%
No Diagnosis	12	3%	20	5%	32	8%	24	6%	32	6%
Admissions With Lengths of Stay That Were										
One Week or Less	66	16%	89	20%	117	28%	75	19%	96	17%
Over 60 Days	140	33%	98	22%	83	20%	84	21%	108	19%

Appendix 2.1 (Continued). Admissions to Inpatient Facilities - FY 1984 through FY 1988

San Antonio State Hospital

	1984		1985		1986		1987		1988	
Total Admissions	3,540		3,085		3,413		3,476		2938	
Commitment Type										
Voluntary	1,380	39%	705	23%	661	19%	937	26%	921	31%
Involuntary	2,156	61%	2,379	77%	2,748	81%	2,440	69%	1,894	64%
Respite	0	0%	0	0%	0	0%	1	0%	0	0%
Ethnicity										
Black	353	10%	284	9%	343	10%	392	11%	392	13%
Hispanic	1,472	42%	1,318	43%	1,544	45%	1,525	43%	1,288	44%
White	1,693	48%	1,459	47%	1,487	44%	1,539	43%	1,245	42%
Other	22	1%	24	1%	39	1%	20	1%	13	0%
Sex										
Female	1,042	29%	980	32%	1,029	30%	1,045	30%	964	33%
Male	2,498	71%	2,105	68%	2,384	70%	2,431	69%	1,974	67%
Unknown	0	0%	0	0%	0	0%	0	0%	0	0%
Diagnosis										
Serious Mental Illness	1,430	40%	1,196	39%	1,134	33%	1,143	32%	1,022	35%
Substance Abuse	1,495	42%	1,297	42%	1,549	45%	1,583	45%	1,205	41%
Other	390	11%	370	12%	372	11%	325	9%	214	7%
No Diagnosis	225	6%	222	7%	353	10%	425	12%	497	17%
Admissions With Lengths of Stay That Were										
One Week or Less	644	18%	456	15%	647	19%	802	23%	638	22%
Over 60 Days	924	26%	864	28%	905	27%	878	25%	673	23%

Terrell State Hospital

	1984		1985		1986		1987		1988	
Total Admissions	2,692		2,764		2,388		2,044		2,210	
Commitment Type										
Voluntary	1,188	44%	1,283	46%	1,056	44%	1,046	51%	1,037	47%
Involuntary	1,503	56%	1,479	54%	1,329	56%	951	47%	1,078	49%
Respite	0	0%	0	0%	0	0%	0	0%	0	0%
Ethnicity										
Black	670	25%	699	25%	540	23%	436	21%	546	25%
Hispanic	107	4%	113	4%	106	4%	73	4%	86	4%
White	1,894	70%	1,932	70%	1,715	72%	1,518	74%	1,560	71%
Other	21	1%	20	1%	27	1%	17	1%	18	1%
Sex										
Female	1,068	40%	1,086	39%	963	40%	830	41%	925	42%
Male	1,624	60%	1,678	61%	1,425	60%	1,214	59%	1,285	58%
Unknown	0	0%	0	0%	0	0%	0	0%	0	0%
Diagnosis										
Serious Mental Illness	1,647	61%	1,628	59%	1,316	55%	977	48%	1,065	48%
Substance Abuse	664	25%	749	27%	773	32%	781	38%	747	34%
Other	307	11%	309	11%	253	11%	242	12%	289	13%
No Diagnosis	74	3%	78	3%	46	2%	44	2%	110	5%
Admissions With Lengths of Stay That Were										
One Week or Less	261	10%	347	13%	258	11%	216	11%	280	13%
Over 60 Days	778	29%	687	25%	656	27%	560	27%	484	22%

Appendix 2.1 (Continued). Admissions to Inpatient Facilities - FY 1984 through FY 1988

Vernon State Hospital

	1984		1985		1986		1987		1988	
Total Admissions	1,038		1,019		949		919		843	
Commitment Type										
Voluntary	475	46%	482	47%	487	51%	507	55%	274	33%
Involuntary	556	54%	534	52%	456	48%	398	43%	547	65%
Respite	0	0%	0	0%	0	0%	0	0%	0	0%
Ethnicity										
Black	78	8%	53	5%	51	5%	68	7%	235	28%
Hispanic	122	12%	142	14%	130	14%	189	21%	164	19%
White	835	80%	807	79%	759	80%	655	71%	436	52%
Other	3	0%	17	2%	9	1%	7	1%	8	1%
Sex										
Female	291	28%	277	27%	225	24%	245	27%	134	16%
Male	747	72%	742	73%	724	76%	674	73%	709	84%
Unknown	0	0%	0	0%	0	0%	0	0%	0	0%
Diagnosis										
Serious Mental Illness	218	21%	223	22%	184	19%	143	16%	339	40%
Substance Abuse	414	40%	396	39%	562	59%	642	70%	337	40%
Other	367	35%	374	37%	134	14%	43	5%	68	8%
No Diagnosis	39	4%	26	3%	69	7%	91	10%	99	12%
Admissions With Lengths of Stay That Were										
One Week or Less	47	5%	58	6%	42	4%	42	5%	33	4%
Over 60 Days	523	50%	529	52%	468	49%	454	49%	493	58%

Wichita Falls State Hospital

	1984		1985		1986		1987		1988	
Total Admissions	1,802		1,657		1730		1,670		1,981	
Commitment Type										
Voluntary	1,169	65%	1,021	62%	989	57%	904	54%	935	47%
Involuntary	632	35%	634	38%	735	42%	724	43%	983	50%
Respite	0	0%	0	0%	0	0%	0	0%	0	0%
Ethnicity										
Black	185	10%	167	10%	165	10%	151	9%	190	10%
Hispanic	61	3%	60	4%	68	4%	59	4%	90	5%
White	1,540	85%	1,420	86%	1,482	86%	1,446	87%	1,693	85%
Other	16	1%	10	1%	15	1%	14	1%	8	0%
Sex										
Female	692	38%	565	34%	636	37%	626	37%	749	38%
Male	1,110	62%	1,092	66%	1,094	63%	1,044	63%	1,232	62%
Unknown	0	0%	0	0%	0	0%	0	0%	0	0%
Diagnosis										
Serious Mental Illness	684	38%	617	37%	676	39%	563	34%	675	34%
Substance Abuse	740	41%	728	44%	761	44%	808	48%	933	47%
Other	330	18%	267	16%	261	15%	260	16%	319	16%
No Diagnosis	48	3%	45	3%	32	2%	39	2%	54	3%
Admissions With Lengths of Stay That Were										
One Week or Less	259	14%	218	13%	216	12%	194	12%	208	10%
Over 60 Days	511	28%	445	27%	507	29%	451	27%	460	23%

Appendix 2.1 (Continued). Admissions to Inpatient Facilities - FY 1984 through FY 1988

	Amarillo State Center				Beaumont State Center				El Paso State Center									
	1987		1988		1987		1988		1984		1985		1986		1987		1988	
Total Admissions	10		3		28		28		6		590		563		546		570	
Commitment Type																		
Voluntary	3	30%	0	0%	0	0%	0	0%	0	0%	192	33%	135	24%	169	31%	216	38%
Involuntary	0	0%	0	0%	10	36%	0	0%	6	100%	396	67%	426	76%	359	66%	333	58%
Respite	7	70%	3	100%	17	61%	22	79%	0	0%	1	0%	1	0%	0	0%	2	0%
Ethnicity																		
Black	0	0%	0	0%	9	32%	6	21%	0	0%	31	5%	23	4%	22	4%	23	4%
Hispanic	0	0%	0	0%	0	0%	0	0%	5	83%	311	53%	328	58%	326	60%	351	62%
White	10	100%	3	100%	19	68%	22	79%	1	17%	239	41%	208	37%	184	34%	189	33%
Other	0	0%	0	0%	0	0%	0	0%	0	0%	9	2%	4	1%	14	3%	7	1%
Sex																		
Female	5	50%	2	67%	12	43%	7	25%	2	33%	238	40%	203	36%	176	32%	197	35%
Male	5	50%	1	33%	16	57%	21	75%	4	67%	352	60%	360	64%	370	68%	373	65%
Unknown	0	0%	0	0%	0	0%	0	0%	0	0%	0	0%	0	0%	0	0%	0	0%
Diagnosis																		
Serious Mental Illness	0	0%	0	0%	0	0%	0	0%	0	0%	242	41%	268	48%	262	48%	255	45%
Substance Abuse	0	0%	0	0%	0	0%	0	0%	0	0%	145	25%	199	35%	198	36%	183	32%
Other	0	0%	0	0%	0	0%	0	0%	1	17%	50	8%	79	14%	67	12%	83	15%
No Diagnosis	10	100%	3	100%	28	100%	28	100%	5	83%	153	26%	17	3%	19	3%	49	9%
Admissions With Lengths of Stay That Were																		
One Week or Less	8	80%	3	100%	8	29%	10	36%	0	0%	78	13%	98	17%	93	17%	85	15%
Over 60 Days	1	10%	0	0%	0	0%	1	4%	3	50%	78	13%	104	18%	69	13%	63	11%

Appendix 2.1 (Continued). Admissions to Inpatient Facilities - FY 1984 through FY 1988

	Laredo State Center										Rio Grande State Center									
	1984		1985		1986		1987		1988		1984		1985		1986		1987		1988	
Total Admissions	20		185		177		219		243		865		973		996		946		1,010	
Commitment Type																				
Voluntary	17	85%	127	69%	141	80%	169	77%	170	70%	498	58%	619	64%	570	57%	442	47%	535	53%
Involuntary	3	15%	58	31%	36	20%	44	20%	64	26%	367	42%	354	36%	426	43%	462	49%	380	38%
Respite	0	0%	0	0%	0	0%	1	0%	0	0%	0	0%	0	0%	0	0%	0	0%	0	0%
Ethnicity																				
Black	0	0%	2	1%	4	2%	3	1%	0	0%	6	1%	5	1%	8	1%	6	1%	7	1%
Hispanic	16	80%	155	84%	142	80%	183	84%	210	86%	611	71%	725	75%	741	74%	728	77%	801	79%
White	3	15%	27	15%	26	15%	26	12%	31	13%	243	28%	241	25%	245	25%	208	22%	179	18%
Other	1	5%	1	1%	5	3%	7	3%	2	1%	5	1%	2	0%	2	0%	4	0%	23	2%
Sex																				
Female	11	55%	55	30%	76	43%	81	37%	104	43%	257	30%	274	28%	302	30%	279	29%	299	30%
Male	8	40%	130	70%	101	57%	138	63%	139	57%	608	70%	699	72%	694	70%	667	71%	711	70%
Unknown	0	0%	0	0%	0	0%	0	0%	0	0%	0	0%	0	0%	0	0%	0	0%	0	0%
Diagnosis																				
Serious Mental Illness	10	50%	158	85%	143	81%	152	69%	139	57%	403	47%	485	50%	445	45%	465	49%	465	46%
Substance Abuse	1	5%	9	5%	1	1%	8	4%	12	5%	292	34%	304	31%	271	27%	320	34%	381	38%
Other	1	5%	15	8%	28	16%	26	12%	22	9%	127	15%	120	12%	90	9%	98	10%	109	11%
No Diagnosis	8	40%	3	2%	5	3%	33	15%	70	29%	43	5%	64	7%	190	19%	63	7%	55	5%
Admissions With Lengths of Stay That Were																				
One Week or Less	9	45%	61	33%	45	25%	48	22%	75	31%	244	28%	314	32%	346	35%	325	34%	384	38%
Over 60 Days	2	10%	32	17%	41	23%	55	25%	34	14%	43	5%	45	5%	15	2%	27	3%	14	1%

69

Appendix 2.1 (Continued). Admissions to Inpatient Facilities - FY 1984 through FY 1988

	TRIMS		Waco Center for Youth				
	1984	1985	1984	1985	1986	1987	1988
Total Admissions	378	363	67	96	140	173	173
Commitment Type							
Voluntary	240 63%	216 60%	65 97%	93 97%	137 98%	164 95%	172 99%
Involuntary	137 36%	147 40%	2 3%	3 3%	3 2%	9 5%	1 1%
Respite	0 0%	0 0%	0 0%	0 0%	0 0%	0 0%	0 0%
Ethnicity							
Black	89 24%	111 31%	6 9%	16 17%	32 23%	22 13%	31 18%
Hispanic	30 8%	14 4%	5 7%	5 5%	10 7%	16 9%	24 14%
White	251 66%	223 61%	56 84%	74 77%	97 69%	132 76%	114 66%
Other	8 2%	15 4%	0 0%	1 1%	1 1%	3 2%	4 2%
Sex							
Female	229 61%	205 56%	24 36%	33 34%	52 37%	76 44%	80 46%
Male	149 39%	158 44%	43 64%	63 66%	88 63%	97 56%	93 54%
Unknown	0 0%	0 0%	0 0%	0 0%	0 0%	0 0%	0 0%
Diagnosis							
Serious Mental Illness	287 76%	224 62%	7 10%	8 8%	11 8%	12 7%	13 8%
Substance Abuse	41 11%	40 11%	0 0%	0 0%	0 0%	0 0%	0 0%
Other	35 9%	42 12%	60 90%	88 92%	124 89%	159 92%	160 92%
No Diagnosis	15 4%	57 16%	0 0%	0 0%	5 4%	2 1%	0 0%
Admissions With Lengths of Stay That Were							
One Week or Less	52 14%	58 16%	1 1%	0 0%	1 1%	0 0%	5 3%
Over 60 Days	79 21%	32 9%	63 94%	82 85%	121 86%	147 85%	103 60%

Appendix 2.1 (Continued). Admissions to Inpatient Facilities - FY 1984 through FY 1988

State Schools

	1984		1985		1986		1987		1988	
Total Admissions	25		14		8		14		14	
Commitment										
Type										
Voluntary	7	28%	0	0%	2	25%	2	14%	1	14%
Involuntary	18	72%	13	93%	5	63%	2	14%	4	14%
Respite	0	0%	0	0%	0	0%	0	0%	0	0%
Ethnicity										
Black	6	24%	2	14%	3	38%	2	14%	1	14%
Hispanic	5	20%	8	57%	2	25%	5	36%	4	36%
White	14	56%	4	29%	3	38%	7	50%	8	50%
Other	0	0%	0	0%	0	0%	0	0%	1	0%
Sex										
Female	10	40%	8	57%	1	13%	9	64%	5	64%
Male	16	64%	6	43%	7	88%	5	36%	8	36%
Unknown	0	0%	0	0%	0	0%	0	0%	0	0%
Diagnosis										
Serious Mental Illness	0	0%	0	0%	0	0%	0	0%	0	0%
Substance Abuse	0	0%	0	0%	0	0%	0	0%	0	0%
Other	5	20%	1	7%	4	50%	1	7%	3	7%
No Diagnosis	20	80%	13	93%	4	50%	13	93%	10	93%
Admissions With Lengths of Stay That Were										
One Week or Less	5	20%	5	36%	0	0%	4	29%	2	29%
Over 60 Days	5	20%	4	29%	4	50%	2	14%	4	14%

Source: TDMHMR, 1988a.

References

Bonner, Julie. 1989. Texas Department of Mental Health and Mental Retardation, Management Information System. Austin, Texas. Telephone interview by Pamela Diamond. November 6.

Crean, Hugh F., Norma Rodriquez, and Rudolfo Vega. 1990. "Concho Valley Center for Human Advancement: A Case Study." In Community Care of the Chronically Mentally Ill in Texas: Four Case Studies. Special Project Report. Austin, Texas: Lyndon B. Johnson School of Public Affairs, The University of Texas at Austin.

Leff, H. Stephen. 1989. "Operational Planning in the Texas Mental Health and Mental Retardation System". Seminar presented by the Human Services Resource Institute, Austin, Texas. (January 12).

Marshall, R. F., and L. F. Bouvier. 1986. Population Change and the Future of Texas. Washington, D.C.: Population Reference Bureau.

Mickel, Virginia F. 1983. Recidivism in Texas State Hospitals During a Five-Year Period: Fiscal Year 1978 through Fiscal Year 1982. Austin, Texas: Texas Department of Mental Health and Mental Retardation.

Miller, Gary E., and William V. Rago. 1987. "Fiscal Incentives to Encourage Non-Institutional Public-Sector Mental Health and Mental Retardation Services." Austin, Texas: Texas Department of Mental Health and Mental Retardation.

Nunn, Bruce. 1990. "Eight State Hospital Bed Days: 1984 through 1989." Faxed Communication, February 5.

Reinstra, Janice. 1990. "Continuity of Care." In Financing the Care for the Chronically Mentally Ill in Texas. Policy Research Project Report. Austin, Texas: Lyndon B. Johnson School of Public Affairs, The University of Texas at Austin.

Rosenstein, Marilyn J., Laura J. Milazzo-Sayre, Robin L. MacAskill, and Ronald W. Manderscheid. 1987. "Use of Inpatient Psychiatric Services by Special Populations." In Mental Health, United States, 1987, ed. Ronald W. Manderscheid and Sally A. Barrett. Washington, D.C.: U.S. Government Printing Office.

Texas Department of Health (TDH). December 1988. "State Health Planning and Resource Development." Austin, Texas.

Texas Department of Mental Health and Mental Retardation (TDMHMR). 1988a. "CARE System Tapes, Campus Data, September 1, 1983 through August 31, 1988." Austin, Texas.

_____. 1988b. "CARE System Tapes, Community Data, September 1, 1983 through September 30, 1988." Austin, Texas.

_____. 1989a. "Client Profile Survey Data." Selected information from data tapes. Austin, Texas.

_____. 1989b. Future Directions for Comprehensive Community-Based Mental Health Services in Texas. Austin, Texas. (Draft.)

_____. 1989c. <u>1989 Directory of Services</u>. Austin, Texas.

Texas Employment Commission (TEC). 1989. "Texas Work Force 2000." Austin, Texas.

Chapter 3. Minority Populations[*]

During the past two decades, there has been a stated policy of improving the acceptability, appropriateness, and cultural relevance of mental health services for members of minority groups, but in reality there are inadequate and culturally insensitive mental health services for members of these groups. Although the 1977 President's Commission on Mental Health provided various recommendations to improve the delivery of mental health care to minority members more than ten years ago, few of these suggestions have been implemented (Shore, 1988). As a result, the minority chronically mentally ill have been historically misdiagnosed, inappropriately served, and disproportionately institutionalized (Rosenthal and Carty, 1988). This is a matter of great concern since the minority population is growing at a much faster rate than that of the general population.

OVERVIEW OF THE LITERATURE FOR MEXICAN-AMERICANS

Over the past thirty years, a great deal of observation and concern has focused on the issue of underutilization of mental health services by Mexican-Americans in Texas (Jaco, 1959; Kruger, 1974; Cuellar, 1977; Dworkin and Adams, 1987). This issue has received much attention because Mexican-Americans experience many difficulties due to problems with acculturation, discrimination, language differences, and poverty, and these difficulties have been associated with a higher incidence of mental disorders, particularly psychoses and other serious mental disorders (Dohrenwend and Dohrenwend, 1969; Robins, 1978). This has led researchers to hypothesize that because Mexican-Americans live under high levels of environmental and psychological stress which are associated with mental disorder, Mexican-Americans should show an increased utilization of mental health services. Paradoxically, however, as was found by Karno and Edgerton (1969) and others (Griffith, 1983, cited in Dworkin and Adams, 1987; and Hough et al., 1987), Mexican-Americans underutilize mental health services.

In a paper commissioned by the Hogg Foundation, Cuellar and Schnee (1987) examined the utilization rates of state hospitals and CMHMRCs in Texas during FY 1985. These investigators found that Mexican-Americans underutilized both of these mental health facilities. Specifically, they found that TDMHMR served a total of 3,458 Hispanics (see Appendix 3.1 for the definitions used in this chapter) in state hospitals, which was only 17 percent of the total population served by the state system during that year.

Of concern, however, in examining the usage patterns of mental health services is the considerable variation in the definition of "underutilization." Early studies in this area have assumed that mental health needs are equivalent across Anglos, blacks, and Hispanics. Thus, in these studies, the number of an ethnic group receiving mental health services was compared against the total number of that particular group in the general population (Dworkin and Adams, 1987). However, there are those researchers who argue that, because Mexican-Americans face additional psychological stressors (e.g., poverty, discrimination, acculturation), even proportional treatment rates signify underutilization (Ramirez, 1980; Griffith, 1983, cited in Dworkin and Adams, 1987).

Another concern is that few studies have examined the utilization of mental health services by ethnicity in terms of established need. Vernon and Roberts (1982) contend that data should be reported for both treated and untreated rates of mental

---

[*]This chapter was written by Norma Rodriquez and Rudolfo R. Vega.

disorders by ethnicity in order to determine to what extent utilization patterns are representative of actual mental health needs (treated rates are based on contacts with a mental health provider, while untreated rates are based on community surveys). An examination of these rates would provide a more accurate account as to whether certain groups are being underserved. Vernon and Roberts indicate that assessments of utilization are presently being made by comparing a subgroup of the treated population with the proportion of that particular group in the general population, which may not say much about actual need.

In a study conducted in Alameda County, California, Vernon and Roberts (1982) examined utilization patterns in terms of need. They found that Anglos and Mexican-Americans underutilize services in relation to established need, but underutilization was greater for Mexican-Americans. Another California study (Vega, Kolody, and Warheit, 1985, cited in Dworkin and Adams, 1987), which also examined service utilization relative to established need, further supported the finding that Mexican-Americans underutilize mental health services.

According to Dr. Fernando Trevino, project director for the Center for Cross-Cultural Research, located in Galveston, Texas, there has yet to be a comprehensive examination in the state of Texas for the rates of mental health needs in comparison to the rates of reported utilization (Trevino, Interview, February 7, 1989). Thus, one of the main goals of this center is to investigate the prevalence, incidence, and treatment of mental disorders of Hispanics in Texas to better serve this segment of the population.

The issue of the underutilization of mental health services by Mexican-Americans has been a fairly consistent finding across studies. Regardless of whether utilization is examined by comparing a subgroup of the treated population with its representation in the general population, or whether it is more accurately examined by comparing treated rates with the actual needs of the general population, the conclusion has been the same-- Mexican-Americans have been found to underutilize mental health services. The following hypotheses have been proposed to account for the underutilization of mental health services by Mexican-Americans (Padilla, Ruiz, and Alvarez, 1975; Ramirez, 1980):

1. Utilization rates have not been adjusted for age;
2. Mexican-Americans experience a lower frequency and severity of mental illness;
3. Mexican-Americans make use of alternate sources of treatment;
4. Mexican-Americans encounter barriers within the traditional mental health system which inhibit utilization.

Utilization Rates Have Not Been Age-Adjusted

Ramirez (1980) addressed the concern that the differential use of mental health services by ethnicity may be due to differences in age distributions. To examine this, he standardized utilization rates by adjusting for age and found that Mexican-Americans under age 21 underutilized services at community mental health centers. However, comparable user rates were found for Mexican-Americans and Anglos over age 21. Ramirez also found that adjusting for age yielded no significant differences between ethnic groups for the use of alcoholism and drug abuse services at CMHMRCs. This is interesting in that other researchers who have not adjusted for age (Cuellar, 1977; Cuellar and Schnee, 1987) have found that Mexican-Americans were overrepresented in alcoholism services and drug abuse services at CMHMRCs.

Stolp, Warner, and Juretic (1989) indicate that age adjustment is very important when examining such services as alcoholism and drug abuse by ethnicity because (1) these services may be used heavily by younger age groups, and (2) the patterns of utilization may be presented inaccurately for youthful populations, such as Hispanics. In illustrating this, they provide the following example: if youths under 25, regardless of ethnicity, tend to use mental health, alcoholism, and drug abuse services heavily, then discharge and utilization rates for Hispanics would be inflated, given the fact that more than 50 percent of Hispanics are under 25.

Lower Frequency and Severity of Mental Illness

The most comprehensive studies on the prevalence of mental disorders among Hispanics in the untreated population have been those studies based on the Los Angeles Ecological Catchment Area (ECA) project data (Roberts, 1980; Hough et al., 1987). Such studies have concluded that Hispanics have at least the same prevalence of severe mental health disorders as the general population. In other words, no statistically significant differences have been found between the prevalence of mental disorders among Hispanics and the prevalence of mental disorders in the general population. It must be noted that generalizing California data to Texas may be a problem in that California Mexican-Americans may not be like Texas Mexican-Americans. However, as was mentioned earlier, there has yet to be a comprehensive mental health needs analysis in the state of Texas. Therefore, because the ethnic composition of California most closely resembles that of Texas and because needs analyses have been conducted in that state, California data will be presented as evidence when Texas data are not available.

One study which used the ECA project data (Hough et al., 1987) examined the utilization of general medical and mental health services by Mexican-Americans and non-Hispanic whites. These researchers found that Mexican-Americans with recent diagnoses for a mental disorder were less likely than non-Hispanic whites to have made a mental health visit during any of the six months prior to the interview. In addition, Mexican-Americans reported half the number of visits of non-Hispanic whites. Given these findings, it could be expected that Mexican-Americans would also have lower rates of hospitalization for physical conditions. However, no significant differences were found between Mexican-Americans and non-Hispanic whites in terms of hospitalization for physical conditions. Nevertheless, Mexican-Americans with recent diagnoses for mental disorder were only half as likely as non-Hispanic whites to make a mental health visit to either a mental health specialist or a general medical care provider. These data suggest that the prevalence of mental disorders among Mexican-Americans in Los Angeles is equivalent to that of Anglos and, therefore, that underutilization cannot be a function of lower need.

Another study, which examined the mental health needs of the community in Alameda County, California, found that the prevalence of psychological distress among Mexican-Americans is comparable to if not higher than that of the overall population (Roberts, 1980). In this survey, Mexican-Americans reported an equal amount of job dissatisfaction, negative affect, and episodes of mental illness as the overall population did, while they reported more episodes of chronic nervous problems, less positive affect, and less happiness. Upon adjustment for age, sex, education, income, marital status, and physical health, many of these differences were reduced, but in no case was the prevalence rate for Mexican-Americans significantly lower than that of the general population.

Alternate Sources of Treatment

Given the findings of Roberts (1980) and Hough et al. (1987) that the prevalence of mental disorders is the same between Anglos and Mexican-Americans, and that Mexican-Americans are underutilizing traditional mental health services, there exists a possibility that Mexican-Americans are receiving services from other, nontraditional sources.

At one time, it was believed that the utilization of curanderos (faith-healers) explained the underutilization of mental health services by Mexican-Americans. However, examination of this notion has shown that curanderismo alone cannot explain the underutilization of mental health services (Edgerton, Karno, and Fernandez, 1970). In their study, Edgerton, Karno, and Fernandez (1970) interviewed Mexican-Americans and Anglos and asked questions about the role psychiatrists play and what they would do if they were suffering from an emotional disorder. These researchers found that Mexican-Americans reacted more favorably toward psychiatrists than did Anglos. Furthermore, they found that Mexican-Americans in Los Angeles had reduced their reliance on curanderos, and they concluded that the underutilization of mental health services by Mexican-Americans cannot be attributed to the use of curanderos.

It has also been suggested that perhaps Mexican-Americans are turning to the use of family physicians for mental health problems. However, this too has been called into question by a recent study. As mentioned earlier, Hough et al. (1987) found that Mexican-Americans with recent diagnoses for a mental disorder were only half as likely as non-Hispanic whites to make a mental health visit to either a mental health specialist or a general medical care provider.

Therefore, it appears that neither the use of curanderos nor the use of family physicians can account for the underutilization of mental health services by Mexican-Americans. However, Mexican-Americans may rely on other alternate sources such as priests, teachers, and beauticians, which have not yet been systematically examined.

Barriers Which Inhibit Utilization of Mental Health Services

According to this hypothesis, Mexican-Americans underutilize the mental health system because of barriers which inhibit utilization, not because of a lower need for services. However, before this hypothesis could be tested, researchers had to determine whether Mexican-Americans recognize mental illness. In examining this, Karno and Edgerton (1969) interviewed Mexican-Americans and Anglos by describing various states of emotional problems. They found that Mexican-Americans were twice as likely as Anglos to recognize mental illness and that Mexican-Americans believed in a more favorable prognosis for mental disorder than did Anglos. Because of their findings, Karno and Edgerton concluded that underutilization of mental health services by Mexican-Americans was not a function of lesser incidence or recognition of mental disorder. Instead, they hypothesized that underutilization could be the result of language barriers between the therapist and the client, a shortage of mental health services in Mexican-American communities, and the role of family physicians in mental health services.

Four barriers to the utilization of mental health services by Mexican-Americans have been identified by minority advocates (Shore, 1988; Valdez, 1980; and Windle, 1980):

1. Geographic inaccessibility of mental health centers;
2. Language barriers between clients and therapists;
3. Class-bound values of therapists; and
4. Culture-bound values of therapists.

With respect to the first barrier, geographic inaccessibility, Valdez (1980) indicates that community mental health centers are generally limited in accessibility or are difficult to access by Mexican-American populations. An examination of the availability and accessibility of community mental health centers in Texas to Mexican-Americans conducted by Valdez revealed that the accessibility of local CMHMRCs was poor across the state. He also found that in metropolitan areas, accessibility was slightly greater but overall accessibility was limited and difficult for Mexican-American populations.

Windle (1980) asserts that services are infrequently located near the target population, and therefore clients do not use them. In addition to transportation difficulties, clients feel uncomfortable when entering an unfamiliar neighborhood or another area of the city because they fear for their own safety or are threatened by the presence of a majority of another ethnic or racial group.

As far as the language barrier is concerned, Torrey (1968) indicated that most Mexican-Americans are bilingual, but a "significantly" small number speak little or no English. This not only creates barriers to the utilization of mental health services, but it can also lead to misdiagnosis. For instance, scientists at the New York Medical College found that Hispanic patients who were interviewed in English by experienced mental health professionals were considered to have greater psychopathology than when they were interviewed in their own native language. They also reported that these patients tended to speak more slowly and to pause longer, thus exhibiting characteristics frequently associated with depressive symptomotology when, in fact, these manifestations were due to shifts in bilingual usage (Marcos, 1979).

Clients continue to be treated by therapists in accordance with middle-class norms even though the use of these norms has proven ineffective for lower-class clients (Trevino, Interview, February 7, 1989). As a result, psychiatrists tend to rely on medication as the treatment of choice when low-income clients fail to respond to therapy.

Studies conducted as far back as 20 years ago have shown that there is a great danger in having therapists from one culture diagnose and treat clients from another culture (Torrey, 1968; Cardenas and Cardenas, 1977). Torrey (1968) presents evidence in which 90 percent of Anglo residents in psychiatry associate "hearing voices" with "crazy" while less than 20 percent of Mexican-American high school students make this association. Similar results were found by Cardenas and Cardenas (1977), who concluded that when the clients' needs are incompatible with the methods of service provision, the services are not only irrelevant but may be detrimental as well. Further expansion on this issue was provided by Kleinman, Eisenberg, and Goode (1978), who indicated that as the cultural incompatibility increases, so does failure to comply.

Studies of community mental health centers in which the four barriers identified by Torrey were reduced have shown an increased utilization rate by Mexican-Americans. For instance, in Denver, Colorado, a community mental health center located in a Hispanic community implemented a program to reach out to this population (Phillipus, 1971). The center was informally decorated and the first person with whom a patient would come in contact was always a Spanish-speaking receptionist. Clients and staff would refer to each other on a first-name basis, and a substantial number of Spanish-speaking Hispanic staff were present. Evaluation of the program revealed that the patient load was representative of the target population in terms of ethnic composition. It was also found that Hispanic self-referrals dropped upon removal of the program renovations, but returned to previous levels as soon as the program changes were reinstated.

Similar results were found in a study conducted in Laredo, Texas, by Trevino, Bruhn, and Bruce (1979). Their results indicated that when the four barriers identified by Torrey were absent, Mexican-Americans utilized mental health services in proportion to their numbers in the population and, in fact, slightly overutilized them. The results of this study are particularly interesting since this study was conducted in a Mexican border town, where possible alternatives to mental health such as folk medicine were readily available across the Mexican border. Moreover, one could expect greater relations among extended family members given the cultural influence and proximity of Mexico. Nevertheless, Mexican-Americans showed a slight overutilization of mental health services.

SOURCES OF DATA

What follows is a discussion of the sources of data and procedures which were used in examining the utilization of mental health services at both inpatient facilities and community programs by Mexican-Americans and by blacks. Data will be examined from five sources: (1) TDMHMR's Client Assignment and Registration (CARE) Data System,[1] (2) TDMHMR's Client Profile Survey,[2] (3) TDMHMR's Data Books for FY 1982-1986, (4) 1980 Bureau of the Census general population statistics, and (5) estimates of the number of illegal migrants in the state of Texas.

Procedures

An unduplicated total number of clients served at inpatient facilities (state hospitals and state centers) during FY 1984-1988 was obtained from CARE data. In addition, CARE data provided information on the services used (Client and Family Support, Residential, and/or Case Management) by clients who were assigned to a community center after having had at least one inpatient admission within the past five years. The Data Books provided information on utilization characteristics of community facilities (state hospital outreach programs, state centers, and community MHMR centers), which was more extensive than that provided by CARE data. In addition, the Data Books provided all of the information regarding types of admission, discharges, and number of residents. The Client Profile Survey provided important client information not currently included in CARE data, such as level of education, source of referral, and length of stay.

Utilization of Mental Health Services by Hispanics

The utilization patterns of mental health services by Hispanics, as defined by the U.S. census, will be examined in this section. The percentage of Hispanics being served in the various facilities (both inpatient and community) will be compared to the percentage of Hispanics in the state of Texas to determine the level and characteristics of utilization. The total number of Hispanics in Texas, which includes persons of Mexican-American, Puerto Rican, Cuban, and other Spanish origins, is 3,735,824. This

---

[1]Data were provided on all inpatient admissions to state-operated facilities from October 1, 1983, through September 30, 1988. For each client admitted during that time period, records of prior admissions (pre-1983) were also appended to the data set. In addition to records of inpatient admissions, records of clients who were active in the community centers were also available from TDMHMR for the same time frame. However, there were some gaps in both databases, since all community centers and all state centers did not begin to utilize this system at the same time.

[2] A regionally representative sample was developed through an interactive sampling technique. The sample for each region was drawn from the population of clients active in state hospitals and community programs on the CARE system of TDMHMR. This population was also stratified by age. If the number of clients selected in the sample from a particular program was relatively high, a second sample on these clients was selected and appropriate weights for the clients in that program were assigned.

figure is a composite of the number of Hispanics included in the 1980 U.S. Census (2,985,824), as well as the 750,000 illegal migrants in Texas identified by Bean et al. (1982). This composite figure (3,735,824) represents 25 percent of the total population of the state of Texas in 1980.

A comprehensive analysis of CARE data revealed that during FY 1984-1988, an unduplicated total number of 62,185 clients were served by TDMHMR at inpatient facilities (TDMHMR, 1988a). Of this number, 11,971, or 19.3 percent, were Hispanics. Of these Hispanics 42 percent were diagnosed as severely mentally ill (those clients diagnosed with schizophrenia and related disorders, depressive disorders, and other nonorganic psychoses), while 37 percent of Hispanics were diagnosed as having a substance abuse disorder (alcohol related or drug related).

As can be seen from Table 3.1, Hispanics proportionately underutilized inpatient services during that five-year period. Upon examination of the different utilization patterns of state hospitals for FY 1982-1986, it becomes evident that Hispanics have maintained a stable utilization of approximately 15 percent in terms of direct admissions, first admissions, readmissions, discharges, and number of residents (TDMHMR, 1988b).

Table 3.1. Unduplicated Total Number of Clients Served at TDMHMR Inpatient Facilities by Ethnicity During FY 1984-1988

Ethnicity	Number Served	Percentage of Total
Anglos	39,673	(.64)
Blacks	9,439	(.15)
Hispanics	11,925	(.19)
Others	561	(.01)
Total	61,598	

Source: TDMHMR 1988a.

The picture for inpatient programs at state centers, however, is somewhat different. Hispanics overutilized state centers when comparing use rates with the percentage of Hispanics in the state of Texas. However, the state centers for which data were available, Laredo, El Paso, and Rio Grande, are located in areas which are densely populated with Hispanics. Thus, these figures actually represent proportional representation. Although it appears that the utilization of state centers by both whites and Hispanics increased by about 50 percent from FY 1984 to FY 1985, this is not the case because, while data were available from Laredo, El Paso, and Rio Grande state centers for FY 1985, information was available only from Laredo and Rio Grande for FY 1984. From FY 1985 to FY 1986, there was a slight decrease of utilization of state centers by Hispanics across all categories.

The CARE data for FY 1984-1988 also revealed that the proportion of Hispanic males to females receiving services was higher than that found for blacks or whites. The respective percentages for this five-year period are 73 percent for Hispanics, 66 percent

81

for blacks, and 64 percent for whites. These results are consistent with previous findings (Bachrach, 1975; Cuellar, 1977; Cuellar and Schnee, 1987).

According to the TDMHMR Client Profile data, of those persons admitted to state facilities, Hispanics were more likely (22 percent) to be referred to a state facility by family and friends than were blacks (9 percent) or whites (13 percent) (TDMHMR, 1988b). Prior to hospitalization, 62 percent of Hispanics lived with their parents, compared with 49 percent for blacks and 33 percent for whites (TDMHMR, 1988b). Although this is in part probably due to the younger age of the average Mexican-American client, these two findings may provide evidence for the hypothesis that Mexican-Americans underutilize mental health services because they receive more emotional support from both immediate and extended family members.

Among those admitted for inpatient services, Hispanics were the least educated. Forty-two percent of Hispanics had not attained more than a junior high level of education, which was more than twice the percentage for blacks (18 percent) and whites (19 percent). Similarly, 26 percent of Hispanics had never worked in contrast to 18 percent for blacks and 15 percent for whites. While in treatment, Hispanics were more likely (21 percent) than blacks (10 percent) or whites (15 percent) to have a short-term stay of one week or less (TDMHMR, 1988b).

The trends for the utilization of state hospital outreach programs indicate that Hispanics were utilizing these services rather proportionately across the categories of mental health, alcohol abuse, drug abuse, and all diagnoses excluding mental retardation during FY 1982-1986, and in all cases, Hispanics' use of these services decreased slightly from FY 1985 to FY 1986.

With respect to state centers, Hispanics were overrepresented, but, as was mentioned earlier, this is not actually the case because the state centers which are being examined are located in areas which are comprised primarily of Hispanics. In addition, only 10 percent of all the Hispanic clients who were served in community programs were provided services at state centers. It should be noted, however, that across the different diagnoses, the percentage of Hispanics using state center services began to decline in FY 1984, with the exception of drug abuse, in which Hispanics' use decreased from FY 1984 to FY 1985 but increased dramatically from FY 1985 to FY 1986.

Eighty-four percent of all Hispanics served in community programs were served at community MHMR centers. Within these centers and across all diagnoses, Hispanics have shown a steady increase in the use of these services, with the greatest increases being for the use of alcohol abuse services. It is interesting to note that Hispanics increased in their use of drug abuse services between FY 1984 and FY 1985, and decreased in their use of these services between FY 1985 and FY 1986 (TDMHMR, 1986).

Utilization of Mental Health Services by Blacks in Texas

According to Williams (1986), research emphasis on the mental health needs of minorities appears to have shifted toward the study of Hispanics. While the underutilization rate of mental health services by Mexican-Americans has been the topic of much research, overrepresentation of blacks in mental health institutions is a research topic which has not received as much attention by scientists. This case is particularly true in Texas, where Hispanics comprise the largest segment of the minority population and their utilization rates of mental health services have been the main focus of investigators as witnessed by the research cited above. Regarding blacks in Texas, no comprehensive research has been undertaken on the mental health needs of this group, which comprises 11.5 percent of the state population (Marshall and Bouvier, 1986). Yet blacks in Texas are proportionally overrepresented in psychiatric institutions;

more often diagnosed with severe mental illness; involuntarily committed at a higher rate than other ethnic groups; and hospitalized for longer periods of time than their white and Hispanic counterparts (Williams, 1986).

Black Clients at TDMHMR Facilities

This section will analyze the characteristics of the black clients served by TDMHMR at inpatient facilities during FY 1982-1986 to the extent made possible by the available data. A shortcoming of this approach is that only limited generalizations can be made to the untreated black population. The information discussed below, however, is the only data available reflecting the use of mental health services by blacks in Texas at a statewide level. When appropriate, relevant findings of the research literature on blacks and mental health will be incorporated within the context of this discussion.

Blacks comprised 15 percent of the TDMHMR inpatient population during FY 1984-1988. Proportionally, they were overrepresented by 3.5 percent since they only comprised 11.5 percent of the Texas population. The majority of the black inpatients were male clients (66 percent), and most of them (58 percent) were in the 26-45 age group (TDMHMR, 1988a).

The number of direct admissions of blacks into state facilities is proportional to the number of residents. However, when the components of the total number of direct admissions is examined, it is revealed that blacks tend to be readmitted at a proportionately higher rate than whites or Hispanics. Specifically, the average percentage of readmissions accounted for by blacks throughout this period (21 percent) is 6 percent higher than the average percentage of first admissions (15 percent) for blacks. In contrast, the average percentage of readmissions accounted for by whites during this period (63 percent) is 8 percent lower than the average percentage of first admissions for whites.

The utilization rate of state center inpatient facilities by blacks was practically negligible. There were only ten black residents at the state centers during FY 1982-1986. The lack of utilization of those facilities by blacks is explained by their geographical inaccessibility to the black population.

The Client Profile Survey indicates that the main source of referral for black inpatients -- aside from state hospitals, which referred 19 percent of them -- were the police and courts, which committed 16 percent (TDMHMR, 1988b). State hospital outreach and community mental health centers referred 12 and 14 percent respectively. Family and friends referred 9 percent, and the rest came from sources such as private hospitals, public hospitals, and private physicians.

During FY 1984-1988, blacks in Texas were committed to state hospitals at a significantly higher rate than could be expected by chance alone (TDMHMR, 1988b). While 73 percent of blacks were committed involuntarily, 55 and 52 percent of Hispanics and whites respectively were committed as such. Nationwide, 56.6 percent of black males are committed involuntarily, compared with 48.9 percent of white males (NIMH, 1986; cited in Rosenthal and Carty, 1988).

Blacks in Texas are also diagnosed with severe mental illness at a disproportionate rate. As revealed by the CARE data (TDMHMR, 1988a), the majority of the black inpatients (63 percent) received a diagnosis under this category compared with 40 percent of whites and 42 percent of Hispanics. The percentage of blacks diagnosed with schizophrenia (26 percent) was more than twice the rate of whites (12 percent) and 12 percent higher than that of Hispanics. Blacks were also least likely to be diagnosed with affective disorders. Whereas 11 percent of whites and 9 percent of

Hispanics receive such a diagnosis, only 6 percent of blacks are classified as such. These figures are congruent with findings cited in the literature on the epidemiology of mental health disorders among blacks.

According to figures provided by the National Institute of Mental Health (1986, cited in Rosenthal and Carty, 1988), black inpatients nationwide are diagnosed with schizophrenia at almost twice the rate of white inpatients (56.6 to 31.5 percent). However, they are underdiagnosed with affective disorders (7.7 percent of blacks compared with 15.6 percent of white inpatients). Three major reasons have been cited to explain the disproportionate diagnosis of severe mental illness among blacks-- all of them plausible explanations for the overdiagnoses of severe mental illness among blacks in Texas: cultural differences between black patients and white clinicians, lack of understanding of black norms, and stereotypic thinking (Jones, Gray, and Parson, 1981).

As stated by Jones and Gray (1986, p. 63): "black patients' use of language, behavior mannerisms and styles of relating may not be understood by non-black mental health providers, and language which is not understood may be considered as evidence for thought disorders. Styles of relating are sometimes misinterpreted as evidence for affective disorder while unfamiliar styles of relating can be construed as bizarre." In addition, many psychotherapists have the stereotypic notion that blacks are happy individuals and thus do not suffer from affective disorders (Jones and Gray, 1986). Compounding these problems is the fact that the true prevalence of mental health disorders among blacks is unknown (Williams, 1986).

The literature on the epidemiology of mental health disorders among blacks is inconclusive (Williams, 1986). Most of the differences in prevalence of mental disorders between blacks and other ethnic groups are accounted for by low socioeconomic status (Williams, 1986). Indeed, as shown by the Client Profile Survey, many of the characteristics of the black inpatient population at TDMHMR are indicative of low socioeconomic status. For instance, 80 percent of the black inpatients, as compared with 62 percent of their white counterparts, have not held a job 12 months prior to hospitalization. Only .07 percent of blacks have held a job for a 12-month period prior to hospitalization. In contrast, 17 percent of whites have worked for the same amount of time. Sixty-one percent of blacks, compared with 44 percent of whites, were unable to work prior to hospitalization.

Black Clients at TDMHMR Community Mental Health Facilities

Most of the blacks' utilization of services by diagnoses was quite stable in that blacks did not show any marked decreases or increases in terms of utilization in any of the diagnostic categories (mental health, drug abuse, substance abuse). Interestingly, blacks were proportionately underrepresented in drug and alcohol categories in all types of community facilities, with the exception of the drug category at community MHMR centers, in which they were proportionally represented (TDMHMR, 1988a). For example, the utilization rates for alcohol and drug abuse at state hospital outreach programs are only 5 and 7 percent respectively. If drugs and alcohol abuse are rampant in the black community, as the popular press has claimed, then blacks in Texas are significantly underrepresented in substance abuse services at community facilities.

From the evidence provided above for the utilization of services by Mexican-Americans and blacks in Texas, it becomes evident that mental health services need to be provided in an acceptable, appropriate, and culturally relevant manner. This is especially important given that this segment of the population is growing at a much faster rate than the general population and that by the year 2015, Mexican-Americans and blacks will comprise over half of the Texas population (Marshall and Bouvier, 1986).

DEMOGRAPHICS

The population of Texas has increased tremendously throughout the years--from 1836 to 1986, the population has doubled eight times. According to the Census Bureau, Texas ranked third in population behind California and New York in 1980. The 1988 population estimates for Texas indicate a census of 17,265,994 (Shore, 1988). The ethnic composition of Texas as of 1985 was 63 percent Anglo, 22.7 percent Hispanic, 12.5 percent black, and 1.8 percent Asian and other. In the decade between 1970 and 1980, Texas became extremely diverse. During this period, the Mexican-origin population increased at the highest rate (70 percent), whereas the black population increased by 22 percent and the Anglo population by less than 15 percent.

In 1985, the median age for Anglos in Texas was 32.1, which was higher than it was for blacks (26.2), Hispanics (24.1), and for Asians and others (27.5). In 1985, Anglos also made up the greatest percentage of people in each of the five different age groups: 0-14 (54.7 percent), 15-24 (56.7 percent), 25-44 (64 percent), 45-64 (71.6 percent), and 65+ (77.9 percent).

In terms of educational attainment, more than 70 percent of Anglos age 25 or older have completed high school and 20 percent have completed four or more years of college, while the respective proportions for minorities are as follows: blacks, 53 percent and 9 percent; Asians and others, 69 percent and 31 percent; and Hispanics, 35 percent and 6 percent.

The differences among the groups also apply to the type of jobs held as well as median income. In 1980, 60 percent of Anglos and 56 percent of Asians were employed in white-collar jobs, while only 35 percent of both blacks and Hispanics were similarly employed. In addition, in 1979, nearly 28 percent of all blacks and 28 percent of Hispanics in Texas were below poverty level, while only 17 percent of Asians and 12 percent of Anglos fell below this level (U.S. Bureau of the Census, 1980, Table 245). Notably, most of the correlates associated with mental health disorders, namely low SES and unemployment, are conspicuously present in this population. Further, this income and employment variation by ethnicity probably also affects the use of private hospitals and therapists. While much of the Anglo and Asian needs may be treated by the private sector, those of Hispanics and blacks are much more likely to be dependent upon the public sector.

Population Projections

Various demographers have made projections of the state's population in terms of size and composition. This section will examine the projections set forth by Ray Marshall and Leon Bouvier. According to their model, there are three scenarios: A--low levels of migration; B--moderate levels of migration; and C--high levels of migration. This section will focus primarily on the middle scenario, B, unless otherwise specified.

While Anglos claimed the majority of the population in Texas in 1985 (63 percent), it is projected that as early as 2000, Anglos will constitute only a little more than half of the population (55.5 percent) and that by 2025 Anglos will no longer be the majority (46.3 percent). In 1985, Hispanics made up 22.7 percent of the population while blacks made up 12.5 percent and Asians and others 1.8 percent. However, by 2000, these trends will change and Hispanics will comprise 28.9 percent, Asians and others 3.4

85

percent, and blacks 12.2 percent. These increases are particularly striking when the number of people is examined in contrast to proportional changes. For instance, Anglos in Texas totaled 10.4 million in 1985; by 2035, they will total 13.1 million while Hispanics numbered 3.7 million in 1985 and will number 12 million in 2035. The respective enumerations for blacks and Asians are as follows: blacks, 2.0 million to 3.3 million and Asians, 0.3 million to 1.9 million. However, it must be kept in mind that some social scientists believe that these projections are somewhat inflated given that the new immigration laws will tend to decrease the influx of immigrants.

Upon examination of the demographic characteristics of the Texas population along with the projections set forth by Marshall and Bouvier, it becomes apparent that the composition of the population is changing dramatically. Of particular interest is the fact that Hispanics are the fastest-growing ethnic group in the state of Texas. This is of great importance in that Hispanics, as mentioned earlier, have lower levels of education and income, and low income and low educational attainment are associated with a higher incidence of mental disorder (Hollingshead and Reidlich, 1968). In addition, because the present mental health system poses certain delivery barriers to special population members, it becomes evident that current and future programs must be molded to cater to this rapidly growing population. Although the knowledge exists to improve services provided to minority populations, such knowledge has not been used to implement the effective delivery of mental health services to minority members (Naranjo and Malone, 1988). Nevertheless, there is a consensus by minority advocates as to the steps which need to be taken to improve service delivery to minorities. Such consensus centers around three main recommendations.

First, states, in this case the state of Texas, should have a statutory requirement mandating the establishment of culturally relevant state mental health plans, reflecting the ethnic and cultural diversity of minority people. Evidence has been found that a state-level policy statement requiring culturally sensitive minority services as well as a separate office of minority affairs are good predictors of successful minority mental health programs (Byrd, 1985). TDMHMR currently has a separate office of minority affairs, but it lacks a statutory requirement to serve minorities (Shore, 1988). To attain this recommendation, the following procedures have been suggested that state mental health plans be revised in accordance with PL 99-660. Such revisions should include the following regulatory standards: (1) provision of culturally relevant services, and (2) assurance of equitable minority representation throughout the mental health system.

Second, administrative actions should be taken to ensure culturally sensitive mental health programs. Such actions would include the following:

1.   Administrative actions to assure compliance with standards for culturally relevant mental health services. For instance, the state of Colorado has a performance contracting arrangement which requires that minorities be admitted in proportion to their numbers in the population (Byrd, 1985). The contract provides incentives and disincentives for the agencies to meet this requirement, e.g., failure to serve the projected numbers of clients in the target group results in an up to 5 percent reduction in funds.

2.   Provision of cross-cultural mental health training for service providers. According to Lefley (1984), cultural sensitivity training for mental health professionals would increase the use of services by minorities and would decrease the drop-out rate from these services. In addition, the work of Bernal and Padilla (1982) has demonstrated that little is being done to prepare clinical psychologists to work with minority groups.

3.   Sponsorship of research initiatives to examine issues concerning the delivery and appropriateness of mental health services to minorities.

4.   Actions to ensure that staff meets minimum criteria on cross-cultural issues regarding mental health, e.g. mandatory cross-cultural training and bilingual abilities for staff serving non-English-speaking clients.

5.   Effective marketing of mental health services, stressing their availability, effectiveness, and accessibility.

6.   A community-based minority needs assessment.

Third, minority representation should be increased throughout the mental health system, including leadership roles and advocacy groups. This could be accomplished by the following:

1.   Enforcement of affirmative actions plans and development of standards to ensure adequate minority representation throughout the mental health system.

2.   Recruitment of minority members in the administrative structure of mental health agencies. According to a case management status report by TDMHMR (1988c), of case management administrators, only 2.8 percent are Hispanics and 4.2 percent are blacks, while 93 percent are whites. In addition, of case managers (MH and MR), 15.6 percent are Hispanics and 23 percent are blacks, while 60.9 percent are whites.

3.   Recruitment of minority members for advocacy groups.

4.   Establishment of a coalition of minority groups (professional, family, consumer, etc.) to educate the community on mental health and service delivery issues.

CONCLUSIONS

It becomes evident that in regard to mental health services, Mexican-Americans are underserved in the state of Texas. The current demographic trends projected by Marshall and Bouvier (1986) indicate that Mexican-Americans are the fastest-growing ethnic group in Texas. As a consequence, there will be an increasing demand to provide mental health services to this population.

Texas has minimal resources to cater to the needs of this growing population. Although certain programs are currently in existence (the Office of Multicultural Services, the Bilingual/ Bicultural Unit in the San Antonio State Hospital, and the Minority Mental Health Research Center at UTMB), there is no comprehensive systematic statewide program to address the mental health needs of this population. Strong efforts should be directed to implement the recommendations which have been laid out by various minority advocates to better serve this growing segment of the population.

APPENDIX 3.1. Definition of Terms (Data Books, 1982-1986).

First Admissions: Direct admissions to a facility of clients who have never been served by that facility.

Readmissions: Direct admissions to a facility of clients who have been served previously by that facility.

Direct Admissions: The sum of first admissions and readmissions.

Discharges: The discharge of clients, with or without medical advice, while in residence or while on leave from a facility.

Residents: Number of clients physically present in a facility as of the last day of the fiscal year.

Inpatient Facilities: These include state hospitals and state centers.

State Hospital: Texas state mental hospital administered by TDMHMR.

State Center (inpatient and community): A TDMHMR-operated facility providing the mentally ill/mentally retarded with services such as diagnosis and evaluation, counseling, day care, training, respite care, and short-term domiciliary care.

Community Programs: These include community MHMR centers, state centers, and state hospital outreach.

Community MHMR Center: Facility receiving grants-in-aid which provides a complex of community-based services (inpatient, outpatient, diagnosis, evaluation, etc.) under the direction of a board of trustees appointed by local governments.

State Hospital Outreach: A community program providing treatment/ training in a noninstitutional setting, under a state hospital following geographic service areas.

Hispanics: This term refers to persons who are of Mexican-American, Puerto Rican, Cuban, and other Spanish origins. The total number of this population consists of 3,735,824. This figure is a composite of the number of Hispanics included in the 1980 U.S. census (2,985,824), as well as the 750,000 illegal migrants in Texas identified by Bean et al. (1982). This composite figure (3,735,824) represents 25 percent of the total population of the state of Texas in 1980.

References

Bachrach, L. L. 1975. <u>Utilization of State and County Mental Hospitals by Spanish-Americans in 1972</u>. NIMH Division of Biometry, Statistical Note 116, DHEW Publication No. ADM 75-181. Washington, D.C.: U.S. Government Printing Office.

Bean, F. D., A. G. King, R. D. Benford, and L. B. Perkinson. 1982. <u>Estimates of the Number of Illegal Migrants in the State of Texas</u>. Austin: Texas Population Research Center, University of Texas at Austin.

Bernal, M. E., and A. M. Padilla. 1982. "Status of Minority Curricula and Training in Clinical Psychology." <u>American Psychologist,</u> vol. 37 (July).

Byrd, C. M. 1985. <u>Project to Review and Describe Mental Health Activities Directed at Chronically Mentally Ill Minority Individuals in CSP Funded States</u>. NIMH Final Report. Rockville, Maryland: National Institute for Mental Health.

Cardenas, J. A., and B. Cardenas. 1977. <u>The Theory of Incompatibilities: A Conceptual Framework for Responding to the Educational Needs of Mexican-American Children</u>. San Antonio, Texas: Intercultural Development Research Association.

Cuellar, I. 1977. "The Utilization of Mental Health Facilities by Mexican-Americans: A Test of the Underutilization Hypothesis." Ph.D. diss., University of Texas at Austin. <u>Dissertation Abstracts International,</u> vol. 38 (1977).

Cuellar, I., and S. B. Schnee. 1987. "An Examination of Utilization Characteristics of Clients of Mexican-Origin Served by the Texas Department of Mental Health and Mental Retardation." In <u>Mental Health Issues of the Mexican Origin Population in Texas: Proceedings of the Fifth Robert Lee Sutherland Seminar in Mental Health.</u> ed. R. Rodriguez and M. T. Coleman. Austin: Hogg Foundation for Mental Health, The University of Texas at Austin.

Dohrenwend, B. P., and B. S. Dohrenwend. 1969. <u>Social Status and Psychological Disorder</u>. New York, N.Y.: Wiley and Sons.

Dworkin, R. J., and G. L. Adams. 1987. "Retention of Hispanics in Public Sector Mental Health Services." <u>Community Mental Health Journal,</u> vol. 23 (Fall).

Edgerton, R. B., M. Karno, and I. Fernandez. 1970. "<u>Curanderismo</u> in the Metropolis: The Diminished Role of Folk Psychiatry Among Los Angeles Mexican-Americans." <u>American Journal of Psychotherapy,</u> vol. 24 (January).

Griffith, J. 1983. "Re-examination of Mexican-American Service Utilization and Mental Health Need." <u>Hispanic Journal of Behavioral Sciences,</u> vol. 5 (June).

Hough, R. L., M. Karno, M. A. Burnam, D. M. Timbers, J. I. Escobar, and D. A. Regier. 1987. "Utilization of Health and Mental Health Services by Los Angeles Mexican-Americans and Non-Hispanic Whites." <u>Archives of General Psychiatry,</u> vol. 44 (August).

Hollingshead, A. B., and F. Reidlich. 1968. <u>Social Class and Mental Illness</u>. New York, N.Y.: Wiley and Sons.

Jaco, E. G. 1959. "Mental Health of the Spanish-American in Texas." In <u>Cultures and Mental Health: Cross-Cultural Studies</u>, ed. M. K. Opler. New York, N.Y.: MacMillan Co.

Jones, B. E., and B. A. Gray. 1986. "Problems in Diagnosing Schizophrenia and Affective Disorders Among Blacks." <u>Hospital and Community Psychiatry</u>, vol. 37 (January).

Jones, B. E., B. A. Gray, and E. B. Parson. 1981. "Manic-Depressive Illness Among Poor Urban Blacks." <u>American Journal of Psychiatry</u>, vol. 138 (May).

Karno, M., and R. B. Edgerton. 1969. "Perception of Mental Illness in a Mexican-American Community." <u>Archives of General Psychiatry</u>, vol. 20 (February).

Kleinman, A. M., L. Eisenberg, and B. Goode. 1978. "Culture, Illness, and Cure: Clinical Lessons from Anthropologic and Cross-Cultural Research." <u>Annals of Internal Medicine</u>, vol. 88 (February).

Kruger, D. 1974. "The Relationship of Ethnicity to Utilization of Community Mental Health Centers." Ph.D. diss., University of Texas at Austin.

Lefley, H. P. 1984. "Cross-Cultural Training for Mental Health Professionals: Effects on the Delivery of Mental Health Services." <u>Hospital and Community Psychiatry</u>, vol. 35 (December).

Marcos, L. R. 1979. "Effects of Interpreters on the Evaluation of Psychotherapy in Non-English Speaking Patients." <u>American Journal of Psychiatry</u>, vol. 136 (February).

Marshall, F. R., and L. F. Bouvier. 1986. <u>Population Change and the Future of Texas</u>. Austin: Population Reference Bureau, The University of Texas at Austin.

Naranjo, D. R., and S. Malone. 1988. <u>Region VI Community Support Program Planning Conference for Minority Long-Term Mentally Ill Clients</u>. President's Commission on Mental Health. Task Panel Reports, vol. 3. Washington, D.C.: U.S. Government Printing Office.

Padilla, A. M., R. A. Ruiz, and R. Alvarez. 1975. "Community Mental Health Services for Spanish-Speaking-Surnamed Population." <u>American Psychologist</u>, vol. 30 (September).

Phillipus, M. J. 1971. "Successful and Unsuccessful Approaches to Mental Health Services for an Urban Hispano-American Population." <u>Journal of Public Health</u>, vol. 61 (April).

Ramirez, D. 1980. <u>A Review of the Literature on the Underutilization of Mental Health Services by Mexican-Americans: Implications of Future Research and Service Delivery</u>. San Antonio: Intercultural Development Research Association.

Roberts, R. E. 1980. "Prevalence of Psychological Distress Among Mexican-Americans." <u>Journal of Health and Social Behavior</u>, vol. 21 (February).

Robins, L. N. 1978. "Psychiatric Epidemiology." <u>Archives of General Psychiatry</u>, vol. 35 (June).

Rosenthal, E., and L. A. Carty. 1988. "Impediments to Services and Advocacy for Black and Hispanic People with Mental Illness." In <u>NIMH Mental Health Law Project</u>. National Institute for Mental Health, Rockville, Maryland: U.S. Government Printing Office.

Shore, S. 1988. <u>Texas State Report</u>. Paper presented at the National Institute for Mental Health-Community Support Program Minority Issues Conference, Austin, Texas. (November 9-10).

Stolp, Chandler, David C. Warner, and M. Juretic. 1989. "Patterns of Inpatient Mental Health, Mental Retardation, and Substance Abuse Services Utilization in California." <u>Social Science Quarterly</u>, vol. 70, no. 3 (September).

Texas Department of Mental Health and Mental Retardation (TDMHMR). 1986. <u>Data Books, Volumes A and B, FY's 1982-1986</u>. Austin.

_____. 1988a. <u>Client Assignment and Registration (CARE) Data System</u>. Austin.

_____. 1988b. <u>Client Profile Survey</u>. Austin.

_____. 1988c. <u>Case Management Six Months Status Report: September 1, 1987, to February, 28, 1988</u>. Austin.

Torrey, E. F. 1968. "Psychiatric Services for Mexican-Americans." (Manuscript.)

Trevino, F. M. 1989. Program Director for the Center for Cross-Cultural Research, Galveston, Texas. Interview, February 7.

Trevino, F. M., J. G. Bruhn, and H. Brunce, III. 1979. "Utilization of Community Mental Health Services in a Texas-Mexico Border City." <u>Social Science and Medicine</u>, vol. 13 (May).

U.S. Bureau of the Census. 1980. <u>General Population Characteristics of Texas</u>. U.S. Department of Commerce, Washington, D.C.: U.S. Government Printing Office.

Valdez, R. 1980. <u>The Location of Community Mental Health Centers in Texas: Some Descriptions and Comparisons</u>. San Antonio: Intercultural Development Research Association.

Vega, W. A., B. Kolody, and G. Warheit. 1985. "Psychoneuroses Among Mexican-Americans and Other Whites: Prevalence and Caseness." Cited in R. J. Dworkin and G. L. Adams. 1987. "Retention of Hispanics in Public Sector Mental Health Services." <u>Community Mental Health Journal</u>, vol. 23 (Fall).

Vernon, S. W., and R. E. Roberts. 1982. "Prevalence of Treated and Untreated Psychiatric Disorders in Three Ethnic Groups." <u>Social Science and Medicine</u>, vol. 16 (August).

Williams, D. H. 1986. "The Epidemiology of Mental Illness in Afro-Americans." <u>Hospital and Community Psychiatry</u>, vol. 37 (January).

Windle, C. 1980. "Correlates of Community Mental Health Center Underservice to Nonwhites." <u>Journal of Community Psychology</u>, vol. 8 (February).

Chapter 4. The Criminal Justice System and Its Impact on the Mentally Ill[*]

RECENT HISTORY

The policies of deinstitutionalization, first implemented over 20 years ago and designed to transfer the care of the mentally ill from the hospitals to local communities, have affected a number of the public and private sectors of society. The criminal justice system is one of these sectors. The criminal justice system has found itself with a disproportionate number of added responsibilities. The means for dealing with these added responsibilities are just now taking shape.

In the past, society has dealt with its mentally deranged by locking them away in what was euphemistically referred to as asylums. This approach effectively insulated law enforcement, and citizens, from the necessity of coping with the bizarre, the messy, and, on occasion, the dangerous behavior of the mentally ill. More recently, however, a different approach has emerged -- one which attempts to maintain a substantial portion of the mentally ill population in community settings. And with this new approach has come a changing role for the police as well as the rest of the criminal justice system (Murphy, 1986).

One unforeseen result of deinstitutionalization has been an increasing number of calls for police assistance from family members no longer able to cope, from businesses being disrupted by street people loitering around their shops, from landlords of buildings in which the mentally ill person resides, and from members of the public who are alarmed by the shabby appearance or bizarre behavior of people they encounter in moving about the community (Murphy, 1986).

In other instances, the police are called because the mentally ill person may be holding someone hostage or threatening violence. Sadly, however, this is more often a case of the misperception among the lay public (and often among mental health professionals as well) that persons with mental illness are often dangerous, violent, and even homicidal (Fox, Erickson, and Salutin, 1972; Sheridan and Teplin, 1981; Teplin, 1984; Jemelka, Trupin, and Chiles, 1989).

For example, Sheridan and Teplin (1981) found that bizarre behavior was the predominant reason for an individual's receiving police attention and being taken to a mental health facility. In their study of data from a mental health intake center, almost 27 percent of the individuals (n=838) were taken to the facility for exhibiting bizarre behavior. The second most prevalent behavior in their study was attempted suicide (12 percent of the cases). This was followed by cases involving destructive, assaultive, or violent behavior (11 percent) and disorderly behavior (6 percent).

Similarly, Fox, Erickson, and Salutin (1972), in a one-year study of police referrals to three Toronto hospitals, examined officer reports to identify the reasons and behaviors that officers cited for bringing subjects in for examination (Table 4.1). A prior history of mental illness was by far the predominant reason for referral.

Finally, Teplin (1984) observed 1,072 police encounters involving some 2,122 citizens. The data revealed the following: very few (85 people or 4 percent of the sample) exhibited signs of serious mental illness; the mentally ill were far less likely to be victims or complainants, but twice as likely as other citizens to be subjects of concern

---

[*]This chapter was written by Hugh F. Crean.

Table 4.1. Behavioral Elements Attracting Police Attention (n=337)

	Behavioral Element	Frequency	Percentage
1.	Prior mental illness	116	22.3
2.	Aggressive behavior against <u>others</u>: overt-actual or attempted	50	9.6
3.	Transportation under warrant or committal papers already signed by a doctor	38	7.3
4.	Bizarre, extremely unusual behavior	38	7.3
5.	Report of hallucinations and/or delusions	34	6.5
6.	Drug or alcohol intoxication-- apparent or reported	32	6.2
7.	In an emotional state (hysterical, incoherent, agitated)	31	6.0
8.	Unusual <u>active</u> behavior (annoyance, yelling, running around, bothering people, disorderly)	30	5.8
9.	Unusual <u>passive</u> behavior (disoriented, disheveled, vagueness, unable to account for self)	27	5.2
10.	Aggressive behavior against <u>self</u>: overt-- actual or attempted	26	5.0
11.	Aggressive behavior against <u>self</u>: potential-- verbal mention only	25	4.8
12.	Destruction or theft of property	23	4.4
13.	Aggressive behavior against <u>others</u>: potential--verbal mention only	15	2.9
14.	Voluntary request for hospitalization or assistance by patient	15	2.9
15.	Other (any residual uncategorizable information)	20	3.8
	Total	520	100.0

Source: Fox, Erickson, and Salutin, 1972, p. 93.

or objects of assistance, and somewhat more likely (35 percent versus 23 percent) to be suspects. The types of violations involved did not differ significantly between the mentally ill and the other subjects. This led Teplin to conclude that " . . . the stereotype of the mentally ill as dangerous is not substantiated by data from police-citizen encounters" (p. 56).

Yet this perception continues. As recently pointed out by Jemelka, Trupin, and Chiles (1989): "The inaccurate caricature of the mentally ill offender as a crazed psychotic killer has fueled policy and statute changes affecting all mentally ill offenders, and effective planning for this population is hampered because of it" (p. 481).

The relatively small number of such violent cases continues to contribute to the public's view that most mentally ill offenders are violent and unmanageable. This, in turn, has impacted and fueled policy making.

Society must understand that the illness of such offenders is key to their criminal behavior. Whitmer (1980), in a study of almost 500 defendants in need of psychiatric

94

treatment, indicated that the offenses of these mentally disordered defendants, whether minor threats to public peace or seriously harmful personal assaults, generally derived from acute psychotic processes or from poor judgment and impulsive behavior that attends chronic mental illness. Half of the offenses were felonies. Some of the defendants had prior arrests, but few had served time in a state prison. All, however, had psychiatric histories of from 1 to 15 psychiatric hospitalizations. Despite the long psychiatric history, almost 60 percent had no outpatient treatment. At the time of arrest, 94 percent were not involved in any outpatient program. Although community services were often offered, one distinct, identifiable, and homogeneous group of chronic mentally ill did not use them. These persons were likely to forget the time of their appointments or the person they were supposed to see; stopped taking their medication because they were convinced it was the source of their difficulties; and/or spent their meager income in a few days and had nothing left for the rest of the month (Whitmer, 1980, cited in Murphy, 1986).

While Whitmer's research points out that few of the defendants studied had served time in a state prison, other research notes the increase in percentage of persons with a criminal history who are committed to mental hospitals (Steadman, Monahan, and Duffee, 1984). Between 1969 and 1978, the Steadman group found that the percentage of male hospital admissions with at least one prior arrest rose from 38 percent to 56 percent. These data suggest the existence of a growing population of individuals common to both the mental health and the correctional systems.

As the police, the various correctional agencies, and the community at large become increasingly aware of the needs and abilities of the mentally ill, an increasing avoidance of the unnecessary involvement of the mentally ill in the criminal justice system will be realized. In Texas, the state's increased reliance on police-affiliated mental health units is a step in that direction.

LOCAL SYSTEMS

Perhaps the most potent reason for police involvement with the mentally ill is that in most communities the police usually have the only 24-hour, seven-day-a-week, mobile emergency response capacity (Levinson, 1984). Add to this the authority that police agencies have and the fact that there is no charge for their services and it becomes easy to understand not only the extent of police involvement in various community services but also the basis of overrepresentation of the mentally ill in the criminal justice system.

Traditionally, police encounters with the mentally ill have been viewed in polar terms: either emergency detention or arrest. Relatively scant attention was given to alternative dispositions. Lacking clear and procedural guidance, officers were often making what we would now consider "bad" decisions. The amount of training in mental illness issues affects such decision-making. For example, in 1978, Patrick found that officers who had received training in how to manage the mentally ill were more accepting of the tenets guiding mental health professionals. Janus et al. (1979) found that 16 hours of instruction in abnormal psychology and psychiatric descriptions and syndromes improved the attitudes of officers toward the mentally ill and the mental health system. More important, officers were better able to perceive, understand, and report psychotic behavior which, in turn, improved their ability to make appropriate referrals for treatment. An examination of police incident reports presented to psychiatrists indicated that referrals from officers with training were accepted 62 percent of the time in contrast to 14 percent for officers who had not received training. Despite such evidence of the benefits of mental health training, Murphy (1986), in a survey of 38 police academies, found that the average length of time devoted to mental health topics during training for recruits was 4.27 hours; the range was from a low of 90 minutes to a high of 22 hours. In Texas, the amount of training in mental health issues varies widely from a low of 4 hours to approximately 20 hours.

In Texas, peace officers have been mandated the responsibility of transporting the mentally ill. When all other forms of transportation are unavailable (e.g., family members, friends, staff members of various mental health agencies, etc.), the police or local sheriff's department must, by mandate, transport such individuals (Churgin, 1988). This is a time-consuming and resource-consuming task, one that is often avoided if possible by many peace officers. It is for these reasons that some of the counties in Texas have moved toward a mental health unit within the local sheriff's department. Presently, Mental Health Deputies Units exit in Galveston, Travis, McClennan, Smith, and Montgomery counties.

Mental Health Deputies Units

The Galveston County Sheriff's Department's Mental Health Deputies Program is widely cited in the literature as having a model program in impacting the mental health and criminal justice interface. Because this is a model program, it will be described in some detail. It is known that more and more counties in Texas are moving to a similarly modeled program.

In Galveston County, five deputy sheriffs certified as Texas Peace Officers, emergency medical technicians, and mental health specialists staff the Galveston County Sheriff's Department's Mental Health Deputies Unit, a 24-hour-response program for managing law enforcement encounters with the mentally ill (Larson, Winburn, and Henry, n.d.). The deputies are law enforcement officers first, but as mental health paraprofessionals (each deputy undergoes nine months of training in casework or services with the Gulf Coast Mental Health/Mental Retardation Center) their goal is to intervene in crises and to determine appropriate preliminary dispositions (Joseph, n.d.). Galveston's program became operational on September 1, 1975.

This program grew out of three predominant needs. First, during the late 1960s and early 1970s, there was a substantial and consistent increase in the number of mentally ill persons entering the criminal justice system. Second, the sheriff's deputies assigned to patrol duties were experiencing problems with this population and with implementing the Texas Mental Health Code as written. According to the code, if an officer learns from a credible source that an individual is believed to be mentally ill and likely to harm himself or herself or others, the officer is authorized to take the person into custody and transport him or her to a psychiatric facility for evaluation.[1] This process took line officers away from their regular duties for a minimum of one and a half to two hours on each occasion. Because of unfamiliarity with the mentally ill and the mental health system, officers were often reluctant to become involved in such a time-consuming task. Likewise, most people (including families) were trying to avoid becoming involved in the civil commitment process. Third, the County Commissioner's Court, particularly the committing judges and the senior county psychiatrist, were also concerned about needless incarcerations and quickly involved themselves in developing a solution (Joseph, n.d.).

The interaction among the various social service and law enforcement agencies and the commitment of those resources at their disposal contributed to a solution with

---

[1]In the past, officers were required to obtain a warrant from a magistrate before action could be taken. This has since been repealed in the Mental Health Code, and peace officers are now authorized to take individuals suspected of having some form of mental illness to a specified psychiatric facility for evaluation.

clearly defined goals and objectives. The first goal of the new program was to improve communication among the various professions involved. The second was to establish a special operations unit to deal with the mentally ill through crisis intervention, special screening, and diversion recommendations. The third goal of the program was to reduce the incarceration and institutionalization of the mentally ill and to provide alternative dispositions.

In some instances, alternative dispositions were not and are not possible. Throughout the criminal justice system, it has become somewhat apparent that, in many instances, those who commit a felony are treated as criminals first and then as mentally ill. In other instances, however, knowledgeable law enforcement personnel will try to get felony charges dropped when deemed appropriate.[2] If a misdemeanor has been committed, law enforcement personnel may again try to get the charges dropped. If unable to do so, however, the proceedings taken become very sporadic throughout the state. In some counties, the probate judge will release such persons to the local mental health authority for treatment. If released before their criminal hearing has begun, such persons are expected to return for criminal proceedings. Counties like Galveston, where such Mental Health Units exist, are reportedly utilizing such a process (Martinez, Interview, August 23, 1989). Sadly, in many other counties, mentally ill misdemeanant defendants receive few or no services while waiting in the county jail for trial dates to be set and proceedings to occur. Many may wait years before finally going to trial where their mental illness may or may not be detected (Hale, 1989). The 71st Legislature has recently addressed this issue, and this resolution as well as other recent legislation impacting the criminal justice system and the mentally ill will be discussed in a later section.

In Galveston County, between 60 and 70 percent of the calls to the unit come from either patrol deputies or from the sheriff's dispatch center. The remainder of the service calls come from the Probate Court, family or friends, emergency medical services, and/or outpatient residence programs. Table 4.2 presents summary data on the source of calls received by the Galveston County Mental Health Deputies Unit.

Table 4.2. Source of Contacts for the Galveston County Mental Health Deputies Unit

Source	Number	Percentage
Police	297	78.0
Judge/Courts	24	6.0
Family	21	5.0
MHMR Center	13	3.0
Self	9	2.0
EMS	7	1.0
Other Agencies	4	1.0
Public Hospital	2	0.5
Friend	2	0.5
Emergency Room	1	0.2
TOTAL	380	

Source: Larson, Winburn, and Henry, n.d., p. 5.

---

[2]This is not all that uncommon; as reported by the Travis County Mental Health Deputies Unit, many citizens recognize the need many of these people have for psychiatric treatment and, in many instances, are willing to drop charges under the assurances that the person will be evaluated and treated (Martinez, Interview, August 23, 1989).

In some instances a mental health deputy goes directly to the scene; in other instances, usually those involving patrol officer contacts, the person is taken to a centralized location for screening by the mental health deputy. Calls from patrol officers involve cases in which the officer is unsure of an appropriate disposition or cases which will require an extended period of time.

Actions that triggered consideration of commitment were actual or threatened violence or suicide; bizarre or socially offensive behavior, especially when displayed publicly; and manifestations of social and personal incompetence and impairment in self-care. Criminal charges usually resulted only when an individual with signs of mental illness had been apprehended after an ineptly executed petty crime (such as shoplifting) and was subsequently identified by law enforcement officials as needing psychiatric evaluation. Table 4.3 presents summary information on the reasons for referral in the Galveston County Mental Health Deputies Unit. Note that the percentages are similar to those found in research presented earlier.

Table 4.3. Reasons for Referral to the Galveston County Mental Health Deputies Unit

Complaints	Number of Patients	Percentage
Assault or Violent Action	43	9.0
Verbal Threats of Assault or Violent Action	35	7.0
Suicide Threats	23	5.0
Suicidal Action	87	19.0
Bizarre or Offensive Behavior	48	10.0
Alcohol Intoxication	66	14.0
Domestic Problems	43	9.0
Disorientation	21	4.0
Depression	35	7.0
Drug Intoxication	24	5.0
Recidivism from State Hospital	11	2.0
Accusation of Sexual Deviance	7	1.0
Criminal Charge	4	0.8
Personal Neglect	4	0.8
Retardation	4	0.8
TOTAL	455	

Source: Larson, Winburn, and Henry, n.d., p. 7.

After a mental health deputy has screened an individual and concluded that no emergency examination is necessary, the deputy has two options. If there is no urgent need for a mental health evaluation, the deputy can arrange for outpatient services, voluntary hospitalization, or assistance from other human service agencies, or can take no further action. If a mental health examination is warranted, the deputy must then transport the individual to an approved psychiatric facility for an emergency evaluation. In about 50 percent of the cases, the deputies request psychiatric evaluation. Of those examined, about half are hospitalized. Hospitalization is usually voluntary, short-term, and done locally at the University of Texas Medical Branch facility in Galveston. Table 4.4 presents dispositions for the Galveston County MH Deputies Unit.

Table 4.4. Disposition of Contacts for the Galveston County Mental Health Deputies Unit

Disposition	Number	Percentage
Emergency Room	98	25.0
Hospitalization	82	21.0
Evaluation Only	88	23.0
Jail	34	8.0
Dead on Scene	26	6.0
Family	16	4.0
GCRMHMR	15	3.0
Other/Community	7	1.8
Outpatient Clinic	5	1.3
Salvation Army	4	1.2
Private Doctor	3	0.7
Alcoholism Detox	2	0.5
Total	380	

Source: Larson, Winburn, and Henry, n.d., p. 7.

Along with responding to calls in the community, the deputies also screen county jail inmates who have been identified by correctional deputies as possibly needing mental health attention. These are inmates who did not exhibit any mental disorder when admitted but appear to have developed problems in confinement.

Table 4.5 presents summary information on the Travis County Mental Health Deputies Unit for the first six months of FY 1989.

Table 4.5. Summary Statistics for Travis County Mental Health Deputies Unit, January through July 1989

	Cumulative	Avg./Month
Total Cases Reviewed	1,135	162.1
No Commitment Action Taken	465	66.4
Committed to ATC Crisis Stabilization Unit	61	8.7
Committed to Austin State Hospital	385	55.0
Transported to PES for Disposition	114	16.3
Committed to Shoal Creek Hospital	60	8.6
Committed to Charter Lane Hospital	18	2.6
Committed to Holy Cross Hospital	3	0.4
Transported to MHMR Centers	9	1.3
Transported to CPC Hospital	8	1.1
Transported to Travis County Jail	9	1.3
Transported to Salvation Army	3	0.4
Cases within City Limits of Austin	991	141.6
Cases within Travis County	144	20.6
Man-Hours Expended	536.8	219.5

Source: Travis County Mental Health Deputies Unit, 1989.

The unit handles, on the average, between 12 and 20 calls in any 24-hour period. Not all of these calls require a strict mental health response; some involve domestic disturbances and other problems of a social service nature (Larson, Winburn, and Henry, n.d.). Travis County utilizes a similar design. The county sheriff's department employs seven mental health deputies, a clerk, a sergeant, and a lieutenant. One assistant county attorney is also budgeted through the Travis County Mental Health Deputies Unit (Martinez, Interview, August 23, 1989).

Various mechanisms are used in Texas by mental health deputies and other peace officers to get individuals into treatment. Here is as summary of these mechanisms and how they are utilized in Travis County, provided by the Travis County Mental Health Deputies Unit:

1. Voluntary -- Adults may voluntarily commit themselves to an inpatient mental health facility. A minor 15 years of age or younger may be admitted to voluntary inpatient mental health services only if the parent, managing conservator, or guardian consents. In all volunteer admissions, the person must first submit to pre-admittance screening by Psychiatric Emergency Services or an MHMR center.

2. Warrant -- An adult may execute an application for the emergency detention of a mentally ill person by contacting the mental health unit and providing a sworn affidavit detailing the behavior of the person in question. The affidavit is then presented to a magistrate and a warrant is issued if the magistrate feels that the information justifies an emergency commitment.

3. Emergency Commitment without Warrant -- Any person may notify the mental health unit of an emergency situation brought on by the behavior of a mentally ill person. The unit will respond to the incident and take the appropriate action. In most situations requiring emergency response the Austin police or Travis County Sheriff's Office will first be notified due to their capacity for quick response and their ability to stabilize a dangerous situation.

4. Order of Protective Custody (OPC) -- After a mentally ill person has been examined by a medical doctor and a certificate of medical examination for mental illness has been completed, an OPC may be filed with the court. The physician's certificate must be dated within five days of the date the OPC is sought. The certificate is taken to the county attorney's office where a motion for an OPC is drafted. The magistrate reviews the motion, and if in agreement he or she enters an order for protective custody. The effect of an OPC is to order the individual in question to submit to psychiatric examination and treatment. An OPC further orders law enforcement officers to ensure that the person is admitted to an inpatient facility and also orders the inpatient facility to accept that person for treatment.

5. Psychiatric Emergency Services (PES) -- Austin-Travis County Mental Health and Mental Retardation Center maintains a crisis stabilization unit on the grounds of the Austin State Hospital. Psychiatric Emergency Services (PES) serves as a screening facility for the Austin State Hospital and the crisis stabilization unit. PES is located at Brackenridge Hospital next to the Emergency Room. Any person feeling the need for emergency psychiatric services may avail himself or herself of these facilities. (Martinez, 1988)

In FY 1989, the budget for the Travis County Mental Health Deputies Unit was $376,276, of which $355,205 represented personnel expenditures alone. The City of Austin as well as Travis County contracts with the Mental Health Deputies Unit to provide these services. The contract with the City of Austin for FY 1989 was $93,500 (this sum was used to provide the salaries of three MH deputies). Pertinent to this is the fact that the City of Austin accounts for more than 85 percent of the calls received and at the same time accounts for only about 25 percent of the budget. Travis County is concerned with accounting for 75 percent of the budget and is looking for the City of Austin to contribute more for such services. At the same time, the city's financial duress makes it unlikely that city funds for this program will increase (Martinez, Interview, August 23, 1989).

The Travis County Mental Health Deputies Unit also works in close conjunction with the Austin Police Department's Victim Assistance Program (VAP). The VAP serves many emotionally disturbed persons (EDPs) in the city of Austin who come into contact with the Austin police. EDP is a catch-all phrase used by the VAP which includes all mentally ill persons and many substance abusers (Reyna, Interview, August 9, 1989). In Austin, there are three main groups of EDPs coming into contact with the police:

1. EDPs who commit crimes. The Mental Health units and the VAP assist the local police in assessing dangerousness to self or others and a proper disposition.

2. EDPs who inappropriately use 911 telephone services, thereby diverting needed resources from the public. Anyone making five or more inappropriate calls within a one-week period is assigned a "worker" who acts in a case management role to provide mental health and social services by referral to appropriate agencies.

3. EDPs who are victims of crimes. Because of their various problems, many of these individuals become easy prey. This phenomenon is often overlooked when speaking of the mentally ill.

For FY 1989, the City of Austin estimates that $205,713 will be expended to support the VAP (City of Austin, 1989). In 1988, 469 EDPs were served, of which 414 were either chronic 911 callers or persons who required commitment. (Since the VAP is not yet automated, data as to the exact committing problem are not available. The VAP hopes to move to an automated data collection system in FY 1989.) These 469 instances represent duplicated cases. It was estimated that the VAP serviced approximately 125 to 150 unduplicated EDPs in 1988 (Reyna, Interview, August 9, 1989). Austin is as yet the only city in the state to have such a Victim Assistance Program.

In Dallas County, the Diagnostic, Assessment, and Treatment Services (DATS/Forensics) of the Dallas County Mental Health and Mental Retardation Center (DCMHMR) provides screening, psychological assessments, medication maintenance, individual and/or group counseling, psychoeducational groups, and referral services for individuals who have a history and/or recent diagnosis of major mental illness and who are currently involved with the criminal justice system for any criminal activity not related to drugs or alcohol (DCMHMR, 1989a; cited in Blasi et al., 1990). DATS was started at the request of the Dallas County Commissioners Court (Cotton, 1989; cited in Blasi et al., 1990). Except for a contract with the Dallas County Community Corrections Residential Facility to provide services for its residents, DCMHMR is totally unreimbursed for this service. In addition to building space, DCMHMR provides the following staff for the DATS unit: a unit coordinator (100 percent), a psychologist (100 percent), an associate clinical psychologist (50 percent), a psychiatrist (25 percent), and two secretaries (150 percent). As of October 1988, there were 302 active DATS clients

(DCMHMR, 1989b; cited in Blasi et al., 1990). The average length of stay is from one to six months, although individuals on probation or parole are eligible to receive services as long as they want to. Most individuals participate in a 60- to 90-minute weekly group session for no less than 16 weeks. DATS clients are reevaluated at the end of the 16 weeks.

The director of Psychiatric Emergency Services at Parkland Hospital has identified various deficiencies in the DATS program. These include a lack of specific programming for sexual offenders and for violent offenders. He also sees a need for more programming for drug and alcohol abusers. Nevertheless, he regards the forensics clinic as "a major and critical resource" for the Parkland Hospital emergency room (Puryear, 1989, p. 6; cited in Blasi et al., 1990).

DCMHMR has also recently implemented a mobile crisis intervention team. The team consists of two mental health professionals trained in psychiatric crisis intervention. The team has been designed to operate from 6:00 p.m. to 2:00 a.m. seven days a week, times when crisis calls are most likely to be made and professional services least likely to be available. The team's duties include aiding the police in family and public disturbances when a person is suspected to have mental illness as well as aiding with suicide attempts and homicide or hostage situations (Gill, 1989; cited in Blasi et al., 1990). According to the Dallas Morning News (1989; cited in Blasi et al., 1990), the City of Dallas and Dallas County agreed to split the costs, approximately $87,000 each, for the initial four months of operation (June 1 through September 30, 1989). The Dallas Alliance for the Mentally Ill has agreed to raise funds for a van for the program, and the Dallas Mental Health Association has conducted much advocacy work important to the success of the program (Boardman, 1989; cited in Blasi et al., 1990).

Lubbock County also has a somewhat unique collaboration between law enforcement personnel and the local providers of mental health services. Lubbock cannot support its own Mental Health Deputies Unit; thus, Lubbock CMHMRC personnel and law enforcement officers cross-train and work side by side with each other (Hale, Interview, August 18, 1989). In Lubbock, the local sheriff's department and the mobile crisis team of the Lubbock CMHMRC both respond to emergency crisis calls. Should either office receive a call where a social service crisis situation is suspected, both units will meet at the scene and proceed as a team. Both understand and are comfortable with each other's roles. Such a program provides the authority and criminal expertise of law enforcement personnel complemented by the expertise of the CMHMRC crisis team in the care and treatment of mental health problems (Hale, Interview, August 18, 1989).

While this is not an exhaustive search of such programming in the state of Texas, we are aware of no other such formalized programs. Training of law enforcement personnel in mental health issues is equally sporadic. In the above mentioned programs, law enforcement and mental health professionals work side by side, almost inevitably resulting in the heavy involvement of mental health service providers with the training and continuing education of local law enforcement officers. Indeed, this is the case in all of the programs described above, and it is somewhat the case in Tarrant and Harris counties. In Tarrant County, the local CMHMRC and the local Mental Health Association are both formally involved in the basic officer training curriculum and in continuing education. This is also occurring with the local CMHMRC and Mental Health Association in Harris County, although in a much more sporadic and less formalized manner (Hale, Interview, August 18, 1989).

COUNTY JAILS

Of the 254 counties in Texas, 244 operate active jails (Crump, Interview, August 15, 1989). As of June, 1989, Texas had a state jail capacity of 33,874 with an average daily population of 35,813. Thus, the local jail system was at 106 percent of capacity. These local jails range from a capacity of 2 in Coke and Loving counties to a capacity of 4,804 in Harris County (Texas Commission on Jail Standards, 1989). The Texas Commission on Jail Standards documents no information regarding mental health services provided through the county jail system.

Reportedly, all of the more urban counties provide mental health screening and services similar in nature to those provided by the Travis County Jail (Crump, Interview, August 15, 1989). For this reason, Travis County will be presented as a case study of the county jail systems. However, much caution is warranted in generalizing from this one system to others throughout the state.

As with all other aspects of the criminal justice system, providing mental health services has become more and more of an issue for the county jails. Illustrative of this is the fact that in Travis County alone, the county jail is the fourth largest purveyor of mental health services in the county (Simmons, Interview, December 5, 1988).

The Travis County Jail has the capacity to house 1,378 inmates. As of December 1988, there were 1,241 inmates serving sentences at this facility, of which approximately 400 would be serving sentences at the Texas Department of Corrections if adequate space were available (Simmons, Interview, December 5, 1988). Of this population, roughly 10 percent are felt to have serious mental health problems; thus, there are typically 100 to 150 inmates with some form of mental illness at the county jail at any one time. Approximately 10 percent are diagnosed with personality disorders and another 50-70 percent are diagnosed with some form of psychotic disorder (schizophrenia, bipolar disorder, etc.). Roughly 50 percent of the inmates are convicted for felonies and 50 percent convicted for misdemeanors. Those felons directly sentenced to the county jails are usually convicted of third degree (F3) felonies. Their crimes usually consist of DWI, burglary, auto theft, etc.

Services for this population are provided by the two part-time psychiatrists (equivalent to one full-time) and 15 master's-level caseworkers on staff at the Travis County Jail. This facility has 36 beds available for the mentally ill. Services include the identification and screening of those with mental health problems. Upon entering the jail, each inmate is administered a medical/mental health screening instrument. In addition, all staff have the duty and responsibility to report any abnormal and/or symptomatic behavior to the counseling and medical sections for evaluation. Once identified, a more formalized evaluation is conducted by a psychiatrist. If an inmate has been identified as having a need for mental health services, treatment for that inmate will be provided by the jail psychiatrist, jail counselors, and the medical section staff. Mental health care may include assessment, counseling, medication, and/or physical intervention for acute psychiatric decompensation depending on need. Once under treatment, the treatment team (which includes the jail psychiatrist and all others directly involved in the delivery of mental health care) meets once a week for review of cases and staff education (Bailey, 1987).

Aftercare for such individuals is based on services provided by the Austin-Travis County MHMR Center. Each offender released is referred to the ATCMHMRC, where both facilities work to obtain any financial benefits available to this population (e.g., SSI, SSDI, Medicaid, etc.). In FY 1988, a total of $11,422,067 was spent to operate the Travis County Jail (Vaughn, Interview, July 19, 1990). Of this, $454,862 (4 percent of the total expenditures) was spent on direct mental health services. This figure includes $54,203 comprising fees for the two consulting psychiatrists. The remaining $400,659 was spent in counseling services. These figures do not include costs for medications, counseling services provided by the chaplaincy department, hospital stays, or transfer costs to various facilities. In FY 1989, a total of $14,056,797 was expended in operating the jail; $492,576 went for mental health services, $423,088 for counseling services, and $69,488 for psychiatrists' fees.

As stated previously, the Texas Commission on Jail Standards informally reported that most if not all of the urban counties of Texas have similar programs (Crump, Interview, August 15, 1989). However, others have suggested that this is not the case and that while Austin represents one of the better systems, few other counties match this program (Kifowit, Interview, July 24, 1989; Hale, Interview, August 18, 1989). It is partly because of this lack of consistent services that one hears stories of those mentally ill persons who have committed a relatively minor violation remaining in county jails for years waiting for their case to go to trial. The Interagency Council on Mentally Retarded, Developmentally Disabled, and Mentally Ill Offenders (to be discussed below) has earmarked such situations as a direct focus of their concerns for the next biennium. The council plans to survey all county jails in the hopes of better identifying the population of mentally ill misdemeanants and the services provided them (Hale, Interview, August 18, 1989).

VERNON STATE HOSPITAL'S MAXIMUM SECURITY UNIT

The state hospital at Vernon is the state hospital operated by TDMHMR which is responsible for those mentally ill who require maximum security.[3] In FY 1988, the Maximum Security Unit was transferred from Rusk State Hospital to Vernon. The Maximum Security Unit (MSU) services all 254 counties of Texas. It is comprised of highly aggressive and, at times, manipulative patients. Because of this population, the hospital is fenced in, is staffed with security personnel, and is patrolled by guards in watch towers. All units are locked units with no off-grounds privileges allowed (Norris, Interview, November 5, 1989).

The MSU has an average daily population of approximately 300 (Norris, Interview, November 5, 1989). Entrance into the unit is typically accomplished through one of two modes: through the county jails or through other state hospitals or community MHMR centers.

Those sent to Vernon via the county jails are usually referred in order to determine competency to stand trial. Such pretrial assessments typically have an upper-limit stay of no more than 21 days; in extenuating circumstances this limit may be exceeded. If it is determined that the person is competent to stand trial, he or she is then transferred back to the county of origin, where the trial will be heard. If incompetency is determined, persons are admitted under several different criteria, including dangerousness to self or others and the likelihood of regaining competency. Should a person regain competency while at Vernon, he or she will then appear in court for the case to be tried. Vernon also has a unit for those found to be "not guilty by reason of insanity," a separate unit of approximately 70 persons that is "full most of the time" (Norris, Interview, November 5, 1989).

In the past, all sections of the Texas Criminal Code were considered appropriate for the MSU. Thus, both misdemeanant and felony offenders comprised this population. However, recent legislation has eliminated misdemeanant offenders from being sent to the MSU. The other mode of entry is through referrals from other state hospitals and/or community MHMR centers. Such referrals are based on the level of dangerousness the person has manifested toward self or others. The huge number of referrals requires that Vernon take only the most aggressive patients from this population. For this group there is no upper limit to length of stay.

---

[3]Vernon State Hospital also operates the statewide drug treatment center for adolescents.

In FY 1988, Vernon State Hospital budgeted the amount of $14,946,609 (TDMHMR, 1988). In FY 1988, MSU costs totaled $9,655,680, representing roughly 65 percent of Vernon's budget (TDMHMR, 1990a). In FY 1988, Vernon State Hospital was in the process of readying itself to serve maximum security patients. Thus MSU patients were treated for approximately half of FY 1988 at Rusk and half at Vernon. Of the 288 patients treated requiring maximum security, 101 were treated at Vernon. This represented a cost of $223.84 per patient per day (TDMHMR, 1989). This figure is quite high due to the transfer of responsibilities from Rusk to Vernon. For example, in FY 1989, 313 patients were treated at Vernon's Maximum Security Unit at an average daily cost of $130.42 (TDMHMR, 1990b),[4] a figure in keeping with past expenditures.

TEXAS ADULT PROBATION COMMISSION

The Texas Adult Probation Commission (TAPC) provides for the improvement of probation services and the establishment of uniform state standards for probation through the disbursement of state aid to local adult probation departments. Approximately 96 percent of TAPC's appropriations is used to fund county probation departments which provide services to offenders placed on probation. TAPC does not provide direct services to probationers (Criminal Justice Policy Council, 1988).

In April 1987, a Specialized Caseload Program was initiated specifically to divert those offenders with mental impairments from entering the Texas Department of Corrections. Statutorily, TAPC is under no mandate to provide services specifically for the mentally ill. This program was initiated primarily for the purpose of aiding with present prison overcrowding. Currently, the Specialized Caseload Program exists in 8 urban counties in Texas (Rodriguez, Interview, November 11, 1988). Where such programs are unavailable, probationers with mental health problems are typically placed under intensive supervision (Pope, Interview, August 16, 1989). Funding for the Specialized Caseload Program stems from appropriations for specialized caseloads (Table 4.6).

Table 4.6. Legislative Appropriations to the Texas Adult Probation Commission for FY 1988

Total Appropriations	$ 50,844,752	
Special Appropriations		
Specialized Caseloads	$ 1,200,000	(2.4%)
Intensive Supervision	$ 7,128,000	(14.0%)
Court Residential Treatment Centers	$ 1,798,000	(3.5%)
Supplemental Grants	$ 83,000	(0.2%)
Total Special Appropriations	$ 10,209,000	(20.1%)

Source: State of Texas, 1987.

Note: This table highlights those programs felt to be affecting the CMI. All funding for TAPC stems from the State of Texas General Revenue Fund.

Other funding impacting the chronically mentally ill (CMI) is felt to come out of TAPC's Intensive Supervision, Court Residential Treatment Centers, and Supplemental Grants appropriations categories. The proportion of these finances going specifically for

---

[4]In FY 1989, 131 drug-dependent youth were also treated at an average daily cost of $124.11.

the CMI is unknown. It is known that from the Supplemental Grants appropriations, an amount not to exceed $76,103 was to be designated to a pilot study conducted by the Interagency Council on Mentally Retarded, Developmentally Disabled, and Mentally Ill Offenders on diverting these populations from TDC.

Local funds are also used to provide adult probation services. State costs are related to central administration costs as well as to state aid provided the local departments. Local funds include probation fees which help to finance various programs. Adult probation departments at the county level administer all direct probation supervision services. Table 4.7 presents average costs per day per client for services provided by TAPC; both state and local costs are provided. As seen, most funding for the Specialized Caseload Program and for the residential program is being provided by the state.

**Table 4.7. Texas Adult Probation Commission Average
Cost per Day per Client (FY 1988)**

<u>Regular Direct Supervision</u>

State Cost	$ .37
Local Cost	.82
Total Cost	$ 1.18

<u>Specialized Caseload</u>

State Cost	$ 4.51
Local Cost	.03
Total Cost	$ 4.54

<u>Court Residential Treatment Centers</u>

State Cost	$27.31
Local Cost	4.60
Total Cost	$31.91

Source: Criminal Justice Policy Council, 1988, p. 12.

The Specialized Caseload Program involves one caseworker per county working with no more than 25 mentally ill probationers (intensive supervision requires that one caseworker work with no more than 40 probationers each). Each specialized caseworker is trained and experienced in dealing with a specific problem area (i.e., mental illness, mental retardation, alcohol and drug abuse, sex offenders, or family violence). The caseworker typically meets with each probationer once a week unless situations deem otherwise. Probationers may remain on a specialized caseload for up to one year, although this term may be extended by the court. The primary role of the mental health caseworker is to act as a broker in obtaining needed services. Probationers in the program receive community services such as outpatient treatment and some housing via contracts between the local probation departments and local providers of services. For example, in Travis County, probationers are seen by Austin-Travis County MHMR caseworkers and psychiatrists, receive medications through the VA system or through the ATCMHMR Center, and those with a history of alcohol or drug abuse problems receive services from the Texas Commission on Alcohol and Drug Abuse. The Travis County program also reports good rapport with ATCMHMR's Crisis Stabilization Unit such that

106

those with acute difficulties receive needed hospitalization with little bureaucratic difficulty (Rodriguez, Interview, November 11, 1988).

The typical crimes committed by these offenders are nonviolent and lower-level felonies. Examples of such crimes include motor vehicle theft, forgery, larceny, etc.

Another primary role of these specialized probation officers is the obtaining of employment and any other available benefits for this population. Since its inception in Travis County, for example, the income received by these probationers breaks down as follows (Rodriguez, Interview, November 11, 1988):

        12 receive SSI
        2 receive VA benefits
        7 are gainfully employed
        5 are supported by their parents and/or family
        1 is in residence at a halfway house for substance abuse
        2 are transient (homeless)

Since its inception, approximately 3,000 persons with mental illness have been successfully diverted from incarceration through the Texas Adult Probation Commission's Specialized Caseload Program for high-risk and high-need offenders.

The Court Residential Treatment Centers provide short-term residential treatment services to felony probationers. Services available in the centers include drug and alcohol treatment, counseling for emotional problems, job skills training, and basic education. Placement in a Court Residential Treatment Center may be up to one year. Three residential centers were in operation in FY 1988. It is unknown how many of those probationers using this program were diagnosed as mentally ill (Pope, Interview, August 16, 1989).

As of FY 1989, all such programming is to be determined by the local probation departments and other providers of services. Each county is to be funded by TAPC in a block-grant distribution. Thus, each county is to use such funds as county needs demand. In many ways, this scheme possesses mechanisms for the development of more creative programming at the local level. While such a mechanism demands more creative usage of financial resources and increased collaboration at the local level, it also possesses the possibility of fragmenting information throughout the state (Pope, Interview, August 16, 1989).

TEXAS BOARD OF PARDONS AND PAROLES

The Texas Board of Pardons and Paroles (BPP) is that state agency which determines which prisoners are paroled from the Texas Department of Corrections and other penal institutions, establishes the conditions of parole, and investigates and supervises persons released on parole. BPP is also constitutionally responsible for investigating and recommending acts of executive clemency by the governor.

At the end of FY 1988, there were 52,047 releasees under BPP's active supervision. Of these, approximately 6,000 were classified as having a moderate to severe problem with emotional stability[5] (Table 4.8). It is unknown to what extent those classified as

---

[5]Within BPP, there is no formal identification of the mentally ill; the only approach available in identifying those with mental illness is through a scale that BPP uses to rank emotional stability.

having problems with emotional stability coincides with the operational definition of the CMI being used throughout this report.

Table 4.8. Estimated Numbers of Those Paroled with a Moderate to Severe Emotional Problem and Recidivism Rates for Those with an Emotional Problem versus Those without Emotional Problem (FY 1988).

Release Population	Estimated Supervision Population	Percentage of Population
Total Number Parolees	52,047	100%
Severe Emotional Stability Problem	1,000	2%
Moderate Emotional Stability Problem	5,000	10%
One Year Recidivism Rate		
No Emotional Stability Problem		16%
Emotional Stability Problem		19%

Source: Texas Board of Pardons and Paroles, 1988.

Pardons and parole services for the mentally ill parolees are limited. Like the Texas Adult Probation Commission, BPP is under no statutory mandate to serve the mentally ill. Although requests have been made, there is no funding which is specifically targeted to serve the mentally ill or others with mental or emotional impairments. Since there are no direct funds for services, these agencies have had to pull resources from other services offered within the agency (Burke, Interview, November 9, 1988).

Services offered include an Intensive Supervision Parole (ISP) program and the Halfway House program. Both services are very similar in nature to TAPC's services provided special-needs offenders.

Like TAPC's Specialized Caseload Program, BPP's Intensive Supervision Parole program began operation in FY 1987. Where available, mentally ill parolees are placed under the ISP program. An emergency appropriation of $700,000 from the legislature enabled the agency to implement ISP programs in Dallas and Harris counties, where 41 percent of the release population reside (BPP, 1987). In FY 1988, the program was expanded to include Tarrant County, making the program operational in the three counties with the highest number of releasees. Forty-nine percent of BPP's release population reside in these three counties (BPP, 1988). Where such programs are unavailable, parolees with moderate to severe problems with emotional stability are placed under the intensive supervision level of parole (BPP, 1988), which is distinct from the Intensive Supervision Parole program.

Officers supervising cases in the ISP program maintain caseloads of no more than 25 releasees (regular parole officers averaged caseloads of 74 releasees per officer in FY 1988, down from 90 in FY 1987). ISP officers are specially trained in their area of concern (i.e., mental illness, mental retardation, substance abuse, etc.). Parole officers in the ISP contact each releasee at least ten times monthly, with a minimum of one face-to-face contact each week. Releasees under intensive supervision are required to meet with their supervising officers three times each month (BPP, 1988). Table 4.9 presents data on the percentage of releasees on intensive, medium, and minimum supervision for those served in FY 1988 as well as releasees' recidivism rate after one year of release by level of supervision.

Table 4.9. Texas Board of Pardons and Paroles Release Population by Levels of Supervision and Recidivism Rates for Those Classifications during FY 1988

Case Classification	Percentage	Recidivism Rate
Intensive Supervision	43%	23%
Medium Supervision	34%	16%
Minimum Supervision	23%	11%

Source: Texas Board of Pardons and Paroles, 1988, p. 30.

Note: Intensive Supervision case classification does not equal Intensive Supervision Parole.
Recidivism rates are calculated as the percentage of cases returned to prison after one year of release. It is interesting to note that while many of the SMI resurfaced under the Intensive Supervision classification, they are acting to bring Intensive Supervision's recidivism rate down--i.e. emotional problem recidivism = 19 percent (Table 4.8); Intensive Supervision recidivism = 23 percent.

Within ISP, mental health counseling, employment, participation in basic adult education, and/or similar efforts are verified frequently. However, in many cases, there are no services available where the person is released or, if services are available, there is often no funding available for the person to obtain such services. While such parolees are technically subject to revocation, all such clients have to state is that either there are no services available or that there is no funding for such treatment.

In FY 1988, BPP allocated $24 million (50.7 percent of the total budget) for parole supervision. It also allocated another $798,278 (1.7 percent of the total budget) for the ISP program.

BPP also provides a halfway house program which is designed primarily for those releasees who have no residential resources in the community. While the mentally ill comprise a large portion of this homeless population, data on what proportion of those using the halfway house program were mentally ill are not collected. Inmates may be released to halfway houses directly from TDC as a condition of release, at the inmate's request, or as an alternative when the inmate is unable to develop or maintain a suitable residential plan. Releasees in halfway houses have an opportunity to look for suitable employment or job training and participate in drug/alcohol treatment programs, counseling, or other social services available in the community or as part of the house's program.

BPP designated $12.3 million (25.9 percent of the total budget) for the Halfway House program in FY 1988.[6] These funds were used to contract for bed space with other agencies (usually private, nonprofit; e.g., Salvation Army). In FY 1988, BPP contracted

---

[6]Funds for this program in FY 1988 are approximately doubled the amount of $6.9 million for the Halfway House program in FY 1987.

with 29 halfway houses across the state for 1,148 beds. A total of 9,552 clients were placed in the Halfway House program in FY 1988. The average cost was $21.41 per day per client. A client typically stayed in the halfway houses an average of 43 days (BPP, 1988).

The Texas Board of Pardons and Paroles provided various cost figures associated with the supervision of parolees and the Halfway House program. The cost figures in the various levels of supervision are listed in Table 4.10.

Table 4.10. Average FY 1988 Cost per Day per Client of the Texas Board of Pardons and Paroles

Service	Cost (FY 1988)
Parole and Mandatory Supervision (Total Average)	$ 1.78
Average by Level of Supervision	
Intensive	$ 2.52
Medium	$ 1.56
Minimum	$ 1.04
Intensive Supervision Parole (ISP)	$ 5.39
Halfway House Program	$26.91

Source: Criminal Justice Policy Council, 1988, p. 19.

Note: Costs per day of the Halfway House program represent the average costs of all halfway and preparole transfer houses.

Table 4.11 presents total FY 1988 expenditures for BPP. Approximately 85 percent of the agency's appropriations are used for direct services for those released from the Texas Department of Corrections.

Table 4.11. Texas Board of Pardons and Paroles Agency Expenditures for FY 1988

Program Area	Amount Budgeted	Percentage of Total
Parole Supervision	$ 24,000,000	(50.7)
Intensive Supervision parole (ISP)	$ 798,278	(1.7)
Halfway House Program	$ 12,300,000	(25.9)
Administration	$ 1,700,000	(3.7)
Parole Selection	$ 3,900,000	(8.3)
Support Services	$ 4,400,000	(9.4)
Executive Clemency	$ 122,361	(0.3)
Total Expenditures	$ 47,220,639	

Source: Texas Board of Pardons and Paroles, 1988, p. 45.

TEXAS DEPARTMENT OF CORRECTIONS

Recent surveys typically suggest that 6 to 8 percent of state prison populations have a serious psychiatric illness (Steadman, Monahan, and Hartstone, 1982; McCarthy and Feder, 1985), and that 15 to 20 percent of all prison inmates need psychiatric treatment at some point in their incarceration (Halleck, 1986; Monahan and Steadman, 1984; Roth, 1980). Such data suggest that the prevalence of mental disorder among prison populations does not greatly differ from rates found in groups of comparable social classes in the community (Monahan and Steadman, 1984).

A local survey conducted by the Texas League of Women Voters found that approximately 10 percent, or 3,800 inmates, of TDC's population was estimated to have some form of serious mental difficulty (League of Women Voters of Texas Education Fund, 1988). While estimates may vary, it is increasingly being recognized by prison administrators that mentally ill inmates in prison are a growing problem. Texas prison overcrowding no doubt plays a part: the mentally ill become much more visible as their stress is exacerbated when living conditions deteriorate and other resources have been stretched beyond limits.

Presently, TDC is the only component of the criminal justice system that is mandated to provide services to the adult mentally ill. Such services have either been initiated or expanded as a direct result of the landmark Ruiz v. Estelle (1980) decision which delineated minimum components necessary for adequate mental health care in TDC.

Senate Bill 245, Section 45, which passed during the 70th Session of the Texas Legislature, mandated that the Texas Department of Corrections identify inmates with special needs and consider the feasibility of transferring those inmates to facilities in the state other than those of TDC. In response to such legislation, TDC has recently completed a study entitled Transferring Special Needs Offenders to Community-Based Programs (TDC and the Criminal Justice Center, 1989), which examines the feasibility of such legislation.

The study included the mentally ill, mentally retarded, mobility impaired, vision impaired, hearing impaired, elderly, and those with significant medical problems. Early on, it was decided that inmates convicted of 3g offenses (i.e., capital murder, aggravated kidnapping, aggravated sexual assault, and aggravated robbery) would be excluded from consideration for transfer to the community. After sampling the remaining special-needs offenders and obtaining survey results from TDC clinical and direct care personnel, it was determined that approximately 2.3 percent of the total TDC population (52 percent of the eligible special needs offenders) or a total of 892 special needs offenders would be recommended for transfer based on the TDC inmate population as of July 1988 (38,000). Estimates were also made for March 1990, at which time TDC's currently approved construction projects would allow an increase of TDC's inmate population to 49,412 (95 percent capacity). It was estimated that 1,274 special-needs offenders would be recommended for transfer based on this total TDC population (TDC and the Criminal Justice Center, 1989).

The operational definition of the mentally ill special-needs offenders used in this study was similar in nature to the definition of the CMI being used throughout this report. The special-needs study identified the seriously mentally ill on the basis of the following criterion:

> Any offender admitted to an inpatient psychiatric facility in
> TDC who has been assessed by the psychiatric facility
> admissions staff as exhibiting a psychotic disorder, major

affective disorder, or other significant psychiatric condition, as defined in the <u>Diagnostic and Statistical Manual of Mental Disorders, Third Edition, Revised</u>. (TDC and the Criminal Justice Center, 1989, p. 11)

The operational definition utilized in this study limited TDC's sample to inpatient offenders. TDC's rationale for this decision related primarily to the increased level of functioning of its outpatient psychiatric patients (TDC and the Criminal Justice Center, 1989).

Of special importance to this report was the determination of the number of offenders in TDC requiring inpatient psychiatric care. Based on the special-needs study, it was determined that 980 offenders (2.6 percent of 38,000 offenders) required inpatient psychiatric care. Although TDC does not currently house that many offenders in an inpatient psychiatric setting, as facilities become available, that number, in all likelihood, will be reached. The inpatient population as of July 1988 consisted of 662 mentally ill inpatient offenders. This figure was used in computing initial transfer decisions (i.e., based on a total population of 38,000), while the 2.6 percent figure was used in computing future transfer decisions (i.e., based on a total population of 49,412).

Currently, TDC has the capacity to house 884 mentally ill offenders in its four inpatient facilities. Table 4.12 presents the capacity and location of these four units. It is important to note that the average daily population had already increased by 74 persons from July 1988 to May 1989.

Table 4.12. Capacity, Location, and Average Daily Population of TDC's Four Inpatient Programs

Unit	Location	Capacity	ADP for May 1989	
Beto I	Palestine	38	23	
Ellis II	Huntsville	510	407	
Mountain View*	Gatesville	32	12	
Skyview	Rusk	304	294	
Total		884	736	(91.5% of capacity)

Sources: Ferrara, Letter, August, 28, 1989; TDC, 1989a.

Note: ADP = Average Daily Population
* female psychiatric facility

The largest number of special-needs offenders came from the counties of Harris, Dallas, Bexar, Tarrant, Travis, and Jefferson, which cumulatively represented a minimum of 50 percent of the total special-needs population. Consequently, inmates from those counties comprised the group from which the sample was taken. The decision to divide the offenders according to county of residence and then sample 50 percent of the cumulative population was based on two considerations. The first was associated with a general consensus that efforts should concentrate on and give close attention to those offenders from large urban areas since these locations typically offer the majority of services needed. The second reason was related to the need to limit the size of the sample to be studied. The total number of offenders in each special-needs category from the most populous counties is shown in Table 4.13.

Table 4.13. Special-Needs Offender Frequency Distribution for Major Texas Counties

County	MI	MR	MoI	VI	HI	El	SMP	Total	Percentage
Harris	158	136	13	3	5	76	62	453	22
Dallas	113	139	8	4	2	46	42	354	38
Bexar	31	30	3	1	2	22	10	99	43
Tarrant	24	25	0	1	1	17	16	84	47
Travis	37	17	1	2	1	9	14	81	51
Jefferson	11	22	1	0	1	8	3	46	53
Galveston	9	6	0	2	2	7	5	31	55
Nueces	12	0	1	2	0	3	7	25	56
Lubbock	8	8	0	0	0	3	5	24	57
Gregg	9	7	1	1	0	3	1	22	58
El Paso	14	3	0	0	0	4	0	21	59
Bell	7	0	2	2	0	4	3	18	60
Williamson	3	4	0	0	0	6	4	17	61
Wichita	5	7	0	0	0	0	2	14	62
Other	221	207	19	7	9	194	141	798	100
Totals	662	611	49	25	23	402	315	2,087	
Percentage	32	29	2	1	1	19	15		

Source: TDC and the Criminal Justice Center, 1989, p. 90.

Note: MI = mentally ill; MR = mentally retarded; MoI = mobility impaired; VI = vision impaired; HI = hearing impaired; El = elderly; SMP = significant medical problems.

Table 4.14 reflects the remaining methodology used in identifying the sample for study in the special-needs report.

Table 4.14. Sampling Procedure Utilized in Special-Needs Offender Study

	MI	MR	MoI	VI	HI	El	SMP	Total
System Total	662	611	49	25	23	402	315	2,087
Total in Six Major Counties	374	369	26	11	12	178	147	1,117
Total-3g Offenders in Six Major Counties	64 17%	77 21%	4 15%	2 18%	3 25%	21 12%	25 17%	196 17.5%
Total in Six Counties Less 3g Offenders	310	292	22	9	9	157	122	921
Final Sample Size x=25.7% of Non 3g Offenders in Six Major Counties	66	75	22	9	9	33	22	236

Source: TDC, 1989a, p. 89.

Note: MI = mentally ill; MR = mentally retarded; MoI = mobility impaired; VI = vision impaired; HI = hearing impaired; El = elderly; SMP = significant medical problems.

For the final sample of 66 psychiatric inpatient offenders, an analysis of several characteristics was compiled and compared to those of the total TDC population.

Figure 4.1. Comparison of Ethnicity in TDC's Psychiatric Inpatient Special-Needs Offender Sample versus TDC's Total Population

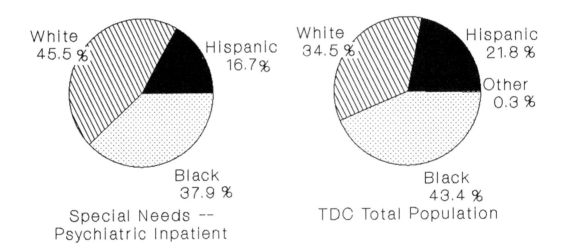

Sources: TDC, 1989b, p. 16;
         TDC and the Criminal Justice Center, 1989, Appendix B.

Note: Psychiatric Inpatient sample is based on July 1988 sample.

114

Figure 4.1 presents a breakdown by ethnicity. As seen, whites and Hispanics appear overrepresented while blacks appear underrepresented.

Figure 4.2 compares committing crimes for the psychiatric inpatient population with those of the total TDC population. Because the statistics for the total population were compiled for the national crime indexes, Texas' 3g crimes are included within the general type of crime committed. Thus, aggravated kidnapping would be included under kidnapping. It is noteworthy that many of the psychiatric inpatients are in TDC because they have committed a serious offense. Some critics have suggested that many of the mentally ill are "locked up" for minor violations such as disturbing the peace and/or vagrancy. While many of those in the county jails may be there for such crimes, many in TDC do appear to be there for serious violations of the law.

Figure 4.3 compares length of sentence for special-needs offenders with that of the total TDC population. There appears to be little difference in the overall patterns among the two groups.

The first results to be analyzed in the study related to the transfer decision. As stated earlier, projections were made from the sample to the July 1988 TDC population (38,000) and the TDC population estimated in March of 1990 (49,412). Tables 4.15 and 4.16 indicate the projected number of initial transfer recommendations assuming the program were to begin at the specific times listed in the table.

Table 4.15. Projected Number of Initial Transfer Recommendations Based on a Total July 1988 TDC Population of 38,000

	MI	MR	MoI	VI	HI	El	SMP	Total
SNO Pop. July 1988	662	611	49	25	23	402	315	2,087
Percentage of 38,000	1.7%	1.6%	.13%	.07%	.07%	1%	.8%	5.5%
Estimated Percentage of 3g Offenders	17%	21%	15%	18%	25%	12%	17%	17.3%
and Number	113	128	7	5	6	48	54	361
SNO Pop. Minus 3g Offenders	549	483	42	20	17	354	261	1,726 (4.5% of 38,000)
Percentage Recommended for Transfer	38%	61%	23%	33%	67%	52%	68%	52%
Estimated Number Recommended for Transfer July 1988	208	295	10	7	11	184	177	892 (2.3% of 38,000)

Source: TDC and the Criminal Justice Center, 1989, p. 92.

Note: MI = mentally ill; MR = mentally retarded; MoI = mobility impaired; VI = vision impaired; HI = hearing impaired; El = elderly; SMP = significant medical problems.

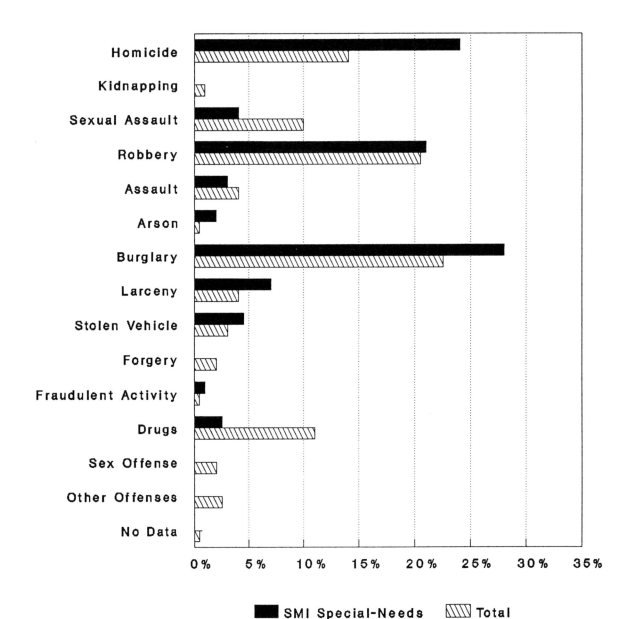

Figure 4.2. Comparison of Types of Crimes Committed by TDC's Psychiatric Inpatient Special-Needs Offender Sample versus TDC's Total Population

Sources: TDC, 1989b, p. 20;
TDC and the Criminal Justice Center, 1989, Appendix B.
Note: Psychiatric inpatient sample is based on July 1988 sample.

116

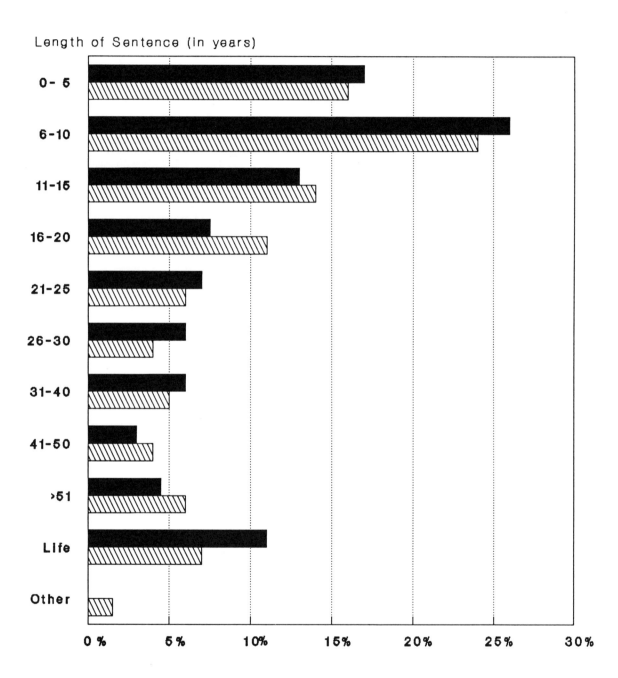

Figure 4.3. Comparison of Lengths of Stay by TDC's
Psychiatric Inpatient Special-Needs Offender Sample
versus TDC's Total Population

Length of Sentence (in years)

■ SMI Special Needs   ⧅ Total

Sources: TDC, 1989b, p. 21;
          TDC and the Criminal Justice Center, 1989, Appendix B.
Note: Psychiatric Inpatient sample is based on July 1988 sample.

117

Table 4.16. Projected Number of Initial Transfer Recommendations Based on a Total TDC Population of 49,412

	MI	MR	MoI	VI	HI	El	SMP	Total
SNO Pop.	1,285	791	64	35	35	494	395	3,099
March 1990 Percentage of 49,4142	2.6	1.6	.13	.07	.07	1	.8	6.3
Estimated Percentage of 3g Offenders	17	21	15	18	25	12	17	17.3
and Number	218	166	10	6	9	59	67	535
SNO Pop less 3g Offenders	1,067	625	54	29	26	435	328	2,564
Percentage Recommended for Transfer	38	61	23	33	67	52	68	52
Estimated Number Recommended for Transfer March 1990	405	381	12	10	17	226	223	1,274

Source: TDC and the Criminal Justice Center, 1989, p. 92.

Note: MI = mentally ill; MR = mentally retarded; MoI = mobility impaired;
VI = vision impaired; HI = hearing impaired; El = elderly;
SMP = significant medical problems.

In addition to the projections based upon the initial population, projections were also made for the number of special-needs offenders who were likely to be eligible for transfer on an annual basis. These projections were based on the estimated number of special-needs offenders who would be admitted to TDC on an annual basis assuming TDC capacity of 38,000 (July 1988) and 49,412 (March 1990). These projections are presented in Tables 4.17 and 4.18.

Table 4.17. Projected Number of Annual Transfer Recommendations Based on a Total July 1988 TDC Population of 38,000

	MI	MR	MoI	VI	HI	El	SMP	Total
Estimated Number of Annual Admissions	111	281	12	2	11	113	69	599
Est. Percentage of 3g	17	21	15	18	25	12	17	17.3
Offenders and Number	19	59	2	.4	3	14	12	109
SNO Pop less 3g Offenders	92	222	10	1.6	8	99	57	489.6
Percentage Recommended for Transfer	38	61	23	33	67	52	68	52
Estimated Number Reccomended for Transfer Annually	35	135	2	.5	5	51	39	267.5

Source: TDC and the Criminal Justice Center, 1989, p. 92.

Note: MI = mentally ill; MR = mentally retarded; MoI = mobility impaired;
VI = vision impaired; HI = hearing impaired; El = elderly;
SMP = significant medical problems.

Table 4.18. Projected Number of Annual Transfer Recommendations Based on a Total TDC Population of 49,412

	MI	MR	MoI	VI	HI	El	SMP	Total
Estimated Number of Annual Admissions	215	367	14	3	15	146	89	849
Estimated Percentage of 3g Offenders	17	21	15	18	25	12	17	17.3
and Number	37	77	2	.5	4	18	15	154
SNO Pop less 3g Offenders	178	290	12	2.5	11	128	74	695.5
Percentage Recommended for Transfer	38	61	23	33	67	52	68	52
Estimated Number Recommended for Transfer Annually	68	177	3	.8	7	67	50	372.8

Source: TDC and the Criminal Justice Center, 1989, p. 92.

Note: MI = mentally ill; MR = mentally retarded; MoI = mobility impaired; VI = vision impaired; HI = hearing impaired; El = elderly; SMP = significant medical problems.

For those offenders who were not recommended for transfer by a staff member, that staff member was asked to provide a reason for nontransfer. An analysis of these responses revealed the following nine reasons, in descending order:

1. Criminal history and prior incarcerations
2. Poor institutional behavior
3. Potential threat to others
4. Non-compliant or unresponsive to treatment
5. Current acute nature of illness
6. Required structured environment with close supervision
7. Poor probability of successful adjustment to a community-based program
8. Special needs being met at TDC
9. No major problem manifested (TDC and the Criminal Justice Center, 1989).

The special-needs study was also charged with making recommendations to the legislature which will impact on transferring such populations into the community. Those recommendations made which impact on the CMI are presented below:

1. Mandatory Presentence Investigations of All Felony Suspects. At the present time, there is no systematic process to identify offenders with mental impairments; therefore, diversion programs cannot be utilized appropriately. It was recommended that the judge's discretion to forgo such investigations be removed and that such investigations include a thorough psychological evaluation and that a copy of the investigation accompany convicted felons upon transfer to TDC. The Code of Criminal Procedure, Article 42.12, Section 4 (b) presently states, "The court is not required to direct a probation officer to prepare a report if: (1) the defendant requests that a report not be made and the court agrees to the request; or (2) the court finds that there is sufficient information in the record to permit the meaningful exercise of sentencing discretion and the

119

court explains this finding on the record" (State of Texas, 1988). Such action would result in several cost-saving measures, including expediting the Texas Department of Corrections diagnostic process. Such reports could also allow for the early identification of persons with mental impairments, for purposes of pretrial diversion.

2.   Establishment of Regional Interagency Human Service Councils. It was recommended that interagency councils be established on a regional basis that would be responsible for coordinating services delivery to special-needs offenders at the community level.

3.   Funding for Community Services. It was recommended that additional contract funds be made available to the Texas Board of Pardons and Paroles and the Texas Adult Probation Commission to enable them to contract for community services for each of the special-needs offender categories.

4.   Establishment of a Special-Needs Parole. It was recommended that a unique type of parole be authorized whereby special-needs offenders could be transferred from the Texas Department of Corrections prior to the normal parole eligibility date. The special-needs parole would be a permanent suspension of incarceration for the purpose of receiving services at the community level. Two options for the legal jurisdiction over an inmate granted Special-Needs Parole were presented:

> Option 1: Offenders under this option would be remanded to the jurisdiction of the Board of Pardons and Paroles. Under this option, the offender would be eligible to receive various forms of state and federal financial assistance which they are ineligible to receive while under the jurisdiction of TDC. However, to transfer such inmates back to TDC would require a formal revocation hearing.

> Option 2: Offenders under this provision would remain under the jurisdiction of TDC and could be transferred back to TDC without the requirement of a formal hearing. However, inmates under TDC's jurisdiction do not qualify for federal and state financial assistance.

5.   Funding for Texas Rehabilitation Commission (TRC) Services. It was requested that additional state monies be made available to the TRC to serve an increased number of special-needs offenders.

6.   Community Facilities for the Mentally Ill. It was recommended that a legislative appropriation be provided to the Texas Board of Pardons and Paroles to fund the development of community residential facilities for mentally ill offenders.

7.   Specialized Parole and Probation Caseloads. Funding for the Texas Board of Pardons and Paroles and the Texas Adult Probation Commission was recommended to expand their Specialized Caseload Programs for offenders with mental impairments and to fund at requested levels for contract services.

8.   Mental Health and Mental Retardation Service Priorities. It was recommended that the Texas Department of Mental Health and Mental

Retardation be directed to reorder service priority populations in such a way that mentally retarded and mentally ill offenders be given a higher priority of service provision in the community (TDC and the Criminal Justice Center, 1989).

Services for the adult mentally ill offender in TDC range from outpatient therapies through extended care. Data available from Ellis II, the largest psychiatric facility in the TDC system, give some indication of the types of services given and average stays in these treatments. Table 4.19 presents this data for September and August of 1988.

Table 4.19. Report on Inpatient Services at Ellis II (TDC)

	Sept. 1988	Aug. 1988
Average Daily Census	485.0	428.0
Average Daily Acute Care Census	43.0	69.0
Average Days Stay in Acute Care	65.0	60.0
Average Daily Intermediate Care Census	217.0	156.0
Average Days Stay in Intermediate Care	302.2	306.5
Average Daily Structured Care Census	169.0	171.0
Average Daily Diagnostic and Evaluation Census	56.0	32.0
Average Daily Extended Care Census	0.0	0.0
Number of Beds in Psychiatric Center	525.0	518.0
Average Number of Cells Available	27.7	81.3

Source: TDC, 1988.

Funds for these services are part of those appropriations designated for psychiatric services in TDC's total budget. Table 4.20 presents these figures. Roughly 85-90 percent of TDC's total budget comes from the state's General Revenue Fund. Presently, there is little federal funding available for the criminal justice system.

Table 4.20. Texas Department of Corrections Total Appropriations and Funds Appropriated for Serving the CMI for FY 1988

TDC Total Appropriations	Psychiatric Services
$ 723,929,974	$ 32,192,516 (4.4%)* 2-^N2

Source: State of Texas, 1987.

> * FY 1988 total budget includes a $250,000,000 bonded construction fund which was not as substantial in the past nor is it as substantial in FY 1989. Without this difference, psychiatric services typically comprise 6.3 percent of TDC's total budget.

Transferring special-needs offenders would impact TDC financially as well. Based on current programming, TDC provides a range of services for the inpatient mentally ill at a cost of $99.96 per day of which $34.00 represents the basic daily cost for incarcerating any offender. If the average annual population of mentally ill inpatient offenders (980) is reduced by 35 inmates (as predicted), the reduction in required funding for the Mentally Ill Inpatient Offender Program has been calculated to amount to 14 full-time equivalent positions and operational costs approximating $295,172 per year (TDC and the Criminal Justice Center, 1989, p. 120).

An ongoing issue concerning services for the mentally ill offender is related to the issue of continuity of care. In the past, coordination between TDC, BPP, TDMHMR, and community MHMR centers has often been lacking. Recently, the 70th Legislature had stipulated under item 44 of TDMHMR's code that

> It is the intent of the Legislature that the Department of
> Corrections and the Department of Mental Health and Mental
> Retardation enter into an interagency agreement which will
> provide for improved services to the mentally ill and
> mentally retarded inmates of the Department of Corrections
> and allow the agency to utilize facilities of the Department
> of Mental Health and Mental Retardation when appropriate
> and feasible. (State of Texas, 1987, p. ii-59)

The recently established Interagency Council on Mentally Retarded, Developmentally Disabled, and Mentally Ill Offenders continues to address this and many other issues surrounding the improved care and treatment of the state's mentally impaired offenders.

INTERAGENCY COUNCIL ON MENTALLY RETARDED, DEVELOPMENTALLY DISABLED, AND MENTALLY ILL OFFENDERS

Proposals submitted to the 70th Legislature became law in Senate Bill 719, which established the Interagency Council on Mentally Retarded, Developmentally Disabled, and Mentally Ill Offenders. The Interagency Council represents an unprecedented legislative charge to criminal and juvenile justice agencies, social service and education agencies, advocacy organizations, and policy councils to collaborate on developing community-based sentencing alternatives for offenders with mental impairments. Significant among the directives to the council were these:

1. to determine the status of offenders with mental retardation, developmental disabilities, and mental illness,

2. to identify the services needed by these offenders and to develop a plan to implement community-based alternatives to incarceration, and

3. to implement a pilot project to demonstrate strategies to implement community alternatives. (Interagency Council on Mentally Retarded, Developmentally Disabled, and Mentally Ill Offenders, 1989a)

The Interagency Council on Mentally Retarded, Developmentally Disabled, and Mentally Ill Offenders was enacted into law on September 1, 1987. The first full meeting of the council was held on June 3, 1988. The council consists of 27 members, 9 of whom are appointed by the governor and serve staggered six-year terms. In addition, the executive director or a designated representative of each of 18 agencies, associations, and councils are also members of the council. Table 4.21 lists those 18 agencies.

Table 4.21. Agencies Comprising the Interagency Council on Mentally Retarded, Developmentally Disabled, and Mentally Ill Offenders

1. Texas Department of Corrections
2. Texas Department of Mental Health and Mental Retardation
3. Board of Pardons and Paroles
4. Texas Adult Probation Commission
5. Texas Juvenile Probation Commission
6. Texas Youth Commission
7. Texas Rehabilitation Commission
8. Central Education Agency
9. Criminal Justice Policy Council
10. Mental Health Association in Texas
11. Texas Commission on Alcohol and Drug Abuse
12. Commission on Law Enforcement Officer Standards and Education
13. Texas Council of Community Mental Health and Mental Retardation Centers
14. Commission on Jail Standards
15. Texas Planning Council for Developmental Disabilities
16. Texas Association for Retarded Citizens
17. Texas Alliance for the Mentally Ill
18. Parent Association for the Retarded of Texas, Inc.

Source: Interagency Council on Mentally Retarded, Developmentally Disabled, and Mentally Ill Offenders, 1989a, p. 8.

To ensure that funds were available to support the implementation of SB 719 in FYs 1988 and 1989, the legislature appropriated by rider specified biennium funding for each of the primary agencies. Table 4.22 lists those agencies and amounts to be funded.

Table 4.22. Specified Biennium Funding for Agencies Associated with the Interagency Council on Mentally Retarded, Developmentally Disabled, and Mentally Ill Offenders

Agency	Funding
Texas Department of Mental Health and Mental Retardation	$ 452,206
Central Education Agency	$ 350,800
Texas Department of Corrections	$ 350,000
Board of Pardons and Paroles	$ 152,206
Texas Adult Probation Commission	$ 152,206
Texas Juvenile Probation Commission	$ 152,206
Texas Youth Commission	$ 152,206
Texas Rehabilitation Commission	$ 152,206
Texas Commission on Alcohol and Drug Abuse	$ 50,000

Source: Interagency Council on Mentally Retarded, Developmentally Disabled, and Mentally Ill Offenders, 1989a, p. 8.

The council made numerous recommendations to the 71st Legislature. Many of these recommendations were supported those made by TDC's special-needs report, including the following:

1. Mandatory presentence investigations for all convicted felons.
2. Establishment of regional Interagency Human Service Councils.
3. Funding for community services.
4. Special-Needs Parole.
5. Funding for Texas Rehabilitation Commission services.
6. Residential community facilities for the mentally ill.
7. Specialized probation and parole caseloads.
8. Mental Health and Mental Retardation service priorities with wording changes.

The council felt that service priorities did not necessarily have to be changed, but rather that a policy prohibiting discrimination was in order. There have been reported situations in which otherwise eligible clients have been denied needed services by community mental health and mental retardation centers because of their status as a parolee or probationer. Jemelka, Trupin, and Chiles (1989) also report such findings in Washington state. A recent survey found that a prior history of incarceration or of felonious criminal behavior was often used as an exclusionary criterion in screening for program eligibility. Thus, the development and dissemination by TDMHMR to its providers and contractees of a policy prohibiting discrimination in eligibility for services against a person with a history as an offender is needed.

The council also made numerous other recommendations to the legislature. A few of the more significant recommendations impacting on the care and treatment of the mentally ill offender are as follows:

1. The Medicaid Plan should be expanded to include rehabilitation and case management service options for offenders with mental impairments. The state's resources should be supplemented whenever possible.

2. Fund and direct the Texas Education Agency, Texas Rehabilitation Commission, Texas Department of Mental Health and Mental Retardation, and the Texas Commission on Alcohol and Drug Abuse to expand their services in such a way that offenders with mental retardation and mental illness be given continued services in the community after parole and probation. This funding scheme should not displace any funds which are ordinarily appropriated for currently designated service populations, but rather be in addition to existing funds.

3. Release of inmates with mental impairments from Texas Department of Corrections with 30 days of medication and the immediate access to a mental health and/or mental retardation authority physician for medication control and continuity of care. Presently, inmates with mental impairments are released with 10 days of medication. Continuity of medication compliance is critical to offenders with mental impairments. (Interagency Council on Mentally Retarded, Developmentally Disabled, and Mentally Ill Offenders, 1989a)

Of these recommendations, only the last was not adopted by the 71st legislature. Currently, the Interagency Council has contracted with the Association for Retarded Citizens -- Austin to conduct a pilot study in Travis County with offenders who are mentally retarded or who have a developmental disability. This pilot project has been in operation for six months. Although the tenure has been brief, statistics highlight several issues:

1. At the time of their arrest, 82.7 percent of the offenders were receiving no services. Offenders with mental retardation/developmental disabilities are

often unable to access social services. The independent case manager is critical in identifying and obtaining services required by the offender.

2. The average offender had completed 9.1 years of education. Most offenders were or are involved in special education and therefore entitled to educational services through their 21st birthday. This suggests that the focus of education should be on the development of retention and dropout prevention strategies.

3. The program has a significantly higher number of adult participants than juveniles. This reflects the existence for at least five years of specialized probation and parole services for adult offenders with mental retardation/developmental disabilities in Travis County. Comparable services for juveniles have been in effect for less than one year. Specialized parole and probation caseloads are clearly having an impact on successful identification of offenders with mental impairments. (Interagency Council on Mentally Retarded, Developmentally Disabled, and Mentally Ill Offenders, 1989b, pp. 11-12)

It is unknown to what extent these results would generalize to the CMI population. However, the implications of such results are significant and indicate the need for evaluating such a program with the CMI.

Fundamental to any success of such a program has been the establishment of an independent case management system to coordinate all related services for those involved in the pilot project. Five case managers have been employed to work with the 45 offenders (41 adults and 4 juveniles) currently in the pilot study. The independent case manager's role is to

... serve as the primary contact person for offenders with mental retardation/developmental disabilities, from time of arrest to post-incarceration. At any point in the criminal justice system, the independent case manager is responsible for identifying the scope and level of needs of the offender with mental impairments. Once the needs and services are identified, the independent case manager, in cooperation with participating agencies, develops an individual justice plan (IJP) .... The IJP serves as the master plan whereby all service needs are identified and responsible service agencies are held accountable for ensuring delivery and/or availability of services. (Interagency Council on Mentally Retarded, Developmentally Disabled, and Mentally Ill Offenders, 1989b, p. 1)

The development of this independent case management system in conjunction with an expanded array of community treatment alternatives in the Travis County pilot project has had a significant impact on the recidivism rate for these offenders. At six months, the recidivism rate for the 41 adults in the project was 7.3 percent. BPP reported a one-year recidivism rate for those with an emotional stability problem to be 19 percent (1988).

The Interagency Council recommends expanding its pilot programs to include the mentally ill. It also recommends expanding these pilot projects to include Harris and Dallas counties. Should this recommendation be enacted by the 71st Legislature, the council believes that a mechanism to provide services to these inmates must be further developed. Such support of these pilot projects also implies that increased funding will be required by any or all human service agencies to provide such services to this population.

The Interagency Council has already begun activities targeted for recommendations to the 72nd Legislature. Activities designed to impact policy regarding mentally ill offenders include

1.   establishing a pilot project with the mentally ill;

2.   formalizing and expanding police officer training in the recognition and handling of those suspected of having emotional problems; and

3.   assessing the number of mentally ill misdemeanants incarcerated in county jails, services provided to such persons, and alternative programming options to more effectively meet the needs of these people (Hale, Interview, August 18, 1989).

THE 71ST LEGISLATURE'S IMPACT ON THE MENTALLY ILL OFFENDER

The Texas Legislature's 71st Session devoted a major portion of its efforts to the criminal justice system. With this has come a fair amount of legislation impacting on the mentally ill in the criminal justice system. Some of the more important resolutions impacting on this population are discussed in this section.

Undoubtedly, the most important legislation affecting the criminal justice system comes out of H.B. 2335. Within this act comes the establishment of the Texas Department of Criminal Justice, the consolidation of the three major state agencies handling the care and supervision of felons throughout the state (TAPC, TDC, and TBPP) into one state agency. Such consolidation is expected to create a single, more uniform, and more streamlined process among the three functions (probation, prison, and parole) and is expected to increase communication among the three. Increased communication along with a more uniform terminology should result in a more consistent identification and treatment of the mentally ill among all three divisions. Increased communication should also be extremely helpful at the transition points. In the past, the transition from TDC's jurisdiction into BPP's was often done in haste, with frequent disregard or unawareness of the recommendations each agency had made. Also ignored were the needs of the felon entering the community (Gilliland, Interview, October 20, 1989). While consolidation will certainly impact all facets of the criminal justice system's administrative and programming procedures, it is felt that this increased and more uniform communication holds tremendous potential for identifying, treating, and planning for the special-needs of the mentally ill offender.

Also included in H.B. 2335 was an article which will require that the Community Justice Assistance Division of the Texas Department of Criminal Justice (formerly TAPC) conduct pretrial service reports on offenders suspected of being mentally impaired. Such passage offers the possibility of diverting from the criminal justice system a significant number of persons with mental impairments who are more appropriate for treatment in the mental health/mental retardation system. Such an enactment, along with any increased communication with the Institutional Division (formerly TDC) also allows for early identification of the mental impairment and an early identification of special-needs should such an offender be sent to the Institutional Division. However, the major benefit in this enactment is the possibility for the diversion of special needs offenders from entering prison unnecessarily.

S.R. 764 is a Senate resolution which acknowledges the fact that a significant number of the inmates in county jails across Texas are believed to be mentally ill and that many of these inmates are arrested for minor, nonviolent misdemeanors. This resolution calls for the cooperation of the Interagency Council and TDMHMR in addressing alternatives for serving those with mental impairments who are charged with and jailed for misdemeanors. S.R. 764 has added a clause which states that any defendant found to be incompetent to stand trial for a misdemeanor because of mental illness shall have an order entered committing the defendant to a mental health facility which serves the catchment area in which the committing court is located for a period not to exceed 18 months. Such care may be at a community mental health center or in a TDMHMR institution, depending on need.

Legislation was also passed which would allow for the expansion of the Medicaid program to include rehabilitation and case management service options. As stated previously, many of those in the criminal justice system feel that the state's resources should be supplemented whenever possible. Currently, TDMHMR is working on plans regarding the proper mechanics for expanding services to this client population group. With this expansion has come the addition of a representative from the Department of Human Services to the Interagency Council.

A mandate that mental health deputies handle substance abuse calls as well as their other social service responsibilities was also passed. Thus, proper dispositions will have to be made regarding substance abusers as well. This legislation will have a significant impact on the number of incidents handled by such mental health units (Martinez, Interview, August 23, 1989).

Finally, legislation was passed allowing for a pilot project with mentally ill offenders to be conducted in Harris County.

These legislative activities concerning the mentally ill offender are not all-inclusive; rather they are felt to represent the major legislation which impacts on the mentally ill offender. Missing from this list is any legislation concerning the transfer of the special-needs offender, on which TDC's study was based. The legislature expressed reservations at releasing violent special-needs offenders (Kifowit, Interview, July 24, 1989).

Nevertheless, many involved in the care and treatment of mentally ill offenders felt that the 71st Legislature was a success. Such major initiatives indicate a progressive move on the part of the legislature to better serve the mentally ill offender.

CONCLUSIONS

Regarding the care and treatment of the mentally impaired offender in the state of Texas, there is, in many ways, a sense of optimism. However, such optimism is tempered by three major concerns:

1. The youthfulness and as yet unproven status of many of the programs throughout the state

2. The lack of a centralized source of information regarding model programming

3. The required ongoing commitment on the part of the legislature, the service agencies involved, and the key stakeholders in better serving the mentally ill offender.

The broad picture of programs and initiatives painted in this report suggest a growing number of efforts directed toward better serving this population. Indeed, the research literature as well suggests that there has certainly been an increased focus on ascertaining an accurate count of and determining effective programming for this population. The increased focus by the state parallels this increased focus nationally.

The mere numbers and types of programs targeted induce this sense of optimism. However, caution is in order. This report has repeatedly alluded to the fact that many of these programs are in an initial phase while many others are still in the planning phase. In many respects, such programs remain unproven.

Another issue which becomes readily apparent in studying such programs is the fragmentation and sporadic nature of the programming. Throughout the state, there is as yet no one single repository of knowledge containing information on those offenders with mental illness. This has the potential for becoming even more problematic as the decision-making process for service planning moves more toward the local level. Many of the agencies studied advocated for the creation and funding of local human service collaboration, a movement desperately needed in order to provide better service coordination for populations in need. Yet, as decision-making becomes increasingly decentralized and more power moves to the local level, a formalized mechanism for information to also move and be utilized at the local level must be in place. While the Interagency Council on Mentally Retarded, Developmentally Disabled, and Mentally Ill Offenders is likely to assume the responsibility for a key role in that mechanism, it does not, as yet, possess that ability to collect and disseminate such information other than through informal networks developed by the various individuals on the council.

For example, currently for one to ascertain whether each county jail is providing any mental health services, one must survey each of the 254 county jails in Texas. The Texas Commission on Jail Standards nor any other agency collects such information. At the local law enforcement level, this becomes even more problematic. While there should certainly be a great deal of flexibility from locale to locale, there is also a need for some formal body to collect, store, and disseminate information regarding various model programs throughout the state. As stated previously, the Interagency Council may fulfill such a role as member agencies gather such information.

A final concern is the continued interest in better serving this population. As recently as five years ago this population was largely ignored. Many were incarcerated in the county jails and state prisons with no mental health services available. Others were relegated to a marginal existence on the streets and under bridges. This recent interest on the part of the state is commendable and it is imperative that such commitment continue. With the consolidation of the three major criminal justice agencies in the state, many newly found possibilities exist for improving the quality and the quantity of services for this population. As previously pointed out, the possibilities for better communication, coordination, and planning among these three entities are greatly facilitated. At the same time, however, possibilities also exist for increased neglect of this population. With such a mega-agency, firmer bureaucratic barriers may be erected. Some experts believe that decreased funding may be a major problem. They also point out that the possibility for implementing some of these special services will be reduced or diluted in such a huge and complicated budget structure. It is imperative that a continued commitment on the part of the Texas legislature, the service agencies involved, and the key stakeholders throughout the state be realized.

In sum, the state of Texas must humanize mental health services to the severely emotionally disturbed offender. Unnecessary arrests and unnecessary jailings must be lessened. A full complement of services to the mentally ill population must be in place. Such services can and should be provided in an environment which preserves the dignity of the person while protecting his or her, in conjunction with the public's, rights and freedoms under the law. Such an environment is necessary in Texas.

References

Bailey, Doyne. 1987. "Travis County Jail Mental Health Procedures." Austin, Texas. (Draft.)

Blasi, Jana, Lynn Parish, Jan Rienstra, and Charles Blissett. 1990. "Dallas County MHMR Center." In <u>Community Mental Health in Texas: Four Case Studies</u>. Special Project Report. Austin: Lyndon B. Johnson School of Public Affairs, The University of Texas at Austin.

Boardman, Diane. 1989. Fiscal Services, Dallas County Mental Health and Mental Retardation Center, Dallas, Texas. Telephone interview by J. Rienstra, June 22. Cited in Jana Blasi, et al. 1990. "Dallas County MHMR Center." In <u>Community Mental Health in Texas: Four Case Studies</u>. Special Project Report. Austin: Lyndon B. Johnson School of Public Affairs, The University of Texas at Austin.

Burke, William. 1988. Director of Personnel, Texas Board of Pardons and Paroles, Austin, Texas. Interview by H. Crean, November 15.

Churgin, Michael J. 1988. <u>An Analysis of the Mental Health Code</u>. Austin, Texas.: Hogg Foundation for Mental Health.

City of Austin. 1989. "City Budget--Police Department--Victim Services." Austin, Texas. (Computer printout.)

Cotton, Larry. 1989. Associate Executive Director, Program Services. DCMHMR. Interview by J. Rienstra. Cited in Jana Blasi, et al. 1990. "Dallas County MHMR Center." In <u>Community Mental Health in Texas: Four Case Studies</u>. Special Project Report. Austin: Lyndon B. Johnson School of Public Affairs, The University of Texas at Austin.

Criminal Justice Policy Council. 1988. <u>Texas Correctional Costs: 1987-1988</u>. Austin, Texas. (Draft.)

Crump, J. 1989. Executive Director, Texas Commission on Jail Standards, Austin, Texas. Telephone interview by H. Crean, August 15.

Dallas County Mental Health and Mental Retardation Center (DCMHMR). 1989a. "Diagnostic, Assessment, and Treatment Services (Forensics)." Dallas, Texas. (Draft.) Cited in Jana Blasi, et al. 1990. "Dallas County MHMR Center." In <u>Community Mental Health in Texas: Four Case Studies</u>. Special Project Report. Austin: Lyndon B. Johnson School of Public Affairs, The University of Texas at Austin.

_____. 1989b. "FY 1988 Cost per Unit of Service, Core and Non-Core Services, Adult Mental Health." Dallas, Texas. (Draft.) Cited in Jana Blasi, et al. 1990. "Dallas County MHMR Center." In <u>Community Mental Health in Texas: Four Case Studies</u>. Special Project Report. Austin: Lyndon B. Johnson School of Public Affairs, The University of Texas at Austin.

Eisenberg, Michael. 1988. Planner, Texas Board of Pardons and Paroles, Austin, Texas. Letter to T. Tompkins, November 16.

Ferrara, Mathew. 1989. Chief Psychologist, Texas Department of Corrections, Huntsville, Texas. Letter, August 28.

Fox, Richard G., Patricia G. Erickson, and Lorne M. Salutin. 1972. <u>Apparently
Suffering from Mental Disorder</u>. Toronto, Canada: University of Toronto, Centre
of Criminology.

Gill, John. 1989. "Mobile Crisis Intervention Team: Executive Summary." Dallas, Texas.
(Draft.) Cited in Jana Blasi, et al. 1990. "Dallas County MHMR Center." In
<u>Community Mental Health in Texas: Four Case Studies</u>. Special Project Report.
Austin: Lyndon B. Johnson School of Public Affairs, The University of Texas at
Austin.

Gilliland, Steve. 1989. Associate Clinical Psychologist, Texas Department of Corrections,
Huntsville, Texas. Interview by H. Crean, October 20.

Hale, K. 1989. Associate Director, Mental Health Association, Austin, Texas. Interview
by H. Crean, August 18.

Halleck, S. 1986. <u>The Mentally Disordered Offender</u>. Pub no. (ADM) 86-1471.
Rockville, Md.: National Institute of Mental Health.

Interagency Council on Mentally Retarded, Developmentally Disabled, and Mentally Ill
Offenders. 1989a. <u>Annual Report from the Interagency Council on Mentally
Retarded, Developmentally Disabled, and Mentally Ill Offenders</u>. Austin, Texas.

_____. 1989b. <u>Pilot Project Overview</u>. Austin, Texas.

Janus, Samuel S., Barbara E. Bess, James Cadden, and Harold Greenwald. 1979. "The
Police Officer as Street Psychiatrist." <u>Police Studies: The International Review of
Police Development</u>, vol. 2 (Fall).

Jemelka, Ron, Eric Trupin, and John A. Chiles. 1989. "The Mentally Ill in Prisons: A
Review." <u>Hospital and Community Psychiatry</u>, vol. 40 (May).

Joseph, Baker T. n.d. "Galveston County Mental Health Deputy Program." Galveston,
Texas. (Draft.)

Kifowit, Dee. 1989. Executive Director, Texas Council on Offenders with Mental
Impairments, Austin, Texas. Interview by H. Crean, July 24.

Larson, David L., G. Michael Winburn, and David Henry. n.d. "Mental Health Deputies
Field Evaluation of High-Risk Individuals." Galveston, Texas. (Draft.)

League of Women Voters of Texas Education Fund. 1988. <u>Services for the Seriously
Mentally Ill in Texas -- Facts and Issues</u>. Austin, Texas.

Levinson, R. 1984. "The System that Cannot Say No." <u>American Psychologist</u>, vol, 39
(July).

Martinez, P. 1988. "Memorandum for the Record -- April 14, 1988." Austin, Texas:
Travis County Mental Health Deputies Unit. (Draft.)

_____. 1989. Lieutenant, Mental Health Unit, Travis County Sheriff's
Department, Austin, Texas. Interview by H. Crean, August 23.

McCarthy, Brian, and Lynette Feder. 1985. "Mentally Ill and Mentally Retarded Offenders in Corrections." In U.S. Department of Justice, 1985. Sourcebook on the Mentally Disordered Prisoner. Washington, D.C.: National Institute of Corrections.

Monahan, J., and H. J. Steadman. 1984. Crime and Mental Disorder. Research in Brief Series. Washington, D.C.: U.S. Department of Justice, National Institute of Justice.

Murphy, Gerard R. 1986. Improving the Police Response to the Mentally Disabled. Washington, D.C.: Police Executive Research Forum.

Norris, Marion. 1989. Public Information Officer, Vernon State Hospital, Vernon, Texas. Telephone interview by H. Crean, November 5.

Patrick, Mary E. McDonald. 1978. "Policemen's Attitudes Toward Mental Illness and the Mentally Ill." Issues in Mental Health Nursing, vol. 1 (Fall).

Pope, Demetria. 1989. Director of Programs, Community Justice Assistance Division, Texas Adult Probation Commission, Austin, Texas. Interview by H. Crean, August 16.

Puryear, Douglas. 1989. Director of Psychiatric Emergency Services, Parkland Memorial Hospital, Dallas, Texas. Letter to J. Rienstra. Cited in Jana Blasi, et al. 1990. "Dallas County MHMR Center." In Community Mental Health in Texas: Four Case Studies. Special Project Report. Austin: Lyndon B. Johnson School of Public Affairs, The University of Texas at Austin.

Reyna, Deborah. 1989. Assistant Coordinator, Victims Services Division, Austin Police Department, Austin, Texas. Interview by H. Crean, August 9.

Rodriguez, G. 1988. Mental Health Probation Officer, Travis County, Austin, Texas. Telephone interview by H. Crean, November 11.

Roth, L. H. 1980. "Correctional Psychiatry." In Modern Legal Medicine, Psychiatry, and Forensic Science, ed. W. S. Curran, A. L. McGarry, and C. S. Perry. Philadelphia, Penn.: Davis.

Ruiz v. Estelle. 1980. 503 F. Supp. 1265, 1323.

Sheridan, Edward P., and Linda A. Teplin. 1981. "Police-Referred Psychiatric Emergencies: Advantages of Community Treatment." Journal of Community Psychology, vol. 9, no. 2 (April).

Simmons, W. 1988. Director of Treatment Programs, Travis County Jail, Austin, Texas. Telephone interview by H. Crean, December 5.

State of Texas. 1987. Text of Conference Committee Report -- Senate Bill No. 1 and Governor's Veto Proclamation. Supplement to Senate Journal, 70th Legislature, 2nd Called Session.

_____. 1988. Texas Criminal Procedure: Code and Rules with Tables and Index: Code as Amended through the 1987 Regular and 1st and 2nd Called Sessions of the 70th Legislature: Rules as Received through October 1, 1987. St. Paul, Minn.: West Publishing Co.

Steadman, H. J., J. Monahan, and B. Duffee. 1984. "The Impact of State Mental Hospital Deinstitutionalization on the United States Prison Populations, 1968-1978." Journal of Criminal Law and Criminology, vol. 75 (Summer).

Steadman, H. J., J. Monahan, and E. Hartstone. 1982. "Mentally Disordered Offenders: A National Survey of Patients and Facilities." Law and Human Behavior, vol. 6, no. 1 (January).

Teplin, Linda A. 1984. Keeping the Peace: The Commonalities and Individualities of Police Discretion. Chicago: Northwestern University Medical School, Northwestern Memorial Hospital.

Texas Board of Pardons and Paroles (BPP). 1987. 1987 Annual Statistical Report. Austin, Texas.

_____. 1988. 1988 Annual Statistical Report. Austin, Texas.

Texas Commission on Jail Standards. 1989. Capacity Report -- 06/20/89. Austin, Texas.

Texas Department of Corrections (TDC). 1988. Psychiatric Services -- Inpatient Report, Ellis II. Huntsville, Texas. (Computer printout.)

_____. 1989a. Psychiatric Services -- Inpatient Report, June 1989. Huntsville, Texas. (Computer printout.)

_____. 1989b. 1988 Fiscal Year Statistical Report. Huntsville, Texas.

_____ and The Criminal Justice Center. 1989. Transferring Special Needs Offenders to Community-Based Programs. Huntsville, Texas. Sam Houston State University.

Texas Department of Mental Health and Mental Retardation (TDMHMR). 1988. Executive Fact Book -- Third Quarter 1988. Austin, Texas.

_____. 1989. Texas Department of Mental Health and Mental Retardation Per Patient Per Day Cost (In-Patient Treatment) For Twelve Months Ending August 31, 1988 by Patient Classification. Austin, Texas.

_____. 1990a. Vernon State Hospital Maximum Security Costs -- Fiscal Year 1988. Austin, Texas.

_____. 1990b. Texas Department of Mental Health and Mental Retardation Per Patient Per Day Cost (In-Patient Treatment) For Twelve Months Ending August 31, 1989 by Patient Classification. Austin, Texas.

Travis County Mental Health Deputies Unit. 1989. Mental Health Unit Statistics. Austin, Texas. (Monthly computer printouts.)

U.S. Department of Justice, National Institute of Corrections. 1985. Sourcebook on the Mentally Disordered Prisoner. Washington, D.C.

Vaughn, Charles. 1990. Budget and Research Analyst, Budget and Research Department of Travis County, Austin, Texas. Telephone interview by H. Crean, July 19.

Whitmer, Gary E. 1980. "From Hospitals to Jails: The Fate of California's Deinstitution-alized Mentally Ill." American Journal of Orthopsychiatry, vol. 50, no. 1 (January).

Section Two. Services

The major state policy directions for the range and types of public mental health services to be provided are found in House Bill 3 and, to a lesser extent, in the Mental Health Code. There are specific, defined requirements for the types of community-based services to be provided. The most explicit language in HB 3 about the types of services to be provided is directed to community-based services and, most directly, to the CMHMRCs. CMHMRCs are to provide prehospital admission screening, hospital discharge planning, and "continuing mental health and physical care services" for persons from their service area entering and leaving state hospitals (TDMHMR, 1988a, pp. 28-29). These services are required by HB 3, the Mental Health Code, and the terms of the 1986 R. A. J. v. Jones settlement order.

The terms of the 1986 order for aftercare services, recently made a part of the CMHMRC contracts, require local mental health authorities (LMHA) to "make a good faith effort to make available and accessible those services specified in the community aftercare plans"; to set a follow-up appointment for each person; to document outreach efforts to these persons; to "make a good faith effort to make case management services available" to qualified persons; and to "make a good faith effort to arrange for such non-clinical support as food, clothing, and shelter" as is necessary for these persons (TDMHMR, 1990, pp. V-6,7).

In 1985, Senate Bill 633 amended HB 3 to require the provision of five services in each local services areas (LSA) and in 1987, SB 257 added two more services to be provided. These are (1) 24-hour emergency screening and rapid crisis stabilization services; (2) psychosocial rehabilitation programs, including social support activities, independent living skills, and vocational training; (3) case management services; (4) family support services, including respite care; (5) medication-related services, including medication clinics, laboratory monitoring, medication education, mental health maintenance education, and the provision of medication; (6) community-based assessments, including the development of interdisciplinary treatment plans and diagnosis and evaluation services; and (7) community-based crisis residential service or hospitalization (TDMHMR, 1988a, p. 30). These seven services are commonly referred to as core services, although the law itself does not include the term (TDMHMR, 1988a, p. 30). CMHMRCs are also to develop standards for, inspect, and certify or register privately operated boarding homes in their area to which the CMHMRCs refer their clients (TDMHMR, 1988a, pp. 38-39). By law, these service requirements also apply to the local LMHAs operated by TDMHMR facilities.

TDMHMR promulgated its administrative definitions for community-based mental health services and its standards for these services in 1986. In the FY 1988 version of the service definitions, 42 different types of community services are listed and defined; 18 of these are required core services. The service definitions are detailed and their accompanying community standards are highly prescriptive (TDMHMR, 1988b). SB 633 also required TDMHMR to apply the community standards to ensure the provision of quality services to the defined priority population. The policy and administrative practice of requiring a large number of specific services to be provided by the CMHMRCs is reminiscent of the earlier federal policy and practice, particularly as expressed in PL 94-63 and its attendant regulations, which required 12 essential services to be provided by federally funded CMHMRCs.

This section examines the core and noncore services required by the legislation listed above. It is hoped that these chapters will give the reader a more thorough understanding of the services provided by TDMHMR and the CMHMRCs. While the primary authors are listed at the beginning of the chapters, it should be noted that Janice Rienstra edited this section and significantly rewrote several of the chapters.

References

Texas Department of Mental Health and Mental Retardation (TDMHMR). 1988a. <u>Texas Laws Relating to Mental Health and Mental Retardation</u>. Sixth Ed. Austin, Texas.

_____. 1988b. <u>TDMHMR Mental Health Community Standards</u>. Austin, Texas.

_____. 1990. "FY 1990 Contract Instructions." Austin, Texas.

Chapter 5. Crisis Response Services[*]

Crisis services have long been recognized as an essential component of comprehensive community mental health services. The first federal community mental health center grants required emergency screening and referral as one of the five essential services to be provided. In 1977, the National Institute of Mental Health (NIMH) listed crisis assistance services as one of ten essential services within its Community Support Program. The purpose of crisis assistance services is to provide 24-hour, quick response crisis assistance to help both the person with serious mental illness and involved family and friends to cope with psychiatric emergencies, while maintaining the person's status as a functioning community member to the greatest possible extent (Stroul, August 1987, p. 6). These services should include round-the-clock telephone services, on-call trained personnel, and options for either short-term or partial hospitalization or temporary community housing arrangements for crisis stabilization (Stroul, August 1987, p. 6). NIMH further defined crisis response services as having four interrelated service elements. These elements are crisis telephone services, walk-in crisis services, mobile crisis outreach services, and crisis residential services (Stroul, August 1987, pp. 27-28).

In 1985, the Legislative Oversight Committee (LOC) on Mental Health and Mental Retardation identified emergency screening and other crisis services as essential for all mental health priority populations in Texas (LOC, February 1985, p. 35). The LOC's report listed its conclusions about the existing screening and other emergency services from the results of the survey. First, those services that were available often operated only Monday through Friday; second, state hospitals were often used inappropriately as a substitute for community-based screening; third, contracts with private providers for screening and emergency services should be an option; and fourth, rural areas usually had too few services to support emergency screening (LOC, February 1985, p. 35). The consensus of the committee was that "the first dollar spent for mental health services must be allocated to the development and implementation of screening and emergency services" (LOC, February 1985, p. 35).

The LOC report listed three major recommendations for emergency screening and other crisis services. The first was that TDMHMR must assure that people in each service area have access to (1) 24-hour emergency screening and rapid stabilization services; (2) crisis hospitalization; and (3) community-based assessment, including development of a multidisciplinary treatment plan. The second recommendation was that TDMHMR's funding to a service area must be contingent upon either the certification of the availability of screening/emergency services in the area or the specific allocation of funds for such services in mental health services budgets. The third major recommendation was that appropriate alternatives to jails, often used as holding facilities, must be developed (LOC, February 1985, pp. 37-38).

A slightly revised version of these recommendations was incorporated in Senate Bill 633, passed in 1985:

> Sec. 4.03. (a) The Department shall insure that at a minimum the following services are available in each service area: (1) 24-hour emergency screening and rapid crisis stabilization services; (2) community-based crisis residential service or hospitalization; (3) community-based assessments, including the development of interdisciplinary treatment plans and diagnosis and evaluation services; . . . (Vernon's, 1988)

---

[*]This chapter was written by Jana Blasi, Carolina Martinez, and Lynn Parish.

These and the other services required by SB 633 were called core services, and were to be made available to persons in each local service area. In its official mental health services definitions for FY 1988, TDMHMR placed 24-hour emergency screening and assessment and multidisciplinary assessment under the Client and Family Support budget category; crisis stabilization services were placed under the Residential Services budget category.

24-HOUR EMERGENCY SCREENING AND ASSESSMENT

TDMHMR includes three services in its definition of 24-hour emergency screening and assessment: crisis hot line, crisis intervention team, and multidisciplinary assessment.

Crisis Hot Line

As defined by TDMHMR, a crisis hot line is the mechanism through which the client population gains access to the services of the crisis intervention team. It must be easily accessible to the public throughout each mental health service area and must operate whenever the center is not operational. It is often operated by volunteers with professional staff support and supervision. Hot lines must have the back up of the crisis intervention team which is on call 24 hours a day for consultation and for immediate face-to-face preliminary assessment of all clients who are (1) apparently experiencing a mental health crisis which could potentially endanger the safety of either the client or another person, or (2) may be experiencing hallucinations, delusions, disorientation, generalized confusion, or bizarre behaviors.

In rural areas or service areas with a low population, this program component may be a substitute for a rurally-based crisis intervention team, with the clear understanding that professional staff must be on call for immediate face-to-face assessment of clients who are demonstrating a safety risk through a centrally located crisis intervention team which is operational 24 hours per day and to which such rural clients demonstrating a risk may be immediately referred (TDMHMR, 1987, p. 10).

Not all calls to a crisis hot line are crisis calls; local mental health authorities are required to have written procedures for distinguishing crisis from non-crisis calls. Persons in a psychiatric crisis are to be assessed immediately by the crisis intervention team. Persons who are not in crisis but in need of and eligible for mental health services are to be assessed within one month of initial contact (TDMHMR, 1989, pp. 13-3, 13-4).

Additional data about the actual availability of crisis hot lines, hours of service provided, or numbers of persons served are not centrally collected. Services reported by local mental health authorities to the CARE system are lumped under three major categories: residential, client and family support, and case management. Therefore, crisis hot line services are not specifically identifiable. A 1986 core services survey found a "substantial increase in effort" in the availability of crisis hot lines in local service areas in that 64 percent of local service areas responding to the survey had crisis hot lines (MHAT, 1986, p. 4). The FY 1988 TDMHMR contract data indicate that all but two community centers provided a crisis hot line and all but two state facilities (as the designated local mental health authority) offered a hot line. In FY 1988, a grand total of $1,274,973, or 0.8 percent of all mental health expenditures, was budgeted for crisis hot lines; this represents an annual per capita expenditure of seven cents. A little more than half of the total, or $640,727, was funded by non-TDMHMR funds from other state, local, and federal sources. Of the total TDMHMR FY 1988 mental health contracts-for-services funds (which include state general revenue, MH block grant, and required local match funds), $546,461 or 0.5 percent was allocated for crisis hot line services.

Crisis Intervention Team

TDMHMR defines a crisis intervention team as

[the] 24-hour face-to-face crisis intervention component which preliminarily assesses all clients who are apparently experiencing a mental health crisis with the potential for 1) life-threatening behavior, or 2) acute psychiatric crisis involving bizarre behavior, hallucinations, generalized confusion, or disorientation . . . Any client who is confirmed by the crisis intervention team to be evidencing such life-threatening and/or acutely dysfunctional behavior must then be assessed by a physician, preferably a psychiatrist. (and others in an multidisciplinary assessment, discussed below) . . . The team consists of two or more persons, one of whom must be a mental health professional, who have on-call medical back-up, who can perform emergency screening on a face-to-face basis and who can make a preliminary plan for care. There is an assigned team on duty on duty 24 hours per day, 7 days per week. The crisis team works in conjunction with the local courts, emergency rooms, jails, and ideally has as a team member a registered nurse trained in assessment of psychiatric crisis. (TDMHMR, 1987, pp. 10-11)

TDMHMR requires that each mental health authority have at least one crisis intervention team, located in the densest population area. The team may be mobile throughout the area, but is not required to be. Mental health authorities may provide this service through a contract or agreement with a local facility such as a hospital emergency room, "provided that the contracted facility has 24-hour on-duty professional physician/psychiatric mental health staff with on-call or on-duty medical back-up" (TDMHMR, 1987, pp. 10-11). The 1986 MHAT survey of core services found that 81 percent of service areas surveyed offered some type of 24-hour emergency screening services (MHAT, 1986, p. 3). TDMHMR's quantitative goal for crisis intervention team services is one 24-hour crisis intervention team for each 150,000 population (TDMHMR, 1987, p. 11). The mental health service budget data indicate that in FY 1988, there were 62 crisis intervention teams across the state, or roughly one team for each 282,000 population. Few of these teams are mobile, as envisioned by the NIMH definitions.

In FY 1988, a grand total of $2,876,954 was budgeted for community-based crisis intervention services. This amount was 1.8 percent of all mental health services funds, or an average statewide expenditure of 16.7 cents per person per year. State general revenue, MH block grant, and required local match funds funded $1,681,964, or 58.5 percent, of the total crisis intervention costs. Other, non-TDMHMR funds supported the remaining $1,194,990, or 41.5 percent of the costs.

Multidisciplinary Assessment

TDMHMR requires that multidisciplinary assessments be provided to all persons experiencing life-threatening behavior or acutely dysfunctional behavior; further, the assessment must be performed within 24 hours of referral by the crisis intervention team. Multidisciplinary assessment differs from emergency screening in that it examines all dimensions of a person with serious mental illness. Emergency screening, as performed by crisis intervention teams, is by definition a rather quick, face-to-face, preliminary assessment (Milton, 1989).

The multidisciplinary assessment is to include an interview with the person, "standardized tests, physical examination, laboratory procedures, etc.," and clarification of the findings and recommendations to the person. "Multidisciplinary" is defined as "a physician (preferably a psychiatric) assessment and one or more of psychological, nursing, or social service assessments" (TDMHMR, 1987, p. 11). The results of the assessment usually provide the basis for additional treatment options for the person in acute crisis. Often the person is already in a community crisis stabilization unit or in a state hospital when the assessment is done. If not, a referral to crisis stabilization or the hospital may be made. Sometimes other less restrictive options may be more suitable.

Although TDMHMR places multidisciplinary assessment under the category of emergency services for both definitional and budget purposes, its community standards require that assessments be performed for all clients, not just those in crisis (TDMHMR, 1989, pp. 11-1, 11-2). The assessments required for all clients are not identified in the community standards as "multidisciplinary" assessments, but are to include information along a number of problem dimensions which are very similar to the official definition of a multidisciplinary assessment; these other assessments are to be completed within 30 days of a person's admission to a facility or to the roster of the CMHMRC's patients.

Both crisis and noncrisis assessments form the basis for the person's treatment plan. The treatment plan delineates problem-related goals to attain, maintain, and/or establish and it specifies intervention strategies for achieving the client's stated objectives. The staff responsible for each strategy are identified as well as the frequency of staff intervention (TDMHMR, 1989, pp. 11-9 to 11-12).

All but three community centers provide multidisciplinary assessment, according to FY 1988 contract data. Only Texoma, Texas Panhandle, and Tropical Texas community centers did not provide multidisciplinary assessment (TDMHMR, 1988a). Many outreach centers rely on the state hospital in their service area to provide this service (Diamond, Griffin, and Hoover, 1990, p. 181).

In FY 1988, a total of $6,156,066 was budgeted for multidisciplinary assessment, which includes noncrisis assessments. TDMHMR contracts-for-services funds totaled $3,665,308; R. A. J. v. Jones funds, $473,083; and other funds, $2,0117,675. Of the total FY 1988 mental health services budget, 3.8 percent was allocated to assessments; statewide, this represents an expenditure of 36 cents per capita per year. There is no separate budget line item for noncrisis assessments. Consequently, funds for all assessment services are typically budgeted under the emergency services' Multidisciplinary Assessment line item. Therefore, the funds spent for multidisciplinary assessments for those persons in crisis are not readily identifiable.

STRUCTURED CRISIS RESIDENTIAL SERVICES

Persons with serious mental illness who are in an acute psychiatric crisis may be referred to a local crisis residential unit for stabilization by the crisis intervention team, the multidisciplinary assessment team, or others. As defined by TDMHMR, structured crisis residential programs provide 24-hour, short-term intensive care to persons experiencing psychiatric crises of moderate to severe proportions (TDMHMR, 1987, p. 2). This service may be provided by mental health authorities in two ways: either they may directly operate a crisis stabilization unit (CSU), or they may contract with a licensed general or private psychiatric hospital to provide this service for them, identified in the budget as "contracted inpatient beds." In FY 1988, about one-third of the community centers operated their own CSU; some of these also contracted for a few crisis residential beds. The rest of the centers contracted for all their CSU beds. Half of the state facilities contracted for crisis beds; the remainder had no crisis residential beds separate from the facility itself (TDMHMR, 1988a).

Table 5.1. Characteristics of Residential Programs Based on Services Definitions FY 1988
Structured Residential Programs

Program	General Staffing Requirements	Medical Support	Nursing Support	Capacity	Length of Stay	Licensing Requirements	Special Characteristics
Contracted Inpt. Beds (MH Crisis Intensive)	Adequate staffing and staff-to-client ratio to ensure safety and provision of programming (16.6 and 16.7)	JCAH and/ or Medicare Standards of Care (16.2)	JCAH and/ or Medicare Standards of Care (16.2)	Varies by hospital	Typically 3-7 days	Licensed as a private psych. hospital by TDMHMR or as a general hospital by TDH.	Children and adolescents requiring crisis stabilization must be served in licensed private psych. hospital.
Crisis Stabil-ization Unit (MH Crisis Intensive)	Adequate staffing and staff-to-client ratio to ensure safety and provision of programming (16.6 and 16.7) Ancillary staff as required (16.22)	MD chief of unit (16.16) MD on-call 24 hours per day (16.18) Daily MD rounds (16.19)	RN unit supervisor (16.20) RN on-call 24 hours per day (16.23) RN or LVN on-duty 24 per day (16.22)	Typically 10-40	Typically 5-14 days	Licensed by TDMHMR as a crisis sta-bilization unit.	Clients may or may not be court-committed. Serves adults only.

139

Source: Pharis, February 1988, Appendix E, p. E-1.

Note: Numbers in parenthesis refer to TDMHMR Mental Health Community Standards.

Table 5.1 compares some characteristics of contracted inpatient beds and CSUs.These programs are structured upon the medical model, are "hospital-like," and are often housed in former hospitals. Persons may or may not be court-committed to these units. Although some CSUs do not admit court-committed clients, crisis stabilization units are more likely to admit these clients than are the contracted inpatient beds service, especially those operated by general hospitals. CSUs that do accept court-committed clients are, by necessity, very restrictive with locked doors, barred windows, and security guards. Some centers, such as Dallas County MHMR, have separate units for their court-committed and voluntary clients, thus allowing those who do not need the extra security to be in a less restrictive environment.

As Table 5.1 shows, a client typically stays 3 to 7 days in contracted bed programs and 5 to 14 days in CSUs. Clients receive physical examinations, laboratory tests, psychiatric evaluations, medication stabilization, 24-hour nursing care, and some amount of casework services. In CSUs and in some contracted bed programs, clients may also be involved in therapeutic groups and classes for a good part of each day. An example of classes that are typically offered are those found at the Acute Inpatient Treatment Center (AITC) at the Dallas County MHMR. These classes typically include classes in stress management, problem solving, relaxation techniques, anger management, and assertiveness (Blasi, Parish, Rienstra, and Blissett, 1990, p. 39). In instances in which only one or two beds are contracted for (especially in general hospitals), clients are less apt to be offered groups or classes and greater reliance is placed on individual therapy. Some units also offer family member programs and most offer discharge planning.

Table 5.2 shows the availability of crisis beds and contracted beds by mental health authority. Six centers have both crisis stabilization units and contracted beds, six have crisis stabilization units only, and twenty-two have contracted inpatient beds only. Six centers have only one crisis bed available (all are contracted beds), and four have only two available (all contracted). This demonstrates the wide range in the availability of this service.

The contract data in Table 5.2 contain some major discrepancies which should be noted. For example, Harris County lists a total of 294 beds under crisis and contracted beds; this number represents the total number of beds made available through the new Harris County Psychiatric Center (a state-operated facility) and the Harris County Hospital District. According to a recent report of the Harris County Mental Health Needs Council, only 8 of these beds are classified as crisis or emergency beds, with an average length of stay of 5 days (Mental Health Needs Council, 1989, p. 15). The remaining beds are nonemergency, longer-term beds, in that the average length of stay is 20 to 40 days. Data for the other large urban centers serve to underscore the variability. Dallas County MHMR has 80 short-term crisis beds, while Bexar County MHMR has 16.

The FY 1988 contract data indicate that a grand total of $25,236,255 was budgeted for structured crisis residential services: $15,659,890 for CSUs and $9,576,365 for contracted inpatient beds. However, because of various budgeting artifacts, this is less than the true cost. State funds for the Harris County Psychiatric Center and the Tarrant County psychiatric hospital are not included in these budgeted amounts. Also not included are various off-budget contributions of local city and county governments to crisis services. In El Paso, all the crisis residential and other inpatient services are provided by Thomasen Hospital; the costs are not reflected in that center's (Life Management) contract. Subtracting the estimated noncrisis beds in Harris and Tarrant counties yields a rough estimation that there were a total of about 500 community-based crisis residential beds throughout the state in FY 1988. This yields a statewide average of 2.9 crisis beds per 100,000 population, although the distribution of these beds is far from even.

Table 5.2. Structured Crisis Residential and Respite Beds, FY 1988

Facility Name	Type	Region	Date	Crisis Beds	Contracted Beds	Brief Respite
State Hospitals						
San Antonio	OUTREACH	3			11	
Terrell	OUTREACH	6	29-Oct-87		1	
Big Spring	OUTREACH	1	30-Oct-87		1	
Austin	OUTREACH	4	30-Oct-87			
Kerrville	OUTREACH	2	12-Oct-87		2	
Rusk	OUTREACH	5	28-Oct-87			
Wichita Falls	OUTREACH	7	30-Oct-87			
State Centers						
Rio Grande	OUTREACH	3	30-Oct-87			2
Laredo	OUTREACH	3	30-Oct-87			
El Paso	OUTREACH	1	30-Oct-87			
CMHMRCs						
Abilene Regional	CMHMRC	1	1-Oct-87		2	
Austin/Travis Co.	CMHMRC	4	16-Nov-87	16		
Bexar County	CMHMRC	3	7-Oct-87	20		
Brazos Valley	CMHMRC	4	9-Oct-87		4	
Central Counties	CMHMRC	4	30-Sep-87	10	4	
Central Plains	CMHMRC	1	6-Nov-87	11		
Central Texas	CMHMRC	4	9-Oct-87		10	
Concho Valley	CMHMRC	1	21-Oct-87		1	
Dallas County	CMHMRC	6	23-Oct-87	80		
Deep East TX	CMHMRC	5	22-Sep-87	20		2
Denton County	CMHMRC	7	19-Nov-87		2	
Gulf Bend	CMHMRC	3	11-Nov-87		12	
Gulf Coast	CMHMRC	4			28	
Harris County	CMHMRC	5	31-Oct-87	40	254	
Heart of Texas	CMHMRC	4	30-Sep-87		2	
Johnson City	CMHMRC	4	1-Oct-87		2	
Life Management	CMHMRC	1	5-Oct-87		34	
Lubbock Regional		1	5-Nov-87		1	
Navarro County	CMHMRC	6	2-Nov-87		1	
Northeast TX	CMHMRC	6	1-Oct-87		3	
Nueces County	CMHMRC	3	9-Oct-87		27	
Pecan Valley	CMHMRC	7	17-Oct-87		1	1
Hunt County	CMHMRC	6	20-Aug-87		2	
Permian Basin	CMHMRC	1	18-Sep-87		8	
Sabine County	CMHMRC	5	15-Oct-87		20	5
Southeast TX	CMHMRC	5	30-Sep-87	64	3	
Tarrant County	CMHMRC	7		56	18	
Texoma	CMHMRC	7	20-Nov-87		3	
Texas Panhandle	CMHMRC	7		24	1	
Tri County	CMHMRC	5	19-Nov-87	18	5	
Tropical Texas	CMHMRC	3	13-Oct-87	9		
Wichita Falls	CMHMRC	7	11-Nov-87		1	
Collin County	CMHMRC	7	20-Oct-87		3	
East Texas	CMHMRC	6	13-Nov-87		4	
State Totals				368	471	10

Source: TDMHMR, 1988a.

TDMHMR defines two additional types of structured crisis stabilization programs which mental health authorities may choose to provide. These are Supervised Family Living/Crisis Stabilization Foster Care and Detoxification centers. The former program is designed for persons experiencing moderate crises. It is structured and provides close supervision by foster care families in a home or homelike setting rather than in a hospital or hospital-like setting. There must be the capacity for at least one member of the foster care family to remain awake at all times. Additionally, there must be 24-hour on-call medical backup. If the program serves children or adolescents, it must be licensed by the Texas Department of Human Services (TDMHMR, 1988b).

According to the contract data, no center provided an identifiable family living/foster care stabilization program, although some centers may be informally providing it in their respite residential programs (Hale, Interview, March 31, 1989).

OTHER APPROACHES TO CRISIS RESIDENTIAL SERVICES

In other states, crisis residential services are provided in a variety of settings and through a variety of approaches. These settings and approaches may be conceptualized as a continuum of approaches which range from the more structured programs with more institutionalized features to the more flexible, normative programs that take place in homelike settings. The two ends of this continuum represent very different approaches to community-based crisis residential services. The institutional approach, based on the structured, medical model, attempts to "define what services are provided by institutions and to provide them in community settings" (Stroul, August 1987). The other end of the continuum is to provide this service in a more homelike setting and to develop an intentional "alternative" community (Stroul, August 1987).

The approaches described below offer true changes from the care offered in institutionalized settings and are generally referred to as alternative crisis residential services. There are actually two different alternative approaches, but they are tied together by a common principle that clients should be treated in the least restrictive setting possible.

Individual Approach

The first group of approaches is collectively called the individual approach. Crisis residential services are provided in the homes of specially selected and trained community families. These settings generally serve only one client at a time. The rationale for using family-based crisis homes is that they offer "accepting, normalized settings for clients in crisis which are thought to be less threatening, disruptive, and stigmatizing than hospitals" (Stroul, August 1987, p. 22). The family sponsors provide housing, meals, transportation, medication monitoring, informal training in living skills, and warmth and support, but they are not considered a formal part of the treatment team.

The treatment team is headed by a clinical case manager who is generally responsible for the client. Upon placement, the case manager will stay with the client until the client is stabilized to the point that the family sponsor can take over (sometimes up to 24 hours later). The clinician visits daily and provides crisis-oriented therapeutic services as well as linkage with community services. Psychiatrists and nursing staff are available and conduct physical and psychiatric examinations as well as prescribe medications. There is 24-hour emergency medical backup.

The Southwest Denver Program, which started in 1972, is the prototype for this kind of program. It allows two clients in each of its two family-based crisis homes. Table 5.3 shows its characteristics.

Table 5.3. Alternative Home ... Program of the Southwest Denver Mental Health Center, Denver, Colorado

Type of Program	Type of Agency	Community	Capacity/ Average Stay	Clients	Diagnosis
Family-Based Crisis Homes	CMHC Private, Nonprofit	Urban	4 Beds 2-3 Weeks	Ages 18-90 60% 18-40 35% 40-65 5% over 65 54% Female 46% Male 64% White 30% Hispanic 3% Native American 2% Black 1% Asian	28% Adjustment Disorder 26% Depression 15% Bipolar 12% Schizophrenia 10% Dual Diagnosis (MH/Substance Abuse) 5% Anxiety 4% Other

Admissions

32% Preventive
30% Direct Diversion
24% Early Discharge
10% Transition
3% Respite

Would not admit:

Homicidal threats or behavior
High suicidal risk and unable to contact
Environmentally destructive, e.g. fire starter
Severe illness or health problem
Past history of behavior unacceptable to home
sponsors, e.g. exposing self, repeatedly leaving AMA,
assaults or threats, history of not benefitting from program.

2% Involuntary admissions

Staffing Patterns

1 FTE

Physician
Nurse
Clinician

3 staff to 1 client

2 Home Sponsors @ $1,300/month
with sick and vacation benefits

Home Sponsors on five year contract
with annual raise

Resources

Cost:
$98.00/day

Funding Sources:
98% Colorado state mental health funds
2% Medicaid

Third Party Revenues:
Medicaid - Therapeutic Visits by Physician, Nurse
and Therapist

(Continued Next Page)

143

Table 5.3 (Continued). Alternative Home Program of the Southwest Denver Mental Health Center, Denver, Colorado

Description

o Family-based crisis home program which provides home-oriented therapeutic atmosphere in which client feels like a guest in the alternative home.

o Client participates in daily home activities and is visited in the home by staff as well as coming to the Center for services of nurse, physician, and clinician.

o Provides medical and nursing services, transportation assistance, relocation and housing referral, daily treatment program coordinated by clinician, and alternative home sponsors.

o Agency also provides crisis walk-in services.

community.

Observations

o Licensed by Colorado Division of Mental Health.

o Has alternative home sponsors who have been with the program for more than years.

o Problem ascertaining whether or not the client is appropriate for the crisis home disposition and projecting benefit.

o Communication between clinician, client, physician, and home sponsor must be worked on consciously.

o Problem encouraging and arranging for use of alternative home by the city hospital which provides 24-hour emergency psychiatric services for the

144

Source: Stroul, August, 1987, pp. 92, 93.

Group Approach

The second alternative crisis residential approach is called the group approach. These are crisis residences that generally serve 8 to 10 people and are located in typical neighborhood homes, duplexes, and apartments. These settings offer a supportive, supervised context for crisis stabilization as well as an "alternative" community. In addition to room and board, the services offered by crisis residential programs generally include the following: (1) a physical examination performed by a doctor or nurse within 24 to 48 hours of admission; (2) psychiatric services; (3) 24-hour emergency medical backup; (4) development of a client service plan; (5) crisis-oriented counseling; (6) family and support system consultations; (7) linkages with the community; (8) social and recreational activities; (9) daily living skills training; and (10) discharge planning and follow-up care. As with the family-based programs, the average length of stay appears to be between seven or eight days and two weeks (Stroul, August 1987, pp. 26-28).

There are many group crisis residences across the country. Tables 5.4 and 5.5 show the characteristics of two of these.

Mosher and Menn (1987) compared alternative programs with hospitals and the comparison is shown in Table 5.6. If the TDMHMR definition of crisis stabilization unit/contracted inpatient bed were applied to this comparison, it would fall in the hospital column in every category except geographical setting. This table, then, concisely distinguishes these two treatment philosophies.

Alternative crisis residential programs have definite advantages. The first is that they are generally less expensive than institutionally-based crisis programs. It is difficult to extract the actual costs of crisis stabilization beds and contracted inpatient beds in Texas (Table 5.7). This difficulty exists for several reasons. First, all structured crisis beds are under one budget category. Therefore, the figures include costs for detoxification beds, many of which are subsidized by the Texas Commission on Alcoholism and Drug Abuse. Second, the centers normally report only the costs to themselves rather than the total costs. For example, the crisis stabilization facilities for both the Harris County and Tarrant County centers are subsidized by the state. Therefore, the costs the centers report, which reflect their own out-of-pocket expenses, seriously underestimate the total costs. Finally, most centers report only direct costs, excluding indirect costs. For example, Concho Valley CMHMRC reports a cost of $250 per client day; however, it reports that once contracted services, staff salaries, professional consultations, transportation, and other hidden costs are included, the total costs per client day is closer to $347 (Crean, Rodriguez, and Vega, 1990, p. 137). For all of these reasons the average cost of $189.59 per client day is probably a serious underestimate of the true costs.

Alternative crisis residential programs are generally less expensive than those in highly structured, hospital-like settings. Southwest Denver CMHC reports a cost of $98 per day for its family care program. Group crisis residential programs are somewhat more expensive but still considerably less expensive than medical model approaches; Crossing Place reports a cost of $114 per day, and PATH's per diem cost is $133. Of the 20 group crisis residences reporting cost information for the NIMH Crisis Residential Services Project, the average cost per client day was $135 (Stroul, August 1987, p. 39).

There is also some evidence that these nonhospital-like alternatives may have somewhat better outcomes than hospital like approaches. They have very low hospitalization rates, encourage less dependency, are less stigmatizing, and--by keeping the client active and connected with community--have a less disruptive impact on the client (Stroul, August 1987, p. 18).

145

Table 5.4. Alternative Home Program of Crossing Place, Wooley House, Washington, D.C.

Type of Program	Type of Agency	Community	Capacity/Avg. Stay	Clients	Diagnosis
Group Crisis Residence	Residential Agency Private, Nonprofit	Urban	8 Beds 34 Days	Ages 18+ 50% 18-40 45% 40-65 5% Over 65 55% Female 45% Male 55% Black 45% White	65% Schizophrenia 25% Major Affective Disorders 10% Other

Admissions	Staffing Patterns	Resources
75% Direct Diversion 25% Preventative Would not admit: Primary diagnosis of substance abuse Actively violent Clients requiring medical resources of hospital No involuntary admissions	8 FTEs 1 M.S.W. 7 Counselors 2 Staff to 8 Clients	Cost: $114/day Funding Sources: 53% District of Columbia 43% St. Elizabeth's Hospital (U.S. Govt.) 4% Private Third Party Revenues: None

Description	Observations
Residential alternative to hospitalization. Non-medical model program in small, family-style setting. Counselors work 24-hour shifts. Provides intense individual, crisis-oriented therapy, psychiatric evaluation and consultation, art therapy, family support. Agency also provides crisis telephone services.	Licensed by District of Columbia. Problem finding housing options for persons who have stabilized. Problem working with persons who have substance abuse and psychiatric problems

Source: Stroul, August 1987, pp. 106, 107.

Note: This program was established in 1977.

Table 5.5. PATH (Positive Alternatives to Hospitalization) Apalachee Center for Human Services, Tallahassee, Florida

ype of Program	Type of Agency	Community	Capacity/Avg. Stay	Clients	Diagnosis
roup Crises esidence	CMHC Private, Nonprofit	Urban/Rural	14 Beds 6 Days	Ages 14-Geriatric 2% Under 18 70% 18-40 25% 40-65 3% Over 65 60% Female 40% Male 80% White 20% Black	50% Schizophrenic 30% Depression 10% Personality Disorders 5% OBS 5% Other

dmissions	Staffing Patterns	Resources
% Direct Diversion % Early Discharge % Preventive % Respite % Transition ould not admit: ute intoxification ute medical problems % Involuntary admissions	23 FTEs 1 M.D. 6 R.N./L.P.N.s 2 M.S.W.s 5 Bachelors Counselors 9 Aides/Technicians 1 staff to 1.6 clients	Cost: $133/day Funding Sources: 60% State 25% Local 15% Fees Third Party Revenues: Medicaid - Psychiatric Day Treatment Other - Outpatient

scription	Observations
spital diversion program which functions as an ernative to psychiatric hospitalization. ovides psychiatric evaluation; medication therapy; ividual, group and family therapy; lab work and eral medical treatment for non-acute problems; ivities therapy; case management; other specialized vices as needed. ency also provides crisis telephone, crisis walk-in, l limited mobile outreach services.	Licensed by State Office of Licensure and Certification Has reduced local inpatient admissions dramatically. Collects utilization data. Problem balancing needs of involuntary and voluntary clients.

rce: Stroul, August 1987, pp. 126, 127.

:e: This program was established in 1978.

147

Table 5.6. Comparison of Alternative Programs and Hospitals

<u>Alternatives</u>   <u>Hospitals</u>

Treatment

Psychosocial model   Medical model
Labeling (stigmatization) minimized   Labeling (diagnosis) emphasized
Residents responsible for own behavior   Staff accountable for patient's behavior

Setting

Community-based   Removed from community
Homelike atmosphere   Institutional atmosphere
Open   Closed, locked, or restrictive

Social Structure

Nonauthoritarian   Authoritarian
Nonhierarchical   Hierarchical
Program flexibility   Inflexibility
Role differentiation minimized   Role differentiation emphasized
  (i.e., "just people")
Client as resident   Client as patient
Continuity of ongoing daily activities   Removal from usual daily activities

Source: Stroul, August 1987, p. 19. As adapted from Mosher and Menn, 1987.

Table 5.7. Residential Services---Capacity and Cost per Day, FY 1988

Facility Name	SC Capacity	SC No.of Clients	SC Client Days	SC Cost/Day
Abilene Regional	2	12	84	$238.10
Austin-Travis County	26	880	8255	$123.91
Bexar County	65	3792	14,584	$106.00
Brazos Valley	4	80	1008	$86.11
Central County	14	140	3500	$158.30
Central Plains	11	250	3000	$141.83
Central Texas	10	10	40	$250.00
Collin County	3	35	841	$338.00
Concho Valley	1	58	405	$250.00
Dallas County	80	1412	19,033	$228.08
Deep East Texas	24	381	6,777	$201.58
Denton County	2	60	598	$400.00
Gulf Bend	12	340	3700	$38.06
Gulf Coast	28	408	6354	$99.78
East Texas	4	110	1250	$151.23
Harris County	294	3608	89,816	$69.97
Hunt County	2	20	145	$275.00
Heart of Texas	2	202	1681	$100.51
Johnson County	2	48	720	$325.00
Life Management	34			
Lubbock Regional	9	324	1944	$174.53
Navarro County	1	20	100	$250.00
Northeast Texas	3	28	291	$271.56
Nueces County	2	57	571	$350.26
Pecan Valley	1	27	105	$237.55
Permian Basin	8	360	2740	$15.63
Sabine Valley	55	816	9039	$144.44
Southeast Texas	68	680	19,700	$106.26
Tarrant County	84	1040	17,040	$227.26
Tx. Panhandle	25	225	5772	$119.21
Texoma	3	72	400	$265.48
Tri-County	25	277	6600	$181.84
Tropical Texas	17	302	5461	$124.82
Wichita Falls	1	31	310	$206.14
Totals	922	16,105	231,864	$6,256.44
Averages	27.12	488.03	7026.18	$189.59

Source: TDMHMR, 1988a.

Note: SC denotes structured crisis and reflects all structured crisis beds,
including detoxification beds.

149

The ideal crisis residential system would offer an array of programs that would include alternative programs as well as the more structured crisis stabilization units. Its guiding principle would be a continuum of responses so that clients could be treated in the least restrictive, most normative setting possible. In order for this continuum to occur, TDMHMR would need to revise its service definitions so that community centers are required to provide more than one kind of crisis stabilization program.

As long as persons with serious mental illness continue to experience periodic crises, the role of crisis residential programs will be crucial to the system of community-based care. It is here that diagnoses are made and that medications and treatment are initiated. It is also here that the client gains temporary asylum and a chance to regain a hold on life in the community. It is where the client and the professionals can evaluate his or her actual situation, reality perception, coping mechanisms, and community supports to make the necessary adjustments. It is a time for recommitment for the client who must recommit to life in the community and for the community mental health authority who must recommit to providing the supports that will enable the client to survive outside an institution.

References

Austin-Travis County Mental Health Mental Retardation Center. n.d. <u>Program Reference Manual</u>. Austin, Texas.

Bellack, Alan, and Kim Mueser. 1986. "A Comprehensive Treatment Program for Schizophrenia and Chronic Mental Illness." <u>Community Mental Health Journal</u>, vol. 22 (Fall).

Bengeldorf, Herbert, and Allen Alden. 1987. "A Mobile Crisis Unit in the Psychiatric Emergency Room." <u>Hospital and Community Psychiatry</u>, vol. 38 (June).

Blasi, Jana, Lynn Parish, Jan Rienstra, and Charles Blissett. 1990. "Dallas County MHMR Center." In <u>Community Mental Health in Texas: Four Case Studies</u>. Special Project Report. Austin: Lyndon B. Johnson School of Public Affairs, The University of Texas at Austin.

Crean, Hugh, Norma Rodriguez, and Rudolfo R. Vega. 1990. "Concho Valley Center for Human Advancement." In <u>Community Mental Health in Texas: Four Case Studies</u>. Special Project Report. Austin: Lyndon B. Johnson School of Public Affairs, The University of Texas at Austin.

Cummings, Louise, and Diane Sheridan, eds. August 1988. <u>Facts and Issues: Services for the Seriously Mentally Ill in Texas</u>. Austin, Texas: League of Women Voters of Texas Education Fund.

Dallas County Mental Health and Mental Retardation Center (DCMHMRC). 1988. "Adult Inpatient Treatment Center." Dallas, Texas: (informational handout.)

Diamond, Pamela M., Minh Ly Griffin, and Nicholas L. Hoover. 1990. "San Antonio State Hospital Outreach." In <u>Community Mental Health in Texas: Four Case Studies</u>. Special Project Report. Austin: Lyndon B. Johnson School of Public Affairs, The University of Texas at Austin.

Hale, Karen. 1989. Associate Director, Mental Health Association in Texas, Austin, Texas. Telephone interview by Lynn Parish, March 31.

Kiesler, C. A. 1982. "Mental Hospitals and Alternative Care: Noninstitutionalization as Potential Public Policy for Mental Patients." <u>American Psychologist</u>, vol. 37 (July).

Legislative Oversight Committee on Mental Health and Mental Retardation (LOC). February 1985. <u>Report to the Legislature. Vol. 1: Mental Health</u>. Austin, Texas.

Mental Health Association in Texas (MHAT). 1986. "Senate Bill 633: Core Services Survey." Austin, Texas.

Mental Health Needs Council, Inc. 1989. <u>Needs for Mental Health Services in Harris County.</u> Houston, Texas.

Milton, Edwina. 1989. Program Consultant, Texas Department of Mental Health and Mental Retardation, Austin, Texas. Telephone interview by Jana Blasi, April 24.

Mosher, L. R., and A. Z. Menn. 1978. "Community Residential Treatment for Schizophrenia: Two-Year Follow-Up." <u>Hospital and Community Psychiatry</u>, vol. 29 (November).

Pharis, David. February 1988. "Characteristics of Residential Programs Based on Service Definitions FY 1988." Austin, Texas: R. A. J. Review Panel.

Stroul, Beth A. August 1987. Crisis Residential Services in a Community Support System: Report on the NIMH Crisis Residential Services Project. Rockville, Md.: National Institute of Mental Health.

Texas Department of Mental Health and Mental Retardation (TDMHMR). 1987. "Mental Health Service Definitions FY 1988." Austin, Texas.

_____. 1988a. "Community Mental Health Center Contract Data." Austin, Texas. (Computer printout.)

_____. 1988b. "Licensure of Crisis Stabilization Units, Chapter 401, Subchapter K." Austin, Texas. (Administrative rule.)

_____. 1988c. "CARE Data." Austin, Tex. (Computer printout.)

_____. 1989. TDMHMR Mental Health Community Standards. Austin, Texas.

Vernon's Annotated Texas Statutes. 1988. Article 5547-204.

Chapter 6. Psychosocial Rehabilitation[*]

Psychosocial rehabilitation is an umbrella term for a variety of relatively discrete services. Academic programs often are included in the rehabilitation process for those clients whose learning was hindered or interrupted by their illness (Dincin, 1975, p. 138). Another basic component is vocational rehabilitation for clients to relearn lost skills or to obtain certain skills for the first time (Dincin, 1975, p. 136). Clients can practice their new skills in sheltered work assignments or as members of work crews organized by the rehabilitation program. Higher-functioning clients may perform voluntary or paid work in the community on a part- or full-time basis (Dincin, 1975, p. 137).

Social rehabilitation is an important part of the rehabilitation process (Dincin, 1975, p. 138). An effective vehicle for this is the formation of activity, problem-solving, and support groups (Dincin, 1975, pp. 139-140). Sometimes social rehabilitation can be facilitated through individual client counseling (Dincin, 1975, p. 140).

Residential services are part of many psychosocial programs (Dincin, 1975, p. 141). In the Fairweather Lodge model, vocational and social rehabilitation are combined in a voluntary, group residential environment which has proven very successful. Fairweather Lodges allow clients to become independent of the public support system for their needs, because they include both housing and employment, which are essential for self-sufficiency in the community.

In Texas, psychosocial rehabilitation programs often include many of the components described above. TDMHMR defines psychosocial rehabilitation as programs designed "to help the high-risk chronic client acquire and maintain life skills that enable him [or her] to cope effectively with the demands of his [or her] personal and social environment. The goal of these services is to improve the overall quality of life and the independence of the severely impaired client who otherwise might be totally dependent upon others for provision of basic day-to-day care and unable to participate within the community setting. Central to the focus of this program is the creation of an environment which empowers the client member and emulates activities found within the community, i.e. a wellness model. These programs increase the control of the client members over their program content and activities and enable them to live more normalized lives than would otherwise be possible. Psychosocial programs provide an array of services which enhance the client's network of social supports; enhance independent living skills; and provide vocational development skills which may include prevocational, vocational skills training, sheltered and supervised employment opportunities as well as transitional and independent employment services" (TDMHMR, 1987, p. 14).

TDMHMR requires three of these program elements: social support activities, independent living skills, and vocational skills development, including prevocational training and vocational training. Other program elements are defined but not required (TDMHMR, 1987, p. 16). Both the required and the optional program elements are described below.

SOCIAL SUPPORT ACTIVITIES

Social support activities are designed to ensure the development of a social network which will provide the client a source of companionship, normalized social

---

[*]This chapter was written by Joellen M. Harper.

activity, and a "support safety net" within the community during times of stress (TDMHMR, 1989, App. E, p. 15).

TDMHMR defines social support activities as "member-organized outings, social clubs, coffee houses, independent member meetings, and other activities such as client-generated newsletters. Evening and weekend operation, in which clients have appropriate staff support available, is necessary to enable informal client gatherings and social activities to occur on a normalized schedule. The availability of social support activities to a given client is not time-limited in the course of a client's chronic mental illness; the chronically ill client requires a viable social network on a permanent ongoing basis in order to remain in the community. A client's need for other elements of the comprehensive psychosocial array may vary from time to time, particularly as his [or her] level of independence increases; however, social support activities are to be ongoing" (TDMHMR, 1987, p. 15).

Despite the demonstrated success and cost-effectiveness of psychosocial rehabilitation programs in general, and of social support activities in particular, a very small portion of the total mental health budget is allocated to them. In FY 1988, a total of $372,847 was budgeted for social support services in the state; this represented 0.2 percent of the total budget for that year and 3.2 percent of the budget for all psychosocial rehabilitation programs (TDMHMR, 1988). During FY 1988, all but two mental health authorities provided some level of social support activities (TDMHMR, 1988). The number of clients served by these programs is not centrally collected.

INDEPENDENT LIVING SKILLS

The second component of psychosocial rehabilitation that TDMHMR requires mental health authorities to provide is called independent living skills. This is defined as those activities designed to increase each client's ability to independently accomplish those tasks required to successfully live in the community. This is to include both critical survival skills and skills typically expected of persons in various age groups. Examples of such activities are the use of public transportation, the management of money, the purchase and preparation of food, the maintenance of a pleasant home environment, and the use of community resources (e.g., assistance programs and health clinics). In addition, independent living skills should assist the client in adopting appropriate social behavior for acceptance and effectiveness in the community environment. This is most often provided by personal social adjustment training which includes assertiveness training and communication techniques (TDMHMR, 1989, App. E, p. 15).

In FY 1988, $697,145 was budgeted for independent living skills programs across the state. This amount represented 6 percent of all funds budgeted for psychosocial programs and 0.4 percent of total mental health funds. During FY 1988, all 34 of the existing community centers contracted to provide independent living skills activities (TDMHMR, 1988). The number of clients served in these programs is not centrally collected.

VOCATIONAL SKILLS DEVELOPMENT

The third required element of psychosocial rehabilitation programs is vocational skills development. Of five specific services within the general category of vocational services, TDMHMR requires mental health authorities to provide two services: prevocational and vocational training. The remaining three optional services are sheltered employment, stations in industry, and transitional or supported employment. Each of these is discussed below.

Prevocational Training

Prevocational training "develops skills prerequisite to learning more formal vocational skills and developing vocational abilities and talents" (TDMHMR, 1989, App. E, p. 16). This training provides opportunities for a client to identify the type of job in which he or she is interested and to learn the responsibilities, tasks, and behavior necessary for the job. Other activities are learning the use of basic tools, acceptable work habits and attitudes, on-task behavior, and other job responsibilities. Specific training is offered in job readiness skills, such as resume preparation, interviewing, and job hunting. Another feature of prevocational training is the opportunity for clients to experience the training on a regular, preferably daily, basis.

In FY 1988, a grand total of $1,346,046 was budgeted for community-based prevocational skills training. This was 11.4 percent of the total psychosocial program budget and 0.8 percent of all mental health funds budgeted that year. The number of clients receiving this training in FY 1988 is not centrally collected. All but three mental health authorities offered some level of prevocational training in FY 1988 (TDMHMR, 1988).

Vocational Training

The focus of vocational training services is on the development of skills in a particular vocational area, either through formalized instruction, practical experience, or actual experience on the job. By definition, this training is more intense than the prevocational training and often involves payment of a wage to the client. Harbor House, operated by the community center in Austin, is the community-based training program for Fairweather Lodge. This program targets adults with moderate to severe mental health problems who need a structured living and work environment. The goal upon completion of the training program is for the members to graduate as a group and move into their own Fairweather Lodge. The lodge members completely support themselves and the lodge through working on one or more janitorial contracts they negotiate with various public agencies and some private businesses.

In FY 1988, $1,138,392 was budgeted for vocational training across the state. This represented 9.6 percent of the budget for all psychosocial programs and 0.7 percent of total funds for all mental health services. The number of persons served in this program in FY 1988 is not centrally available. All but three mental health authorities provided some level of this service in FY 1988 (TDMHMR, 1988).

Sheltered Employment

Sheltered employment generally means employment in segregated settings for persons with serious mental illness who do not yet have skills to move to supported or independent employment (TDMHMR, 1989, App. E, p. 16). Clients in sheltered workshops do real work, secured by contracts with various manufacturers, such as IBM, to perform various tasks, such as mechanical assembly, collating, sorting, labeling, packaging, and bulk mailing. Clients usually are paid on a piece-rate basis (a specific amount for each piece completed), according to guidelines established by the U.S. Department of Labor. Participating clients are considered by staff to be not

155

competitively employable; for those unable to learn the skills to move up to other work settings, the sheltered workshop may be a more or less permanent employment placement.

Although mental health authorities are not required to offer sheltered employment, 21 of the 34 community centers provided some level of this service in FY 1988. In FY 1988, $1,161,391 was budgeted for sheltered workshops across the state. This amount was 1.0 percent of total mental health funds and 13.7 percent of all psychosocial funds budgeted for FY 1988. The number of clients served in sheltered workshops is not centrally collected.

Stations in Industry

Stations in industry offer an alternative between the sheltered workshop environment and competitive employment. Community centers may obtain contract employment, as the sheltered workshops do, for clients who are willing and able to begin to take on responsibility and make a commitment to work. While this is still structured, supervised work, clients earn at least minimum wage and commit to work a certain amount of time each week.

Mental health authorities are not required to provide a stations-in-industry program, although 16 of the 34 community centers contracted to offer this work opportunity in FY 1988. A small amount of funds, $98,662, was budgeted for this service in FY 1988, less than 1 percent of the psychosocial program budget.

Transitional Employment

A transitional, or supported, employment program is actually located in normal places of business. A client begins to work at an entry-level position at regular prevailing wages, sometimes on a temporary, transitional basis. It is an opportunity for a client to obtain necessary experience on a short-term (three to nine months) basis. The goal is to prepare clients for "eventual successful and unsupervised work adjustment on a permanent basis" (TDMHMR, 1989, App. E, p. 17). This service has a variety of interpretations from center to center. Many centers consider their work crews to be "transitional employment," in that they prepare clients to go on to competitive employment after a period of time. Another type of transitional employment is the pairing of a client with a job coach. The coach accompanies the client to his or her job on a daily basis, gradually decreasing the number and duration of visits.

Although transitional employment is not required by TDMHMR, more than half of the total psychosocial program funds were spent for transitional employment services, which were provided by less than half of the community centers. In FY 1988, $6,533,655 was budgeted for transitional employment services. In several cases the programs received much of their funding from the Texas Rehabilitation Commission. This represented 55 percent of the total psychosocial programs budget, and 4 percent of the total mental health services budget in that year. These funds were allocated to 15 of the 34 community centers to provide transitional employment in FY 1988. As in other psychosocial program components, the number of clients served in transitional employment is not centrally collected.

AVAILABILITY OF PSYCHOSOCIAL REHABILITATION

The FY 1988 community center contract data provide information on whether the various psychosocial components are available, as well as on the total level of psychosocial funding per community center. Table 6.1 shows the total and per capita community center funding for psychosocial programs. The level of funding ranges from $0.00 to $2.57 per capita. According to the FY 1988 contract data, the Abilene center has allocated no funds to psychosocial programs, but does provide all of the required components of this core service. Conversely, the Texoma center has above-average per capita funding for psychosocial programs, but lacks two of the required components. These may be errors in the data.

Even allowing for extremely limited funds for all community center programs, the funding level for psychosocial programs appears to indicate that these programs have a very low priority. The FY 1988 total budget for psychosocial rehabilitation programs was $11,808,138, or 7.3 percent of all mental health services funds that year (TDMHMR, 1988).

CONCLUSIONS

There are many criteria by which to evaluate the effectiveness of psychosocial rehabilitation programs for persons with serious, long-term mental illness. It is difficult to evaluate the programs from a strict cost-effectiveness approach, since many of the benefits are intangible and unquantifiable, such as improved quality of life. However, it is clear that psychosocial programs are worthwhile when they empower clients to work to become more self-reliant and less dependent on the public support system. Numerous studies on psychosocial rehabilitation programs reflected in the literature in recent years demonstrate their long-term effectiveness.

From the information provided above, it is apparent that there are only a few psychosocial rehabilitation programs in the state; those service areas which do have these kinds of programs cannot provide them in sufficient quantity to meet their own local needs. Although some centers offer extensive services, others provide only the minimum accepted by TDMHMR. Apparently a small minority provide none at all.

The primary reason behind this situation is insufficient funds. Community centers are required to provide seven core services, in addition to other so-called noncore services required by TDMHMR. With a fixed amount of funding, centers must choose which services will be offered, in what amounts, for how many clients, and for which types of clients. It is difficult to say that the core services are available to all clients when clients must wait months to obtain them or when they are not eligible for them because only the most disabled clients can be served.

Table 6.1. Texas CMHMRC Total and Per Capita Psychosocial Funding

L S A # CMHMRC	1988 Total Psychosocial Funding	1988 Estimated Population*	1988 Psychosocial Total Funding Per Capita
1 Abilene	0	165,366	$0.00
2 Texas Panhandle	148,772	378,560	$0.39
3 Austin Travis	462,508	537,630	$0.86
4 Bexar County	463,275	1,158,478	$0.40
5 Brazos County	188,651	247,942	$0.76
6 Central Counties	222,309	299,489	$0.74
7 Central Plains	54,339	105,481	$0.52
8 Central Texas	68,335	104,128	$0.66
9 Concho Valley Center	140,963	124,368	$1.13
10 Dallas County	630,984	1,810,294	$0.35
11 Deep East Texas	254,725	375,339	$0.68
12 East Texas	185,543	291,746	$0.64
13 Life Management	326,772	577,511	$0.57
14 Gulf Bend	73,378	171,788	$0.43
15 Gulf Coast	1,099,325	427,792	$2.57
16 Harris County	3,318,072	3,004,791	$1.10
17 Heart of Texas	259,638	292,607	$0.89
18 Lubbock	102,220	279,458	$0.37
19 Navarro County	46,000	39,992	$1.15
20 Collin County	101,130	210,097	$0.48
21 Northeast Texas	110,520	130,915	$0.84
22 Nueces County	18,689	318,227	$0.06
23 Pecan Valley	290,802	145,268	$2.00
24 Permian Basin	215,016	284,795	$0.75
25 Sabine Valley	166,831	304,988	$0.55
26 Southeast Texas	635,746	380,116	$1.67
27 Tarrant County	682,352	1,077,631	$0.63
28 Texoma	124,250	151,908	$0.82
29 Tri County	56,380	325,852	$0.17
30 Tropical Texas	254,034	657,129	$0.39
31 Wichita Falls	189,744	132,353	$1.43
34 Johnson City MHMR	71,898	88,519	$0.81
61 Denton County	52,630	192,390	$0.27
62 Hunt County	155,243	67,180	$2.31
Total	$11,171,074	14,860,128	$0.75

Source: TDMHMR, 1988.

*July 1986 estimate by Texas Dept. of Health of 1988 population.

References

Dincin, Jerry. 1975. "Psychiatric Rehabilitation." <u>Schizophrenia Bulletin</u>, vol. 13 (Summer).

Texas Department of Mental Health and Mental Retardation (TDMHMR). February 1989. <u>TDMHMR Mental Health Community Standards</u>. Austin, Texas.

_____. 1988. "Fiscal Year 1988 Community Center Contract Data." Austin, Texas. (Computer Printout.)

_____. 1987. "Mental Health Services Definitions: FY 1988." Austin, Texas.

Chapter 7. Case Management[*]

There is no single definition of case management; the definitions which are most commonly accepted in theory and in practice are substantively different. The following general definition of case management was proposed in 1976, according to criteria established by the Joint Commission on Accreditation of Hospitals as part of an ideal balanced service system of community mental health services:

> Case management services are activities aimed at linking the service system to a consumer and coordinating the various system components in order to achieve a successful outcome. The objective of case management is continuity of services . . . Case management is essentially a problem-solving function designed to overcome systems rigidity, fragmented services, misutilization of certain facilities and inaccessibility. (Levine and Fleming, May 1986, p. 7)

Current literature outlines six functions of case management: client identification and outreach, client assessment, service planning, linkage with requisite services, monitoring of service delivery, and client advocacy.

The literature also outlines common problems which hinder the growth of case management. For example, the Montana Department of Institutions (MDI) concluded that major problems in implementing community-based case management originated from insufficient funds, staff, and time. In addition, the MDI pointed out that the multiple definitions, priorities, and guidelines for case management were an impediment to the successful implementation of a case management program (MDI, September 1982, p. 44). A more subtle issue is that the practice of effective case management appears to thwart the traditional office-based practices that mental health professionals are trained to do. Effective case management most often occurs outside of offices in a fairly nonstructured manner that is not appointment-based (Collins, 1989b).

A second problem area is the caseload size of individual case managers. Studies have shown that the effectiveness of case management decreases as caseload size increases. According to Rubin, the ideal caseload size is 15 to 30 "under normal circumstances" (Rubin, 1987, p. 10). However, it has been noted that case managers often perform functions which are beyond the scope of case management activities. This over-extension of duty is prevalent because case managers take it upon themselves to ensure that their clients are receiving appropriate services and care. As a result, case managers have multiple roles, such as that of counselor, advocate, administrator, planner, broker, consultant, therapist, social skills teacher, and diagnostician (Rubin, 1987, p. 5; Intagliata, 1982, p. 659; Levine and Fleming, May 1986, p. 9).

A further impediment to the viability of an effective case management program is that case managers experience high rates of burnout, resulting in excessive turnover among case managers. Case managers consistently state that one of the most debilitating aggravations for them is the amount of paperwork involved. Other negative aspects include the frustrations of dealing with the numerous bureaucracies, the low salaries, and the wear and tear on personal automobiles.

Although case management is perceived to be a cornerstone in bridging the gaps among community services, current literature reveals conflicting findings as to the effectiveness of case management. Studies have not demonstrated consistency and

---

[*]This chapter was written by Lynn Parish. The section on Medicaid and case management was written by Nicholas L. Hoover.

conclusiveness in reduction of recidivism and treatment costs. As stated previously, a major reason for discrepancies in the findings is the different definitions or models of case management. Systematic, comparative evaluation of case management is difficult given the wide variation in case management models which exist (Borland, McRae, and Lycan, 1989, p. 374).

The literature also reflects the continuing efforts to develop consistent guidelines for case management programs which are effective, yet sufficiently flexible to accommodate local variations. A typology of case management was prepared by the National Institute of Mental Health (NIMH) in its recent review of case management models. NIMH categorized the prevailing case management programs into four basic models: the Expanded Broker Model, the Personal Strengths Model, the Rehabilitation Model, and the Full Support Model (Robinson and Bergman, March 1989, p. 1).

The implementation of case management programs is a relatively young phenomenon. For example, the TDMHMR case management program is in its fourth year and is still being evaluated and assessed. Evidence suggests a desire for a dynamic case management system which will effectively coordinate the disjointed services, prevent misutilization and duplication of services, and realize the philosophy of continuity of care for persons with serious and long-term mental illness.

CASE MANAGEMENT IN TEXAS

In 1985, TDMHMR implemented a statewide case management program as part of its effort to successfully shift services from institutions to the community. It budgeted $900,000 for the design of the program, $300,000 of which came from NIMH grants. TDMHMR's stated purpose was to develop a statewide system of services that would be comprehensive, individualized, and long term for mentally ill and mentally retarded individuals (TDMHMR, 1987b).

By initiating a statewide program and setting guidelines for the program, TDMHMR hoped to ensure uniformity of service across the state. Local providers were required to design their services according to these guidelines, listed in Table 7.1. TDMHMR issued standards for program design and entry eligibility, such as 24-hour availability of services, a maximum caseload size of 40, with case managers devoting their full time to case management. In addition, TDMHMR developed a career ladder for case managers, a self-instructional core curriculum for training staff, and an annual evaluation to assess needs and the degree of compliance with the guidelines.

The program began with certain restrictions that have shaped its development. The most important of these is that the legislature did not appropriate any new funds for case management. Instead, funds were taken from other parts of the community-based budget; case managers were conscripted from other community programs. Thus, funding and manpower constraints were with this program from its conception. So in Texas, from the very beginning, because of the money and manpower constraints, the population targeted to receive case management was extremely small. Eligibility criteria for the program were strictly defined and tightly interpreted. The result is that only the neediest of the needy had access to these services.

A study done by TDMHMR in 1988 demonstrates just how limited the access is to this service. It showed that even though 70 percent of those who were discharged from the state hospitals in a one-year period met both the chronicity and at-risk requirements, only 21 percent of that 70 percent received case management (Ganju, 1988, p. 4). The same study showed that, in the entire system, only 11.9 percent of the chronic population receives case management (Ganju, 1988, p. 6).

162

Table 7.1. Case Management: Departmental Requirements

LMHAs shall implement a case management system for members of the priority population.

Case management must be an identifiable unit within the organizational structure and not exceed two levels below the chief executive officer.

Case managers perform exclusively only those functions within the purview of case management.

Clients of priority population must be screened according to case management eligibility criteria.

Policy must be implemented for monitoring and reassessing all clients who need, but currently are not receiving, case management services.

Case management services must be available 24 hours a day, 7 days a week.

Caseload must not exceed one full-time case manager for every 40 MH clients and 30 MR clients.

Plans must exist for expansion of case management program to serve clients who are identified as needing, but not presently receiving, case management services.

Cooperative agreements must be developed with other appropriate agencies at regional/local levels.

Policies and procedures must be implemented for expending client services funds.

Individuals working within the various components of case management unit(s) must be trained adequately.

Mechanisms must be implemented for identifying and resolving service delivery constraints.

Case management unit and agency must meet all applicable community standards. See Chapter 8, Case Management, TDMHMR Community Standards.

Source: Collins, Interview, November 8, 1988b.

The other idiosyncracy of the case management program is that it started in an atmosphere of resentment and resistance, much of which persists today. To some extent this resentment can be attributed to the fact that case management was the first, and is still the only, core service to be this tightly delineated, regulated, and monitored. The extent of the rules and regulations made some centers feel that TDMHMR was imposing a single, unjustifiably uniform model on very diverse centers and populations. They questioned whether a uniform statewide system was even desirable in a state as large and diverse as Texas.

Another reason for the resentment was the fact that no new funds were allocated for this service. Some centers had to disband existing programs in order to establish this one. This was particularly wrenching because centers have historically adjusted to underfunding by efficiently using available resources, including personnel. Case management, if it is long term and intensive, uses large numbers of personnel for very few clients. Thus it delivers very little punch for the dollar when viewed from a short-term perspective of resource allocation.

Finally, the resentment toward TDMHMR's insistence on its model can be attributed to the very real conflict that occurs when an "ideal" model is imposed on real conditions. The validity of TDMHMR's model of high-intensity, long-term case management is rarely disputed in the field. As one center director observed, when explaining why his center provides mostly short-term case management, "If you have ten people in front of you, each of whom needs case management, but you only have the resources to provide pure, long-term case management to one of them, you can either opt to provide it to the one and tell the others you can't help them, or you can give all of them at least a 'have-to-have' level of service" (Gill, Interview, April 24, 1989).

While there is little doubt that TDMHMR's guidelines impose uniformity, there are certain advantages to a uniform statewide system that cannot be disputed. First, it begins to ensure a minimum level of acceptable case management services across the state. Second, it attempts to ensure that the service reflects current literature on what makes an effective case management program. Third, the standardized rules and regulations are reassuring to the legislature, which has often been reluctant to appropriate funds to the community-based sector because of the perceived lack of uniformity and accountability.

Structural Organization of Case Management

There are 77 case management units throughout the state. Of these, 30 are mental health (MH) units, 31 are mental retardation (MR) units, and 16 are combined MH and MR units. These units are housed in 60 facilities, including local community centers, state hospital outreach centers, and state centers (TDMHMR, 1988b, p. 1). Organizationally each unit is under the auspices of its own mental health authority.

Case management is the only core service that has its own special office at TDMHMR. The Case Management Office is located within the Division of Training and Staff Resources. It is here that guidelines are issued, compliance is measured, and recommendations are made. However, the Case Management Office has no line authority over the units in the field. Rather, it advises TDMHMR on case management issues, provides technical assistance and training, and acts as a liaison between the units, their centers, and TDMHMR. TDMHMR attempts to issue clear-cut policy directives and detailed budget instructions. Standards designed to ensure the consistency and quality of case management services are present in the TDMHMR community standards, and specific performance measures are included in all local provider contracts.

While substantive conformity is difficult to measure, the Case Management Office attempts to assess at least some areas of conformity and uniformity through periodic surveys it asks the centers to complete. The results of these surveys indicate that although local providers are not currently in full compliance with departmental guidelines, they are moving in that direction. Several examples will serve to illustrate this point. One regulation requires that each mental health authority implement an areawide case management system; there was 73 percent compliance in 1987 and 83 percent compliance in 1988. Still, this means that in FY 1988, 17 percent of the units were not providing case management services to their entire service area (TDMHMR, 1988b, p. 5). Another requirement is that case management be an identifiable (separate) unit within the organizational structure, not to exceed two levels below the chief executive officer. In FY 1987, 75 percent of the units met this requirement; in FY 1988, 83 percent did. Still, in FY 1988, 51 percent of case management supervisors supervised more than the case management unit, suggesting that many of these units are not entirely separate from the center's other activities (TDMHMR, 1988b, p. 9). Thus, while progress has been made in the last three years, even the components easiest to assess do not show complete uniformity.

Funding for Case Management

In FY 1987, 5.6 percent of the community-based budget went to case management (MH and MR). In FY 1988, $8.8 million was budgeted for MH case management services and in FY 1989, $9.8 million was budgeted (Table 7.2). Assuming the 7,716 mental health clients served by case management in the first and second quarters of FY 1988 remained constant throughout the year, the $8.8 million budgeted for 1988 is approximately $1,140 per case-managed client. The requests for MH case management for FY 1990 and 1991 are $14.5 million and $17.5 million respectively (Table 7.2).

In the past few years, case management has received more than 90 percent of the funds it has requested. If this trend continues, there will be a dramatic increase in the amount of funds going to case management in the next few years, especially if Medicaid expansion for case management becomes a reality in the near future.

In FY 1988 state hospitals received 16 percent of the MH case management funds, state centers received 2 percent, and community centers received 82 percent. Of all of the clients receiving case management in the first and second quarters of FY 1988, 18 percent were served at state hospitals, 0.4 percent were served at state centers, and 81.6 percent were served at community centers (TDMHMR, 1988b, Appendices B-2 and B-3).

The state was the sole funding source of case management at state hospitals and state centers, but local funds made up 11 percent of the funds going to community centers for case management. Case management is labor intensive: in FY 1988, over 80 percent of all case management funds was budgeted for salaries (Roberts, Interview, November 18, 1988a).

Tables 7.3, 7.4, and 7.5 illustrate the allocation of FY 1988 budgeted funds by provider. The most obvious conclusion that can be drawn from Table 7.5 is that great discrepancies exist in the amount of money each service provider budgets for case management (Tables 7.3 and 7.4). In general, providers with a large number of case-managed clients tend to spend less per client than those with fewer case managed clients. From whatever angle one examines the dollars spent by each local provider on case management, the essential fact remains that there are great variations in the amount of funds available to each local case management program. As Table 7.5 shows, there are wide variations among the centers in both the size of their caseloads and in the proportion of clients admitted to case management of the total population served at the center.

Table 7.2. FY 1988 Statistics for the Texas Case Management Program

CMHMRC	MH Served	Screened for Case MGMT	Added to Case MGMT	No. Added/ # Screened	MH Receiving Case MGMT	Case-Managed Total Served	# of MH Case Managers	Average Caseload Size	Discharge Rate	Amount Budgeted	Budgeted Clients Case-Managed
Abilene	982	107	16	14.95%	46	4.68%	2	23	17.4	$88,845	$1,931
Austin - Travis	4,192	42	7	16.67%	240	5.73%	9 (1)	26.55	22.10	$371,105	$1,546
Bexar County	3,030	313	112	35.78%	477	15.74%	21 (2)	22.62	37.50	$585,286	$1,227
Brazos Valley	1,057	224	34	15.18%	160	15.14%	7	22.86	22.50	$151,140	$945
Central Counties	3,161	115	51	44.35%	230	7.28%	8	28.75	23.90	$274,416	$1,193
Central Plains	1,086	11	11	100.00%	73	6.72%	2	36.50	9.60	$96,687	$1,324
Central Texas	830	14	7	50.00%	130	15.66%	4 (1)	32.25	4.60	$150,093	$1,155
Collin County	914	387	70	18.09%	70	7.66%	3	23.33	22.90	$85,372	$1,220
Concho Valley	472	77	15	19.48%	57	12.08%	2		N/R	$66,367	
Dallas Co.	7,423	733	173	23.60%	706	9.51%	15	47.07	5.00	$595,060	$843
Deep East Texas	1,818	143	129	90.21%	204	11.22%	10	20.40	56.90	$247,298	$1,212
Denton Co.	853	63	49	77.78%	73	8.56%	3	24.33	15.10	$109,496	$1,500
East Texas	3,060	125	108	86.40%	108	3.53%	4	27.00	11.10	$106,067	$982
Gulf Bend	1,668	52	20	38.46%	113	6.77%	3	37.67	18.60	$159,056	$1,408
Gulf Coast	1,419	94	92	97.87%	212	14.94%	6	35.33	4.70	$178,024	$840
Harris Co.	9,371	297	217	73.06%	427	4.56%	22	19.41	36.30	$726,627	$1,702
Heart of Texas	1,240	160	50	31.25%	150	12.10%	6	25.00	4.70	$166,409	$1,109
Hunt Co.	971	41	15	36.59%	40	4.12%	1	40.00	22.50	$28,304	$708
Johnson Co.	354	78	2	2.56%	49	13.84%	1	49.00	18.40	$56,971	$1,163
Life Mgmt Center	3,949	262	120	45.80%	210	5.32%	6 (9)	40.00	96.20	$242,782	$1,156
Lubbock Regional	2,398	806	18	2.23%	340	14.18%	9	37.78	5.30	$299,478	$881
Navarro Co.	405	17	17	100.00%	53	13.09%	2	26.50	37.70	$61,209	$1,155
Northeast Texas	836	13	9	69.23%	84	10.05%	3	28.00	3.60	$76,754	$914
Nueces Co.	2,115	263	157	59.70%	105	4.96%	2 (3)	51.00	13.30	$110,252	$1,050
Pecan Valley	981	N/A	N/A		175	17.84%	7		N/R	$231,974	$1,326
Permian Basin	1,774	84	35	41.67%	105	5.92%	3 (6)	33.00	2.90	$94,756	$902
Sabine Valley	4,194	64	52	81.25%	269	6.41%	8		25.70	$290,383	$1,079
Southeast Texas	3,728	35	11	31.43%	201	5.39%	7		2.50	$192,784	$959
Tarrant Co.	8,244	378	199	52.65%	356	4.32%	9		33.70	$383,103	$1,076
Texas Panhandle	2,285	158	63	39.87%	261	11.42%	8		18.40	$304,750	$1,168
Texoma	1,536	86	21	24.42%	151	9.83%	5		13.90	$136,949	$907
Tri-county	1,570	10	7	70.00%	61	3.89%	4 (4)	14.25	86.90	$165,088	$2,706
Tropical Texas	3,294	647	15	2.32%	243	7.38%	7		0.00	$220,055	$906
Wichita Falls	1,191	10	8	80.00%	95	7.98%	3		7.40	$218,930	$2,305

State Facilities

CMHMRC	MH Served	Screened for Case MGMT	Added to Case MGMT	No. Added/ # Screened	MH Receiving Case MGMT	Case-Managed Total Served	# of MH Case Managers	Average Caseload Size	Discharge Rate	Amount Budgeted	Budgeted Clients Case-Managed
Austin		93	86	92.47%	258		11		16.30	$282,678	$1,096
Big Spring		66	36	54.55%	274		9		26.30	$285,532	$1,042
Kerrville		149	15	10.07%	62		6		33.90	$170,990	$2,758
Rusk		26	21	80.77%	145		5 (3)	14.25	17.20	$158,301	$1,092
San Antonio		206	63	30.58%	139		7		43.90	$173,991	$1,252
Terrell		63	36	57.14%	104		4		30.80	$180,106	$1,732
Wichita Falls		173	58	33.53%	239		8		3.80	$179,468	$751
El Paso		23	9	39.13%	28		3		3.60	$36,415	$1,301
Laredo		50	25	50.00%	160		4		20.60	$91,798	$574
Rio Grande		62	15	24.19%	33		1		3.00	$39,128	$1,186

Source: TDMHMR, 1988a.

166

Table 7.3. CMHMRC Mental Health Case Management FY 1988
Amounts Budgeted

CMHMRC	Amount Budgeted for MH Case Management
Abilene	$ 88,845
Austin-Travis	371,105
Bexar County	585,286
Brazos Valley	151,140
Central Counties	274,416
Central Plains	96,687
Central Texas	150,093
Collin County	85,372
Concho Valley	66,367
Dallas County	595,060
Deep East Texas	247,298
Denton County	109,496
East Texas	106,067
Gulf Bend	159,056
Gulf Coast	178,024
Harris County	726,627
Heart of Texas	166,409
Hunt County	28,304
Johnson County	56,971
Life Mgmt Center	242,782
Lubbock	299,478
Navarro County	61,219
Northeast Texas	76,754
Nueces County	110,252
Pecan Valley	231,974
Permian Basin	94,756
Sabine Valley	290,383
Southeast Texas	192,784
Tarrant County	283,103
Texas Panhandle	304,750
Texoma	136,949
Tri-County	165,088
Tropical Texas	220.055
Wichita Falls	$ 218,930
Total	$ 7,171,880

Source: Roberts, Letter, December 8, 1988b.

Table 7.4. FY 1988 Budgets for State Hospitals and State Centers for Mental Health Case Management

State Hospitals	Amount Budgeted
Austin	$282,678
Big Spring	$285,532
Kerrville	$170,990
Rusk	$158,301
San Antonio	$173,991
Terrell	$180,106
Wichita Falls	$179,468
Total	$1,431,066
State Centers	
El Paso	$36,415
Laredo	$91,798
Rio Grande	$39,128
Total	$167,341

Source: Roberts, Letter, December 8, 1988b.

Table 7.5. Case Management Provider Data for the First and Second Quarters of FY 1988

MRC	Total MH Served (A)	MH Case Managed (A)	CM / Total Served (A)	# MH Case Managers (B)	Caseload Size (G)
ne	982	46	4.68%	2	23.00
n Travis	4,192	240	5.73%	9	(1) 26.55
r County	3,030	477	15.74%	21	(2) 22.62
s Valley	1,057	160	15.14%	7	22.86
al Counties	3,161	230	7.28%	8	28.75
al Plains	1,086	73	6.72%	2	36.50
al Texas	830	130	15.66%	4	(1) 32.25
a County	914	70	7.66%	3	23.33
no Valley (I)	472	157 (57)	33.26% (12%)	2	78.5 (28.5)
s County	7,423	706	9.51%	15	47.07
East Texas	1,818	204	11.22%	10	20.40
on County	853	73	8.56%	3	24.33
Texas	3,060	108	3.53%	4	27.00
Bend	1,668	113	6.77%	3	37.67
Coast	1,419	212	14.94%	6	35.33
s County	9,371	427	4.56%	22	19.41
of Texas	1,240	150	12.10%	6	25.00
County	971	40	4.12%	1	40.00
on County	354	49	13.84%	1	(9) 40.00
Mgmt. Center	3,949	210	5.32%	6	35.00
ock Regional	2,398	340	14.18%	9	37.78
ro County	405	53	13.09%	2	26.50
east Texas	836	84	10.05%	3	28.00
s County	2,115	105	4.96%	2	(3) 51.00
Valley	981	175	17.84%	7	25.00
ian Basin	1,774	105	5.92%	3	(6) 33.00
e Valley	4,194	269	6.41%	8	33.63
east Texas	3,728	201	5.39%	7	28.71
nt County	8,244	356	4.32%	9	39.55
Panhandle	2,285	261	11.42%	8	32.63
na	1,536	151	9.83%	5	30.20
ounty	1,570	61	3.89%	4	(4) 14.25
cal Texas	3,294	243	7.38%	7	(37) 29.43
ta Falls	1,191	95	7.98%	3	31.67
	82,401	6,374 (6,274)		212	
ge	2,424	187 (185)	9.68%	6.24	29.78(H)
Facilities					
		(D)		(E)	
n	N/A	258	N/A	11	23.45
pring	N/A	274	N/A	9	30.44
ille	N/A	62	N/A	6	10.33
	N/A	145	N/A	5	(3) 14.25
ntonio	N/A	139	N/A	7	19.86
	N/A	104	N/A	4	26.00
ta Falls	N/A	239	N/A	8	29.88
o	N/A	28	N/A	3	9.33
	N/A	160	N/A	4	40.00
rande	N/A	33	N/A	1	33.00
		1442		58	
ge		144.2		5.8	24.86

(Continued Next Page)

169

Table 7.5 (Continued). Case Management Provider Data for the First and Second Quarters of FY 1988

CMHMRC	Discharge Rate (C)	$ Budgeted 1988 (f)	$Budgeted/ Total Served	$Budgeted/ To CM Clients	
Abilene	17.4	$88,845	$90.47	$1,931	
Austin - Travis	22.10	$371,105	$88.53	$1,546	
Bexar County	37.50	$585,286	$193.16	$1,227	
Brazos Valley	22.50	$151,140	$142.99	$945	
Central Counties	23.90	$274,416	$86.81	$1,193	
Central Plains	9.60	$96,687	$89.03	$1,324	
Central Texas	4.60	$150,093	$180.83	$1,155	
Collin County	22.90	$85,372	$93.40	$1,220	
Concho Valley	N/R	$66,367	$140.61	423(1164)	
Dallas County	5.00	$595,060	$80.16	$843	
Deep East Texas	56.90	$247,298	$136.03	$1,212	
Denton County	15.10	$109,496	$128.37	$1,500	
East Texas	11.10	$106,067	$34.66	$982	
Gulf Bend	18.60	$159,056	$95.36	$1,408	
Gulf Coast	4.70	$178,024	$125.46	$840	
Harris County	36.30	$726,627	$77.54	$1,702	
Heart of Texas	4.70	$166,409	$134.20	$1,109	
Hunt County	22.50	$28,304	$29.15	$708	
Johnson County	18.40	$56,971	$160.94	$1,163	
Life Management Center	96.20	$242,782	$61.48	$1,156	
Lubbock Regional	5.30	$299,478	$124.89	$881	
Navarro County	37.70	$61,219	$151.16	$1,155	
Northeast Texas	3.60	$76,754	$91.81	$914	
Nueces County	13.30	$110,252	$52.13	$1,050	
Pecan Valley	N/R	$231,974	$236.47	$1,326	
Permian Basin	2.90	$94,756	$53.41	$902	
Sabine Valley	25.70	$290,383	$69.24	$1,079	
Southeast Texas	2.50	$192,784	$51.71	$959	
Tarrant County	33.70	$283,103	$34.34	$795	
Texas Panhandle	18.40	$304,750	$133.37	$1,168	
Texoma	13.90	$136,949	$89.16	$907	
Tri County	86.90	$165,088	$105.15	$2,706	
Tropical Texas	0.00	$220,055	$66.80	$906	
Wichita Falls	7.40	$218,930	$183.82	$2,305	
Sum	701.30	$7,171,880	$3,612.65	$40,638	(41,379)
Average	21.90 (J)	$210,938	$106.25	$1,195	(1,217)

State Facilities

	(D)				
Austin	16.30	$282,678	N/A	$1,096	
Big Spring	26.30	$285,532	N/A	$1,042	
Kerrville	33.90	$170,990	N/A	$2,758	
Rusk	17.20	$158,301	N/A	$1,092	
San Antonio	43.90	$173,991	N/A	$1,252	
Terrell	30.80	$180,106	N/A	$1,732	
Wichita Falls	3.80	$179,468	N/A	$751	
El Paso	3.60	$36,415	N/A	$1,301	
Laredo	20.60	$91,798	N/A	$574	
Rio Grande	3.00	$39,128	N/A	$1,186	
Sum	199.4	$1,598,407		$12,782	
Average	19.94	$159,841		$1,278	

Source: TDMHMR, 1988b.

170

Who Receives Case Management?

The case management program is intended to serve those individuals who are part of TDMHMR's priority population (Service Groups I-IV) and are most in need of community support in order to live in the community. This does not mean that every person with serious, long-term mental illness receives case management. In order to be referred to case management, clients must meet three requirements (Table 7.6). First, they must meet a chronicity requirement, whereby the client must have a mental disorder (excluding mental retardation only and substance abuse only) of at least two years' duration. Second, they must meet an at-risk for hospitalization criterion whereby their history of hospital and community services is examined. Third, they must demonstrate a need for case management by showing a deficiency in three or more areas considered to be crucial to living in the community. These include, but are not limited to, a lack of basic living skills, housing, employment, and income support.

Clients who meet these three criteria are referred to the case management unit. At this point either the supervisor or the case management team "verifies" their eligibility. It is at this second screening that many patients are deemed ineligible for case management. Of the 6,820 clients referred to case management, 2,274 (33 percent) were admitted to the program, 858 (12.5 percent) were placed on a waiting list, and 3,688 (54 percent) were rejected (TDMHMR, 1988a, Section F, p. 7).

There are currently 1,126 clients on waiting lists for case management; when supervisors were instructed to disregard the lack of resources and estimate the number of additional MH case managers needed to serve those in need, they indicated the need for an additional 188 case managers for FY 1988 (TDMHMR, 1988b, pp. 5, 13). Based on a ratio of 1 to 28, this means that an additional 5,264 clients would receive services. Several case managers and supervisors interviewed for this report expressed the opinion that, but for a lack of resources, most clients referred would be assigned a case manager.

In addition, it should be noted that while an average 9.68 percent of those mental health clients seen by community centers are admitted to case management, this proportion varies a great deal (Table 7.5). For example, the Pecan Valley MHMR Center admitted almost 18 percent of its clients to case management, while the East Texas center (in Tyler) provides fewer than 4 percent of its clients with case management. Nor can this variation be related to differences in the prevalence of serious mental illness; some of the largest urban centers are among those with the lowest proportion of clients admitted to case management.

In addition to the two-thirds of the client population who are referred to case management programs but are either rejected or put on a waiting list, 17 percent of the case management units reported that they were not currently providing case management services to their entire service area. This suggests the existence of a pool of possibly eligible individuals who have never even been assessed for case management (TDMHMR, 1988b, p. 5).

Finally, it should be noted that while the chronicity requirement is currently in effect, there are many clients receiving case management who do not meet this requirement. One Texas study found that, of those discharged from the state hospitals in a one-year period who met the at-risk requirement but failed to meet the chronicity requirement, 13 percent were admitted to case management programs (Ganju, 1988).

Of the 7,716 MH clients who presently receive case management, the majority are part of the intended population; 91 percent of them have been previously admitted to a state hospital; 56 percent have a diagnosis of schizophrenia, and 18 percent have a diagnosis of major affective disorders (Figure 7.1); 26 percent have a chemical abuse

Table 7.6. Mental Health Eligibility Criteria for
Case Management Services

<u>Screening Requirements:</u>

All MH clients in Service Groups I-IV who are not currently assigned to a case management must be screened at least annually for case management services using the MH eligibility criteria for case management. Any client in a state facility who is not currently assigned to as case manager must be screened or rescreened for case management prior to their discharge. Screening is the responsibility of the MH Authority's designated staff unless they have an interagency agreement or contract with the state facility. Designated staff includes such professionals as the client's continuity of services person, liaison staff or primary therapist.

<u>Screening Procedures:</u>

Step I: Determine if the person has a <u>chronic mental disorder</u> or a combination of a chronic mental disorder, substance abuse and/or other disabilities. Chronic mental disorder is defined as any disorder (except mental retardation or substance abuse) or a combination of disorders diagnosable on Axes I or II of the DSM-III-R which is two years duration (or six months duration, if a disorder of infancy, childhood or adolescence.)

Step II: For clients who meet the above definition, determine if <u>one or more of the following</u> applies. The listing below does not imply priority order and includes people of any age group. The client:

1. Has received inpatient* psychiatric treatment on multiple occasions, and/or

2. Has received inpatient* psychiatric treatment requiring continuous care for six months or longer within the last year, and/or

3. Is an identified but unsuccessfully involved recipient of community agencies' services including, but not limited to MHMR. Unsuccessfully involved client is defined as a client whose prescribed treatment and care plan has not resolved the identified problems and the client is high risk for inpatient psychiatric treatment, and/or

4. Has received inpatient* psychiatric treatment in a state hospital, having been involuntarily committed for reasons of dangerous to self or others, within the past six months.

*This term means hospital based inpatient care and mental health treatment services such as emergency or crisis stabilization units, or inpatient hospitalization.

(Continued Next Page)

172

Table 7.6 (Continued). Mental Health Eligibility Criteria for Case Management Services

Step III: Clients who meet the criteria in the Steps I and II <u>must</u> be evaluated for the following functional/skill areas. If they meet <u>three or more</u> of the following criteria of need and require assistance to receive or maintain services in these areas, they should be referred to the case management unit.

1.   Requires help in basic living skills or has severe physical health problems.

2.   Emotional and/or social disabilities consist of severe, persistent problems in functioning in school, work, personal relationships, family roles, and as a member of society.

3.   Basic life support needs such as food and housing are not met or are met only as a result of continuous or intermittent linkages with community support services such as family, social services, SSI, or medication.

4.   Requires public financial assistance for maintenance and is unable to procure financial assistance without help.

5.   Is unemployed or has markedly limited skills in acquiring and maintaining employment.

6.   Exhibits inappropriate social behavior which results in demand for intervention by the mental health and/or law enforcement/judicial system.

7.   Requires community resources which are unavailable.

8.   Other reasons which must be specified when referring.

Referral Procedures:

The person or team referring a client who meets eligibility criteria in above steps 1-3 should identify the specific needs in writing and refer the client to the case management unit.

Case Management Assignment Procedures:

The case management unit supervisor will determine if the client is to be assigned to a case manager or placed on a waiting list if a case manager is not available. When the client is on a case management waiting list, the continuity of services staff person maintains responsibility until the client is assigned to a case manager. If the supervisor determines the client is not in need of case management, the supervisor will return the referral with a written explanation.

Source: TDMHMR, 1988a, Appendix A.

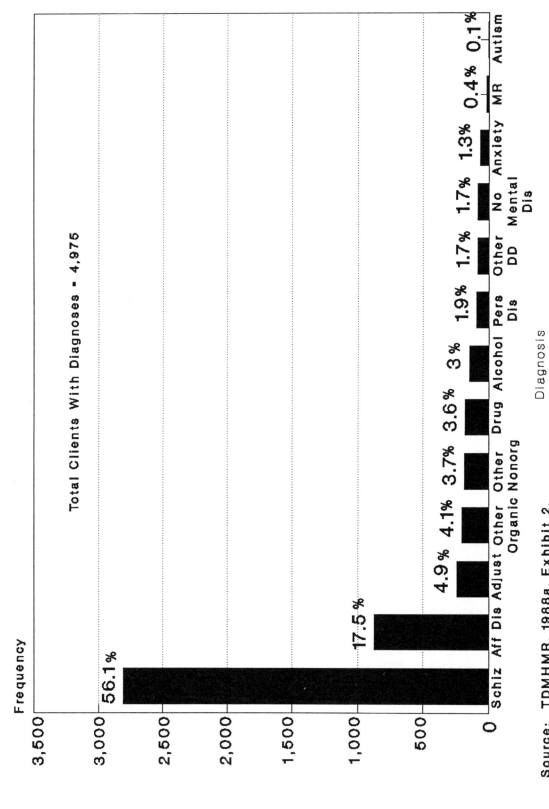

Figure 7.1. Diagnoses of FY 1988 Mental
Health Case Management Clients
with a Diagnosis Report on CARE

Source: TDMHMR, 1988a, Exhibit 2.

problem in addition to their mental disorder; 13 percent have been homeless at least once during the last two years; 80 percent are in Service Groups I through IV, which speaks to their chronicity; and 35 percent of them go well beyond the eligibility requirements (TDMHMR, 1988b, p. 3: Collins, Interview, November 8, 1988b). Thus, those who "win" a place in case management are desperately in need of the service.

Case Management in Action

Once a client enters the program, he or she is assigned a case manager. TDMHMR defines a case manager as a single accountable individual who locates, coordinates, and advocates for services on the client's behalf.

Initially, the case manager performs a life needs assessment for the client (Appendix 7.1), which suggests where the case manager's energies should be directed and whether the client will need high-, moderate-, or low-intensity management.

Usually, the first issue that needs to be addressed is housing. Housing is a particularly difficult problem for these clients, not only because there is a serious housing shortage for persons with serious mental illness in the state, but also because these clients, with their multiple problems, are often ineligible for housing arrangements that require a degree of independence, such as Fairweather Lodges. Housing was listed by case managers as the number one resource needed but unavailable in the community.

The second concern is usually establishing eligibility for income from government programs such as Social Security, SSDI, SSI, AFDC, Veterans' disability payments, Medicaid, and food stamps. This requires establishing and maintaining good relations with other government agencies. Since SSI takes at least three months to obtain, the case manager must find funds for the client in the interim. This calls for creative solutions, and each unit handles the problem differently.

Only a small percentage of clients in case management are considered by staff to be capable of working, but if the client is work-ready, the case manager may find him or her a job. Usually this is at a sheltered workshop. On the rare occasion in which a client is ready for competitive employment, the case manager may work with the Texas Employment Commission.

The case manager, then, is a long-term facilitator. He or she is responsible for connecting clients to the community in which they live and ensuring that the connection remains sound.

Effectiveness of the Case Management Program

Few studies have been done to determine the effectiveness of case management in Texas because of the difficulty of finding a control group. Two studies would indicate that the program is achieving a measure of success. One study showed that individuals who were case managed received more community-based services than did a similar group that was not. Another study, completed by TDMHMR in August 1986, showed that individuals who were assigned a case manager spent 11,664 fewer days in state hospitals than they would have if they had not had a case manager (TDMHMR, 1987b, p. 3).

Despite the dearth of research, there are some agreed-upon attributes that affect the success of case management programs and that can be used as a basis for evaluating the Texas model. The first of these is caseload size. Research shows that 15 to 30 clients is the optimal caseload under normal conditions (Rubin, 1987, p. 10), when case managers have more responsibility, higher-intensity clients, less authority to hold service providers accountable, fewer community resources, or less expertise, the caseload should be lowered (Rubin, 1987, p. 10). The MH caseload ceiling in Texas has been 40 clients; this will be reduced to 35 in FY 1990. The average caseload size is 29, but this average is deceptive. The range is from a low of 14, at Tri County, to a high of 51, at Nueces County (Table 7.5). Fourteen of the 34 centers had average caseloads of more than 30, nine had caseloads of 35 or more, and four had caseloads of 40 or more (Table 7.5). A review of the literature found almost no instances in which caseloads of this size were found to be effective. Furthermore, because of the policy of admitting only the neediest of the needy to case management, case managers in Texas are burdened with an exceptional number of high-intensity clients.

Another factor that affects success is the quantity and quality of community resources. In general, those studies showing the effectiveness of case management were done in a context of relatively comprehensive, well-funded community support systems (Rubin, 1987, p. 12). When case managers in Texas were asked to evaluate the effectiveness of the case management service, the area they rated as least effective was in developing community resources to meet client needs (TDMHMR, 1988b, p. 12).

Case managers identified the top three services needed but unavailable in the community as housing, day activity/social programs, and crisis stabilization services (TDMHMR, 1988b, p. 4). The budget for case management is expected to more than double in the next three years, and 8,000 to 10,000 more clients are expected to be served. These additional clients will drive the need for community resources even higher. Community resources must expand hand in hand with case management.

A third attribute affecting success is program continuity. Continuity has two aspects, the first of which is continuity of care from the case manager. In order for the program to achieve its ultimate goal of moving the client toward reasonable independence, there must be a long-term relationship between the case manager and the client. Yet, in Texas, the turnover rate for case managers (MH and MR) is 37 percent a year, significantly higher than the 22 percent turnover rate for that of the entire system (TDMHMR, 1988b, p. 7). It is not meaningful to talk about long-term case management while the case manager turnover rate is this high. The high turnover rate not only significantly increases costs, it also disrupts the client's progress toward independent living. To get at the root of this high turnover, TDMHMR surveyed case managers for sources of stress. The top five sources of stress reported by case managers were inadequate salary, paperwork overload, lack of resources, large caseloads, and personal transportation expenses.

The typical case manager is between the ages of 25 and 49, is college educated (79 percent), and has 4.1 years of experience in case management or related areas. Yet 77 percent of all case managers make below $19,403 per year (TDMHMR, 1988a, Section E, p. 5). This salary is far too low to retain the best and the most experienced case managers.

Paperwork overload is not only a source of stress for case managers in itself, but it also reduces the time they can spend with clients and service providers. It may be caused by unnecessary or duplicative paperwork and/or lack of clerical support. The first problem should be examined in TDMHMR's next survey of case managers. As for the lack of clerical support, there are 46 positions listed as clerical support for the 326 case managers and supervisors, a ratio of 1 to 7. Fifteen units have no clerical support at all (TDMHMR, 1988a, Appendix D).

The size of a case manager's caseload seems to have a significant effect on turnover rates. TDMHMR conducted a stress survey of case managers in March of 1988 which showed that the turnover rate among MH case managers increased as the MH caseload size increased (TDMHMR, 1988b, p. 7).

176

One indirect measure of the length of time clients remain in case management is the annual discharge rate, the annual rate at which clients are discharged from a particular case management unit. The Texas MH case management program has an average annual discharge rate of 23 percent at community centers and 20 percent at facilities (TDMHMR, 1988b, Appendix B), compared with 6 percent and 4 percent discharge rates for the MR program. But 26 percent of the facilities are discharging more than a third of their clients per year and 12 percent have a discharge rate above 50 percent (Table 7.5).

Finally, examining the effectiveness of the program for those who are in it is only half the story. Of equal importance is how effective the program is at providing services to all of the priority population who need them and would benefit from them. In this area, the Texas program is clearly deficient. Some parts of the priority population are not even assessed for case management. Of those who are evaluated and referred, more than half are turned away and others are placed on the waiting list. Thus, there remains a large unserved population.

Future Changes in Texas Case Management

There are several changes in the Texas case management program that are either being contemplated or actively pursued; if implemented, they will have a direct impact on the program. The first of these will affect who will receive case management. Since at least its tenth report to the court, the R. A. J. Review Panel has been expressing its concern that the chronicity requirement is denying case management to some acutely ill individuals who are at serious risk for hospitalization. The panel has asked TDMHMR to abandon its chronicity requirement. This change has been accepted and became effective in September 1989. TDMHMR has studied the likely impact of this change and has concluded that the number of persons who might be eligible for case management will expand by 9 to 22 percent, with a figure closer to the lower end more likely (Ganju, 1988). Case management costs are projected to increase by 10 to 25 percent (again with a proportion of 10 percent being more realistic).

This is likely to have an impact on the number of persons with serious and long-term mental illness who will receive case management. Presently only 21 percent of persons with chronic mental illness discharged from the hospitals and at risk for rehospitalization are receiving case management. If the funds requested through 1991 are available, this percentage should rise dramatically. But if those funds are not appropriated or if a significant portion of those funds is used to meet this change in criteria, with more acute, nonchronic clients being admitted to case management, the proportion of persons with long-term mental illness admitted to case management will remain low.

Another change that has affected the accuracy of data collected by TDMHMR about the individual case management units is the CARE system. In the past, the only way of collecting data from the individual units about caseload sizes, clients being served, and their profiles was through survey instruments sent directly to the local units. When the CARE system is fully hooked up to the case management units, information should become more consistent and accurate and clients can be tracked to determine recidivism rates and other information.

Another change expected within the next two years is the advent of an expert system for case management. An expert system is a computer program that attempts to replicate the decision-making and problem-solving functions of knowledgeable and effective experts. An expert system is being developed for case management to help screeners to determine whether a client is eligible for case management and to walk them through a detailed needs assessment. This will promote greater uniformity in program admissions and better tracking. With the expert system in place, for instance, it will be easier to differentiate between those clients rejected for service because they are ineligible and those who are rejected simply because there is no room for them. There are likely to be many changes in the next few years, but these three are the most imminent.

EXPANSION OF THE TEXAS MEDICAID PLAN TO INCLUDE CASE MANAGEMENT

The expansion of Medicaid to cover the costs of targeted case management services was added to Section 1915(g), Title XIX, of the Social Security Act with the passage of the Consolidated Omnibus Budget Reconciliation Act of 1985. The ability of the states to work with this option was facilitated with the passage of Section 4118(i) of PL 100-203, part of the Omnibus Budget Reconciliation Act of 1987, which allows states to limit the providers of case management to the state mental health authority (TDMHMR, 1989, p. 4). This change in policy arose out of the dissatisfaction with the Home and Community Based Waiver (2176 waiver) program passed with the Omnibus Budget Reconciliation Act of 1981. The waiver, which included case management services, offered under this act proved to be increasingly restrictive, difficult to administer, and ineffective. As stated in recommendations from Touche-Ross to TDMHMR, "HCFA's [Health Care Financing Administration] dealings with other states suggest that the waiver application process could be a lengthy one with no guarantees of success" (Touche-Ross & Co., April 1987, p. 78). Because of these changes in Title XIX of the Social Security Act, case management can now be included as an optional service in a state's Medicaid plan.

Limitations to Reimbursement

In Texas, the target populations chosen for coverage under the case management option, along with persons with mental retardation, are persons who are Medicaid-eligible and who have a chronic mental disorder or a combination of chronic disorders and are at risk of long-term institutionalization (TDMHMR, 1989).

Many of the current duties of a case manager would be eligible for Medicaid reimbursement. It should be noted that since the mental health portion of the proposed amendment to the Texas Medicaid plan has not yet been approved by HCFA, some revisions in the definition of reimbursable activities may occur. The current draft of the state plan amendment includes the following reimbursable activities: Case Management Intake; Crisis Intervention; Comprehensive Assessment; Service Planning; Monitoring/Advocacy; Reassessment; and Staff Consultation (TDMHMR, 1989, pp. 1a-1c).

There are several services performed by case managers which would not be reimbursable under the new Medicaid option. These services include (1) outreach activities that are designed to locate individuals who are potentially eligible for Medicaid and (2) any medical evaluation, examination, or treatment that is already billable as a distinct Medicaid-covered benefit; however, referral arrangements and staff consultation for such services are reimbursable as a case management service (TDMHMR, 1989).

Even with the limitations on reimbursable activities, this new option could significantly increase funds so as to expand the availability of case management to those who are most in need. The process which states must follow to receive HCFA approval to add this option to a state Medicaid plan is outlined below.

State Medicaid Plan Amendment Process

If a state wishes to include this option in its state Medicaid plan, it must submit a state Medicaid plan amendment to HCFA for approval. Only after the amendment is approved by HCFA can optional services be eligible for Medicaid reimbursement. A state's proposal to HCFA must contain specific information in the following areas:

Target Group. A state must specify the target group that would be eligible to receive case management services. The group may be identified by age, type, or degree of disability, illness, or other conditions "or any other identifiable characteristic or combination thereof." A separate amendment must be submitted for each target group. The law places no limit on the number of target groups which may receive case management services, or on the number of recipients included in any particular target group.

Comparability. A state must invoke Section 1915(g)(1) of the Act (regarding the provision of services on a non-comparable basis), unless it intends to furnish case management services in the same amount, duration, and scope to all eligible Medicaid recipients.

Statewide Availability. A state must indicate whether case management services would be made available to all members of the target group in the state, or alternatively, if such services will be offered on less than a statewide basis. If the latter option is selected, the state must invoke Section 1915(g)(1) of the Act and specify those geographic areas or political jurisdictions in which such services would be available.

Freedom of Choice. A state must give assurances that case management services would be provided in accordance with the requirements of Section 1902(a)(23) of the Act, which specifies that no restrictions may be placed on a recipient's free choice of providers. In order to meet this statutory requirement, a state must provide assurance to HCFA that: (a) no Medicaid recipient would be forced to receive case management services; (b) each recipient would be free to receive case management services from any qualified provider (e.g., a recipient may not be limited to services provided by a designated county agency or clinic, even if he or she receives all other services from this provider); (c) any individual or entity meeting state standards for the provision of case management would be given the opportunity to qualify as a Medicaid provider of such services; and (d) case management services would not be used to restrict any individual's access to other state plan services. This last point in the guidelines does not take into account an amendment included in the 1987 Reconciliation Act (P.L. 100-203), which authorizes states to restrict the number and type of case management providers in any given geographic area of the state when it elects to provide such services to persons who are developmentally disabled or mentally ill.

Provider Qualifications. A state must specify the minimum standard it would use to govern the provision of case management services. Provider qualifications must be " . . . reasonably related to the case management functions that a provider would be expected to perform". Providers may not be " . . . arbitrarily limited . . . to state or other public agencies"; instead, any person or entity that meets the qualification standards must be permitted to act as a provider of case management services. In addition, a " . . . client may not be prohibited from receiving case management services

179

from a qualified provider in a locality other than that in which he or she resides."

Nonduplication of Payments. "Payments for case management services under Section 1915(g) may not duplicate payments made to public agencies or private entities under other program authorities for the same purpose." In addition, "separate payment cannot be made for case management-type services which are an integral and inseparable part of another Medicaid covered service." A state, therefore, must "differentiate case management services . . . from other Medicaid services and from case management activities which are necessary for the proper and efficient administration of the State plan."

Other Medicaid Services. The cost of any necessary physical or psychological examinations/evaluations should be billed under the appropriate Medicaid service category, rather than as part of the cost of providing case management services. In addition, service referrals may be treated as a component of case management services for billing purposes, but the actual provision of services is not to be treated as a billable case management cost.

Referral for Treatment. When a Medicaid eligible client is found to require medical treatment or referral, the arrangements for such treatment are an allowable case management cost, but the actual treatment is not.

Administrative Activities. Activities associated with administering the state Medicaid plan may not be treated as case management costs, including costs related to: (a) determination/redetermination of Medicaid eligibility; (b) Medicaid intake services; (c) Medicaid preadmission screening; (d) prior authorization for Medicaid services; (e) Medicaid utilization review; (f) EPSDT administration; and (g) activities in connection with "lock-in" provisions under Section 1915(a) of the Act.

Institutional Discharge Planning. For all skilled nursing facilities (SNFs), intermediate care facilities (ICFs), and intermediate care facilities/mental retardation(ICF-MR) providers, discharge planning is a required condition for receipt of Medicaid payment; therefore, such costs cannot be billed separately as targeted case management services.

Client Outreach. Efforts to identify and contact potential recipients do not constitute a billable case manager service. Such outreach activities may be considered necessary for the proper and efficient administration of the state Medicaid plan. If so, Federal Fund Participation must be claimed at the administrative rate (i.e. 50 percent).

Payment Methodology. A state must specify the methodology it will use to establish case management payment rates.

Documentation of Claims. A state must be prepared to fully document all claims for case management reimbursement at the federal medical assistance program (FMAP) rate. Unless a state pays for such services under a capitation or prepaid health plan arrangement, it must be able to document: (a) the date of service provision; (b) the name of the recipient; (c) the name of the provider agency and the person providing the service; (d) the nature, extent, or units of service provided; (e) the place of service. A state may document case management claims at the administrative rate through the use of time studies, random motion studies, or cost allocation plans when such services are performed as part of administration of the state plan, but this type of documentation will not be considered sufficient support of case management claims under Section 1919(g) or 1905(a)(19) of the Act. (NASMRPD, 1987, pp. 3-6)

It is important to note that HCFA has not expected a large number of states to target persons with serious mental illness under this option. "The CBO [Congressional Budget Office] expected this option to have a zero dollar impact on Medicaid expenditures. If in fact this option is pursued in a big way [by the states], we can expect strict regulatory and legislative restriction" (Toff, December 1987, p. 1-6).

HCFA approved Texas' state plan amendment to add targeted case management of the chronically mentally ill as of March 12, 1990. TDMHMR is now billing back to July of 1989 for reimbursement of case management services (Dittmar, Interview, May 14, 1990a) Texas is planning to bill Medicaid on a "per-client contact" basis. Every time that a case manager has some kind of contact with a client, no matter the length or substance of the contact, Medicaid will be billed. The per-client contact payment for mental health case management is $31 for a personal contact and $11 for a telephone contact (Dittmar, Interview, January 12, 1990b).

TDMHMR would use existing state funds to "soft-match" federal dollars available for case management. In FY 1989, $9.7 million was budgeted for mental health case management services. For FY 1990, the very earliest that Medicaid funds for case management services could start coming into the state, TDMHMR requested $14.5 million (TDMHMR, 1988b).

By using the "soft-match" approach to Federal Fund Participation, state funds would be reallocated from existing, fully funded state/local case management programs and used as match funds under the new Medicaid option. Most states using this approach have reallocated funds for services that are similar, or identical to, the new or expanded Medicaid services (NASMRPD, 1986, p. 33). Current estimates by TDMHMR indicate that 55 percent of clients currently receiving case management are Medicaid-eligible (Collins, Interview, November 8, 1988b). This could mean an extremely significant increase in funds for case management services.

Potential Benefits for Case Management

There are several potential benefits as a result of the projected increase in funds for case management services: (1) an increase in services to individuals currently eligible for case management but presently on waiting lists; (2) provision of a better case manager to clerical staff ratio; (3) an increase in the salaries of case managers; and (4) reduction of the caseloads of the case managers who have maximum caseloads (Collins, Interview, November 8, 1988b; Collins, 1989b).

Currently, the ratio of case managers and supervisors to clerical staff is approximately 7 to 1 (582 to 81). The ratio of case managers to clerical staff expressed as ideal by Janet Collins is 3 to 1. It is also felt that there should be a 30 to 50 percent increase in the number of case managers in order to serve the needs of the client populations adequately (Collins, Interview, November 8, 1988b). This would mean an increase in the number of case managers from 582 to between 656 and 873, and a corresponding increase in the number of clerical staff from 81 to between 219 and 291, or a 170 to 260 percent increase in clerical staff. This would free the case managers to do more duties directly associated with serving clients instead of spending a significant of time with routine record keeping. Expansion of Medicaid to case management would further increase the amount of paper work required of the case managers, which serves to emphasize the need for a better ratio of case managers to clerical staff.

The current pay structure was listed as the primary source of stress among case managers. As pointed out in the previous section, in order to increase job satisfaction and decrease turnover, higher salaries for case managers are needed. With current restrictions in state funding, the most promising way for TDMHMR to increase salaries is with new Medicaid funds. Salaries would need to be increased from pay groups 9 through 14 to groups 12 through 18 (Collins, Interview, November 8, 1988a). This would mean an increase in yearly salary ranges from between $16,332 and $21,132 to between $19,788 and $30,336 (Collins, Interview, June 26, 1989a).

The third goal is to lower the caseload size. The maximum caseload size has been 40, to be reduced to 35 in FY 1990. Many case managers believe that this should be further reduced to 28 to 30 clients (Collins, Interview, November 7, 1988a). Expansion of Medicaid for case management is expected to increase the total number of people served by approximately 60 percent, from 7,816 to about 12,500. As stated above, the projected increase in the number of case managers is going to be only 30 to 50 percent (Collins, Interview, November 7, 1988a). This would ultimately mean an increase in caseload size unless the number of case managers is increased to an even higher number. However, because of the projected increase in clerical staff, case managers would be relieved of much of the paperwork duties, leaving more time to devote to clients.

The projected 60 percent increase in clients to be served is derived from (1) the number of clients who are currently on waiting lists, although not all community centers keep formal waiting lists, and (2) the estimated number of persons with serious mental illness that case managers and supervisors think could be served if adequate funding were available. The reason for not projecting a greater increase in clients to be served is that the eligibility requirements for case management would not be changed. The same priority population would still be served.

CONCLUSIONS

Because outreach activities are not eligible for Medicaid reimbursement, clients would be referred from most of the same sources that they are referred from now. However, case managers would be better able to serve those who are admitted to case management. With targeted case management, this can be done with smaller waiting lists and with greater efficiency.

Approval of the addition of targeted case management to the state Medicaid plan means that critically needed new funds would be available. However, in these times of fiscal stress in Texas, there is the possibility that future Texas legislatures could use the increase in federal funds as a reason to reduce the level of state funding for case management services. This could potentially take case management back to where it started: underfunded, understaffed, and incomplete.

The changes that could be brought about by this option could significantly improve the ability of the case managers to serve persons with serious mental illness. However, as has been discussed earlier in this section, if this Medicaid option is over-utilized by the states, it could face severe cutbacks in scope and promise.

Appendix 7.1. Case Management Assessment Form

DATE_____MHMR#_____ASH#_____SEX_____ETHNICITY_____

NAME_____D.O.B._____SS#_____

ADDRESS_____
   Street   City   State   Zip Code

PHONE_____   _____   _____
   Home   Work   Other (specify)

NEXT OF KIN_____ PHONE_____

   ADDRESS_____

REFERRAL SOURCE_____PRIMARY OPC_____

                        CASEWORKER_____

REASONS FOR REFERRAL TO C.M./PRESENTING PROBLEM:

PSYCHIATRIC HISTORY FOR THE PAST YEAR (include dates & locations of past treatment):

Present Medication

Present Diagnosis

Suicidal/Homicidal Ideations

Pattern of Violent Behavior (specify events)

(Continued Next Page)

183

Appendix 7.1 (Continued). Case Management Assessment Form

Client Name_____ Client#_____

DESCRIBE PRESENT STATUS OF CLIENT IN RELATION TO EACH AREA LISTED BELOW:

Primary Support System

Financial Resources (Source/Amount)

Ability to Access Social Agencies

Social/Recreational

Food/Clothing

Drug/Alcohol Issues

Employment History and Current Status

Current Housing Situation (include trends, if any, that seem to result in losing placements

(Continued Next Page)

Client Name_____ Client #_____ Medical Needs

Educational History & Current Needs (if any)

Transportation Needs (include ability to access transportations systems)

Medication/Non-Compliance

Emotional Issues

Community Living Skills (i.e. cooking, laundry)

Strengths

Weaknesses

Comments

STAFF MEMBER COMPLETING ASSESSMENT_____DATE_____

STAFFING   Level of Difficulty   1   2   3   (circle one) 1 = high
                                                                                2 = medium
____Waiting List   3 = low

____Rejected

____Assigned Case Manager

                    _____ DATE_____
                              signature
                    _____ DATE_____
                              signature

(Continued Next Page)

185

Departmental Requirements

Client exhibits problem behavior or emotional disturbance which interferes significantly with daily living or training activities.	1
Client exhibits problem behaviors which interfere partially with daily living or training.	2
Client occasionally exhibits problem behaviors or emotional distrubances which can be modified in the course of routine activities.	3
Client exhibits no problem behaviors or emotional disturbances which interfere with daily living or training.	4

*PRIMARY SUPPORT SYSTEMS

Client has no effective system of primary emotional support. Active intervention must occur to develop system. Client is socially isolated.	1
Client has minimal system of primary emotional support. Client is partially isolated but system can be maintained or developed with intervention to prevent isolation.	2
Client has semi-permanent system of emotional support. Guidance can remediate occasional difficulties with support system.	3
Client has stable, optimal system of long-term primary emotional support.	4

*STABILITY OF LIVING ENVIRONMENT

Client can no longer be maintained in present living environment.	1
Living environment in crisis. Special intervention with client and/or environmental system must occur in order for client to be maintained in environment.	2
Difficulties occasionally arise. Intervention with client and/or environmental system must occur to prevent environmental difficulties.	3
Living environment is stable and optimal for long-term maintenance of client.	4

*HEALTH/PHYSICAL

Client has medical problems, physical constraint or sensory deficit which totally interferes with participation in activities.	1
Client has medical problems, physical constraint or sensory deficit which interferes significantly in activities.	2
Client has medical problems, physical constraint or sensory deficit which interferes minimally with participation in activities.	3
Client in good health; any existing physical constraints do not interfere with participation in activities.	4

*VOCATIONAL

Client can no longer be maintained in work area/currently unemployed.	1
Work context in crisis. Special intervention with client or work system must occur for client to be maintained in work situation.	2
Difficulties occasionally arise in work situation. Intervention must occur in these instances to prevent crisis.	3
Work situation stable, optimal for long-term employment of client (infants, retired, housewives included at this level) or client does not require employment at this time.	4

MEDICATION

Client does not have the ability to self medicate. Is non-complient or supervision required.	1
Client can self medicate with guidance.	2
Client can medicate independently as needed but cannot order his medication.	3
Client can medicate independently as needed and order his medication or medication is not needed.	4

KNOWLEDGE OF COMMUNITY AND COMMUNITY RESOURCES

Client is unable to process social servies within the community.	1
Client has minimal knowledge of other agency services.	2
Client is able to process social services with help.	3
Client is able to utilize other social service agencies without help.	4
	TOTAL CIRCLED #'s

CASEMANAGEMENT LEVEL RATING

Instructions: If the client receives a 1 in two of the #'ed areas above, a rating of HIGH INTENSITY will <u>automatically</u> be assigned. otherwise use the ranges specified below to rate the client's casemanagement level.

_____HIGH INTENSITY (7-14)   _____MODERATE INTENSITY (15-21)   _____LOW INTENSITY (22-28)

CIRCLED #'S   Tot:

Source: TDMHMR, 1988c.

References

Borland, Andrew, John McRae, and Cecile Lycan. 1989. "Outcomes of Five Years of Continuous Intensive Case Management." Hospital and Community Psychiatry, vol. 40, no. 4 (April).

Collins, Janet. 1988a. Director, Case Management Services, Texas Department of Mental Health and Mental Retardation, Austin, Texas. Interview by Nicholas Hoover, November 7.

_____. 1988b. Director, Case Management Services, Texas Department of Mental Health and Mental Retardation, Austin, Texas. Interview by Ly Griffin, Nicholas Hoover, and Lynn Parish, November 8.

_____. 1988c. Director, Case Management Services, Texas Department of Mental Health and Mental Retardation, Austin, Texas. Telephone interview by Nicholas Hoover, November 17.

_____. 1989a. Director, Case Management Services, Texas Department of Mental Health and Mental Retardation, Austin, Texas. Telephone interview by Nicholas Hoover, June 26.

_____. 1989b. Director, Case Management Services, Texas Department of Mental Health and Mental Retardation, Austin, Texas. Critique of draft, July 5.

Dittmar, Nancy. 1990a. Director, Special Programs, Texas Department of Mental Health and Mental Retardation, Austin, Texas. Telephone interview with Nicholas Hoover, May 14.

_____. 1990b. Director, Special Programs, Texas Department of Mental Health and Mental Retardation, Austin, Texas. Telephone interview with Nicholas Hoover, January 12.

Ganju, Vijay. 1988. An Analysis of Changes in Case Management Eligibility Criteria. Austin, Texas: Office of Strategic Planning, Texas Department of Mental Health and Mental Retardation.

Gill, John. 1989. Director, Adult Mental Health Services, Dallas County MHMR, Dallas, Texas. Telephone interview by Lynn Parish, April 24.

Intagliata, James. 1982. "Improving the Quality of Community Care for the Chronically Mentally Disabled: The Role of Case Management." Schizophrenia Bulletin, vol. 8, no. 4. (Winter).

Levine, Irene Shiflen, and Mary Fleming. May 1986. Human Resources Development: Issues in Case Management. University of Maryland: Center of Rehabilitation and Manpower Services.

Montana Department of Institutions (MDI). September 1982. A Study of Case Management Practices in Community Mental Health Centers. Final Report. Helena, Montana.

National Association of State Mental Retardation Program Directors (NASMRPD). 1986. Intelligence Report, Bulletin No. 88-16. Alexandria, Virginia.

Roberts, Chuck. 1988a. Budget Analyst; Management, Analysis, and Reporting Unit, Texas Department of Mental Health and Mental Retardation, Austin, Texas. Telephone interview by Lynn Parish. November 18.

_____. 1988b. Letter to Lynn Parish, December 8.

Robinson, Gail K., and Gail Toff Bergman. March 1989. "Section 1: Choices in Case Management: Summary Report." In Choices in Case Management: A Review of Current Knowledge and Practice for Mental Health Programs. Contract no. 278-87-0026 (PA). Washington, D.C.: National Institute of Mental Health.

Rubin, Allen. 1987. "Case Management: A Viable Concept?" University of Texas at Austin, School of Social Work. (Manuscript).

Russell, Rush. 1989. Revenue Officer, Texas Department of Mental Health and Mental Retardation, Austin, Texas. "Case Management Medicaid Workshop," Austin, Texas. (June 12.)

Texas Department of Mental Health and Mental Retardation (TDMHMR). 1987a. Case Management Manpower Report. Austin, Texas.

_____. 1987b. Texas Case Management. Austin, Texas: (Handout.)

_____. 1988a. "Evaluation for Fiscal Year 1988." Austin, Texas. (Draft.)

_____. 1988b. Case Management Six Month Status Report, September 1, 1987-February 28, 1988. Austin, Texas. (October 4.)

_____. 1988c. "Case Management Assessment Form." Austin, Texas.

_____. 1989. "Case Management and Medicaid in Texas." Austin, Texas (Handout).

Toff, Gail E. December 1987. "Financing Mental Health Services under Medicaid: Proceedings from a Roundtable on Mental Health Policy Issues." Washington, D.C.: Intergovernmental Health and Policy Project, The George Washington University.

Touche Ross and Company. April 1987. "Final Report on Review of Opportunities for Prospective Medicaid Funding for Mental Health and Mental Retardation Services in Texas." Austin, Texas: Texas Department of Mental Health and Mental Retardation.

Chapter 8. Family Support Services[*]

In 1979 the family advocacy movement was organized into the National Alliance for the Mentally Ill (NAMI). The following decade witnessed dramatic changes in understanding the dimensions of need among those who are chronically mentally ill and among those whose lives are most affected: their families. A major catalyst was the phenomenal growth of the family movement. In 1986, NAMI reported 650 affiliate groups; by 1987, NAMI reported that a new affiliate group was formed every 36 hours. The mental health system began to view the needs of family members as legitimate and enduring system concerns (Bachrach, 1987, p. 459).

THE ECONOMIC BURDEN ON FAMILIES

Studies by Hoenig and Hamilton indicated that of the participating families of persons with serious mental illness, 30 percent reported their financial status had deteriorated and 7 percent reported lost earnings (Hoenig and Hamilton, 1969). Measures of economic burden have been included in recent studies but have not been gathered in a systematic manner. In their random sample of relatives of patients being discharged from three state hospitals, Thompson and Doll found that 38 percent reported feeling a financial burden (Thompson and Doll, 1982). Holden and Lewine reported that 32 percent of NAMI members surveyed said that their economic problems were "serious" and, in all, 74 percent of their sample reported being affected financially by the mental illness (Holden and Lewine, 1982).

Hatfield's study of families found that 18 percent wanted some type of financial assistance to ease the financial burden (Hatfield, 1979). In 1984, Lefley surveyed those who had a mentally ill family member and attempted to make an estimate of the costs for hospitalization and treatment not covered by insurance. Estimates ranged from $300 to $150,000 with a mean of $44,080 (Lefley, August 1984). An apparent problem with the survey was that many people did not respond with a dollar figure but simply indicated it cost a "great deal." It also appears that the estimates given greatly underestimate the actual cost of caring for a mentally ill person, considering that only hospitalization and treatment costs were included in the estimates. The estimates did not include costs such as attorneys' fees for getting the person out of jail, airline tickets used to bring the person back home, food, clothing, and alternate housing.

It is evident from these surveys that families of persons with serious mental illness suffer a financial burden, but a definitive analysis of the actual financial burden of mental illness on families has not been done. The extent of the burden depends on many factors, including whether the mentally ill person is the primary wage earner, whether extensive community assistance is available, and the overall financial condition of the family.

LEGISLATIVE MANDATE FOR FAMILY SUPPORT SERVICES

Senate Bill 633, passed in 1985, mandated that "family support services, including respite care," be available to residents in each of the local service areas throughout the state. The official TDMHMR definition of family support services is that they "provide support and counseling to a client's family members through sponsoring advocacy meetings, self-help groups for family members, and counseling. All of the these activities promote improved coping and problem solving skills on the part of the family and the client; strengthen constructive bonding within the family; and, provide the opportunity for sharing of emotional support among families" (TDMHMR, 1987).

---

[*]This chapter was written by Timothy J. Tompkins.

In the field of mental health, both nationally and in Texas, family support services, other than mutual support groups, are not widely available. Nationwide it is estimated that 40 percent of individuals with long-term mental illnesses reside with their families. Torrey and Wolfe estimate as many as 64,000 families in Texas may need some form of family support services (Torrey and Wolfe, 1986).

The TDMHMR budget category for Family Support Services includes family support programs, in-home respite care, and the HB 1154 in-home and family support program. In FY 1988, a grand total of $9,855,830 was budgeted for family support programs across the state, or 57 cents per capita. Forty percent of these funds came from sources other than contracts for services and R. A. J. funds.

FAMILY SUPPORT: A MODEL PROGRAM

Family support programs are as diverse as the communities they serve. The model program described below illustrates the variety of services and activities that can be included.

In 1986, a local family needs assessment was conducted by the Austin-Travis County MHMR Center to identify the needs of family members of persons with serious, long-term mental illness. A number of needs were identified; the following list of needs is ranked in order of frequency with which they were identified and by the emphasis placed on them by the respondents:

1. Information/Education - Almost everyone identified family education about mental illness as an important need. Families feel uninformed and frequently have difficulty getting information from mental health professionals. Without information and knowledge, the families are unable to properly assist in the treatment and recovery of their mentally ill family member.

2. Mutual Support Family members feel alone, isolated, discouraged, depressed, embarrassed, guilty, and stigmatized. They have a need to know that they are not alone, to learn from each other, and to gain support, acceptance, and encouragement from each other.

3. Strategies for Handling Mentally Ill Family Members -They want to know how to deal with lack of motivation, social withdrawal, carelessness, and aggression. They are frustrated with the lack of daily living skills and self-care skills and need to be aware of effective strategies for handling these problems.

4. Treatment/Discharge Planning - Families are frequently left out of both treatment planning and discharge planning even when the client or patient is living at home or will return home after discharge from the hospital. The families feel a lack of value when treated in this manner by the mental health professionals.

5. Residential Placement - This is vital for mentally ill family members when families are unable or unwilling to provide placement, especially following discharge from the hospital.

6. Job Placement and Job Training - Families expressed approval of the Fairweather program but wanted other kinds of job training and placement to be available since many family members are capable of doing more than janitorial work.

190

7. Hope - Family members commonly feel depressed, discouraged, devastated, hopeless and guilty, and they need counselling and other professional support to help them deal with these feelings.

8. Advocacy - Many family members have found an outlet for their needs and emotions through the Austin Alliance for the Mentally Ill. There needs to be more support for such groups to assist the family.

9. Treatment Programs for Dual-Diagnoses - The young mentally ill are increasingly involved with alcohol and other drugs and need unified programs that will treat both.

10. In-Home Care - Expressed needs ranged from occasional, brief services to brief, live-in services, to ongoing, several hours weekly services.

11. Education/Support Groups for Children and Adolescents The children and siblings of the mentally ill have their own set of problems which need to be addressed and separate groups should be available to them.

12. Family Education Groups for Affective Disorders Most identified needs addressed the schizophrenic disorders, but there are also the same needs for families of the depressed or manic persons. (ATCMHMRC, n.d., pp. 2-3).

With this information, the staff developed the specific goals and objectives for this model of the Austin MH Family Support Program, which is considered one of the best in the state. The overall goal of the Family Support Program is to provide support and education to the families, thereby improving their lives and increasing their ability to cope with mental illness in the family. There is now a strong body of research which indicates that an effective family support program not only improves the families' lives, but also significantly reduces the recidivism rate of the family member with serious mental illness. These programs can ease the costs incurred by both families and providers.

The Austin MH Family Support Program provides a variety of services and activities designed to fulfill the objectives listed above. These services include Family Education Groups; an Alumni Group; a Family Education Handbook; an Open Forum; Family Consultations; In-Home Family Respite Care; Client Group Therapy; Clinical Staff Training; and Advocacy services.

The program has proven to be quite successful given the diversity of services offered. According to the staff, there has been particular success and praise for the Family Education Groups and Family Consultation services. These give the families the opportunity to learn more and be able to talk openly about the problems.

RESPITE CARE

Respite care is a relatively new concept that grew out of the national movement in the 1970s to deinstitutionalize and provide treatment settings for disabled persons which are the least restrictive and which most closely resemble normal community living. The main purpose of respite care is to provide families with the opportunity to get away for an evening, a weekend, or several days or to provide backup to families in emergency situations, such as the illness or hospitalization of the primary caretaker or the death or serious illness of another family member which requires the attention of the caretaker.

TDMHMR defines three types of respite care; none of the three types is identified as a required, core service. The first type, in-home respite care, is included under Family Support Services. In-home respite is defined as those services which "include home health aid, homemaker, and supervision services for a mentally disabled individual in his or her mutual or surrogate family home during the day to allow the caretaker(s) to be absent to conduct necessary and normal personal tasks, or overnight and/or weekends in order to provide a period of relief" (TDMHMR, 1987, p. 13).

Two other types of respite programs are listed under TDMHMR's Residential Services category. Brief Respite Foster Care is defined as a supervised program "designed to offer support and relief to the family or usual caretaker(s) through 24-hour supervision of the client outside of his or her own home on a non-crisis basis, i.e., when the client is not exhibiting a psychiatric crisis which presents a possible danger to self or others. The foster care respite provider is unrelated to the client and typically takes care for 24 or more consecutive hours. 24-hour awake supervision is not typically required but could be provided as needed" (TDMHMR, 1987, p. 5).

The third type of respite care defined is Residential Respite during Periods of Client Stress. TDMHMR defines this as a program which "allows the client to reside, temporarily, in a more restrictive residential environment that he or she has been accustomed to during periods of stress which could lead to a state of psychiatric crisis. The program allows the client to re-integrate and stabilize quickly in any appropriate moderately to mildly structured residential setting and is typically based is a small group home setting of 2 to 8 clients" (TDMHMR, 1987, p. 5).

In FY 1988, $26,798 was budgeted statewide for in-home respite care; $61,851 for brief respite foster care; and $652,757 for respite care during client stress. Information about the types and numbers of persons served in these programs is not centrally collected. It is evident that respite care programs are not uniformly available throughout the state.

CONCLUSIONS

Since there are not enough staff or program resources to serve all the needs of persons with serious mental illness, it is especially important that the families are viewed as allies, rather than as adversaries, in the treatment process. Many professionals do encounter families whose actions are contrary to their treatment interventions and who therefore prove detrimental to their efforts. However, in most cases this negative contribution from the family is a result of ignorance and not of calculated intent.

Since very few people know anything about mental illness until they are faced with it, families cannot be expected to know what to do and what not to do in response to their mentally ill family member. However, education alone is not enough. Families need active, ongoing support from mental health professionals and other families in order to best cope with, and help, their mentally ill member. Therefore, it is essential that the mental health system be available to the families in a substantive fashion.

References

Austin-Travis County Mental Health and Mental Retardation Center (ATCMHMRC). n.d. "Mental Health Family Support Program." Austin, Texas.

Bachrach, Leona. 1987. "Family Support Programs in a Regional Mental Health System." Hospital and Community Psychiatry, vol. 38, no. 5 (May).

Hatfield, A. B. 1979. "Help-Seeking Behavior in Families of Schizophrenics." American Journal of Community Psychology, vol. 7, (October).

Hoenig, J., and M. Hamilton. 1969. The Desegregation of the Mentally Ill. London: Routledge and Kegan Paul.

Holden, D. F., and R. R. J. Lewine. 1982. "How Families Evaluate Mental Health Professionals, Resources, and Effects of Illness." Schizophrenia Bulletin, vol. 8 (December).

Lefley, H. P. August 1984. "Practitioners with Mentally Ill Relatives: A View from the Bridge." Paper presented at the convention of the American Psychological Association, Toronto, Canada.

Texas Department of Mental Health and Mental Retardation (TDMHMR). 1987. "Mental Health Service Definitions: FY 1988." Austin, Texas.

Thompson, E. H., and W. Doll. 1982. "The Burden of Families Coping with the Mentally Ill: An Invisible Crisis." Family Relations, vol. 31 (July).

Torrey, E. F., and S. M. Wolfe. 1986. Care of the Seriously Mentally Ill: A Rating of State Programs. Washington, D.C.: Public Citizens Health Research Group.

Chapter 9. Medication-Related Services[*]

While not nearly the curative "wonder drugs" they promised to be initially, antipsychotic and antidepressant agents used to treat the most severe mental illnesses have had a remarkable impact on psychiatric practice and theory--an impact that can be called revolutionary. While pharmacotherapy does not cure mental disorders in the same sense that antibiotics cure infectious diseases, the available drugs do control most symptomatic manifestations and behavioral deviances, facilitate the patient's tendency toward remission, and improve his or her capacity for social, occupational, and family adjustment. For example, the treatment of schizophrenic symptoms such as anxiety, delusions, hallucinations, paranoid states, catatonia, social withdrawal, and autonomic nervous system dysfunctions has been markedly changed by pharmacotherapy. The widespread use of these relatively safe compounds has greatly reduced the number of chronic patients residing in public mental hospitals, shortened the duration of hospitalization for acute episodes, and shifted the focus of treatment of mental disorders from institutional care to community-based ambulatory treatment programs.

COMMUNITY MENTAL HEALTH AND MENTAL RETARDATION CENTERS (CMHMRCs)

As part of this study, the medication clinics of 28 of the 36 CMHMRCs were interviewed by phone and two were visited. Twenty-five of the respondents were registered nurses and three were psychiatrists. All had five or more years of experience in the mental health field. Each person interviewed indicated that the center provided the five (required core) medication-related services.

Medication Clinic

A periodic review of psychiatric status and psychotropic medication was conducted by a physician (either full or part time) with frequencies being determined by diagnosis and client's condition.

Laboratory Monitoring and Physical Examinations

Physical exams were conducted on all new patients by center or private physicians. Thereafter, physicals were performed every 6 to 12 months, including tests for abnormal involuntary muscle movement (usually the AIMS test). Laboratory tests appropriate to the patient's condition were performed by laboratories from the following sources:

1.	Contract with private laboratory	54 percent
2.	Contract with public laboratory	11 percent
3.	Referral to a private laboratory	11 percent
4.	University hospital laboratory	7 percent
5.	Local hospital laboratory	7 percent
6.	In-house laboratory	10 percent

Medication Education

All centers indicate that the physician would review the medication with the client, including indications, adverse side-effects, and symptomolgy that would indicate medication reappraisal. Most clients were given printed handouts containing pertinent

---

[*]This chapter was written by Charles Blisset.

information on the drug utilized, and the client was required to sign a statement of understanding.

Mental Health Maintenance, Education, and Counseling

Most frequently the nurse discussed the stress-coping mechanisms with the client, the critical nature of medication compliance, and the role of proper nutrition in mental health maintenance. Networking with clinic and community groups was approached as dictated by local resources. Centers utilized various combinations of the following approaches to form support groups:

1. Clinic group therapy sessions conducted by nurses and/or caseworkers
2. Religious and civic groups
3. Local mental health volunteer groups
4. Family participation

Medication Provision

Essentially all centers except one (which lamented the fact that it could not always provide medication due to lack of resources) reported some mechanism for providing drugs to the indigent or having a sliding fee scale for those of limited financial means. The survey revealed the following sources of supplying medication(s) to non-Medicaid clients:

1.	In-house pharmacy	38 percent
2.	Local hospital	4 percent
3.	University hospital	4 percent
4.	Local pharmacies	32 percent
5.	Local pharmacies dispensing state contract medication	14 percent
6.	State hospitals	8 percent

Compliance was noted as one of the greatest problems existing in the CMHMRCs. All respondents indicated the use of injectable drugs for noncompliant clients and those who are unable or unwilling to take oral medications. Whenever a client does not appear for an appointment, he or she is contacted by phone or mail up to three times. In the event the client fails to appear after three notifications, the case manager will try to reach the client in the field (often, the family is helpful in locating the mentally ill person).

When the CMHMRCs were contacted, each interviewee was asked to estimate the percentage of Texas mentally ill currently being reached by TDMHMR. Approximately 50 percent stated that they had no estimate, but interestingly, almost all who ventured a guess suggested that only 20 to 30 percent of the mentally ill population is being served by the system.

STATE MENTAL HOSPITALS

Eight TDMHMR hospitals were contacted by phone. Three psychiatrists and five nurses were interviewed. One hospital was visited on four occasions. Each respondent indicated that the hospital was providing the (required core) medication services (see medication services listed under CMHMRCs). All hospitals contacted had in-house pharmacies and laboratories. The state hospitals for the mentally ill have not been able to keep abreast with technological advances in pharmacy services seen in most private and public hospitals primarily due to inadequate funding.

TDMHMR does not have any community-based clinical pharmacy services. Increased patient compliance, decreased use of medication, and patient counseling could be achieved through clinical services. Assuming logistics could be resolved, one clinical pharmacist might serve several community-based services. Of the community centers interviewed, 39 percent have their own in-house pharmacies which dispense medication in the traditional manner with counseling provided by the pharmacist. The smaller units usually contract with a local pharmacist who dispenses the medication, which is stored at the facility. Medication education is essential to patient compliance. The need to explain the importance of talking medication at correct intervals and dosages must be enforced with the community based patient. This reinforcement is an ongoing project, and involvement of the family, friends, and peers in the learning process is helpful.

PROVIDER RECOMMENDATIONS

Recommendations were solicited from all interviewed, and many excellent suggestions were obtained. A few of the most commonly mentioned observations follow:

1. Early preventive care--especially needed for indigent and low-income families.
2. Public and family education is needed regarding mental illness.
3. Work more with families to prevent "burnout" (provide some form of respite for families caring for the mentally ill).
4. As state adds more services/standards, there should be accompanying commensurate funding.
5. There needs to be safe housing for all clients--more halfway houses are needed, as well as three-quarter houses for those requiring 24-hour supervision for medication monitoring.
6. Additional staff is needed at all levels.
7. Routine/ongoing counseling is needed, along with more broad-based care.
8. There is also a need for additional social outlets for clients.

Chapter 10. Continuity of Care[*]

As currently used, the term "continuity of care" has both a broad and a specific definition. The broad definition refers to continuity among services of a comprehensive, community-based treatment program. Linkages between social, medical, and other support services are essential for a community treatment program to be effective for persons with long-term serious mental illness. Simply making all the necessary services available does not ensure that they will be most appropriately used by persons with serious mental illness. There must be active coordination of services--specifically directed toward the needs of each person with serious mental illness--so that these persons do not "fall through the cracks."

Seven dimensions of the broader definition of continuity of care have been identified (Bachrach, 1981). The *longitudinal* dimension means that the services provided vary in accordance to patient needs over time. The *individual* nature of continuity of care refers to treatment programming that is oriented to a specific patient and his or her family. *Comprehensiveness* requires a multidisciplinary treatment approach, including medical care, economic supports, and social skills training. *Flexibility* and *accessibility* of care are necessary to assure a rapid response to sudden changes in a person's medical, psychiatric, or social needs. Finally, the *relationship* between the patient and the care providers should be constant, and *communication* channels should remain open and supportive. A comprehensive service system serves as a treatment coordinator, guiding patients to available resources when they are needed and maintaining contact during periods of stabilization as well as crisis (Bellack and Mueser, 1986, p. 186).

COORDINATION BETWEEN HOSPITAL AND COMMUNITY SERVICES

The more specific definition of continuity of care refers to certain necessary coordinating activities on behalf of clients at the interface of the community service system and the state hospital system. TDMHMR defines this as an activity which "provides an assigned person(s) [the hospital liaison] who is responsible for tracking clients as they enter the state hospital and then prepare to return to the community. The person(s) is responsible for the joint treatment plan process between center and facility; and facilitates the timely return of a client to community services. The primary focus of activities occurs at the juncture between facility and center transition; services are time-limited and short-term in nature" (TDMHMR, May 1987, p. 12).

In Texas, the more specific definition of continuity of care is more commonly used, is required by state law and departmental rule, and is measured by several performance measures in community center contracts for services. An early criticism of community center operations was that there was little to no formal connection between hospital and center services, and that center clients did not necessarily include persons discharged from state hospitals. Senate Bill 791 amended the Texas Mental Health Code to require community centers to perform certain services on behalf of persons at both the front door, through preadmission screening, and the back door, through discharge planning, to the state hospitals.

First, for persons for whom an application for court-ordered mental health services (in a state hospital) had been filed, centers were required to prepare and file with the court "a recommendation for the most appropriate treatment alternative for the proposed patient." Except in an emergency, a hearing on an application cannot be held before this recommendation is filed. Second, the law requires that "before the furlough

---

[*]This chapter was written by Janice Rienstra and Carolina L. Martinez.

or discharge of a patient, the head of the mental health facility (state hospital) shall, in consultation with the patient and the mental health authority in the area in which the patient will live after discharge, . . . develop a plan for continuing care for a patient for whom he [or she] determines the care is required. The plan will address the mental health and physical needs of the client" (Article 5547, 1-100, VTCS).

The TDMHMR rule on continuity of care broadened these responsibilities. Under the rule, centers were responsible for preadmission screening of all persons (with certain exceptions) admitted to state hospitals, both voluntary and involuntary. Before a patient's furlough or discharge from a hospital, the patient, the patient's family (if appropriate), and the hospital and mental health authority staff are to develop a discharge or community support plan. The rule specifies the contents of this plan. Facilities are to notify the local mental health authority at least 24 hours in advance of the furlough or discharge of a patient from its area; the authority is responsible for implementing the community support plan from the time that furlough or discharge begins. Patients discharged from the hospitals are to be contacted, by phone or face to face, within 10 days of discharge by staff of the responsible authority. Further, centers are held responsible for auditable documentation of their own performance, as well as that of the hospitals, in compliance with the rule (TDMHMR, 1988).

A number of factors mitigate against the practice, if not the theory, of continuity of care thus defined. First, persons with mental illness have the right to refuse preadmission screening and discharge planning services, and some do so. Second, the sheer volume of admissions and discharges to state hospitals--averaging 17,000 to 20,000 a year for the past several years--coupled with the relatively short lengths of hospital stay for many, overwhelms the system. In FY 1988, all community programs in Texas had 92.4 staff members whose job was hospital liaison/continuity of care.

A third factor is the relatively large number of involuntary commitments to hospitals. Although hospitals *may* discharge an involuntarily committed person before the commitment expires if the person is found to no longer meet the criteria for hospital care, hospitals *must* discharge persons on expiration of their commitment, whether or not that person is ready for discharge to community services.

A fourth factor is the great geographic distance between many of the state hospitals and the mental health authorities in their service area. Although electronic and telephone communication is invaluable in this instance, it cannot substitute for important direct face-to-face contact between the person to be discharged from the hospital and the community services staff. A person with long-term, serious mental illness is unlikely to respond to a card, listing an appointment three weeks hence with an unknown staff member, in a distant town.

Although community hospital liaison staff regularly visit the state hospital to provide continuity of care services, this may be as infrequent as twice a month in some areas; people are admitted to and discharged from hospitals daily. A fifth factor impeding continuity of care is that although the system has a defined geographic structure, originally based on the notion that persons in a given geographic area are to receive services from providers in that area, things do not always work this way. For example, if a person with mental illness from Dallas is admitted to and discharged from the hospital in San Antonio, the Dallas community center is held responsible for preadmission screening and discharge planning for this person.

Given all the factors which work against effective continuity of care, it has reportedly worked fairly well, within funding constraints. In FY 1988, performance measures reported by community centers indicate that the percentage of persons screened prior to admission to a state hospital ranged from 100 percent to 44 percent; most centers

200

reported screening 80 to 90 percent of all hospital admissions. Similarly, the reported percent of persons discharged from hospitals with a joint discharge plan ranged from 100 percent to a low of 42 percent. Again, most centers reported joint discharge plans for 80 to 90 percent of persons discharged from hospitals (TDMHMR, 1989).

Requiring local mental health authorities to screen hospital admissions is, in a sense, a mechanism for establishing a single point of referral and screening. This concept is fundamental to the more formal and more complex single-portal-of-entry mechanism. However, persons can enter state hospitals in a number of ways which circumvent the preadmission screening process. The TDMHMR rule states that for persons admitted voluntarily to state hospitals, preadmission screening is not required when (1) the person is referred by a (private) physician; (2) the admission is an emergency admission; (3) the person is physically present at the hospital and community services are not readily available; or (4) the hospital and the LMHA have an agreement whereby the hospital performs the screening. Persons may enter the hospital involuntarily, without community-based preadmission screening, if brought by a peace officer for emergency detention. Some local mental authorities have negotiated agreements with their local law enforcement agencies and courts to involve the local LMHA staff in involuntary admissions to state hospitals. In addition, hospitals and committing courts cooperate by holding commitment hearings at the hospital.

COORDINATION WITHIN AND AMONG COMMUNITY SERVICES

The broader definition of continuity of care is also used in Texas, called "caseworker assignment" by TDMHMR. This service provides "an assigned professional staff person who is known to the client within the agency and who serves as a point of contact and an advocate for the client in obtaining services he [or she] needs within the agency. Services will be provided which are less intensive than case management, less comprehensive than full case management, and with limited contact with clients" (TDMHMR, May 1987, p. 12).

The TDMHMR Mental Health Community Standards further define this kind of service and its purpose: "Each [community mental health authority] has comprehensive policies and procedures which address the assignment, reassignment, and communication to the client and others, as appropriate, of a single continuity of services staff person who is responsible for overall program coordination for each client across all community-based services" (TDMHMR, 1989, p. 12-1). The continuity of services staff person is assigned to each client at admission and at all times, regardless of transfer between services, at least until discharge from the mental health authority. The staff person is responsible for facilitating appropriate linkages within local mental health services and with other programs, agencies, and services in the community at large. As with the hospital liaison function described above, the level of continuity of services, or "caseworker assignment," is inadequate. In FY 1988, all community-based programs reported 72.1 staff in caseworker assignment services; that year, more than 106,000 adults were served by these community-based programs.

References

Bachrach, Leona. 1981. "Continuity of Care: A Conceptual Analysis." <u>American Journal of Psychiatry</u>, vol. 138 (May).

Bellack, Alan, and Kim Mueser. 1986. "A Comprehensive Treatment Program for Schizophrenia and Chronic Mental Illness." <u>Community Mental Health Journal</u>, vol. 22, no. 3 (Fall).

Texas Department of Mental Health and Mental Retardation (TDMHMR). May 1987. Mental Health Service Definitions. Austin, Texas.

_____. 1988. <u>Continuity of Services -- Mental Health</u>. Austin, Texas.

_____. 1989. <u>TDMHMR Mental Health Community Standards.</u> Austin, Texas.

Chapter 11. Residential Services and Other Community Housing Alternatives for Persons with Chronic Mental Illness[*]

The lack of adequate community-based housing is arguably the most critical unmet need of persons who are chronically mentally ill (CMI). This critical shortage of housing has been officially recognized as a priority at the federal, state, and local levels for more than a decade. The 1975 amendments to the Community Mental Health Center Act, the 1977 Comptroller General Report to the Congress, the 1978 report of the Presidential Commission on Mental Health, the Community Support Program literature, and HUD/HEW demonstration grants have all identified the same range of housing options as priority needs for the CMI (Lamb, 1984). Yet federal Section 8 housing subsidies and public housing funds have dropped from $26.7 billion in 1980 to $8.6 billion in 1983. In 1983, no funds were allocated for construction of new public housing, compared with $3.7 billion allocated in 1980 (Paterson and Craig, 1987). In 1988, Texas received $3.4 million for HUD programs for assistance to homeless persons (i.e., Section 8 Single Room Occupancy, Transitional Housing Demonstration, Permanent Housing for the Handicapped) (Mattox-Ulmer, Interview, November 21, 1988).

In addition to lack of low-income/public housing, poverty, and discrimination, the increase of homelessness among persons with CMI is often attributed to other factors such as deinstitutionalization and demography. Although the numbers vary, between 20 and 40 percent of the nation's homeless men and between 50 and 80 percent of the homeless women are estimated to be chronically mentally ill (Paterson and Craig, 1987). One study indicates that roughly 15 percent of the nation's total chronically mentally ill population is homeless (Paterson and Craig, 1987). There are varying levels of analysis to the homeless problem: it is a housing problem, an employment problem, a substance abuse problem, and a problem created by cutbacks in social welfare spending. But very few are "homeless by choice."

Deinstitionalization is often cited as a major cause of homelessness among persons with CMI. Two or three decades ago a majority of persons with CMI were admitted to institutions for an indefinite length of time, but today 80 percent of former institutionalized patients are now being placed in the community (Jones, 1986). Generally it is believed that the philosophy of deinstitutionalization was a positive step, but the lack of sufficient funding, community-based housing, and mental health support services has left jails and families with the job of caring for and treating these persons (Paterson and Rhubright, 1987). Families have the additional problem of being severely constrained by the legal system from asserting control over their adult family member.

The level of disability of most homeless persons with CMI is usually substantial enough to qualify them for Supplemental Security Income (SSI) or Social Security Disability Insurance (SSDI) (Jones, 1986). Yet, they are often excluded from income maintenance, health insurance, and food stamp programs because these programs require proof of residence and a mailing address in order to qualify (Jones, 1986). Health insurance is a crucial support, yet most homeless persons with CMI have no medical insurance. As a result, they are excluded from treatment in most voluntary and private facilities.

Because of the severe shortage of housing alternatives for adults with serious mental illness, Senate Concurrent Resolution 63 was passed during the 69th legislative session which set a goal of providing 60 community-based beds per 100,000 population in Texas. At that time there were approximately 12.5 adult community-based housing alternatives (beds) available per 100,000 population in Texas.

---

[*]This chapter was written by Jana Blasi and Carolina Martinez.

Persons with serious mental illness need a continuum of living arrangements, ranging from highly structured and supervised settings to more autonomous living arrangements. There are many different types of residential services, including structured residential programs, intermediate residential programs and semi-independent residential programs. The most common types of alternative housing programs include supervised apartments, unsupervised apartments, supervised group homes, halfway houses, foster care programs, personal care/nursing homes, Fairweather Lodges, clubhouse programs, shelters for the homeless, and board and care homes.

TYPES OF RESIDENTIAL SERVICES

Residential programs provide living and sleeping arrangements as well as services such as extended treatment or training services. There is an array of residential programs, from restrictive and highly structured to semi-independent. In the last several decades, there have been many positive and programmatic developments within the mental health field in its attempt to meet the housing needs of people with CMI. TDMHMR requires that there be availability of at least some element of residential services in addition to the required core crisis stabilization beds for clients of each service area (TDMHMR, 1988a).

Structured residential programs include both crisis and noncrisis treatment settings. These residential programs maintain 24-hour supervision for clients and are very structured. A medical component is often part of structured residential programs. Activities for clients are usually highly structured and include medical supports operated under certain standards. Only one residential program, crisis stabilization, is a required core service. This can either be operated directly by the mental health authority or provided in a licensed hospital under contract with the authority.

Intermediate residential programs offer moderate supervision and moderately structured activities for clients. Twenty-four-hour supervision offers support and relief to the family by providing care for the client. Brief respite foster care homes, personal care homes, therapeutic group homes, and halfway houses are commonly identified as intermediate residential programs.

Semi-independent residential programs offer limited supervision and structure to clients on an as-needed basis. Supervised group homes, board and care homes, quarterway homes, and co-op apartments are examples of semi-independent residential programs.

Nursing homes, according to the 1988 TDMHMR service definition, "are programs which are non-hospital, licensed residential settings providing nursing, personal and other related care services on a short-term, intermediate or long-term basis" (TDMHMR, May 1987, p. 14). *Personal care homes* are residential settings licensed as a personal care home providing life support services to meet the generic need of the client for food, shelter, and safety. Twenty-four-hour supervision is required, although the need for awake staff at night is determined by the characteristics of the resident(s). *Therapeutic group homes* "are residential living programs for two to eight clients offering a therapeutic/ training/educational program. There is on-duty staff awake 24 hours per day" (MHAT, June 1984, p. 7).

Halfway houses are "living environments for two or more individuals which have paid staff on the premises. There must be staff awake 24 hours each day to provide rehabilitative and supportive services to assist the clients from institutional living to community living. Clients often work part or full-time outside the residence" (TDMHMR, May 1987, p. 15).

Supervised family living encompasses three different levels of residential services. If the client is in crisis, supervised family living/crisis stabilization foster care facilities may be used. According to the TDMHMR service definition, "these structured programs are offered to clients who are demonstrating a psychiatric crisis of <u>moderate</u> proportions and are designed to offer close supervision within a family-type atmosphere" (TDMHMR, May 1987, p. 15).

Supervised apartments are housing facilities in which clients live in apartments in the community, usually with community center staff living in an adjoining apartment. *Unsupervised apartments* are housing facilities that are designed for the client who does not need 24-hour supervision. The staff does not live in but is available when needed and visits the client regularly.

Fairweather Lodge is a psychosocial rehabilitation program for a small group of consumers who move out of the hospital to live and work together on a long-term basis. These groups of people have received continuous long-term care in state hospitals, received intensive training in specialized hospital units, and then "graduated" to community living. There are Fairweather Lodges in five areas in Texas. The program provides consumers with training in vocational skills, group-based problem-solving skills, and the option of seeking a long-term and autonomous living arrangement.

Shelters for the homeless are generally found in the larger cities in Texas. Most of these programs are funded by private nonprofit organizations. Many churches become involved with helping the homeless, which includes a subpopulation of people with CMI. The Salvation Army operates shelters in many Texas communities.

Board and care homes are facilities which provide room and board and sometimes custodial care for a fee. Paid staff on the premises prepare meals as needed and ensure maintenance of the home. Care in the board and care home usually does not include medical supervision, social activities, or counseling.

In 1987, Senate Bill 257 was passed which states that before any community center client can be placed in a board and care home by a local mental health authority, the home must be registered by the authority (Petty, Interview, November 13, 1988). The registration process ensures that a board and care home complies with local building and fire codes and meets other basic standards of health and safety.

FUNDING FOR RESIDENTIAL SERVICES AND OTHER HOUSING

Texas receives a variety of funding sources to provide residential services to persons with serious mental illness. However, the demand for the development of new housing facilities far exceeds current revenues. Current sources of funds to limited areas of the state include the Robert Wood Johnson Foundation's program for the mentally ill, the Lower-Income Rental Assistance (Section 8 program), the Stewart B. McKinney Homeless Assistance Act, and community block grants.

The program of the Robert Wood Johnson Foundation for the chronically mentally ill is one source of private funding for housing for the mentally ill in several states. In Texas, the Austin-Travis County MHMR Center was selected to receive $2.5 million in grant monies over a five-year period. Austin also received a $1 million low-interest loan from the foundation to assist in the Austin housing plan. HUD is also assisting in this housing effort by providing 125 Section 8 subsidies for persons with mental illness (RWJF, 1987, p. 4).

The Lower-Income Rental Assistance (Section 8) program is a federal revenue source for housing. Subsidies are given to the household in the form of a commitment by the federal government to pay part of the household's rent. The recipient can then use the subsidy to seek his or her own housing and negotiate a rental agreement with the landlord. To be eligible for the Section 8 program, the housing unit has to meet certain quality standards that are defined by the local public housing authority which administers the program on the local level. Eligible families and individuals in need of Section 8 subsidies must go to the local public housing authority and get on a list to receive the certificate. The length of the waiting list varies with each community; however, the waiting lists are generally quite long. For example, Dallas has a waiting list of 1,579 families for Section 8 vouchers (Ramos, Interview, April 6, 1989).

Most Section 8 subsidies are family-based. Recipients of this housing subsidy must be a family or, if single, a person who is handicapped or over the age of 62. If handicapped, a person must qualify for "independent living" (Ramos, Interview, April 6, 1989). HUD recognizes that "independent living" will mean different things for different groups among the homeless. A homeless person who is mentally ill may be considered living independently if he or she is living in a permanent arrangement in a supervised group home for the chronically mentally ill (HUD, July 1988, p. 2). For a family or handicapped individual to be eligible for the Section 8 housing subsidy, the recipient must meet the low-income criterion of making less than 50 percent of the local median income (Ramos, Interview April 6, 1989). The income median varies with each community.

The Stewart B. McKinney Homeless Assistance Act provides federal monies for the support of homeless individuals with serious mental illness. Congress authorized McKinney grants in the spring of 1987, and then added federal FY 1988 funds in a supplemental appropriation bill. The first award to the states, then, combined awards for two federal fiscal years. In Texas, FY 1987-1988 funds totaled $2.8 million.

COMMUNITY-BASED RESIDENTIAL PROGRAMS IN TEXAS

Every community center provides some kind of residential services. Some centers spend more money on residential services than others and have a wider spectrum of housing available for their clients. TDMHMR contract data list residential services offered by CMHMRCs in Texas. These data are helpful in analyzing the priorities for CMHMRC residential services, number of clients served, client bed days, total capacity, funding, and costs per day. These data do not include clients who are living in housing which is not operated by or contracted by the CMHMRC, nor does it take into account the large number of mentally ill who live at home with relatives and friends. Currently, community centers are providing 20 beds per 100,000 population in Texas (TDMHMR, 1988a).

In 1988, 22,277 clients were served in residential programs at the community centers in Texas. As mentioned earlier in this report, there are four basic categories of residential services offered by community centers in Texas: structured crisis, structured noncrisis, intermediate, and semi-independent. The TDMHMR contract data enable a comparison of total capacity, clients served, client bed days, and cost per day by residential category type. Tables 11.1, 11.2, 11.3, and 11.4 summarize these data.

206

Table 11.1. Structured Crisis Residential Programs

Facility Name	Client Capacity	Number of Clients	Days	Cost/Day
Abilene Region	2	12	84	$238.20
Austin-Travis Co.	26	880	8,255	123.91
Bexar County	65	3,792	14,584	106.00
Brazos Valley	4	80	1,008	86.11
Central Counties	14	140	3,500	158.30
Central Plains	11	250	3,000	141.83
Central Texas	10	10	40	250.00
Collin County	3	35	841	338.00
Concho Valley	1	58	405	250.00
Dallas County	80	1,412	19,033	228.08
Deep East Texas	24	381	6,777	201.58
Denton County	2	60	598	400.00
Gulf Bend	12	340	3,700	38.06
Gulf Coast	28	408	6,354	99.78
East Texas	4	110	1,250	151.23
Harris County	294	3,608	89,816	69.97
Hunt County	2	20	145	275.00
Heart of Texas	2	202	1,681	100.51
Johnson County	2	48	720	325.00
Life Mangement	34			
Lubbock Region	9	324	1,944	174.53
Navarro County	1	20	100	250.00
Northeast Texas	3	28	291	271.56
Nueces County	2	57	571	350.26
Pecan Valley	1	27	105	237.55
Permian Basin	8	360	2,740	15.63
Sabine Valley	55	816	9,039	144.44
Southeast Texas	68	680	19,700	106.26
Tarrant County	84	1,040	17,040	227.26
Texas Panhandle	25	225	5,772	119.21
Texoma	3	72	400	265.48
Tri County	25	277	6,600	181.84
Tropical Texas	17	302	5,461	124.82
Wichita Falls	1	31	310	206.14
Totals	922	16,105	231,864	$6,256.44

Source: TDMHMR, 1988b.

Table 11.2. Structured Noncrisis Residential Programs

Facility Name	Client Capacity	Number of Clients	Days	Cost/Day
Abilene Region	6	6	1,300	$ 19.23
Austin-Travis Co.	10	136	3,175	55.43
Bexas County	63	75	23,890	22.11
Brazox Valley				
Central Counties	1	1	365	49.18
Cemtral Plains	8	115	2,600	49.04
Central Texas	7	110	2,300	61.95
Collin County				
Concho Valley				
Dallas County	115	115	33,588	48.11
Deep East Texas	44	140	4,200	331.75
Denton County	9	57	2,200	122.11
Gulf Bend	43	182	13,568	26.79
Gulf Coast				
East Texas	4	4	1,460	30.00
Harris County	81	155	22,751	9,649.00
Hunt County				
Heart of Texas	20	135	5,745	18.42
Johnson County				
Life Managment	7	21	2,840	29.05
Lubbock Region	35	96	10,920	20.79
Navarro County	5	5	1,825	19.56
Northeast Texas	10	10	3,000	31.15
Nueces County	27	62	9,363	60.04
Pecan Valley				
Permian Basin				
Sabine Valley	17	190	5,706	54.75
Southeast Texas	23	353	6,800	61.40
Tarrant County				
Texas Panhandle	21	72	4,740	44.83
Texoma	6	9	1,800	34.44
Tri County	20	206	5,260	
Tropical Texas				
Wichita Falls				
Totals	582	2,255	169,826	$10,839.13

Source: TDMHMR, 1988b.

Table 11.3. Intermediate Residential Programs

Facility Name	Client Capacity	Number of Clients	Days	Cost/Day
Abilene Regional	26	76	6,595	$76.92
Austin-Travic Co.	69	180	21,910	28.22
Bexar County	54	85	23,505	40.58
Brazos Valley	14	30	3,577	74.96
Central County	10	21	2,555	35.48
Central Plains	24	48	7,000	35.88
Central Texas	4	12	430	81.09
Collin County	12	48	3,655	65.00
Concho Valley				
Dallas County				
Deep East Texas	28	55	6,771	51.09
Denton County	4	4	1,460	12.00
Gulf Bend	3	3	729	16.44
Gulf Coast	6	6	613	40.78
East Texas	24	86	7,300	40.17
Harris County	23	66	7,383	55.23
Hunt County	9	24	3,261	43.73
Heart of Texas	18	78	4,080	62.07
Johnson County				
Life Management	63	121	18,943	30.56
Lubbock Regional	30	192	9,840	24.02
Navarro County	1	1	365	13.54
Northeast Texas	3	3	900	17.41
Nueces County	42	215	14,564	46.58
Pecan Valley	12	120	4,000	56.67
Permian Basin	34	78	8,313	45.29
Sabine Valley	36	185	105,589	36.95
Southeast Texas	23	32	7,440	17.07
Tarrant County	4	20	1,329	84.01
Texas Panhandle	26	156	8,640	44.83
Texoma	12	21	2,710	44.67
Tri County	14	25	4,500	33.35
Tropical Texas	16	260	4,672	42.92
Wichita Falls	24	27	7,884	13.41
Totals	668	2,278	205,483	1,310.92

Source: TDMHMR, 1988b.

Table 11.4. Semi-Independent Residential Programs

Facility Name	Client Capacity	Number of Clients	Days	Cost/Day
Abilene Regional	26	76	6,595	$76.92
Austin-Travis Co.	69	180	21,910	28.22
Bexar County	54	85	23,505	40.58
Brazox Valley	14	30	3,577	74.96
Central Counties	10	21	2,555	35.48
Central Plains	24	48	7,000	35.88
Central Texas	4	12	430	81.09
Collin County	12	8	3,655	65.00
Concho Valley				
Dallas County				
Deep East Texas	28	55	6,771	51.09
Denton County	4	4	1,460	12.00
Gulf Bend	3	3	729	16.44
Gulf Coast	6	6	613	40.78
East Texas	24	86	7,300	40.17
Harris County	23	66	7,383	55.23
Hunt County	9	24	3,261	43.73
Heart of Texas	18	78	4,080	62.07
Johnson County				
Life Management	63	121	18,943	30.56
Lubbock Regional	30	192	9,840	24.02
Navarro County	1	1	365	13.54
Northeast Texas	3	3	900	17.41
Nueces County	42	215	14,564	46.58
Pecan Valley	12	120	4,000	56.67
Permian Basin	34	78	8,313	45.29
Sabine Valley	36	185	10,559	36.95
Southeast Texas	23	32	7,440	17.07
Tarrant County	4	20	1,329	84.01
Texas Panhandle	26	156	8,640	44.83
Texoma	12	21	2,710	44.67
Tri County	14	25	4,500	33.35
Tropical Texas	16	260	4,672	42.92
Wichata Falls	24	27	7,884	13.41
Totals	668	2,278	205,483	$1,310.92

Source: TDMHMR, 1988b.

The funding from general revenue, R. A. J. funds, and other monies vary with the type of residential services offered. Total funds and average funding tend to be greater in the structured crisis category than in the structured noncrisis, intermediate, or semi-independent categories because crisis stabilization beds are a mandatory core service and are the most expensive type of residential service.

All community centers offer some crisis stabilization beds. But the quantity available varies from center to center. For example, the Concho Valley, Navarro County, Pecan Valley, and Wichita Falls CMHMRCs have only one crisis stabilization bed.

CONCLUSIONS

There is a need for a comprehensive statewide study on available housing for the chronically mentally ill in Texas. The public needs information and education about the facts of mental illness to replace the common stereotypes of mental illness. Otherwise, there will continue to be discrimination and stigma against persons with mental illness. It is also necessary to begin to explore more innovative funding programs. Low-interest loans to provide funding for housing is one alternative. The Robert Wood Johnson Foundation Program for the Mentally Ill is an example of the potential for private/public collaboration.

TDMHMR has been working to reduce the number of persons in the state hospitals and to support individuals in the community. At the very least, these persons must have a place to live to accomplish this goal. In addition to a roof over their heads, many people need a variety of support services if they are to remain in the community. Residential programs can either provide these services or ensure that the clients will receive them from another source. Today in Texas there is a critical lack of residential services for persons with serious mental illness. There is great demand for increased funding for the very basic need of housing for this population.

References

Jones, Billy E., ed. 1986. <u>Treating the Homeless: Urban Psychiatry's Challenge</u>. Washington D.C.: American Psychiatric Press, Inc.

Lamb, Richard H., ed. 1986. <u>The Homeless Mentally Ill</u>. Washington, D.C.: American Psychiatric Association.

Mattox-Ulmer, Nancy. 1988. Regional Homeless Coordinator, U.S. Department of Housing and Urban Development, Washington, D.C. Telephone interview by Jana Blasi, November 21.

Mental Health Association in Texas (MHAT). June 1984. <u>Community Residential Services Survey</u>, Austin, Texas.

Paterson, Andrea, and Rebecca Craig. 1987. <u>The Homeless Mentally Ill: No Longer Out of Sight Out of Mind</u>. Report to the State Legislatures. Washington D.C.: National Conference of State Legislatures.

_____ and Ellen Rhubright. 1987. <u>Housing for the Mentally Ill: A Place to Call Home</u>. Report to the State Legislatures. Washington D.C.: National Conference of State Legislatures.

Petty, Cheryl. 1988. Discharge Planning Specialist, Austin-Travis County Mental Health and Mental Retardation Center, Austin, Texas. Interview by Jana Blasi, November 13.

Ramos, Angelina. 1989. Regional Program Director, U.S. Department of Housing and Urban Development, Washington, D.C. Telephone interview by Jana Blasi, April 6.

Robert Wood Johnson Foundation (RWJF). 1987. <u>Robert Wood Johnson Program for the Chronically Mentally Ill: Overview.</u> Boston, Mass.: Massachusetts Mental Health Center. (Pamphlet.)

Texas Department of Mental Health and Mental Retardation (TDMHMR). May 1987. <u>Mental Health Service Definitions</u>. Austin, Texas.

_____. 1988a. <u>Community Center Contract Data: FY 1988.</u> Austin, Texas.

_____. 1988b. "Care System Tapes, Community Data." Austin, Texas.

U.S. Department of Housing and Urban Development. July 1988. <u>Homeless Assistance Programs</u>. Washington, D.C.: U.S. Government Printing Office.

Chapter 12. Income Support Services[*]

SSDI AND SSI PROGRAMS

Social Security Disability Income (SSDI) and Supplemental Security Income (SSI) are programs administered by the Social Security Administration (SSA) as authorized under Titles II and XVI (respectively) of the Social Security Act. These entitlement programs offer direct financial payments and health insurance to qualified disabled persons (USDHHS, January 1988a).

Both programs use the same medical definitions of a disability. The SSA authorizes specific state agencies to act as the Disability Determination Service (DDS). In Texas the authorized state agency is the Texas Rehabilitation Commission (TRC). Though both share the requirements for determination of disability, they have very different eligibility requirements.

SSI is designed to serve aged, blind, and physically and mentally disabled individuals who have limited or no income and assets and do not have a work history which qualifies them for SSDI. SSI is financed from general funds of the U.S. Treasury and is the primary form of federal income support for persons with chronic mental illness (CMI). SSDI is, technically, an insurance program for those who have contributed a minimum amount into the Social Security Trust Fund. While the existence of income and assets do not affect eligibility for SSDI, the existence of income may affect the determination of disability. This program is not used as much by the CMI because the psychopathology of their illness often has prevented them from holding down regular employment, thus affecting eligibility or reducing the extent of benefits (Torrey, 1988, p. 250). Some persons whose onset of chronic mental illness began before the age of 22, and who are unmarried, may be able to gain eligibilty for SSI through their parents' participation in Social Security.

Both programs are very important for the seriously mentally ill who are able to live in community settings. SSI and SSDI allow for a transition period for those who will eventually be able to earn a subsistence wage or those who will never be able to hold regular employment but do not require structured hospital settings for continued improvement. It also allows the disabled individual to live outside of a family setting and to achieve some sense of independence. Both also offer special problems to the CMI throughout the application and renewal process. Although improvements have been made in these processes, including the establishment of a trial work period under which recipients can work and still receive benefits, they still provide problems for the CMI.

Disability is defined as the inability to do any <u>substantially gainful activity</u> by reason of any medically determinable physical or mental impairment which can be expected to result in death or which can be expected to last for a continuous period of not less than 12 months. To meet this definition, the disabled person must have a <u>severe impairment</u> which makes him or her unable to do his or her previous work or any other substantial gainful activity which exists in the national economy. To determine whether he or she is able to do any other work, the DDS considers his or her <u>residual functional capacity</u> and age, education, and work experience (USDHHS, December 1987b, p. 6).

Disability Determination

It is important to note that mentally disabled persons are now likely to be more carefully scrutinized when applying or appealing for benefits (Okpaku, 1988). The

---

[*]This chapter was written by Nicholas L. Hoover.

applicant for either program starts this process by filing forms with his or her local Social Security office. If the applicant meets the work history and income and/or asset requirements for eligibility for SSI or SSDI, his or her file is sent to the state's disability determination service (DDS) in their state (USDHHS, December 1987b, p. 6). In Texas the file would go to the Texas Rehabilitation Commission.

A DDS adjudication team consists of a disability analyst, who is not a physician, and a psychiatrist or clinical psychologist. The applicant submits to the disability analyst evidence in the form of reports from a physician and/or other relevant sources. If this evidence is incomplete or contradictory or not readily available, the DDS may have the applicant examined by a consulting psychiatrist or psychologist at the expense of the DDS (USDHHS, January 1988a). The evaluation of a disability on the basis of mental disorders requires the documentation of medically determinable impairment(s) as well as consideration of the degree of limitation that this impairment will impose on the individual's ability to work. Mental impairments are currently classified under the following eight categories:

1. Organic mental disorder
2. Schizophrenic, paranoid, and other psychotic disorders
3. Affective disorders
4. Mental retardation and autism
5. Anxiety-related disorders
6. Somatoform disorders
7. Personality disorders
8. Substance addiction disorders. (USDHHS, December 1987b)

"A" Criterion. The first set of criteria that the DDS team examines are the clinical signs or symptoms of a particular category of a disorder. One or more of these criteria must be met to establish the existence of a disorder. For evidence of schizophrenic, paranoid, and other psychotic disorders the disabled person must meet one or more of the following clinical criteria: (1) delusions or hallucinations; (2) catatonic or other grossly disorganized behavior; (3) incoherence, loosening of associations, illogical thinking, or poverty of content of speech if associated with blunt affect, flat affect, or inappropriate affect; or (4) emotional withdrawal and/or isolation (USDHHS, December 1987b, p. 72).

"B" Criterion. The second set of criteria refer to the limitations of functioning which are the result of the mental impairment and are the same for all eight categories of mental disorders. In order to be considered disabled, the person must have marked difficulty in two or three (depending on the disorder) of these four functional limitations caused by the disorder:

1.   Marked restrictions of activities of daily living (cleaning, shopping, cooking, paying bills, using a telephone directory, grooming and hygiene, etc); or

2.   Marked difficulties in maintaining social functioning (the capacity to interact appropriately and communicate effectively with others); or

3.   Deficiencies of concentration, persistence, or pace resulting in frequent failure to complete tasks in a timely manner (in a work setting or elsewhere); or

4.   Repeated episodes of deterioration or decompensation in work or work-like settings which cause the individual to

withdraw from that situation or to experience exacerbation of signs and symptoms (which may include deterioration of adaptive behaviors). (USDHHS, December 1987b, p. 72).

"C" Criterion. The SSA came to realize that there were particular problems involved in evaluating mental impairments in individuals who have long histories of repeated hospitalizations or prolonged outpatient care with supportive therapy and medication. In 1985 a third set of criteria was added so that those individuals who show signs of partial recovery and the ability to function in a normal competitive and stressful environment would not have their benefits disallowed because they had complied with their medication and treatment program and had experienced some recovery. These individuals often have periods of wellness followed by psychotic episodes. The new criteria are a medically-documented history of one or more episodes of acute symptoms, signs and functional limitations which at the time met the first two sets of requirements, although these signs or symptoms are currently attenuated by medication or psychosocial support, and one of the following:

1. Repeated episodes of deterioration or decompensation in work or work-like settings which cause the individual to withdraw from that situation or to experience exacerbation of signs and symptoms (which may include deterioration of adaptive behaviors); or

2. Documented current history of two or more years of inability to function outside of a highly supportive living situation. (USDHHS, December 1987b, pp. 68-74)

Eligibility for SSI

Because of the work history requirements for the SSDI program, SSI is the primary form of income support for the CMI. This program is designed for blind, aged, and disabled persons who are not eligible for SSDI or old-age benefits. The program is funded through general funds of the U.S. Treasury and is administered by the Social Security Administration (USDHHS, December 1987b). To be eligible for benefits, which include cash payments and Medicaid coverage, the applicant must meet specific income and resource limits and must also have a severe disability.

Before the determination of disability, the SSA screens the applicant's income and resources to see whether he or she meets the minimum qualifications for eligibility. The maximum amounts that a person or couple can have in income and assets is very restrictive and specific. Income cannot exceed, after exclusions and deductions, current benefit levels of $4,248 per year ($354 per month) for an individual or $6,384 per couple ($532 per month). For each "essential" person living in the home, $178 per month extra income is allowed (Vischi, June 1988, p. 77). In no case may an individual receive benefits if income or resources are greater than the benefit levels. If the income or resources are greater than zero but less than the benefit amounts, he or she will receive partial benefits (USDHHS, June 1988).

Even if income amounts are high enough not to receive any benefits, applicants should still go through the process since eligibility on all other counts may entitle the disabled person to benefits such as food stamps, Medicaid, and other social support services (Torrey, 1988, p. 251). Countable income includes earned and unearned income such as wages or cash in any form; net earnings from self-employment; food, shelter, clothing, and funds to help pay for them; Veterans Administration compensation; annuities, union benefits, public or private pension benefits, Social Security benefits; gifts, prizes, proceeds from life insurance policies; support and alimony payments; and inheritances, interest on bank accounts, and rental income (USDHHS, June 1988).

Some earned income is excluded from being counted. A few of these major exclusions include $65 per month of earned income; earned income used to pay impairment-related work expenses; one-half of the remaining earned income per month; and earned income that is used to fulfill an approved plan to achieve self-support (USDHHS, June 1988).

Some items are not considered income by the SSA and are not counted as such. These include medical care and services, social services; income tax refunds; proceeds of a loan; replacement of lost or stolen income; weatherization assistance; food stamps, federally donated food, housing subsidies; and education and training grants and loans. Food, clothing, shelter, or home energy assistance provided in kind by private, nonprofit organizations are also not counted as income, but all of these need to be reported to the SSA (USDHHS, June 1988).

Maximum resource amounts are $1,900 for an individual and $2,800 for a couple in order to receive SSI checks. Not all resources count toward these limits. The home and land it is on are exempted, along with one automobile with a maximum value of $4,500. Depending on the value, most household goods and personal property are not counted as assets. Examples of items that are counted as assets are easily liquefiable items such as stocks, bonds, mutual fund shares, promissory notes, mortgages, and life insurance policies and bank accounts (USDHHS, June 1988).

When the resources of an individual exceed the allowed limits, that individual will receive no SSI payments unless the resources do not exceed $3,000 for an individual or $4,500 for an individual and spouse and an individual agrees in writing to dispose of nonliquid resources within a specified time period and repay SSI overpayments (Vischi, June 1988, p. 74).

These income/resource requirements mean that if a person with serious mental illness is not already destitute, he or she must become destitute, or hide or transfer assets in order to be eligible for subsistence income support. Once financial eligibility has been established, the file is then sent to the local Disability Determination Service for evaluation.

Eligibility for SSDI

Requirements for SSDI eligibility are fairly straightforward. Workers under 65 (workers 65 and older qualify for Social Security retirement benefits) who have worked long enough and recently enough, and contributed to the Social Security Trust Fund, are insured. Eligible disabled family members may also receive benefits by qualifying on the worker's work history. Eligible family members include a qualified worker's unmarried son or daughter (including stepchild, adopted child, and, in some cases, a grandchild) who is under 18 or under 19 if in high school full time; a qualified worker's unmarried son or daughter disabled before 22 (benefits may start as early as age 18); a qualified worker's spouse who is caring for the qualified worker's child who is under 16 or disabled and also receiving checks or a spouse who is age 62 or older; a qualified worker's disabled widow or widower (benefits are payable at age 50) if the disability occurred before the qualified worker's death or within seven years after death; and a qualified worker's disabled surviving divorced wife or husband (if the marriage lasted ten years or longer) -- benefits are payable at age 50 on the same basis as to a disabled widow or widower (USDHHS, January 1988a, pp. 6-7).

In 1988, a worker would earn one "credit," or quarter, of coverage for every $470 in earnings, up to four credits of coverage with annual earnings of $1,840 or more. This amount increases each year as the general wage rate increases. The number of years of work credits needed for disability depends on the age of the applicant when he or she became disabled (USDHHS, January 1988a, pp. 6-7).

If the applicant is younger than 24, he or she needs to have six credits in the three-year period ending when the disability starts. If the applicant is 24 to 31 years of age, he or she needs credit for having worked half the time between age 21 and the time he or she became disabled. When the applicant is over 31, the number of credits needed is shown in Table 12.1.

Table 12.1. Work Credits Needed for SSDI Eligibility

Born after 1929, Disabled at Age	Born before 1930, Disabled before Age 62	Credits Needed
31 through 42		20
44		22
46		24
48		26
50		28
52		30
53		31
54		32
55		33
56		34
57	1986	35
58	1987	36
59	1988	37
60	1989	38
62 or older	1991 or later	40

Source: USDHHS, January 1988a, p. 7.

Unlike the regulations for SSI, income and resources will not affect an applicant's eligibility for SSDI or the amount of the payment. However, income may affect the determination of disability. In addition to cash benefits, an individual who receives SSDI benefits is eligible for Medicare benefits after he or she has received SSDI cash payments for at least 24 months during the last five years. After the disabled person has submitted his or her application to the SSA office and has met the financial/work history requirements for SSI or SSDI, the file is sent to the DDS. This is the point in the application process at which the disability is determined. It generally takes two to three months to process a disability claim. If the application is approved, monthly benefits will generally start with the sixth full month of disability in the case of SSDI. The waiting period for SSI is normally shorter.

If the applicant's claim is disapproved there are four levels of appeal. The first is reconsideration, which gives the applicant an opportunity to submit any new evidence not previously considered. The second level of appeal is an administrative law judge who is empowered to consider any new evidence. The third level is the SSA Appeals Council in Baltimore. The last level of appeal is the Federal District Court (Torrey, 1988, p. 252).

Benefits usually continue unless the beneficiary's condition medically changes and he or she can perform substantially gainful activity. SSI applicants must immediately report any changes in their financial situation. There are continuing disability reviews which are conducted periodically to check whether or not the disabled person's ability to perform SGA has improved. These are conducted every 6 to 18 months for those expected to improve and every five to seven years for those persons not expected to improve (USDHHS, January 1988a, pp. 6-7).

Benefit Levels

SSI. In 1988 benefits for a person receiving no income and assets under acceptable levels were $354 per month for an individual living alone and $240 per month for an individual living with his or her family. Benefits will normally be less than this amount. For those individuals with a mental illness diagnosis receiving SSI benefits in Texas in December 1988, the average monthly benefit was $228.68 (Schmulowitz, Interview, November 15 and 21, 1988).

There are some "work incentives." The following will not be deducted from the SSI benefit check: $65 earned income per month; or $1 for every $2 earned over that amount. If a disabled person works where the wages are subsidized, only one-half of the unsubsidized wages are deducted from the SSI check (USDHHS, June 1988). Medicaid benefits will not be discontinued when an individual receives income that reduces his or her SSI benefits.

The Program for Achieving Self Support (PASS) allows disabled SSI recipients to set aside income for a specific work goal, such as education, training or the purchase of specific tools. Applicants must submit a work plan; if approved, they are exempt from the income limits for the duration of the plan (Craig and Wright, 1987, p. 83).

Table 12.2. Approximate Monthly Disability Benefits If the Worker Became Disabled in 1988 and Had Steady Earnings

		Disabled Worker's Earnings in 1987						
Worker's Age	Worker's Family	$10K	$15K	$20K	$25K	$30K	$35K	$43K+
25	Disabled Worker	$459	$ 595	$ 731	$837	$837	$964	$1,076
	Disabled Worker Spouse and Child	689	894	1,098	1,256	1,351	1,447	1,615
35	Disabled Worker	449	579	710	824	885	941	1,005
	Disabled Worker Spouse and Child	674	870	1,066	1,237	1,328	1,413	1,509
45	Disabled Worker	447	578	708	821	869	900	936
	Disabled Worker Spouse and Child	672	867	1,063	1,233	1,304	1,351	1,404
55	Disabled Worker	446	577	707	810	842	862	886
	Disabled Worker Spouse and Child	670	866	1,061	1,215	1,263	1,294	1,330
64	Disabled Worker	435	562	689	785	813	832	853
	Disabled Worker Spouse and Child	653	843	1,034	1,178	1,221	1,248	1,280

Source: USDHHS, January 1988a, p. 14.

218

SSDI. Table 12.2 illustrates monthly disability benefits for workers who had steady work histories. The amount of monthly benefits is based on a worker's lifetime average earnings covered by Social Security. The average monthly benefit for a disabled worker early in 1988 was $508; the average payment to a disabled worker with a family was $919 (USDHHS, January 1988b, p. 13). Since most CMI have unstable work histories, the amount of their benefits, if they are eligible at all, will generally be less than the amounts shown above. According to the most recent information from the SSA, the average benefit amount for SSDI recipients with a mental illness diagnosis receiving benefits in December of 1987 in Texas was $473.10 (Schmulowitz, Interview, November 21 and November 28, 1988).

There is a trial work period for SSDI recipients during which payments are maintained at their current levels even though there is income from other sources. For 15 months after the trial period ends, SSDI can supplement work earnings if they slip below $300 a month. After SSDI ends, Medicare continues for two years (Craig and Wright, 1987, p. 83). People can receive both SSI and SSDI at the same time, but the amount of the SSDI benefit will be subtracted from the SSI check. Since the waiting period for SSDI is so long, people can receive SSI benefits until they start receiving SSDI checks if they are eligible for both (USDHHS, June 1988).

How Many Persons with Mental Illness Use SSI and SSDI?

The most current statistics available from the Social Security Administration's Office of Research and Statistics in Baltimore are from December of 1987. These numbers come from a representative sample consisting of one percent of all people in Texas getting SSI and SSDI benefits as of December 1987.

It should be noted that there are two problems with identifying the CMI who are receiving SSI and SSDI (Tables 12.3 and 12.4). First, only 80 percent of the SSDI files and 70 percent of the SSI files list a diagnosis of any kind. Although the SSA began keying the diagnosis into the system in 1969, it did not start requiring states to provide this information until 1983. Since those people with chronic disorders are required to have disability reviews at five- to seven-year intervals, these 1987 data will not include all who have a mental disorder diagnosis. Second, when diagnosis was first keyed into the files in 1969, the entire International Classifications of Diseases (ICD-9) diagnosis code was used. However, in 1985, an abbreviated form listing only the broad categories of disabilities (e.g., mental retardation; mental disorders other than MR) was implemented. So these data will include other people besides the CMI. Table 12.3 shows the number of SSI and SSDI recipients in Texas as of December 1987 with an MH diagnosis, the percentage of total Texas recipients, and the national percentage of recipients with an MH diagnosis.

Table 12.3. SSI and SSDI Recipients in Texas in December of 1987

Program	Total Number in Texas	Files with Diagnosis	Percentage with MH Diagnosis	National Average	Total with MH Diagnosis in Texas
SSI	152,000	112,000	17.2	24.1	19,264
SSDI	130,700	122,000	18.6	18.4	22,692

Source: Schmulowitz, Interview, November 21, and 28, 1988.

Table 12.4 shows the national distribution of SSDI recipients with a diagnosis of schizophrenia between 1978 and 1985. The numbers in this table are based on a 20 percent sample of all SSDI recipients. In 1987 5.6 percent of SSDI recipients had a diagnosis of schizophrenia. In 1981 this level fell 39.6 percent to 3.4 percent of SSDI recipients and stayed near that low level through 1982. For FY 1983, rule changes precipitated by the dramatic number of appeals of disability determinations dramatically increased the number of schizophrenics approved for disability payments.

Table 12.4. Number and Percentage of the National Distribution of SSDI Recipients with Schizophrenia by Year*

Year	Total Files	Files with Schizophrenia	Percentage of Total with Schizophrenia
1978	464,415	25,900	5.6
1981	345,252	11,762	3.4
1982	298,531	9,545	3.2
1983	311,490	18,340	5.9
1984	357,140	21,781	6.1
1985	377,371	21,889	5.8

Source: USDHHS, December 1987, p. 132.

Note: *Based on a 20 percent sample.

There are no data immediately available as to the number of SSI recipients with schizophrenia. The percentage of these recipients will be greater for SSI than for SSDI for reasons stated earlier in the text. Table 12.5 which further illustrates this point, indicates the number of case-managed MH clients who received federal support during FY 1988.

Table 12.5. Texas Mental Health Case-Managed Patients Receiving Federal Support During FY 1987

Program	Number Receiving Benefits
SSI	5,529
SSDI	1,331
Food Stamps	1,893

Source: Collins, Interview, September 28, 1988.

Note: There were 7,816 MH clients within the case management system during FY 1987.

Problems with SSI and SSDI for the CMI

The primary problem that the CMI have with these two programs is that the application, eligibility, review, and appeal processes were not designed with the CMI in mind. Though the evaluation process has been modified to be more accommodating, it is still a very complicated and confusing process that most persons with mental illness have to be guided through or that has to be handled by a representative. This prevents some mentally ill persons from applying for assistance.

The level of payment for SSI recipients is sharply reduced when an individual receives support or in-kind benefits from a household provider. SSI benefits are cut by one-third when the recipient is living with his or her family. Families of the CMI often feel that this is a form of discrimination against them for trying to take responsibility to care for their family member in the community. The eligibility requirements for SSI make for hardship, and there is not enough flexibility in considering wages and resources. This can be a problem with the CMI when they have periods of wellness followed by periods of psychotic episodes in which they cannot work.

An important issue among some case managers has been the problem of dependence by the CMI on income support programs. The case management team at Tri-County CMHMRC in Conroe expressed the philosophy that their job was to get their clients as independent as possible as quickly as prudent. They feared that by getting their clients dependent upon SSI or SSDI, they would have no incentive to find work, since that would lead to cessation of cash benefits and Medicaid coverage. While there are those who should never be dropped from the welfare roles, there are many who can benefit from self-dependence that these income support systems might sabotage (Young, Interview, October 4, 1988).

There are several possible actions to help alleviate some of these problems. Expansion of the case manager program could reach more of the CMI and help others through the eligibility and disability process. The possibility of using the proposed expansion of Medicaid to cover case management and rehabilitation services could aid greatly in delivery of benefits to the CMI. Furthermore, advocacy/outreach programs could locate and aid those CMI who are eligible for benefits but are not currently receiving them. Finally, use of SSI Clinics could help those who are homeless or are not being served by the mental health system in getting through the applications and disability determination process (Farr, 1986, p. 77).

SSI Supplementation

Many of the chronically mentally ill in Texas do receive assistance from the federal government through the SSI program. One avenue to increase the number of persons eligible for SSI, and therefore for Medicaid, is for the state to supplement the federal portion of the SSI check with state funds. By increasing the total amount given to SSI recipients, the maximum total income that a recipient could receive would be larger. This would make many applicants eligible who are currently ineligible for SSI benefits because they have a slightly higher income than allowed. The extension of Medicaid benefits to those receiving only the state supplement is optional (U.S. Congress, House of Representatives, Committee on Energy and Commerce, November 1988, p. 57).

The importance of state supplementation lies in increasing the number of eligible recipients and increasing the benefits for existing or targeted recipients. The increase in the amount received by seriously mentally ill individuals leads back to one major problem faced by deinstitutionalized persons -- housing. Increases in available funds to the CMI and other disabled persons would give them more flexibility in finding adequate housing. In California, the state supplement is specified to be used for housing. Other states give supplements specifically to SSI recipients living in specific types of licensed personal care homes.

Such a stipulation would give owners and operators of board and care homes the financial incentive to improve their facilities and services and obtain licenses. This could be a way of eliminating or registering many of the unregistered board-and-care homes in the state which provide minimal care at the price of the entire SSI check.

As of January of 1988 27 states had some kind of state supplementation of SSI. This supplementation ranged from $2 per month in Oregon to $393 in Connecticut. By increasing the total amount of the benefit given to SSI recipients, the increase in the maximum allowable income is also increased. Table 12.6 shows the SSI maximum allowable income limits for individuals in selected states as of January 1988.

Table 12.6. SSI Maximum Allowable Income Limits for Individuals for Selected States in January of 1988

State	SSI Income (Maximum Benefit)		With Earned Income	
	Monthly Income*	% of Poverty**	Monthly Income***	% of Poverty**
California	575	119.58	1,235	256.85
Colorado	412	85.68	909	189.05
Connecticut	747	155.36	1,579	328.39
Massachusetts	483	100.45	1,051	218.58
Michigan (Wayne Co.)	384	79.86	853	177.40
New York (NYC)	426	88.60	937	194.87
Oklahoma	418	86.93	921	191.54
Pennsylvania	386	80.28	857	178.23
Texas	354	73.62	793	164.92

Source: U.S. Congress, House of Representatives, Committee on Energy and Commerce, November 1988, pp. 289-290.

Notes: *   Monthly income estimate is maximum SSI benefit. Generally, SSI eligibility rules allow an additional $20 monthly income.
          **   Percentage figures are based on the annual 1988 federal poverty guidelines for an individual.
          ***   Monthly income estimate assumes that $20 monthly income disregard is in effect. In addition, the estimate assumes that the first $60 of earned income and one-half of remaining earned income is disregarded.

In addition to the added amount spent on supplementing SSI checks, there would be other costs associated with such a plan. If Texas chooses to extend Medicaid eligibility to those receiving only the state supplement, the amount Texas would have to spend on Medicaid would also increase. There would also be the nominal expense of establishing and administering such a program.

While the addition of funds for SSI supplements and related costs would be a hard fiscal pill for Texas legislators to swallow, additional obstacles would have to be dealt with before implementation. There are specific provisions within the state constitution limiting the amount of funds which can be spent on assistance grants to the needy. The Texas constitution was amended in 1982 to raise the limit on assistance payments to a maximum amount not to exceed one percent of the state budget (Texas State Constitution, 1982, p. 620). During the 1990-1991 biennium the budget for Texas is $46.5 billion (Texas H.B. 222, 1989, p. xi). In accordance with the constitutional limitations, Texas welfare agencies can only disburse $465 million per biennium, or an average of $232.5 million per year.

The amount estimated previously of $217 million approaches this constitutionally mandated limitation on state grants in aid. If a supplementation plan similar to the one outlined above were to be considered, an additional set of steps would have to be taken. In order for these funds to be released, the legislature would have to approve an amendment to the constitution to increase the ceiling on assistance grants to the needy

222

for the voters of Texas to approve. Only when the Texas voters approve the amendment may the legislature raise and appropriate the funds necessary for SSI payments to be supplemented by Texas general revenue funds. While this would be difficult, supplementation of SSI payments is an option that should be considered when discussing the improvement of services to the mentally ill.

If supplementation were to be granted only to specific groups of persons for the purpose of housing, the cost could be much less. Estimates would depend on the number of SSI recipients living in currently licensed personal care homes. A 1988 study by TDHS estimated that there would be 3,262 aged and disabled persons in licensed personal care homes in Texas during FY 1990. The impetus for this study was that the implementation of a state supplementation program would enable SSI recipients and low-income individuals to increase their disposable income, thereby allowing them to purchase more adequate housing. The study found that the additional cost to the state during FY 1990 would be $5,540,045 (TDHS, June 1988).

THE FOOD STAMP PROGRAM IN TEXAS: IMPLICATIONS FOR THE CHRONICALLY MENTALLY ILL

Food stamps can be an important tool for the CMI while living in a community-based setting. They provide the mentally ill person with benefits which smooth the transition from institutional settings, or give the needed resources to ease financial pressures that might force the individual to abandon an otherwise successful life in the community.

The program is administered by the United States Department of Agriculture (USDA) at the federal level. It is responsible for the printing and distribution of the stamps to the states and oversees participation by retail food stores and other food outlets. The Federal Reserve System is also involved in that food stamps are deposited in banks by food outlets and redeemed and converted into cash. The Treasury Department and Social Security Administration both provide some information used by states in verifying a recipient's income and assets (Richardson and Falk, 1985, p. 4). In Texas, this program is administered by the Texas Department of Human Services (TDHS), which is responsible for determining eligibility and issuing benefits.

The Food Stamp Act provides for 100 percent federal funding of benefits. Federal funds also pay for federal administrative costs and for 50 percent of the state and local administrative costs. "State and local costs associated with computerization and fraud control activities are eligible for 75 percent federal funding" (Richardson and Falk, 1985 p. 4).

In FY 1988, the food stamp program distributed $12.4 billion nationally in food stamp benefits to an average of 18.6 million people per month (Smith, Interview, November 30, 1988). The level of benefits in Texas in May of 1988 was $81,255,064 worth of food stamps distributed to 1,547,963 people. The average household size was 3.1 persons (TDHS, June 1988, p. 5).

Eligibility and Benefits

Eligibility for this program is determined by household, not by individuals within the household. Except in special circumstances, the tests for eligibility apply to the aggregate income and assets of all household members. The food stamp program imposes three major tests for eligibility: household income limits, liquid asset limitations, and work registration and job search requirements. Some cash welfare recipients are exempt from work requirements or the asset test on the assumption they meet similar tests under the welfare program.

Those beneficiaries who are disabled are exempted from many work and household income requirements. This is especially important when there are several eligible disabled beneficiaries living in the same household (i.e., a board and care home). In this case, each person is considered a separate household. For the purpose of this discussion it is assumed that those people receiving food stamps who are CMI have gone through the disability determination process and are receiving some level of SSI or SSDI assistance.

In order to qualify for food stamps, a household must have gross monthly income below 130 percent of the federally mandated poverty levels for that size household and countable monthly income at or below the poverty level. For FY 1989, the maximum gross (130 percent of the poverty rate) income that a single-person household could have and still be eligible for food stamps was $626 per month. Income after deductions and exemptions would have to be less than $482 per month to still be eligible. Each additional person in the household adds $212 gross ($162 countable) income to still be below the poverty line (TDHS, June 1988, p. 8).

To be eligible, households must not have liquid assets exceeding $2,000. Liquid assets refer to any item easily converted into cash. However, calculation of liquid assets "excludes the value of a residence, a portion of the value of motor vehicles, business assets, household belongings and certain other resources" (TDHS, June 1988, p. 11).

Maximum benefits are based on the costs of the USDA's "Thrifty Food Plan." This is the amount of food needed for a family to have a nutritious, low-cost diet. Benefits for a single eligible person in Texas range from $10 (minimum benefit for those eligible) to $87, depending on the monthly countable income (Table 12.7).

Table 12.7. Food Stamps Monthly Allotment by Monthly Countable Income and Household Size as of May 1988

Household Size

Countable Income	1	2	3	4	5	6	7	8
$0	$87	$159	$228	$290	$344	$413	$457	$522
24-26	77	151	220	282	336	405	449	514
47-50	72	144	213	275	329	398	442	507
74-76	64	136	205	267	321	390	434	499
97-100	57	129	198	260	314	383	427	492
124-126	49	121	190	252	306	375	419	484
147-150	42	114	183	245	299	368	412	477

Source: TDHS, June 1988, p. 4.

Food stamps are issued monthly. In most states (including Texas) they can be picked up at any U.S. Post Office or TDHS local office. TDHS is required by federal law to determine eligibility within 30 days of application. There is an "expedited" process (5-day service) for those families with little or no income or assets (TDHS, July 1986).

Typically, participating households use their allotment in grocery stores that have been approved to accept food stamps. To be approved, a store must demonstrate that 50 percent of its food sales are staple foods. In addition, wholesalers may be approved to accept food stamps from retailers, and participating meal service programs in certain instances (e.g., Meals on Wheels) may also be approved to accept food stamps. Once they have accepted food stamps, retailers, wholesalers, and approved meal service programs deposit the stamps in banks, where they convert immediately to cash and are eventually redeemed, through the Federal Reserve System, by the U.S. Treasury.

Table 12.8 shows an example of how a particular applicant would be evaluated. This case involves a single male with schizophrenia receiving an SSI check for $354 per month and no other income; he lives in a board and care home which charges $250 a month rent and has $33 in out-of-pocket medical expenses.

Table 12.8. Example of the Calculation of Monthly Food Stamp Benefit

Gross Income	$ 354
Less "Standard deduction"	$ 106
Less 18% of earnings	$ 63
Less Medical expenses over $38	$ 0
Less dependent-care expenses	$ 0
Less shelter expenses over 50% of income remaining after above deductions have been applied	$ 157
Countable Income	$ 28
Maximum monthly Benefit	$ 77
Less 30% of countable income	$ 8
Benefit	$ 69

Source: TDHS, July 1986.

Food stamps may be used to purchase the following items: (1) food for home preparation and human consumption, not including alcohol, tobacco, or hot foods intended for immediate consumption; (2) seed and plants for use in gardens to produce food for personal consumption by the eligible household; (3) meals prepared and served through approved communal dinning programs for the elderly and disabled, including meals in senior citizens centers, meals served in restaurants at concessional prices under an agreement with the appropriate state agency, and meals served through similar programs directed at the elderly and disabled; (4) meals prepared and served in approved drug addiction and alcoholic treatment programs, small group homes for the disabled, and shelters for battered women and children; and (5) equipment for procuring food by hunting and fishing (excepting firearms, ammunition, explosives, and equipment for transportation, clothing, or shelter) where the household lives in certain remote areas of Alaska (Richardson and Falk, 1985, p. 22).

Food stamps are issued in booklets and in several denominations, the lowest of which is $1. When change is necessary, all change of $1 or more must be in food stamps; change of $0.99 or less is in cash (TDHS, June 1988, p. 17).

Food Stamps and the CMI

There are several problems in studying food stamp use by the CMI. The primary one is that TDHS does not list a specific diagnosis in the files of those receiving food stamps. It does list sources of income so that the number of SSI and SSDI recipients who are getting food stamps is determinable. Another problem is that the food stamp program is primarily designed with families in mind. As Table 12.9 shows, 53.8 percent

(805,535) of the recipients were children and 40.9 percent were under 13. Only 24.5 percent (114,873) were single-person households. If it is assumed that most CMI will be listed as single-member households, their potential eligibility and level of benefits could be sharply reduced when some income is earned beyond their SSI checks.

The only statistics currently available concerning the use of food stamps by the CMI are through the case management program (Table 12.5). Of the 7,816 people who had case managers in FY 1988 in Texas, 1,893 (24.2 percent) were receiving some level of food stamp benefits. As noted earlier in this chapter, 6,860 of those in the case management program were receiving SSI or SSDI. With this wide variation in numbers, it cannot be assumed that, because a person is receiving SSI or SSDI, he or she will automatically be receiving food stamps.

Of the 499,280 households receiving food stamps in Texas during FY 1988, 40.7 percent were receiving SSI or SSDI benefits. If it is assumed that 18.6 percent of the total number of SSI and SSDI recipients will have a mental illness diagnosis (Table 12.3), the approximate number would be 37,796 (roughly the total number of SSI/SSDI recipients with a mental illness diagnosis in Texas) with an average benefit of $55.08 per person. In order to fully estimate the current and future costs and sources of funding for the CMI in Texas a better accounting of the use of food stamps is needed. There is not enough information currently available to make confident assumptions as to the number of CMI currently receiving food stamps.

As with SSI and SSDI, there can be a problem with dependence on government assistance. When the assistance becomes an impediment to living a full and productive life, this income support can be a destructive force to the adjustment of individuals with serious mental illness into society.

THE IN-HOME AND FAMILY SUPPORT PROGRAM

The Texas In-Home and Family Support Program was created by House Bill 1154, passed by the 70th Texas Legislature on June 19, 1987, and implemented on September 1, 1987. The goal of the program is "to enable persons with mental disabilities [mental illness/retardation] or developmental disabilities to purchase services that support them in living as independently as possible in the community" (TDMHMR and TDHS, 1989, p. 1). The program is administered by two state agencies, the Texas Department of Human Services (TDHS) and the Texas Department of Mental Health and Mental Retardation (TDMHMR). TDMHMR provides this program to mentally ill or retarded citizens and their families, and TDHS serves those with developmental disabilities.

The TDHS component consists of a pilot program in Bexar County for persons with developmental disabilities not served by TDMHMR. This program is funded by a $315,000 grant from the Texas Rehabilitation Commission, on behalf of the Texas Planning Council for Developmental Disabilities, for each year of the biennium. TDMHMR's In-Home and Family Support Program (informally known as the "1154" program) is a unique program for financing care for the CMI. It is unique for several reasons. It is the only income support plan for the CMI that is paid out of the Texas

Table 12.9. Texas Food Stamp Client Profile
State Totals, December 1987

1. | Sex | Male | Female |
   |---|---|---|
   | Head of Household (HH) | 29.5% | 70.4% |
   | All Recipients | 42.3% | 57.6% |

2. | Age | 0-5 | 6-12 | 13-17 | 18-29 | 30-39 | 40-49 | 50-59 | 60-64 | 65+ |
   |---|---|---|---|---|---|---|---|---|---|
   | HH | 0 | 0 | 0.5 | 30.0 | 25.8 | 13.6 | 9.7 | 4.7 | 15.7 |
   | All | 20.4 | 20.5 | 11.7 | 16.9 | 11.6 | 6.2 | 4.5 | 2.1 | 6.0 |

3. Children

Average # of Children/Households with Children	2.53
Percentage of Households with Children	67.70
Total # of Children	805,535

4. Family Size

   Average Family Size = 3.12

Number in Household	1	2	3	4	5	6	7	8+
Percentage of Households	24.5	19.3	18.6	15.7	10.6	6.0	3.0	2.3

5. | Ethnicity | Households | Recipients |
   |---|---|---|
   | Anglo | 27.8% | 21.5% |
   | Black | 28.4% | 26.1% |
   | Mexican-American | 41.5% | 50.7% |
   | Indian | 0.2% | 0.2% |
   | Asian | 0.7% | 0.7% |
   | Other | 1.4% | 0.8% |

6. Income

Earned $ Average	=	577.42	31.8%	have earned income
Total $ Average	=	440.68	87.2%	have income

7. Recipient Status in Household

	Number	Percentage
Head of Household	468,872	31.3
Other Adult	222,467	14.9
Child	805,535	53.8
Total	1,496,874	100.0

(Continued Next Page)

227

Table 12.9. (Continued) Texas Food Stamp Client Profile
State Totals December 1987

8. Employment Status

	Head of Household	Other Adult	All Recipients	Avg. Coupon Value By Work Reg. of HH
Full-time Employed	13.2	13.5	6.2	$177.36
Part-time Employed	3.9	4.6	1.9	195.53
Seeking Work	23.6	35.9	12.7	192.94
Over Age 60	17.6	9.7	6.9	51.63
Disabled	11.2	8.2	4.7	114.75
Caring for Child	26.4	20.4	11.3	228.54
Caring for Disabled	0.7	1.7	0.5	172.19
Rehab. Treatment	0.3	0.0	0.1	84.80
Other	3.0	6.1	1.8	170.25
Children Under 18	0.0	0.0	53.8	0.00

Average Coupon Value for all Households = $165.57

9. Food Stamp Caseload

	Households
Percentage with SSI	19.2%
Percentage with SSDI	21.5%
Percentage with AFDC	25.4%
Total SSI Benefits/Month	$19,860,046

10. Caseload Data

	Households	Recipients	Benefits
FY 1987	475,139	1,524,039	$868,699,269
FY 1988	499,280	1,601,473	$949,609,532

Source: TDHS, December 1987.

228

State Treasury. It is also uncommon in originating outside of TDMHMR. Implementedat the request of consumers of MHMR and developmental disability services, their families, and various advocacy groups, the program "meets the criteria of flexibility, simplicity and personal autonomy requested by consumers, families and advocates because it combines a powerful, humane set of values with a responsive service delivery system" (TDMHMR and TDHS, 1989, p. 1).

The purpose of this legislation is to "foster independent choice by persons with a mental disability in the selection of services to be provided; to assist such persons to be able to live independently in situations most like those experienced by persons without disabilities; to uphold the value of the family and the human dignity, pride, and independence of the individual; and to recognize the family as the primary mainstay for many persons with mental disabilities" (TDMHMR, 1988, p. 3).

This program is also unique among income support programs in that it does not exclude middle-income families served by TDMHMR and TDHS. All people at or below the median income for the state (Table 12.10) will have 100 percent of their approved request paid. For those whose income is above this level a copayment is required.

Table 12.10. Median Family Income for Participation in the 1154 Program with No Copayment Required

Family Size	Median Income
1	$16,738
2	$21,889
3	$27,039
4	$32,189
5	$37,339
6	$42,489

Source: TDMHMR, 1988, p. 5.

Note: For each additional family member, add $ 1,900.

Table 12.11 shows the maximum copayment range based on a family's median income. If a family's income is below 105 percent of the state's median income, there is no copayment. When the family has income above the state's median income, the copayment range goes up as listed in Table 12.11.

Table 12.11 Maximum Copayment Range by Percentage of Median Income

Income:	Maximum Copay Range
105% of Median	$ 360-$ 720
125% of Median	$ 1,800-$ 3,600
150% of Median	$ 3,600-$ 7,200

Source: TDMHMR, 1988, p. 5.

This is not an entitlement program. A specific amount of money is budgeted, and once that money is exhausted, all requests are denied (TDMHMR, 1988, p. 2). There are many advantages and disadvantages to this type of program. Issues of dependency, fairness, and efficacy have been brought up and will be discussed later in this section.

The program is administered through the community mental health centers, which are given broad latitude in the determination of eligibility, payment rates, and copayments (if any) and provide proper documentation for the program. Not all CMHMRCs participate in this program. The program is currently available only in certain locations. For mental health clients in FY 1988 there were 14 CMHMRCs providing this program and 19 in FY 1989. Table 12.12 is a listing of all the CMHMRCs that have 1154 programs and the amounts appropriated for 1988 and 1989. The aggregate number of clients served during FY 1988 by each of the centers has been included in order to compare the centers.

**Table 12.12. H.B. 1154 Obligation for Mental Health
Services for FY 1988 and 1989**

Participating CMHMRC	FY 1988	FY 1989	Biennium Total	Clients Served by All Funds In FY 1988	$ FY 89/ Clients Served
Austin-Travis	$ 0	$ 55,000	$ 55,000	6.223	8.84
Bexas County	51,000	20,000	71,000	10,948	1.83
Brazos Valley	66,000	75,000	141,000	1,687	44.46
Collin County	66,000	68,000	134,000	2,264	30.04
Concho Valley	9,000	22,000	31,000	611	36.01
Dallas County	125,000	263,000	388,000	11,441	22.99
Deep East Texas	0	66,000	66,000	2,522	26.17
Denton County	60,000	60,000	120,000	1,461	41.07
Gulf Bend	0	6,000	6,000	2,401	2.50
Gulf Coast	104,000	199,000	303,000	2,200	90.46
Harris County	125,000	235,000	360,000	13,564	17.33
Heart of Texas	0	23,000	23,000	1,622	14.18
Johnson County	28,000	43,000	71,000	479	89.77
Life Management Center	81,000	156,000	237,000	5,739	27.18
Lubbock	0	33,000	33,000	3,327	9.92
Permian Basin	21,000	96,000	117,000	2,701	35.54
Tarrant County	83,000	181,000	264,000	12,529	14.45
Tri County	44,000	117,000	161,000	2,262	51.72
Tropical Texas	137,000	282,000	419,000	4,863	57.99
Totals	$1,000,000	$2,000,000	$3,000,000	88,844	22.51

Source: TDMHMR, 1988.

Through this program, eligible persons and/or their families can receive up to $3,600 per fiscal year for various support services in order to help a client better cope with community living. These support services can include (1) medical, surgical, therapeutic, diagnostic, and other health services related to a person's mental disability, including medication; (2) original or unique services consistent with the intent of the enabling legislation and as negotiated between the family or person and the administering agency; and (3) architectural modifications to the home and/or purchase or lease of special equipment or supplies that improve or facilitate the care, treatment, therapy, general living conditions, or access of the person with a mental disability (Moore, Interview, April 11, 1989).

The $3,600 can be paid out in one lump sum or spread over a fiscal year. Eligible services have been reported to vary from buying tires for cars to having dental work done (Young, Interview, October 4, 1988). An additional $3,600 can be paid for architectural modifications to the consumer's residence or for special equipment. It is up to the staff of the CMHMRC to determine whether the service requested by the client or family falls within the guidelines set forth by TDMHMR.

Eligibility for the program is determined by the CMHMRC based on rules promulgated by TDMHMR. A request for money must be made on an individual basis by the person or family. Upon receiving the request for support, a local committee at the CMHMRC must first determine whether the client is eligible and then whether the service requested for payment is appropriate. Eligibility is determined by meeting the four criteria of diagnosis, residency, income, and need (TDMHMR and TDHS, 1989, p. 5).

"In-Home and Family Support offers flexibility to truly individualize the service options to meet the consumers' needs" (TDMHMR and TDHS, 1989, p. A-2). Because the eligible services are broad enough, the mental health authority has a great deal of latitude in what services will be provided. Persons who are being served in a 24-hour residential treatment program are not eligible. The funds cannot be used to augment services provided through other local, state, or federal programs, but participation in any other government entitlement does not affect eligibility. Receipt of 1154 funds does not affect the amount of support given to the person by federal income support programs.

A person or family who is denied eligibility can request a hearing. The CMHMRC must provide documentation as to why the application was denied. (Denial of a request for services due to lack of available funding is not considered grounds for appeal.) Each CMHMRC must set up its own payment system based on TDMHMR guidelines. The rules for establishment of a payment method are as follows:

1. Support for services. The amount of support, not to exceed $3,600 in each fiscal year for each person with a mental disability or family, will be determined on an individual basis. Another rule is that funds may be disbursed in a lump sum or on a periodic basis. With the agreement of the family or the person with a mental disability, as appropriate, payment may be made to the person with a mental disability, the family, or the vendor. The amount of support shall be reduced by the appropriate copayment, if any, and additional amounts may be granted on an individual basis by the commissioner or designee.

2. Support for architectural modification and/or the purchase or lease of equipment or supplies. Additional support may be awarded as a one-time grant of not more than $3,600. Upon specific request and with the agreement of the administering agency, funds may be encumbered for this purpose as monies are available. All architectural modifications, equipment, and supplies purchased with these funds become the property of the person with a mental disability or family and shall not be inventoried by the administering agency or TDMHMR. Architectural modifications on leased property shall be the property of the owner of the property.

3. Determination of the amount of support and copayment. This determination shall be based on the income of the primary recipient of services as documented in the written plan (between the applicant and the CMHMRC), either the person with the mental disability or the family. If the primary recipient is a person with a mental disability who is under 18 years of age, the determination shall be based on the family's income. The administering agency shall base its determination of income from the previous year's income tax

return or other locally acceptable and documented indicator, excluding income from fixed assets such as real property or trusts. The administering agency shall determine the percentage of copayment required using a sliding scale with a base for full compensation that corresponds to Texas median income levels established by TDHS, without adjustment for present or future expenses [Table 12.11]. The amount of the copayment shall be the appropriate percentage of the total cost of services requested. The administering agency uses the base for full compensation as shown above, but can use its own scale to determine the amount of copayment required of participants with income above the median [Table 12.10].

4.   Accountability. The disbursement of support shall be in accordance with the laws of the state and shall include documentation that permits auditing by TDMHMR and the administering agency.

5.   Payment rates. Funding for services or architectural modifications and special equipment shall not exceed the prevailing rates for the area as determined by the administering agency. (TDMHMR, 1988, p. 7)

Use of 1154

This program has been used by 1,432 mental health clients between September 1988 through the first quarter of FY 1989 (TDMHMR and TDHS, 1989, p. A-9). 1154 funds have been allocated as a part of the CMHMRC equalization monies. These are additional funds appropriated and used to ensure that CMHMRCs with different amounts of per capita state support receive a more equal level of per capita funding from the state. CMHMRCs cannot participate in the 1154 program at the expense of other programs for the mentally ill. Funds are distributed to the various CMHMRCs in the program through a very complicated formula. This formula uses the percentage of state/federal funds of the total budget for the CMHMRC, the factors that go into affecting the level of local match, and other considerations. One result of this process is apparent inequities; for example, Johnson County, which has 10 percent of the population of Travis County, will receive 30 percent more 1154 funds than Travis County (Table 12.12).

There are some additional variations in the amounts of funding between CMHMRCs. Bexar County receives one-third of the funds that the Life Management Center receives, even though Bexar County has more than double the population of El Paso. This can be seen in several instances. The inconsistencies in funding were explained by TDMHMR staff as a result of using the formula mentioned above, along with tying the funds to appropriations from equalization monies. It is not so much that these funds are being specifically appropriated for the 1154 program as that a specific percentage of the equalization monies are to be used for the 1154 program. If a center's percentage of equalization monies goes up, the amount for that center's 1154 programs will go up. This still points to some lack of fairness and efficacy in the distribution of the 1154 funds. Those areas that may need the program the most cannot offer it because they would have to sacrifice other programs paid for through monies from the equalization fund (Moore, Interview, April 11, 1989).

Future Directions of 1154

Appropriations for FY 1990-1991 for this program, for mental health clients, is the same as for the FY 1988-1989 biennium: $2 million for each year. Before the session adjourned, mental health advocacy groups said that they would not push 1154 at the expense of other programs for the mentally ill. It was seen as an important program, but not as important as others (Moore, Interview, April 11, 1989).

One innovation for this program is the potential use of an Electronic Voucher System (EVS). The EVS uses debit cards given to program participants. TDMHMR explains the system in this way:

> [EVS] enables individuals and their families to obtain products or services by presenting the card to service providers mutually agreed upon with MHMR. The EVS is handled by contract with FundsNet, a Dallas based company. The debit card identifies the consumer, projected services to be delivered, and the percentage of copayment the consumer must make. When purchasing products or services, the consumer presents the cared to the provider. The provider contacts FundsNet using a toll-free number to request payment for the services or products. Approved transactions are electronically debited from the CMHMRC's bank account and credited to the provider's bank account . . . MHMR maintains control through enrollment of the mutually agreed upon providers and conscientious case coordination. (TDMHMR and TDHS, 1989, p. A-13)

The EVS system has yet to be implemented on a system-wide basis. There are some problems with this system, and some TDMHMR staff have been less than enthusiastic about its implementation. It is felt that start-up costs could be much higher than expected and implementation much more complicated than anticipated by its proponents (Moore, Interview, April 11, 1989). If only 2,000 people are going to be using this system, it may not be efficient to set up EVS for so few clients.

Yet some advantages for this system have been identified by TDMHMR. It may minimize the paperwork of creating a check. Reduced paperwork can mean less cost to provide services. EVS also reduces transaction costs compared with the traditional voucher system. The cost per debit card transaction is $1.14 or less depending on volume, while some estimates put the cost for paying providers by state check at approximately $6 to $10 per check. The system provides accurate, fast reporting through daily transaction reports and effective, efficient administrative controls (TDMHMR and TDHS, 1989, p. A-14).

Potential Problems

While the 1154 program has been a valuable tool for the CMHMRCs to use in helping their clients, it is not universally praised. Critics of the program complain that this is just another "handout" by the state. Some CMHMRC staff have expressed the feeling that the program destroys initiative and allows recipients to become overly dependent on state funds. Tri-County MHMRC personnel operate under the philosophy that it is the job of the staff to get their clients on their feet as quickly as possible. They think it is best that the clients learn to rely on themselves and not upon the help of others. It is felt that the availability of 1154 funds undermines this initiative: "The word gets around pretty quick that there's free money to be had" (Young, Interview, October 4, 1988).

Some CMHMRC staff have called the 1154 program an "administrative nightmare." The complaints stem from TDMHMR taking on a program that in practice does not fit the purpose for which the department was created. TDMHMR is designed to provide mental health services and not act as a distributor of cash benefits. Staff must take out time to verify the validity of claims as well as the eligibility of the recipient and the providers. Case managers are not trained to be eligibility workers. Staff must also expend a great deal of effort in researching the most cost-effective purchase and do some of the leg work that the clients are not able to do (Cotten, Interview, April 12, 1989).

There is a conflict between the desired flexibility and the required accountability. Extensive paper trails have to be left concerning receipts, verification of income, verification of need, appropriateness of the service requested, amount of copayment required, etc. In theory, these services could be handled over the phone (as is proposed in the Electronic Voucher System). However, in practice it is quite another matter. The CMHMRC staff has to make sure that the funds are being spent for appropriate reasons in an appropriate manner (Cotten, Interview, April 12, 1989).

This program was actually designed for clients with mental retardation. The needs of mentally ill clients are not always as clear. The local committees that make the decisions as to what the program will and will not pay for do not have clear definitions of what should be used to keep people out of the state hospital or what might be used to relieve stress. There are no suitable definitions as to what can be paid for that fulfill the goals of the program. This means that a person in Dallas may have a service paid for while a person in Houston could have the same service denied (Cotten, Interview, April 12, 1989).

CMHMRC personnel also stated that it is more difficult to determine whether an MH client is trying to abuse the system than for the MR clients. Many clients cannot work or will not work, and they use the program to get as much out of it as they can. Another complaint aired was that those in residential programs are not eligible for the program. Yet, many of these people have similar or the same needs as those in the community. Many of these needs cannot be paid for through other programs. Some simple needs such as eye glasses, certain medications, and transportation costs do not qualify for payment under existing programs. Making these services available to people in residential programs would aid in keeping them out of the state hospital. The CMHMRCs are keeping these people out of the state hospitals by keeping them in residential programs, so they should be eligible (Cotten, Interview, April 12, 1989).

In the first quarter of 1989, the number of applications for 1154 had already reached the level for all of FY 1988. For all of 1988, 700 applications for funds for mental health clients were approved. During the first quarter of FY 1989, 732 applications were approved. This represents a 418 percent rise in approvals. The amount of 1154 funds available for mental health clients was raised by only 100 percent.

CONCLUSIONS

The 1154 program has a great deal of potential for alleviating some of the short-term needs for the CMI. The flexibility of the program is one of its main advantages, but it also may turn into its main undoing. The needs of the CMI are many. A program that can provide so many services to those in need will have to have either a much higher level of funding or many more restrictions on its use. With the low level of federal support to the disabled, through SSI and food stamps, there are basic needs that cannot be met for people who may not be able to hold down steady employment because of their particular illness. The services that are not covered by present government programs (such as dental care, respite care, transportation costs) are so numerous that the 1154 program can become easily overloaded.

The overuse of this program may lead to more restrictions and complications for the applicants. This would take away some of the advantages of this program. As the program grows, the potential for abuse grows also. If there are just a few dramatic cases of abuse of this program, the restrictions to its use will increase. As long as the CMHMRCs stay within their allotted budgets and give out funds with some care, the program will survive and thrive. This program could become a model in aiding the CMI in their efforts to achieve and maintain self-sufficiency. The more that Texas can do for mentally ill persons to avoid hospital admissions (or readmissions), the better chance these persons have of becoming productive citizens, which will help the state of Texas overall.

References

Collins, Janet. 1988. Director, Case Management Services, Texas Department of Mental Health and Mental Retardation, Austin, Texas. Telephone interview with Nicholas Hoover, September 28.

Cotten, Larry. 1989. Director, Dallas County Community Mental Health and Mental Retardation Authority, Dallas, Texas. Telephone interview by Nicholas Hoover, April 12.

Craig, R. T., and B. Wright. 1987. <u>Mental Health Financing and Programming: A Legislator's Guide</u>. Washington, D.C.: National Conference of State Legislatures.

Farr, Rodger K. 1986. "A Mental Health Treatment Program for the Homeless Mentally Ill in the Los Angeles Skid Row Area." In <u>Treating the Homeless: Urban Psychiatry's Challenge</u>, ed. Billey E. Jones. Washington, D.C.: American Psychiatric Press, Inc.

Moore, Carolee. 1989. Assistant Director, Special Projects, Texas Department of Mental Health and Mental Retardation, Austin, Texas. Telephone interview by Nicholas Hoover, April 11.

Okpaku, Sam. 1988. "The Psychiatrist and the Social Security Disability Insurance and Supplemental Security Income Programs." <u>Hospital and Community Psychiatry</u>, vol. 39, no. 8 (August).

Richardson, Joe, and Gene Falk. 1985. "How the Food Stamps Program Works." Report #84-190 EPW. Congressional Research Service, Library of Congress, Washington, D.C. (November 1).

Schmulowitz, Jack. 1988. Chairman, Social Security Administration Supplement Committee, Office of Research and Statistics, Social Security Administration, Baltimore, Maryland. Telephone interview with Nicholas Hoover, November 15.

_____. 1988. Chairman, Social Security Administration Supplement Committee, Office of Research and Statistics, Social Security Administration, Baltimore, Maryland. Telephone interview with Nicholas Hoover, November 21.

_____. 1988. Chairman, Social Security Administration Supplement Committee, Office of Research and Statistics, Social Security Administration, Baltimore, Maryland. Telephone interview with Nicholas Hoover, November 28.

Smith, John R. 1988. Information Officer, United States Department of Agriculture, Regional Office, Austin, Texas. Telephone interview with Nicholas Hoover, November 30.

Texas Department of Human Services (TDHS). July 1986. "What You Need to Know About Food Stamps and Aid to Families with Dependent Children." Stock code 20549-0000 PSD 75,000. Austin, Texas. (Pamphlet.)

_____. December 1987. "Texas Food Stamp Client Profile: State Totals December 1987." Austin, Texas. (Unpublished report.)

_____. June 1988. <u>The Quarterly Blue Book; A Compilation of DHS Statistics for May 1988</u>. Austin, Texas.

Texas Department of Mental Health and Mental Retardation (TDMHMR). 1988. <u>In-Home and Family Support Program</u>. Austin, Texas. (September 6.)

_____ and TDHS with the Texas Planning Council for Developmental Disabilities. 1989. <u>Texas In-Home and Family Support Program: Report to the 71st Legislature</u>. Austin, Texas. (February 1.)

Texas H.B. 222. 1989. 71st Legislature, Reg. Sess. Austin, Texas.

Torrey, E. Fuller. 1988. <u>Surviving Schizophrenia; A Family Manual</u>. New York, N.Y.: Harper and Row Publishers.

U. S. Congress, House of Representatives, Committee on Energy and Commerce, Subcommittee on Health and the Environment. November 1988. <u>Medicaid Source Book: Background Data and Analysis</u>. A Report Prepared by the Congressional Research Service. Washington, D.C.: U.S. Government Printing Office.

U.S. Department of Health and Human Services (USDHHS). December 1987a. <u>Social Security Bulletin: Annual Statistical Supplement, 1987</u>. Washington, D.C.: Social Security Administration.

_____. December 1987b. <u>Social Security Regulations: Rules for Determining Disability and Blindness</u>. SSA Pub. No. 64-014 1987. Washington, D.C.: Social Security Administration.

_____. January 1988a. <u>Disability</u>. SSA Pub. #05-10029. Washington, D.C.: Social Security Administration. (Pamphlet.)

_____. January 1988b. <u>SSI</u>. SSA Pub. #05-11000. Washington, D.C.: Social Security Administration.

_____. June 1988. <u>What You Have to Know About SSI</u>. SSA Publication No. 05-11011. Washington, D.C.: Social Security Administration.

_____. December 1989. <u>Social Security Bulletin: Annual Statistical Supplement, 1989</u>. Washington, D.C.: Social Security Administration.

Texas State Constitution. 1982. Article III, Sec. 51-A. (Vernon's Texas Statutes. 1984). Austin, Texas.

Vischi, Thomas R. June 1988. <u>Financing Community Services for Persons with Severe and Disabling Mental Illness: A Technical Assistance Manual</u>. Washington, D.C.: National Institute of Mental Health, and Alcohol, Drug Abuse, and Mental Health Administration, Department of Health and Human Services.

Young, Dot. 1989. Associate Executive Director, Tri County Mental Health Mental Retardation Services, Conroe, Texas. Interview by Nicholas Hoover, October 4.

Section Three. Financing Trends and Arrangements

Financing for the chronically mentally ill in Texas is provided by a variety of sources and through a complex delivery system.   A recent study estimated all public expenditures on behalf of the CMI in Texas including entitlement programs and Medicaid received by private providers (Warner, Crumpton, and Watts, 1989). That study estimated total public expenditures outside the formal TDMHMR-CMHMRC system on behalf of the CMI in Texas to have been approximately $270 million in 1987 (Warner, Crumpton, and Watts, 1989). If Medicare and housing subsidies had been included, the figure would have been at least $50 million more. With the addition of portions of the mental health budget at TDMHMR, which exceeded $300 million in 1987, and the local mental health authority budgets at the CMHMRCs which were spent on the CMI, total publicly funded expenditures for the CMI in Texas would have probably exceeded $600 million for 1987. Our focus in this section of the report will be on financing the public system of care for the chronically mentally ill in Texas.

The State of Texas funds over 90 percent of the cost of the Texas Department of Mental Health and Mental Retardation (TDMHMR), whose mental health facilities include eight state hospitals, three state centers, and two specialty institutions for youth. TDMHMR is also the primary funding source for the 35 community mental health and mental retardation centers (CMHMRCs). Other state mental health funds flow through the Texas Department of Human Services to provide the state match for Medicaid programs, the Texas Rehabilitation Commission, the Texas Department of Highways, and the Texas Commission for Alcohol and Drug Abuse (TCADA). The state also provides direct services to the chronically mentally ill incarcerated in the Texas Department of Corrections.

At the local level, the 35 CMHMRCs located throughout the state provide an assortment of services for the mentally ill. These entities are funded by federal and state funds, local fees and tax dollars, and contracts with state and other agencies. Local hospital districts also provide services to the chronically mentally ill in the form of indigent care. A number of private treatment centers and hospitals have been established that care for some of the chronically mentally ill along with other clients. Voluntary and charitable entities also provide both direct service and funding to the chronically mentally ill.

Federal funds provide block grants for government activities in mental health and substance abuse. Federal funds are also available for income support through disability entitlement programs which also entitle the recipient to Medicare or Medicaid coverage. Food stamps, veterans benefits, veterans hospitals, and some housing programs round out the federal entitlement programs which many of the chronically mentally ill may access by virtue of their income, past work history, or veteran status along with their disability. These are not programs exclusively for the mentally ill, however, and the entitlement programs can be used to purchase services in the private sector from private hospitals, board and care homes, or the neighborhood grocery.

Chapter 13 in this section examines the Texas Department of Mental Health and Mental Retardation's funding of mental health services. In particular, trends in funding the agency, which is the primary public source of services for the mentally ill, and trends in funding community-based services are documented. This chapter also looks at the contracting process by which TDMHMR attempts to assure that core services are being provided to TDMHMR's priority population through the community centers. Next, a unique mechanism of financing by TDMHMR to fund community-based care is examined. The $35.50 program was developed in response to federal court orders to reduce the ratio of clients to staff in the state hospitals and encourage care for the mentally ill in the community. Trends in this program are analyzed. Finally the equalization funding incentives by the state are examined.

Chapter 14 looks at financing of community-based care through the CMHMRCs throughout the state. The many sources of funds which finance these centers are detailed and the general financial conditions of the CMHMRCs are analyzed based on an examination of their audited annual financial reports.

Chapter 15 presents trends in federal funding of care for the chronically mentally ill. This includes a discussion of the Alcohol, Drug Abuse, and Mental Health Block Grant and the Stewart B. McKinney Homeless Assistance Act Block Grant in so far as it is directed to the mentally ill. This chapter concludes with a discussion of the Medicaid program and the options available for Texas to expand its Medicaid programs to cover services currently paid only from state general revenues.

Chapter 16 looks at the role of voluntary organizations in providing direct and indirect care to the mentally ill in Texas. State efforts are supplemented through a variety of religious and secular nonprofit organizations and foundations which devote funds and volunteer time to this effort.

Breaking this public funding out by federal, state, and local services will probably amount to federal funding of roughly 35 percent, mostly for entitlement programs with a modest amount for the VA and block grants, a state portion of about 54 percent, mostly for delivery of services and funding local centers, a local portion of roughly 5 percent, and a private or voluntary portion of a comparable level.

The financial data for Chapters 13 and 14 were gathered from a variety of sources. The objective was to do a longitudinal analysis of the funding trends for mental health services in Texas. Information had to be put together about TDMHMR and the CMHMRCs with a five-year trend perspective that was consistent and accurate. An explanation of how these figures were derived and a list of sources can be found in the appendix for Chapter 14.

References

Warner, David C., Laurie Crumpton, and Gary Watts. 1989. "Financial Costs of Caring for the Chronically Mentally Ill in Texas." In <u>Community Care of the Chronically Mentally Ill,</u> ed. Charles Barjzan, Marian Coleman, and Ira Iscoe. Austin, Texas: Hogg Foundation for Mental Health.

Chapter 13. Texas Department of Mental Health and Mental Retardation[*]

The Texas Department of Mental Health and Mental Retardation was established to provide a comprehensive range of services for mentally ill and mentally retarded persons who are in need of publicly supported care, treatment, or rehabilitation. In providing these services, TDMHMR attempts to coordinate services and programs with other governmental entities to minimize duplication and to maximize services available to the targeted population (VATCS, 1984).

In mental health, TDMHMR operates seven state hospitals, three state centers, and two specialty institutions for youth. TDMHMR also operates some community services through outreach units attached to these institutions. It serves most of its clients at the community level by contracting directly with the CMHMRCs for specific services. The mental health services provided by TDMHMR are as follows:

1. Program Administration -- Program Administration for Mental Health Services provides for organizational and programmatic direction and coordination of MH programs in state hospitals, state centers, contracted CMHMRCs, and other multi-service providers.

2. State Mental Hospitals -- State Hospitals and Waco Center for Youth provide a variety of services including 24-hour care and supervision, room and board, a wide array of diagnostic and therapeutic modalities, supportive ancillary services, continuity of care planning with local mental health authorities, and training and rehabilitation.

3. Harris County Psychiatric Center -- This facility, managed and operated by the University of Texas, provides a complete array of psychiatric services, including 24-hour care and supervision, diagnosis, therapy, ancillary services, and continuity of care.

4. State Centers -- State Centers provide a variety of services including 24-hour care and supervision, room and board, a wide array of diagnostic and therapeutic modalities, supportive ancillary services, continuity of care planning with the local mental health authority, and training and rehabilitation as specifically indicated.

5. Tarrant County Psychiatric Hospital -- Residents of Tarrant County, children, adolescents, and adults, who otherwise would be court-committed to state facilities, receive inpatient psychiatric care at this 50-bed facility.

6. Contracted Community Centers -- CMHMRCs provide, through a contract for services, community-based services for the chronically mentally ill, for substance abusers, and for dually diagnosed clients with mental retardation combined with mental illness. Services include residential care, client and family support, and case management. (TDMHMR, 1988)

---

[*]This chapter was written by Joellen M. Harper and Ronnie Jung.

OPERATIONS

Combined funding for mental health and mental retardation at TDMHMR has increased from approximately $710 million in 1984 to $840 million in 1988. This increase of $130 million represents a five-year growth rate of 18.3 percent. Mental health expenditures have increased by 13 percent from $307 million in 1984 to $353 million in 1988. As a percentage of total departmental expenditures the portion attributable to mental health has remained fairly constant over the last five years at 43 percent of total funding (see Chapter 14).

TDMHMR is almost totally dependent upon the state's General Revenue Fund for financing, which provided TDMHMR with $670 million in funds for 1984 and $815 million in funds for 1988. In addition to the state providing 95 percent of funds for TDMHMR, the federal government provided approximately $20 million per year in block grants for the five-year period ending on August 31, 1988. The remaining revenues received from various sources are very insignificant (see the audited financial statements in Chapter 14).

Expenditures by TDMHMR for mental health services over the last five years are summarized in Table 13.1. The above amounts represent the total cost to the state's General Revenue Fund for mental health services provided by TDMHMR. These costs include payroll-related costs such as retirement matching, social security matching, and group insurance costs.

Table 13.1. Expenditures for Mental Health Services Through TDMHMR, FY 1984 to 1988

Location	Fiscal Year 1984	1985	1986	1987	1988
TDMHMR					
Central Office					
Unallocated	$ 29,755,740	$ 29,798,998	$ 23,362,127	$ 11,795,079	$ 18,745,239
State					
Hospitals	209,544,456	222,472,235	230,782,763	233,970,578	235,040,979
Houston Psych.					
Hospital	0	0	5,000,000	13,090,000	15,702,973
Tarrant Co.					
Psych.	0	0	0	713,333	2,651,876
TRIMS	14,677,576	14,421,834	5,635,053	2,145,000	0
State Centers	8,886,687	9,300,324	9,825,748	10,401,694	10,695,722
Subtotals	$261,864,459	$275,993,391	$274,608,691	$272,115,684	$282,836,789
Community Centers					
Contracted Svc.	45,709,068	46,534,304	46,317,794	46,451,995	54,680,941
Staff to Patient	0	7,400,278	10,315,858	13,353,715	16,304,646
Total	$307,576,527	$329,927,973	$331,242,070	$331,921,394	$353,822,376

Sources: Texas Senate Bill 1, 1987; Texas Senate Bill 222, 1989.

It is interesting to note that expenditures for state hospitals increased gradually during this five-year period while the number of patients' days in the hospitals decreased as a result of the movement toward deinstitutionalization. Payments to CMHMRCs for mental health services have increased at a more rapid pace from $45 million in 1984 to $71 million in 1988. This increase in funding is consistent with measures mandated by the federal court to improve staff-to-patient ratios in the state hospitals and with the general trend to move more patients into the community and out of state institutions.

ACTION OF THE 71ST TEXAS LEGISLATURE

The trend toward more funding for community centers is consistent with the overall direction taken by TDMHMR and the Texas Legislature. The 71st Texas Legislature appropriated $729 million for mental health expenditures for the 1990-1991 biennium, compared with $628 million for the 1988-1989 biennium, a total increase for mental health funding of 16 percent (Texas Senate Bill 1, 1987; Texas Senate Bill 222, 1989). The details of the appropriations are listed in Table 13.2.

Table 13.2. TDMHMR General Revenue Fund Legislative Appropriation Biennial Funding for FY 1988-1989 and 1990-1991

Mental Health Funding

Appropriation	Senate Bill 1 70th Legislature		Senate Bill 222 71st Legislature	
	8-31-88	8-31-89	8-31-90	8-31-91
Program Adm.	$ 1,030,293	$ 1,030,293	$ 1,743,889	$ 1,743,889
State Hosp.	176,391,437	172,597,702	197,959,092	204,186,979
Harris Co. Ctr.	18,198,382	18,198,382	19,103,486	19,103,486
State Centers	7,898,097	8,158,497	10,721,328	12,384,919
Contract Svc.	90,359,323	99,939,037	121,928,475	131,407,456
MH Staff-to- Patient Ratio	8,328,064	11,697,015	0	0
Subst. Abuse Ratio	6,568,723	6,568,723	0	0
TDC Support	0	0	2,692,368	2,692,368
Home & Family Support	0	0	2,000,000	2,000,000
Total	$308,774,319	$318,189,649	$356,148,638	$373,519,097
Biennium Total		$626,963,968		$729,667,735

Percentage Increase <u>16</u> Percent

Sources: Texas Senate Bill 1, 1987; Texas Senate Bill 222, 1989.

The portion of funds to be contracted for services has been increasing each year from $98 million in 1988 to $110 million in 1989 for contracted services and staff-to-patient ratio payments to $122 million in 1990 to $131 million in 1991. The funding for contracted services increased by more than 20 percent in the 1990-1991 biennium.

REACTION OF THE COURT-APPOINTED MONITOR

David Pharis, the court-appointed monitor in the R. A. J. v. Jones suit, has asked U.S. district judge Barefoot Sanders to reject the settlement covering operation of TDMHMR because he believes that the 71st Legislature appropriated too little money. The reason for this negative reaction to the budget approved by the 71st Legislature is that TDMHMR officials requested $106 million to comply with court-ordered terms of the lawsuit, but the legislature only approved $60 million for this purpose. Pharis stated that this $45 million shortfall leaves "major areas of inadequate funding" such as "the residential sections of the state hospitals, the outreach departments of the state hospitals which provide community services in rural areas, and some aspects of community programs provided by the community centers." The result of this action is that resolution to the 15-year-old lawsuit has continued to elude lawmakers and TDMHMR officials (Ward, 1989, p. B1).

FUNDING PROCESS

As noted above, TDMHMR is almost totally dependent upon appropriations from the state's General Revenue Fund. Each biennium TDMHMR submits a legislative budget request to the Legislative Budget Board for funding for the next two fiscal years. This budget request is considered along with all other state agencies' requests for education, human services, highways, etc. The Texas legislature approves a budget package for TDMHMR and all state agencies which becomes subject to the governor's veto. Absent the governor's veto, the amount in the appropriation act becomes the spending limit for the next two years. In determining the amount of monies to be appropriated to TDMHMR, the legislature considers the possible impacts of lawsuits as well as constitutional spending limits for state government as a whole. In other words, TDMHMR's budget request is not considered on its own merits but in relation to the total needed for all of state government.

Once the total funding for TDMHMR is established, the department has some discretion in how it allocates money between mental health and mental retardation. It has some discretion, subject to court-mandated ratios, to determine how much of the mental health money is allocated to state hospitals and state centers and how much is contracted out to CMHMRCs. A portion of the money was earmarked for incentive funding ($35.50 program) in the 1988-1989 biennium, but this was not the case for the FY 1990-1991 budget, and a portion is set aside for direct contracts with community centers. The contracting and incentive funding processes, then, are ways to allocate money among community centers. The details of the contracting process are found in Chapter 14. The following section provides additional detail on the incentive funding program initiated by TDMHMR.

THE CLASS ACTION SUIT

Jenkins v. Cowley was a class action suit filed in 1974 in the U.S. District Court in Dallas. Now known as R. A. J. v. Jones, it was filed against all Texas state hospitals on behalf of all past, current, and future state hospital patients. The allegations in the suit maintained that the rights of involuntarily committed patients were being violated. No progress was made in the case until 1980, when the U.S. Department of Justice entered the case as amicus curae, friend of the court, to review the state hospitals. In 1981 the case was settled out of court. The Settlement Agreement, signed March 2, 1981, requires the following:

1. Protection of patients rights;
2. Provision of individualized treatment planning and programming;
3. Adequate staffing to produce 30 hours of appropriate programming per patient per week;
4. Renovations for compliance with Life Safety Codes;
5. Development of guidelines for appropriate provision of psychotropic medications;
6. Development of specialized treatment programs for the mentally retarded who need psychiatric inpatient treatment;
7. Placement of those mentally retarded who no longer need psychiatric inpatient treatment in appropriate programs for the mentally retarded;
8. Retention of Joint Commission on Accreditation of Hospitals (JCAH) accreditation for all state hospitals;
9. Development of aftercare plans and programs for patients discharged from hospitals;
10 Seeking of appropriate funding from the legislature for implementation of these improvements; and
11. Establishment of a three member panel to monitor compliance and to semi-annually report to the court both progress toward compliance and remaining deficiencies. (R. A. J. v. Kavanagh, 1981)

After receiving three reports from the R. A. J. panel, Judge Sanders ruled in April 1984 that the staff-to-patient ratios had to be improved. Sanders established that "absolute minimum" ratios of 1:5 for the day shift were needed to provide safe conditions and effective treatment for state hospital patients (LOC, 1985, p. A-2). To comply with these ratios, given the level of staffing in the state hospitals at that time, TDMHMR could reach these goals by hiring 1,095 new mental health workers, reducing the average daily census by 1,288 patients (as long as they were discharged to appropriately staffed services), or a combination of the strategies. The court asked the parties for a solution to enable compliance. This request was the impetus for the $35.50 program.

THE $35.50 PROGRAM

Gary E. Miller, commissioner of TDMHMR at the time of required compliance, approved an idea to transfer the funds that would have been used for the hiring of new staff to comply with state hospital ratios to the community mental health programs. The funds needed were obtained through an emergency appropriation from the Texas legislature during a special session in January 1985 (R. A. J. Review Panel, 1984, p. 4). TDMHMR requested and received legislative authority for unprecedented transfer flexibility to help fund the community placements required for staffing ratio compliance. A new line-item appropriation, staff-to-patient ratios, was created during the 1985 legislative session as a mechanism to direct funds either to community centers or to hospital staffing, as necessary to meet the required ratios.

The transfer of funds described above evolved into the $35.50 program. The appropriated funds were to be paid to the local mental health authorities (LMHA)[1] that earned them, or made available for hiring additional hospital staff if an insufficient number of clients was released. TDMHMR implemented the $35.50 program in September 1984. The program as designed paid $35.50 to LMHAs for each state hospital bed-day

---

[1] The distinction between CMHMRC and LMHA is quite important. All LMHAs, including the state hospital outreach and state centers outreach, were eligible to earn $35.50 funds.

below the number used by clients who listed a county in that LMHA as their county of residence during the fourth quarter of 1983. The intent was to provide incentives to community-based programs to reduce utilization of state hospital beds and thus comply with staff-to-patient ratios without great additions of staff at the state hospitals. With some modifications, the program continues to operate in this manner.

The rationale behind the program was that it would solve the staffing ratio problem, create an incentive to treat in the community, and provide funds to the CMHMRCs with which to expand services for the mentally ill. Commissioner Miller and some other TDMHMR officials devised a system that would accomplish several goals simultaneously.

Their method was as follows. They identified the annual cost of salary and benefits of hiring a direct mental health care worker, $15,240 (1984 dollars). The cost was multiplied by 1,095, the number of workers necessary to comply with the staffing ratios. The product, $16,687,800, represents the total cost of compliance with the ratios. The cost of the new staff was then divided by the alternative reduction in patients, 1,288. The result, $12,955.74, is the total yearly cost per patient of hiring the 1,095 new employees. Finally, that number was divided by the number of days in the year, yielding $35.50, the cost per patient per day (or cost per bed-day) of complying with the court-ordered ratios. TDMHMR decided that this amount would be paid to the LMHAs for each bed-day reduction in their state hospital utilization.

A baseline number of bed days was established for each LMHA, based on the number of bed days used by clients from each service area who were in specific units of the eight state hospitals during the fourth quarter of FY 1983 (TDMHMR, 1984, p. 4). The units included under the $35.50 program were

1. Adult General Psychiatric,
2. Children and Adolescents,
3. Geriatrics,
4. Medical and Surgical, and
5. Behavior Therapy (at San Antonio State Hospital). (TDMHMR, 1984, p. 2)

State hospital units not falling under the program were

1. Multiple Disability,
2. Maximum Security,
3. Substance Abuse,
4. State Centers (Inpatient),
5. Waco Center for Youth,
6. Texas Research Institute for Mental Sciences (TRIMS), and
7. Vernon South and Vernon South Medical and Surgical. (TDMHMR, 1984, p. 2).

Also not included under the program were the hospitals operated by the Harris County MHMRA and the Tarrant County MHMRA.

For each bed-day from participating units that the LMHA reduced below its baseline, it earned $35.50. TDMHMR acknowledged that the $35.50 payments would not be sufficient to finance community services for all patients whose state hospital admission was prevented (Miller and Rago, 1988, p. 595). Nor does $12,957.50, for keeping one state hospital bed empty for one year, necessarily represent the savings to the hospital for it being empty. The average cost of serving a patient in a state hospital for one year costs much, much more. However, the marginal savings from the reduction

248

of one hospital bed day is probably minimal. True savings from reduced bed-day utilization is not experienced until an entire ward, building, or hospital is closed.

TDMHMR chose the fourth quarter of FY 1983 as the baseline period of bed-day utilization because it had some "fat" on it, meaning there was a relatively higher overall level of bed-day utilization during that quarter. This strategy would allow the LMHAs to begin earning funds under the program immediately (Nunn, Interview, March 3, 1989). The baseline figure for each LMHA, it is important to note, is not permanently fixed. The baseline fluctuates if one of those original clients subsequently changes his or her county of residence. Such an occurrence would drive one LMHA's baseline up, and another's down, by the original number of bed-days used by the particular client on a R. A. J. unit during the baseline period. However, there are no adjustments for clients who entered the mental health system after the baseline period, nor for those who were not residents in a state hospital during that quarter. Furthermore, there is no adjustment to a LMHA's baseline for changes in the population of its local service area.

Payments under the $35.50 program began during the first quarter of FY 1985. TDMHMR authorized a one-time advance payment to the LMHAs to provide the resources needed to reduce the number of bed-days. This advance payment was intended as "seed money with which the LMHAs can begin to accomplish the goal of bed-day utilization reduction" (TDMHMR, 1984, p. 8). The advance payment was calculated by comparing the number of bed-days used in the fourth quarter of FY 1984 to the baseline utilization of the fourth quarter of FY 1983. Theoretically, the reduction in bed-days during that period "represents the number of bed-days the LMHA should be able to reduce in the first quarter of fiscal year 1985" (TDMHMR, 1984, p. 8). Each LMHA was eligible to receive the greater of either (1) $35.50 multiplied by the number of bed-days actually reduced in the fourth quarter of FY 1984, or (2) $17,750 (equivalent to a reduction of 500 bed-days). If the estimated reduction was not achieved by the LMHA in the first quarter of FY 1985, it had until the end of the second quarter to do so. At that time, if the LMHA still had not achieved the reduction, it was required to refund the money not earned.

TDMHMR had until January 1985 to meet the required staffing ratios by means of the $35.50 program process. In December 1984, it was clear that sufficient patients had not been discharged, thus perpetuating noncompliance. Therefore, TDMHMR was required to hire 650 workers in order to comply with the staffing ratios.

THE INCENTIVE DIVERSION PROGRAM

In September 1987 the $35.50 program was renamed and restructured into the Mental Health Incentive Diversion Program (MHIDP). The theory behind the new program is the same as that behind the original. The department explained the changes in terms of "new R. A. J." and "classic R. A. J." (Nunn, Interview, February 27, 1989). The new R. A. J. program continued to compare total R. A. J. bed days in each quarter for each LMHA with a baseline figure to determine the amount to be paid to the authority. The changes under the "new R. A. J.," while significant, did not change the premise of the program as originally created. These changes are summarized as follows:

1. The R. A. J. units included in the program were expanded to include substance abuse units in the state hospitals and centers, and the mental health units in the state centers.

2. As a result, the original baseline was adjusted to accommodate for the addition of the new units. The original baseline for each LMHA was adjusted by averaging the bed

days used on the substance abuse units and state centers'
mental health units during the first and second quarters of
fiscal year 1987. These beds were then added to the original
R. A. J. baseline, creating the "adjusted fiscal year 1983
baseline."

3.   A new incentive baseline was established, and three distinct levels
        of incentive payments per bed day reduction were introduced. The
        new "incentive baseline" is based on the average bed days during
        first and second quarters of fiscal year 1987 on the original R. A. J.
        units, substance abuse units, and state centers' mental health units.
        (Nunn, Interview, March 13, 1989)

Under "new R. A. J.," for each bed day reduced below the adjusted FY 1983
baseline, the LMHA earns $35.50, the same as under the "classic R. A. J." system. In
addition, if a LMHA reduces its bed days below the incentive baseline, it can earn
$35.50, $45, or $60 per bed-day, depending upon its bed-day utilization per 100,000
population in its service area. First, the bed-day utilization level per 100,000 population
of the LMHA's incentive baseline is calculated. (The Texas Department of Health's
population projections for 1988 were used and continue to be used for calculation of
utilization level per 100,000 population [Nunn, Interview, March 3, 1989]). The
utilization level determines whether the incentive payments will start at $35.50, $45, or
$60. For bed-day utilization above 17 per 100,000 population, the LMHA earns the
standard $35.50 per bed-day. If the bed-day utilization rate is between 13 and 17 per
100,000 population, the LMHA earns $45 per bed-day. If the bed-day utilization per
100,000 population is between 0 and 13 per 100,000, the LMHA earns $60 per bed-day.
TDMHMR has calculated, for each LMHA, the breakpoint in bed days at which the
LMHA's incentive baseline bed-day utilization per 100,000 population is equal to 17.0
and 13.0 for 90-, 91-, and 92-day quarters (Table 13.3).

In contrast to the adjusted FY 1983 baseline, which can fluctuate, the incentive
baseline is frozen in time, with no adjustment for changes in county of residence. The
decision was made to average two quarters' bed-day utilization in determining it, so as to
make the level slightly less arbitrary (Nunn, Interview, February 27, 1989).

One of the goals of restructuring the $35.50 program was to create an incentive to
LMHAs to continue reducing state hospital bed-day utilization. The state center units
were added because, under the classic R. A. J. program, it was possible for some LMHAs
to place clients in state center inpatient beds and not lose $35.50 per day for doing so.
This action was originally recommended by the Sunset Advisory Commission "to
encourage more cost-effective treatment of these patients and ensure that the state center
areas receive the same incentives to develop community resources as other areas of the
state" (Sunset Advisory Commission, September 1986, p. 23).

The changes made to the program were politically viable because they benefited
almost all of the LMHAs, without negatively impacting any of them. If a LMHA was
earning $35.50 funds prior to the changes, it would continue to do so afterwards, and
very possibly begin earning more.

Has the $35.50 Program Been a Success?

The $35.50 financing mechanism was created in order to enable compliance with
the staffing requirements of the R. A. J. settlement agreement. A related goal was to
provide money to the community centers as an incentive to provide care in the
community and to enhance their services and programs.

Table 13.3. Texas Local Mental Health Authorities' Adjusted FY 1983 Baseline and Incentive Diversion Program Baseline

#	LMHA	FY 1983 Bed Day Baseline	Incentive Bed Day Baseline	Percentage Decrease in Bed Day Baseline
	CMHMRC			
1	Abilene	4,966	4,065	18.14
2	Texas Panhandle	12,886	8,484	34.32
3	Austin-Travis	16,853	11,167	33.74
4	Bexar County	37,706	32,585	13.58
5	Brazos Valley	4,088	3,746	8.37
6	Central Counties	6,480	2,766	57.31
7	Central Plains	3,701	1,158	68.71
8	Central Texas	3,881	3,191	17.78
9	Concho Valley Center	3,443	3,091	10.22
10	Dallas County	41,765	30,618	26.69
11	Deep East Texas	11,338	5,516	51.35
12	East Texas	11,388	5,169	54.61
13	Life Management	12,250	9,454	22.82
14	Gulf Bend	4,841	2,772	42.74
15	Gulf Coast	4,128	2,913	29.43
16	Harris County	26,202	20,237	22.77
17	Heart of Texas	4,182	2,984	28.65
18	Lubbock	8,621	6,004	30.36
19	Navarro County	2,317	1,053	54.55
20	Collin County	3,258	2,870	11.91
21	Northeast Texas	3,770	1,962	47.96
22	Nueces County	5,132	3,910	23.81
23	Pecan Valley	4,067	1,708	58.00
24	Permian Basin	3,747	3,755	-0.21
25	Sabine Valley	10,124	4,439	56.15
26	Southeast Texas	6,066	2,088	65.58
27	Tarrant County	18,727	14,575	22.17
28	Texoma	7,099	4,234	40.36
29	Tri County	5,631	1,553	72.42
30	Tropical Texas	5,792	5,773	0.33
31	Wichita Falls	10,702	6,309	41.05
34	Johnson City MHMR	541	279	48.43
35	Riceland	5,243	2,087	60.19
61	Denton	3,167	2,963	6.44
62	Hunt County	2,943	1,770	39.86
63	Hotexia-Heart of Texas	2,137	922	56.86
	Subtotal CMHMRCs	319,182	218,150	31.65

(Continued Next Page)

251

Table 13.3 (Continued). Texas Local Mental Health Authorities' Adjusted FY 1983 Baseline and Incentive Diversion Program Baseline

#	LMHA	FY 1983 Bed Day Baseline	Incentive Bed Day Baseline	Percentage Decrease in Bed Day Baseline
	State Hospital Outreach			
32	Blanco/Hays-ASH	759	657	13.44
33	Austin/Waller-ASH	440	261	40.68
36	Capital Area-ASH	6,112	2,326	61.94
37	Great Plains-BSSH	4,883	3,574	26.81
38	Staked Plains/Caprock-BSSH	1,751	1,393	20.45
39	Schleicher/Sutton-KSH	474	276	41.77
40	Hill Country-KSH	23,899	23,706	0.81
41	Anderson/Cherokee-RSH	4,963	2,448	50.67
42	Balcones Area-KSH	1,919	1,089	43.25
43	Val Verde County-KSH	1,016	627	38.29
44	Guadalupe Valley-SASH	2,508	2,090	16.67
45	Brushland/Coastal-SASH	6,152	5,078	17.46
47	Atascosa/Wilson-SASH	1,773	1,334	24.76
48	Gonzales-SASH	935	535	42.78
49	Post Oak-TSH	9,620	5,033	47.68
50	Camp County-TSH	19	124	-552.63
51	Ellis County-TSH	2,230	1,358	39.10
52	Rolling Prairies-WFSH	2,388	1,663	30.36
53	Childress County-WFSH	1,015	717	29.36
54	Pecos River-BSSH	1,831	1,225	33.10
55	Wichita River-WFSH	5,676	3,853	32.12
56	Shackelford/Stephens-WFSH	531	208	60.83
57	Grasslands Area-WFSH	2,789	2,156	22.70
	State Center Outreach			
58	El Paso State Center	1,018	914	10.22
59	Laredo State Center	3,955	2,139	45.92
60	Rio Grande State Center	2,215	1,444	34.81
	Subtotal State Hospital and State Center Outreach	90,871	66,228	27.12
	Subtotal CMHMRCs	319,182	218,150	31.65
	Totals	410,053	284,378	30.65

Source: TDMHMR, 1988.

Note   ASH - Austin State Hospital, BSSH - Big Spring State Hospital
        KSH - Kerrville State Hospital, SASH - San Antonio State Hospital
        RSH - Rusk State Hospital, TSH - Terrell State Hospital
        WFSH - Wichita Falls State Hospital.

The $35.50 program was the first to direct money to the LMHAs based on their performance. These funds are not linked to a specific service provision nor are they included in the state funds that require local matching funds. The program is significant because it was originally envisioned as a vehicle for compliance which would increase funding to community mental health programs. However, it has become a major financing mechanism and for some LMHAs the major source of new funding for programs.

The $35.50 program accomplished more than state hospital compliance with staffing ratios. It helped promote deinstitutionalization of the mentally ill by providing LMHAs an incentive to serve clients in the community. Furthermore, it provided new funds for the LMHAs with which to expand community programs.

The average daily census (ADC) in the state hospitals in R. A. J. units has decreased dramatically since the beginning of the $35.50 program. The fourth quarter FY 1983 baseline for the R. A. J. ADC in the state hospitals was 3,913 (Figure 13.1). In March 1989 the R. A. J. ADC had decreased to approximately 2,560.

New Funds for the Community Programs

Over the life of the $35.50 program the LMHAs have earned nearly $70 million through reduced bed-day utilization (Table 13.4). The majority of these funds, $55,191,514.50, went to community centers. Prior to the program, TDMHMR provided funding to the community centers via grant-in-aid allocations. When the $35.50 program was created as the vehicle for compliance with court-ordered ratios, the legislature was forced to appropriate new funds. There is no way of knowing with certainty whether additional funds would have been appropriated to community programs without the lawsuit and the $35.50 program. These funds of nearly $70 million have been used to create many new programs for care of the mentally ill in the community. However, it must be noted that TDMHMR does not place any restrictions upon a LMHA's $35.50 program earnings. A LMHA does not have to spend the funds on priority population clients, nor even on programs for the mentally ill.

CONCLUSIONS

With the shift toward community-based care, the role of TDMHMR in financing this care is evolving. Its new role is no longer as the primary deliverer of care. Instead, it is the overseer of the caregivers, both at the state hospital and in the community. In order to fulfill this role, TDMHMR must follow certain principles in order to facilitate community-based mental health care.

The first principle is that it must guarantee that the core services are provided to the priority population. Through the contracting and contract review process, the department must make sure that there is uniform delivery of core services throughout the state. This needs to apply equally to the rural outreach areas as well as the CMHMRCs. Further, TDMHMR must insure that these core services are delivered near the homes of those in the priority population if community-based care is to be effective.

Incentives need to be provided to the LMHAs in order to enhance the quality of care provided in the community. The $35.50 program is a unique incentive approach which was designed to fulfill the short-term goal of reducing the census in the state hospitals. While this is laudable, incentives are needed which emphasize longer- term goals to maintain a high quality of care and continuity of care. There should be inducements to insure that there is equitable treatment throughout the state. While the LMHAs should be rewarded for treating people in the community and not in the state

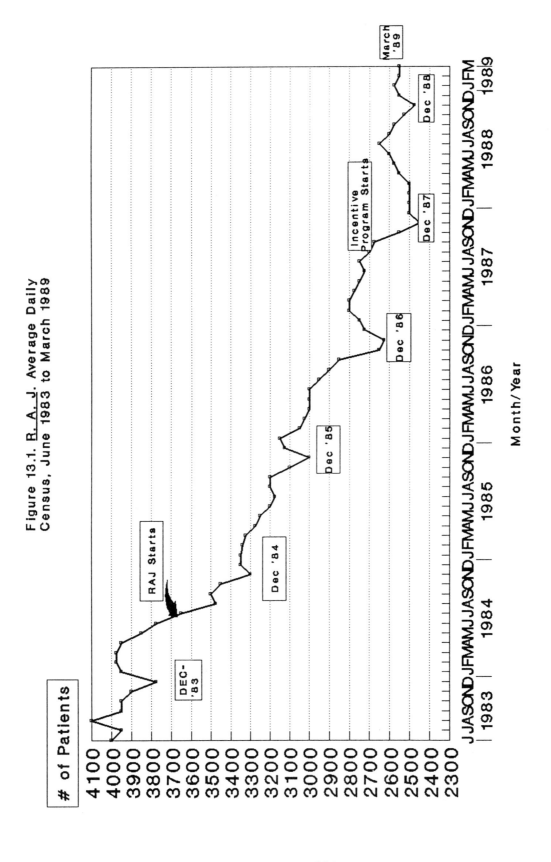

Figure 13.1. R.A.J. Average Daily
Census, June 1983 to March 1989

# of Patients

4100
4000
3900
3800
3700
3600
3500
3400
3300
3200
3100
3000
2900
2800
2700
2600
2500
2400
2300

RAJ Starts

DEC-
'83

Dec '84

Dec '85

Dec '86

Incentive
Program Starts

Dec '87

Dec '88

March
'89

J JASONDJFMAMJJASONDJFMAMJJASONDJFMAMJJASONDJFMAMJJASONDJFM
1983 | 1984 | 1985 | 1986 | 1987 | 1988 | 1989

Month/Year

——— Daily Census

Source: Nunn, Interview, April 12, 1989.

254

Table 13.4. Total $35.50 Program Earnings

Quater/Year	Community Centers	Outreaches	Combined Earnings	Bed Day Reduction
1 Q 85	$ 1,292,342.00	$ 303,844.50	$ 1,596,186.50	44,963
2 Q 85	1,755,546.00	432,993.50	2,188,539.50	61,649
3 Q 85	1,593,666.00	483,084.00	2,076,750.00	58,500
4 Q 85	1,908,764.00	546,664.50	2,455,428.50	69,167
Total				
FY '85	$ 6,550,318.00	$ 1,766,586.50	$ 8,316,904.50	234,279
1 Q 86	$ 2,341,970.50	$ 612,659.00	$ 2,954,629.50	83,229
2 Q 86	2,664,381.50	652,809.50	3,317,191.00	93,442
3 Q 86	2,611,841.50	684,156.00	3,295,997.50	92,845
4 Q 86	2,741,097.00	765,664.00	3,506,764.00	98,782
Total				
FY '86	$ 10,359,290.50	$ 2,715,288.50	$ 13,074,579.00	368,298
1 Q 87	$ 3,161,665.50	$ 976,605.00	$ 4,138,270.50	116,571
2 Q 87	3,507,897.00	1,034,079.50	4,541,976.50	127,943
3 Q 87	3,232,736.50	907,522.00	4,140,258.50	116,627
4 Q 87	3,346,975.50	1,002,697.50	4,349,673.00	122,526
Total				
FY '87	$ 13,249,274.50	$ 3,920,904.00	$ 17,170,178.50	483,667
1 Q 88	$ 3,789,649.00	$ 984,198.00	$ 4,773,847.00	131,733
2 Q 88	4,375,057.00	1,133,834.00	5,508,891.00	149,785
3 Q 88	4,169,465.50	986,850.50	5,156,316.00	138,479
4 Q 88	4,091,579.50	903,368.50	4,994,948.00	132,307
Total				
FY '88	$ 16,425,751.00	$ 4,008,251.00	$ 20,434,002.00	552,304
1 Q 89	$ 4,271,916.50	$ 1,051,259.50	$ 5,323,176.00	139,047
2 Q 89	4,459,960.00	1,092,028.50	5,551,988.50	145,155
Total				
FY '89	$ 8,731,876.50	$ 2,143,288.00	$ 10,875,164.50	284,202

Grand Total $ 69,870,828.50

Source: Nunn, Interview, March 15, 1989.

hospitals, there should also be disincentives for the opposite mode of treatment. One of the main impediments to community-based care is housing. The LMHAs often need to set up community placements for their clients when they are released from the state hospital or in order to prevent institutionalization. Currently, not all LMHAs have the resources to be able to fulfill this basic need.

The problem that TDMHMR has in fulfilling these principles are the constraints on funding. Because state funds are the primary source of revenue, TDMHMR must convince a reluctant legislature to spend millions of dollars on the mentally ill, a constituency with limited support. It has only been through the threat of court orders that the level of funding has increased as much as it has. When this is combined with the less than adequate role of the federal government, exacerbated by the state's lack of aggressiveness in going after Medicaid and other funds, it becomes clear that more local resources and local initiatives will have to be developed if continuous high-quality care for most of the CMI in the community is to become a reality.

References

Legislative Oversight Committee on Mental Health and Mental Retardation (LOC). 1985. *Report to the Texas Legislature, February 1985: Vol. 1, Mental Health*. Austin, Texas.

Miller, Gary E., and William V. Rago. 1988. "Fiscal Incentives to Development of Services in the Community." *Hospital and Community Psychiatry*, vol. 39, no. 6 (June).

Nunn, Bruce. 1989. Systems Analyst, Management Analysis and Reporting Unit, Texas Department of Mental Health and Mental Retardation, Austin, Texas. Interview by Joellen M. Harper, February 27.

——————. 1989. Interview by Joellen M. Harper, March 3.

——————. 1989. Telephone interview by Joellen M. Harper, March 13.

——————. 1989. Interview by Joellen M. Harper, March 15.

——————. 1989. Interview by Joellen M. Harper, April 12.

R. A. J. Review Panel. 1982. *Report to the Court, April 1982-November 1982*. Dallas, Texas: U.S. District Court.

——————. 1984. *Fourth Report to the Court, November 1, 1983-June 1, 1984*. Dallas, Texas: U.S. District Court.

R. A. J. v. Kavanagh. 1981. CA-3-74-0394-H. U.S. Court of the Northern District of Texas.

Sunset Advisory Commission. September 1986. *Staff Evaluation: TDMHMR*. Austin, Texas.

Texas Department of Mental Health and Mental Retardation (TDMHMR). 1984. "Retroactive Reimbursement Program," Attachment A. (November 13.) (Obtained from Bruce Nunn.)

——————. 1988. "Quarterly Incentive Program Report." (December 12.) (Obtained from Bruce Nunn.)

Texas Senate Bill 1. 1987. 70th Leg., Reg. Sess.

Texas Senate Bill 222. 1989. 71st Leg., Reg. Sess.

Vernon's Annotated Texas Civil Statutes (VATCS). 1984. Article 5547-201.

Ward, Mike. 1989. "MHMR Settlement Opposed: Court-Appointed Monitor Faults State Appropriations." *Austin American-Statesman* (June 30.)

Chapter 14. Community Mental Health and Mental Retardation Centers[*]

Historically in Texas, responsibility for the care of the mentally ill has fallen to the state. With the establishment of community mental health and mental retardation centers beginning in the 1960s, their proper role in providing care for the mentally ill was unclear. Initially much of their funding came directly from the federal government, bypassing the state. Therefore, the CMHMRCs' relationship with TDMHMR was ambiguous: it was not clear whether centers were to be the "arms" of the department or independent entities (Laritz, Interview, March 30, 1989). In the best of all possible worlds, CMHMRCs are the primary providers of public mental health care in the community. The financing structure of these entities is very complex. Funding comes from federal, state, and locally generated revenues and varies widely among the community centers. This chapter will attempt to analyze the various sources of revenues and expenditures. There will also be some discussion of alternative sources of funding such as organizing the community centers into bonding authorities.

PURPOSE

Article 5547-203 of Vernon's Texas Civil Statutes authorizes certain local agencies to establish and operate community centers. The local agencies are limited to counties, cities, hospital districts, school districts, and any organizational combination of two or more of these. Community centers may provide mental health services, mental retardation services, or a combination of both (VATCS, 1988).

Community centers are intended to be vital components in a continuum of services for mentally ill and mentally retarded individuals of this state. It is the policy of the state of Texas that community centers strive to develop services for the mentally ill and mentally retarded that are effective alternatives to treatment in large residential facilities (VATCS, 1988).

A community may provide services to persons voluntarily seeking assistance and to persons legally committed to that center. A board of trustees may, with the approval of the state mental health authority, contract with the governing bodies of other counties and cities to provide services to such cities and counties. Community centers shall provide screening services for persons seeking voluntary admission to a state facility as well as for those persons for whom proceedings for involuntary commitment to a state facility have been initiated. Community centers shall also provide continuing mental health and physical care services to persons referred to the center by a state facility and for whom the state facility superintendent has recommended a continuing care plan. The TDMHMR commissioner may designate a facility other than a community center as a provider of continuing care services when local conditions indicate that these services could be more economically and effectively delivered by that facility or when the commissioner determines that local conditions may impose an undue burden on the community center (VATCS, 1988).

CONTRACTING

State funding to the centers reflects the ambiguous authority of these entities. For the most part, state grant-in-aid funds were distributed to the CMHMRCs each year based partially on historical funding and mostly on political influence and arrangements made between each center and TDMHMR (Roberts, Interview, April 13, 1989). There

---

[*]This chapter was written by Joellen M. Harper and Ronnie Jung.

was no real link with specific service provision. Nevertheless, the CMHMRCs reported to TDMHMR every service that was delivered and every client that was served (Laritz, Interview, March 30, 1989). The centers spent an excessive amount of time and money gathering and reporting information which TDMHMR did not use. Around 1980, this flow of information from the CMHMRCs to TDMHMR virtually ceased (Laritz, Interview, March 30, 1989). There was a need for some sort of structure through which the centers and the department could communicate.

With the passage of S.B. 633 in 1985, as a result of the Legislative Oversight Committee's report, TDMHMR eliminated the grant-in-aid method of funding CMHMRCs and began a performance-based contracting system in FY 1986. (TDMHMR did not, however, move to a system of contracting for services with the state-operated community programs, a situation which continues to exist.) At first, the contract negotiation process was not a true negotiation for services (Laritz, Interview, March 30, 1989). This was and is partially due to the lack of a unit cost accounting system whereby community mental health services are priced uniformly across the state. Currently, each center reports how much it costs to provide its programs for each service. Depending upon the specific programs offered, the cost of providing a specific service can vary dramatically from one center to the next. For example, the cost per client-day for structured crisis services during FY 1988 ranged from $15.63 in the Permian Basin service area to $350.26 in the Nueces County service area. The average cost of all CMHMRCs for these services was $169.60 (LBB, 1989, pp. 138-139).

Each year the contracting process improves, as TDMHMR has become more specific with its requirements and the consequences of noncompliance. The CMHMRCs are required to provide local matching funds for the contracted services. The amount of local match required of each CMHMRC is based on a formula that includes, among other variables, socioeconomic factors. Currently the required local match ranges from 14 percent to 27 percent (Laritz, Interview, March 30, 1989). Some think that the main weakness that remains in the contracting system is the monitoring of CMHMRC performance (Laritz, Interview, March 30, 1989) and the lack of resources to actually fulfill the contract requirements.

Given that for many years there was no established basis for the funding each center received, there was a need to equalize the level of funding across the state. TDMHMR worked with the community centers to develop a formula that would equalize the disparity in the distribution of state funds per capita in the CMHMRC service areas. This has not been accomplished by reducing one CMHMRC's budget to increase another's. TDMHMR calculated the average CMHMRC per capita amount of state funding. Beginning in FY 1987, all centers below the average have received equalization funds. Only newly appropriated funds have been included in equalization, making it a slow process.

Table 14.1 presents total and per capita TDMHMR funding for each CMHMRC for FY 1987 and 1988, and the dollar and percent increase in funding between the two years (Roberts, Interview, April 13, 1989). In FY 1987, the average amount of TDMHMR funds for mental health services per capita was $5.84. Only centers below that level were eligible for equalization funds in FY 1988. For fiscal year 1988, all CMHMRCs were brought up to a minimum per capita level of $5.93, increasing the average per capita funding to $6.45.

The state funds "equalized" in this process are general revenue, Alcohol Drug Abuse and Mental Health block grants, budgeted R. A. J./$35.50 monies, state hospital contract funds, and state center contract funds and community and hospital support (Roberts, Interview, April 13, 1989). The theory behind the $35.50 program is to provide an incentive to the CMHMRCs to decrease bed-day utilization because their performance

Table 14.1. Local Mental Health Authorities' Total and Per Capita TDMHMR Funding for FY 1987 and FY 1988

#	LMHA	FY 1987 Total MH Funding*	1987 MH Per Capita**	1988 Est. Pop.***	Maximum FY 1988 Funding	1988 MH Per Capita	Funds Increase From 1987
1	Abilene	$ 1,075,484	$ 6.50	165,366	$ 1,075,484	$ 6.50	$ 0
2	Texas Panhandle	2,660,200	7.03	378,560	2,660,200	7.03	0
3	Austin-Travis	3,562,511	6.63	537,630	3,562,511	6.63	0
4	Bexar County	6,414,362	5.54	1,158,478	6,869,128	5.96	454,766
5	Brazos Valley	879,216	3.55	247,942	1,470,158	5.93	590,942
6	Central Cos.	2,244,037	7.49	299,489	2,244,037	7.49	0
7	Central Plains	1,131,970	10.73	105,481	1,131,970	10.73	0
8	Central Texas	854,484	8.21	104,128	854,484	8.21	0
9	Concho Valley	651,770	5.24	124,368	737,433	5.93	85,663
10	Dallas County	9,640,239	5.31	1,810,294	10,734,033	5.93	1,123,794
11	Deep East Texas	2,277,596	6.07	375,339	2,277,596	6.07	0
12	East Texas	2,092,131	7.17	291,746	2,092,131	7.17	0
13	Life Management	2,696,935	4.67	577,511	3,424,318	5.93	727,383
14	Gulf Bend	1,061,530	6.18	171,788	1,061,530	6.18	0
15	Gulf Coast	1,603,036	3.75	427,792	2,536,568	5.93	933,532
16	Harris County	16,694,471	5.56	3,004,791	17,816,732	5.93	1,122,261
17	Heart of Texas	1,934,184	6.61	292,607	1,934,184	6.61	0
18	Lubbock	1,676,299	6.00	279,458	1,676,299	6.00	0
19	Navarro County	450,885	11.27	39,992	450,885	11.27	0
20	Collin County	655,540	3.12	210,097	1,245,758	5.93	590,218
21	Northeast Texas	886,636	6.77	130,915	886,636	6.77	0
22	Nueces County	2,327,977	7.32	318,227	2,327,977	7.32	0
23	Pecan Valley	1,480,442	10.19	145,268	1,480,442	10.19	0
24	Permian Basin	1,501,172	5.27	284,795	1,688,675	5.93	187,503
25	Sabine Valley	2,487,412	8.16	304,988	2,487,412	8.16	0
26	Southeast Texas	3,503,856	9.22	380,116	3,503,856	9.22	0
27	Tarrant County	5,646,621	5.24	1,077,631	6,389,750	5.93	743,129
28	Texoma	1,474,330	9.71	151,908	1,474,330	9.71	0
29	Tri County	1,537,625	4.72	325,852	1,932,121	5.93	394,496
30	Tropical Texas	2,662,962	4.05	657,129	3,896,408	5.93	1,233,446
31	Wichita Falls	1,472,761	11.13	132,353	1,472,761	11.13	0
34	Johnson County	270,148	3.05	88,519	527,686	5.93	543,655
61	Denton	597,110	3.10	192,390	1,140,765	5.93	543,655
62	Hunt County	722,337	10.75	67,180	722,337	10.75	0
	Total	$86,798,269	$5.84	14,860,128	$95,783,777	$6.45	$8,985,508

Source: Roberts, Interview, April 13, 1989.

* FY 1987 total MH funding includes budgeted FY 1987 general revenue, budgeted FY 1987 block grant, budgeted FY 1987 $35.50 funds, and community and hospital support.
** As of May 14, 1987, using 1988 population figures.
*** July 1986 estimate by the Texas Department of Health of the 1988 Texas Population

261

Table 14.2. Listing of CMHMRCs and Location

Center Name	Location
Abilene Regional MHMR Center	Abilene
Austin-Travis County MHMR Center	Austin
Bexar County MHMR Center	San Antonio
MHMR Authority of Brazos Valley	Bryan
Central Counties Center for MHMR Services	Temple
Central Plains Comprehensive Community MHMR Center	Plainview
Central Texas MHMR Center	Brownwood
Collin County MHMR Center	McKinney
Concho Valley Center for Human Advancement	San Angelo
Dallas County MHMR Center	Dallas
Deep East Texas Regional MHMR Services	Lufkin
Denton County MHMR Center	Denton
MHMR Regional Center of East Texas	Tyler
Gulf Bend MHMR Center	Victoria
Gulf Coast Regional MHMR Center	Galveston
MHMR Authority of Harris County	Houston
Heart of Texas Region MHMR Center	Waco
Hunt County Family Services Center, Inc.	Greenville
Johnson County MHMR Center	Cleburne
Life Management Center	El Paso
Lubbock Regional MHMR Center	Lubbock
Navarro County MHMR Center	Corsicana
Northeast Texas MHMR Center	Texarkana
Nueces County MHMR Community Center	Corpus Christi
Pecan Valley MHMR Life Skills Center	Stephenville
Permian Basin Community Centers for MHMR	Midland
Riceland Regional Mental Health Authority	Wharton
Sabine Valley Center	Longview
MHMR of Southeast Texas	Beaumont
Tarrant County MHMR Services	Fort Worth
Texas Panhandle Mental Health Authority	Amarillo
MHMR Services of Texoma	Denison
Tri-County MHMR Services	Conroe
Tropical Texas Center for MHMR	Edinburg
Wichita Falls Community MHMR Center	Wichita Falls

Source: TDMHMR, 1989.

can increase their earnings under the program. TDMHMR decided to include these budgeted "incentive" earnings in the equalization formula to limit the total amount of dollars that could be earned under the program (Laritz, Interview, April 13, 1989). According to the director of contracting, TDMHMR was concerned that if the $35.50 earnings were left out of the formula, there was the potential for very high earnings which the department could not afford.

The inclusion of these funds in the equalization formula may diminish the incentive to earn under the $35.50 program for those centers below the state per capita average. And it certainly encourages centers to budget unrealistically low estimates for their projected earnings. However, for those centers above the average, the $35.50 program is the only mechanism through which they can obtain "new" state funds each year, so the incentive remains strong.

ADMINISTRATION

The Board of Trustees is responsible for the administration of community centers and for developing policies that are consistent with the rules and regulations of TDMHMR. The trustees appoint an executive director. The trustees may delegate certain responsibilities to the executive director (Laritz, Interview, April 13, 1989).

OPERATIONS

As of August 31, 1988, 34 CMHMRCs scattered throughout the state were making available various levels of service to a total population of 14,800,895 Texans (80 percent of the total population) who lived in their service areas (Table 14.2). These centers took in and expended approximately $250 million in FY 1988. Expenditures of the community centers over the last five years increased from $143 million in 1984 to $250 million in 1988 (see Appendix 14.1). As shown in Table 14.3, the expenditures for mental health services have also increased but at a slower pace.

Table 14.3. Expenditures by Texas CMHMRCs for Mental Health Services FY 1984 Through FY 1988

Year	Total	$ - MH	Percentage
1984	$142,797,000	$ 87,106,000	61
1985	158,791,000	96,862,000	61
1986	177,850,000	108,488,000	61
1987	204,033,000	118,339,000	58
1988	249,838,000	134,789,000	54

Source: Audited and unaudited financial statements of the CMHMRCs. See Appendix 14.2.

The amount of expenditures for mental health services has decreased as a percentage of total community centers' expenditures for the last two years. Funds available for mental retardation have increased more rapidly than those for mental health.

It is worthwhile to analyze not only program expenditures but also the object of expenditure. Salaries and wages comprised 58 percent of the total expenditures for 1988, followed by consulting or professional fees at 15 percent. Supplies, capital outlay, and rent and repairs made up only a total of 13 percent of the total expenditures.

Table 14.4. CMHMRC Mental Health Expenditures by Object for FY 1988

CMHMRC	Personnel Wages	Travel	Consumable Supplies	Capital Outlay	Rent and Repairs	Consultants	Other Operating Expenses	Total
Abiline	$ 3,117,063	$ 58,873	$ 223,560	$ 142,615	$ 343,192	$ 867,766	$ 597,857	$ 5,350,926
Austin-Travis	8,370,351	93,480	867,626	295,999	745,445	774,045	1,378,840	12,525,786
Bexar County	9,289,063	219,681	698,154	231,149	816,331	1,891,129	1,761,967	14,907,474
Brazos Valley	2,046,389	82,667	150,746	240,183	46,697	472,097	583,775	3,622,554
Central Cos.	4,097,858	99,843	279,177	436,204	180,589	346,284	924,350	6,364,305
Central Plains	2,276,440	72,624	225,802	69,420	195,443	128,099	418,187	3,386,015
Central Texas	2,136,595	20,987	248,162	37,495	104,312	94,635	819,310	3,461,496
Collin County	1,277,898	30,130	61,236	151,412	139,155	461,161	204,050	2,325,042
Concho Valley	1,296,956	19,374	113,486	57,006	131,787	685,906	437,261	2,741,776
Dallas County	13,745,211	137,266	905,480	805,482	899,155	5,164,586	1,463,470	23,120,650
Deep East Texas	5,293,026	147,886	538,383	1,503,718	370,8580	1,007,418	1,631,346	10,492,627
Denton County	1,262,766	43,077	94,205	196,037	162,508	772,030	263,162	2,793,785
East Texas	4,836,817	134,914	445,683	104,185	688,152	912,343	905,891	8,027,985
Gulf Bend	2,003,196	54,320	228,173	88,597	118,050	268,343	409,905	3,170,584
Gulf Coast	3,364,896	124,885	261,586	339,713	416,926	1,703,940	1,120,122	7,332,068
Harris County	17,633,043	390,011	1,720,075	267,317	3,223,888	13,483,843	4,466,424	41,184,601
Heart of Texas	3,542,265	86,547	329,292	118,261	136,163	354,365	916,772	5,483,665
Hunt County	1,216,651	28,926	35,487	40,922	37,658	424,669	348,825	2,133,138
Johnson County	709,715	24,631	65,316	17,389	138,146	550,938	150,601	1,656,736
Life Management	5,048,432	81,669	374,203	446,579	277,652	581,783	1,209,226	8,019,544
Lubbock	4,246,529	77,087	350,369	43,990	352,404	1,234,939	889,140	7,194,458
Navarro County	338,577	4,704	32,109	3,499	32,963	124,717	31,980	568,549
Northeast Texas	871,463	16,782	51,010	87,810	115,641	319,005	253,829	1,715,540
Nueces County	3,712,983	50,872	186,300	132,474	318,505	440,728	710,218	5,552,080
Pecan Valley	1,730,956	95,449	278,576	146,029	221,487	423,955	585,723	3,482,175
Permian Basin	2,617,366	97,844	334,765	134,278	112,722	575,876	686,367	4,559,218
Sabine Valley	5,022,800	151,687	537,871	178,558	585,005	323,482	1,449,883	8,249,286
Southeast Texas	3,141,757	44,290	278,074	40,620	95,793	925,693	823,122	5,349,349
Tarrant County	12,098,298	87,179	940,729	456,616	761,247	906,236	1,593,241	16,843,543
Texas Panhandle	1,912,360	72,863	371,033	22,939	183,029	629,626	302,911	3,494,761
Texoma	2,235,571	37,178	211,909	78,023	236,010	369,558	466,561	3,634,810
Tri County	5,326,361	191,332	452,253	206,539	435,605	419,699	1,977,855	9,009,644
Tropical Texas	5,634,341	174,692	513,478	228,992	208,185	644,134	1,183,012	8,586,834
Wichita Falls	2,307,116	39,853	196,242	75,279	236,809	263,809	379,572	3,497,954
Total	$143,761,109	$3,093,603	$12,600,547	$7,425,329	$13,066,778	$38,546,837	$31,344,755	$249,838,958
Percentage	58	1	5	3	5	15	13	100

Source: 1988 audited financial reports (see appendix 14.2) except for Austin-Travis County and Harris County. For these two centers the 1987 percentages were used times the total 1988 budgeted revenue.

Table 14.5. CMHMRC Mental Health Expenditures by Program for FY 1988

CMHMRC	Resi-dential	Client & Family Support	Case Mgmt	Mgmt Support	Total	1988 Est. Pop.	MH Funding Per Capita
Abiline	$ 592,873	$ 812,605	$ 82,459	$ 163,766	$ 1,651,703	165,336	$ 9.99
Austin-Travis	2,232,095	3,246,683	473,475	811,671	6,763,924	537,630	12.58
Bexar County	3,686,449	4,282,527	624,835	1,212,768	9,806,579	1,158,478	8.47
Brazos Valley	340,865	989,658	185,364	224,700	1,740,587	247,9472	7.02
Central Counties	812,181	1,571,827	279,885	424,455	3,088,348	299,489	10.31
Central Plains	739,880	525,422	92,876	338,019	1,696,197	105,481	16.08
Central Texas	194,099	613,960	165,801	243,626	1,217,122	104,128	11.69
Collin County	414,322	602,651	87,887	150,663	1,255,523	210,097	5.98
Concho Valley	240,428	675,191	74,121	129,964	1,119,704	124,368	9.00
Dallas County	6,743,068	7,188,189	522,499	1,550,444	16,004,200	1,810,294	8.84
Deep East Texas	3,465,374	1,296,110	243,626	428,798	5,433,908	375,339	14.48
Denton County	441,770	719,540	98,258	162,230	1,1421,798	192,390	7.39
East Texas	644,878	2,094,289	88,204	404,998	3,232,366	291,746	11.08
Gulf Bend	564,998	821,815	119,848	205,454	1,712,115	171,788	9.97
Gulf Coast	730,080	2,202,449	224,467	491,809	3,648,805	427,792	8.53
Harris County	7,339,096	10,675,049	1,556,778	2,668,762	22,239,685	3,004,791	7.40
Heart of Texas	472,839	1,650,041	161,107	386,472	2,670,459	292,607	9.13
Hunt County	144,501	571,699	36,924	125,977	879,101	67,180	13.09
Johnson County	127,219	226,428	53,589	114,852	522,088	88,519	5.90
Life Management	831,474	2,787,966	266,095	566,162	4,451,697	577,511	7.71
Lubbock	1,035,384	1,262,480	308,973	219,202	2,826,039	279,458	10.11
Navarro County	58,958	346,898	58,965	103,728	568,549	39,992	14.22
Northeast Texas	164,327	756,413	108,280	161,916	1,190,936	130,915	9.10
Nueces County	1,446,043	1,245,513	141,152	316,601	3,149,309	318,227	9.90
Pecan Valley	280,501	1,118,359	212,249	214,310	1,825,419	145,268	12.57
Permian Basin	444,747	1,391,338	94,660	316,222	2,246,967	284,795	7.89
Sabine Valley	2,156,299	1,925,085	313,172	337,362	4,731,918	304,988	15.52
Southeast Texas	2,721,413	1,839,213	212,651	576,072	5,349,349	380,116	14.07
Tarrant County	1,381,602	3,860,733	304,490	653,279	6,200,104	1,077,631	5.75
Texas Panhandle	378,431	1,296,704	1,517,343	302,283	3,494,761	378,560	9.23
Texoma	307,542	169,268	134,643	195,577	1,807,030	151,908	11.90
Tri County	1,216,803	2,619,044	186,108	482,436	4,504,391	325,852	13.82
Tropical Texas	1,038,756	2,263,791	212,648	866,418	4,741,613	657,129	7.22
Wichita Falls	186,199	938,675	211,371	260,671	1,596,916	132,353	12.07
Total	$43,575,494	$64,947,613	$9,454,803	$15,811,667	$134,789,210	14,860,098	$ 9.07

Source: 1988 audited financial reports (see appendix 14.2) except for Austin-Travis, Collin County, Gulfbend, and Harris County. For these centers 54 percent of the total expenditures was allocated for MH. MH was allocated to residential 33 percent, client and family support 48 percent, case management 7 percent, and management support 12 percent.

The remaining 14 percent was expended for travel and other operating expenses. A breakdown by center is shown in Table 14.4.

For FY 1988, mental health expenditures were grouped into the four program areas of Residential, Client and Family Support, Case Management, and Management Support. As shown on Table 14.5 approximately 80 percent of expenditures were for Client and Family Support and Residential. Only 7 percent of the expenditures were for Case Management. The remaining 12 percent was expended for Management Support.

TOTAL REVENUES FOR MENTAL HEALTH AND MENTAL RETARDATION

The sources of funding for the centers includes various federal, state, and local and private sources. Revenues by fiscal year by source are summarized in Table 14.6.

Table 14.6. Total CMHMRC Revenue by Source, Summary of FY 1984 Through 1988

FY	Federal	State	Private & Local	Total
1984	$ 6,742,000	$ 94,386,000	$ 45,387,000	$ 146,515,000
1985	7,247,000	104,463,000	51,031,000	162,741,000
1986	14,782,000	106,463,000	58,886,000	180,131,000
1987	15,217,000	122,132,000	68,936,000	206,285,000
1988	17,400,000	147,677,000	82,558,000	247,635,000

Source: Audited and unaudited financial statements of the CMHMRCs. See Appendix 14.2.

A summary of total revenues, for both MH and MR, by centers for FY 1988 is given in Table 14.7. While it should be noted that these amounts do include money for mental retardation, it is interesting to note the dramatic fluctuations in the per capita revenues among the centers. As noted above, the State of Texas provides the largest portion of funds to the community centers. Other sources include federal block grants, local taxes, insurance reimbursements, and a large number of other miscellaneous sources. Included under the heading of local funds are various reimbursements for grants and contracted services with other state agencies. This table shows the significant difference among the CMHMRCs in getting local funds and in receiving extra funding from agencies other than TDMHMR. As can be seen by the per capita funding column, even with the increases in funding for the centers there is still a great deal of variability among the centers. While all centers have reached a minimum funding level of $5.93 per capita, the rate is considerably different among the centers.

LOCAL TAX EFFORT

Tax support at the local level for the community centers has remained at approximately 10 percent of total funding over the last five years. The amounts and percentages of total funding are shown in Table 14.8.

Table 14.7. CMHMRC Mental Health Revenue by Source for FY 1988

CMHMRC	Local	Per Capita Local Funding	State	Per Capita State Funding	Federal	Per Capita Federal Funding	Total	Per Capita Total Funding	1988 Est. Pop.
Abiline	$ 1,228,884	$ 7.43	$ 3,942,183	$23.84	$ 222,533	$1.35	$ 5,393,600	$32.62	165,336
Austin-Travis	4,670,866	8.69	6,981,873	12.99	873,047	1.62	12,525,786	23.30	537,630
Bexar County	2,997,979	2.59	11,709,245	10.11	352,300	0.30	15,057,524	13.00	1,158,478
Brazos Valley	691,713	2.79	2,780,164	11.21	326,016	1.31	3,797,893	15.32	247,942
Central Cos.	1,147,784	3.83	4,028,839	13.45	736,514	2.46	5,913,137	19.74	299,489
Central Plains	807,846	7.66	2,411,087	22.86	175,102	1.66	3,394,035	32.18	105,481
Central Texas	1,242,812	11.94	1,597,296	15.34	481,077	4.62	3,321,185	31.90	104,128
Collin County	420,605	2.00	1,701,447	8.10	443,478	2.11	2,565,530	12.21	210,097
Concho Valley	705,883	5.68	1,908,429	15.35	148,694	1.20	2,763,006	22.22	124,368
Dallas County	6,944,247	3.84	16,100,815	8.89	1,111,413	0.61	24,156,475	13.34	1,810,294
Deep East Texas	4,756,704	12.67	5,020,421	13.38	679,845	1.81	10,456,970	27.86	375,339
Denton County	1,073,739	5.58	1,639,506	8.52	322,478	1.68	3,035,723	15.78	192,390
East Texas	2,781,812	9.54	4,968,043	17.03	441,260	1.51	8,191,115	28.08	291,746
Gulf Bend	1,045,913	6.09	1,955,185	11.38	175,165	1.02	3,176,263	18.49	171,788
Gulf Coast	2,585,894	6.04	4,574,787	10.69	520,313	1.22	7,680,994	17.95	427,792
Harris County	17,783,511	5.92	20,682,907	6.88	2,718,183	0.90	41,184,601	13.71	3,004,791
Heart of Texas	1,488,982	5.09	3,370,034	11.52	727,915	2.49	5,586,931	19.09	292,607
Hunt County	750,508	11.17	992,483	14.77	346,026	5.15	2,089,017	31.10	67,180
Johnson County	403,456	4.56	1,078,903	12.19	199,831	2.26	1,682,190	19.00	88,519
Life Management	2,472,195	4.28	161,935	0.28	505,132	0.87	3,139,262	5.44	577,511
Lubbock	2,596,692	9.29	4,160,755	14.89	378,245	1.35	7,135,692	25.53	279,458
Navarro County	81,296	2.03	447,330	11.19	7,520	0.19	536,146	13.41	39,992
Northeast Texas	318,389	2.43	1,351,181	10.32	66,915	0.51	1,736,485	13.26	130,915
Nueces County	1,554,216	4.88	3,960,847	12.45	416,736	1.31	5,931,802	18.64	318,227
Pecan Valley	445,863	3.07	2,021,894	13.92	738,657	5.08	3,206,414	22.07	145,268
Permian Basin	958,144	3.36	2,941,403	10.33	678,434	2.38	4,577,981	16.07	284,795
Sabine Valley	3,686,446	12.09	4,018,518	13.18	801,347	2.63	8,506,311	27.89	304,988
Southeast Texas	1,349,791	3.55	4,363,286	11.48	120,829	0.32	5,833,906	15.35	380,116
Tarrant County	6,462,498	6.00	9,610,623	8.92	1,149,773	1.07	17,222,894	15.98	1,077,631
Texas Panhandle	431,941	1.14	3,028,967	8.00	89,695	0.24	3,550,603	9.38	378,560
Texoma	1,094,229	7.20	1,900,574	12.51	790,898	5.21	3,785,701	24.92	151,908
Tri County	5,215,737	16.01	3,759,087	11.54	329,781	1.01	9,304,605	28.55	325,852
Tropical Texas	2,730,711	4.16	5,022,035	7.64	1,318,288	2.01	9,071,034	13.80	657,129
Wichita Falls	1,582,841	11.96	2,113,230	15.97	110,623	0.84	3,806,694	28.76	132,353
Total	$84,510,124	$5.69	$146,305,312	$9.85	$18,504,066	$1.25	$249,319,505	$16.78	14,860,098
Percentage	34		59		7		100		

Source: 1988 audited financial reports (see appendix 14.2) except for Austin-Travis County and Harris County. For these two centers the 1987 percentages were used times the total 1988 budgeted revenue.

Table 14.8. Local Tax Effort of the CMHMRCs and Percentage of Total CMHMRC Budgets

Year	Amount	Percentage
1984	$14,919,696	10.2
1985	17,796,234	10.9
1986	21,358,962	11.8
1987	25,169,880	12.2
1988	25,466,704	10.2

Sources: ATCMHMRC, 1984, 1985, 1986, and 1987; audited and unaudited financial reports of the CMHMRCs (Appendix 14.2).

Local tax revenues come mainly from cities and counties. Local school districts do provide some nonfinancial support in the form of services. Other benefits such as free or reduced rents are provided by various local governmental entities; however, the value of these benefits is difficult to quantify.

Of the total financial assistance provided by local taxes, approximately one-half went from Harris County to the MHMR Authority of Harris County. Another center, Lubbock Regional MHMR Center, received no local tax support in 1988. If these two centers are excluded, the remaining centers received approximately 6 percent of their total funding from local taxes.

As noted earlier in the section on contracting, community centers are required to provide a certain percentage of local funds for matching purposes. TDMHMR has allowed other types of local funds to be counted in computing the local match. These include but are not limited to private insurance reimbursements and reimbursements on state contracts for services rendered and federal ICF-MR, Medicaid, Medicare, etc..

BONDING AUTHORITY

On December 22, 1988, the Texas Council of Community Mental Health and Mental Retardation Centers (TCCMHMRC) officially closed a transaction to sell $37,610,000 in bonds for the benefit of 15 community centers. Roughly half of the money is to be used to refinance current debt at lower interest rates, and the remainder will be used to acquire or renovate facilities and/or major equipment items (Pettit, 1989, p. 1).

These bonds are unique in that they are the first pooled bond financing program in the country where the community centers are the direct recipients and guarantors of the bonds and where the state was not required to provide guaranty for the bonds. The breakdown of the centers participating in this venture and the amount of funds provided to each center are listed in Table 14.9.

**Table 14.9. CMHMRCs Participating in the CMHMRC
Acquisition Program**

Participating Center	Bond Money Received
Abilene	$ 595,000
Austin-Travis Co.	$ 5,040,000
Bexar County	$ 6,115,000
Central Counties	$ 1,015,000
Central Plains	$ 250,000
Collin County	$ 435,000
Dallas Co.	$ 8,620,000
Deep East Texas	$ 655,000
Life Management	$ 1,220,000
Gulf Coast	$ 3,380,000
Johnson Co.	$ 1,535,000
Lubbock	$ 1,485,000
Southeast Texas	$ 1,810,000
Sabine Valley	$ 1,500,000
Tri-County	$ 3,955,000
Total	$37,610,000

Source: Pettit, 1989.

This program will be administered by the TCCMHMRC. For its part in the program TCCMHMRC will receive a closing fee to be paid by the issuer of the bonds as part of the $507,000 delivery costs, and will receive ongoing compensation from the participating CMHMRCs for administrative services (Pettit, 1989, p. 2).

While this is an unusual financing mechanism for CMHMRCs, it is one that should be explored further. The possibilities of the creation of bonding and/or taxing authorities out of the LMHAs could have a significant impact on delivery of mental health care in the community as more funds are made available for this purpose.

OTHER STATE AGENCY REVENUE

Community centers receive a significant amount of revenues from state agencies other than the Texas Department of Mental Health and Mental Retardation. These monies are generally reported under the "local funds" category. The largest amount of other state funds comes from the Texas Department of Human Services, much of which is reimbursement of ICF-MR costs. TCADA funds represent the drug abuse portion of federal alcohol and drug abuse block grant monies allocated to the community centers. The Highway Department contracts with several centers for litter pick-up services on the roads and highways. Although it is difficult to be precise, Table 14.10 illustrates the magnitude of funds involved for FY 1988.

The amounts for the Texas Highway Department appear to be understated by several million dollars based upon cash basis reports. It is very likely that the Highway Department monies are included in the other categories of many of the centers' annual financial reports.

269

Table 14.10. CMHMRC Revenue from Other State Agencies for FY 1988

CMHMRC	TDHS ICF-MR	TRC Rehab	TDH ECI	TCADA	TDHS	TEA	HWY	Other	Total
Abiline	$ 437,925	$ 65,187	$ 233,892	$ 110,394	$ 192,882	$ 0	$ 0	$ 11,279	$ 1,051,55
Austin-Travis	211,086	91,008	304,218	423,972	528,069	68,288			1,626,64
Bexar County	169,541	12,760	75,815	866,619	268,536	18,699		75,000	1,486,97
Brazos Valley	114,894	15,659	227,200	41,880	137,326	37,703			574,66
Central Cos.		146,701	258,348	54,878	111,000				570,92
Central Plains	171,765	1,050	92,275	124,480	81,156	22,540	110,349	8,909	612,52
Central Texas	502,652		93,839		89,478	9,516			695,4
Collin County		12,037		140,368	79,243		15,840	3,644	251,13
Concho Valley		8,520			127,940				136,46
Dallas County	763,389	208,656	449,027		563,749	68,647			2,053,46
Deep East Texas	543,451	33,570	358,066	279,192	567,332	63,527	547,717		2,392,85
Denton County		14,395		255,122	510,962		68,073		848,55
East Texas	739,069	95,510	234,605	74,075	331,053				1,474,31
Gulf Bend	233,249	129,083		21,859	101,470				485,66
Gulf Coast	303,986	34,038		70,000	452,417		848,173		1,708,61
Harris County	371,131	2,482	225,895		709,397	150,926			1,459,83
Heart of Texas	349,261	229,636	245,115	33,315	193,096	43,188			1,093,61
Hunt County	317,231	9,011	125,612		92,899		101,488		646,24
Johnson County	104,340	3,134			24,831				132,30
Life Management	350,248	204,239	161,935	145,503	177,278	46,743	76,476		1,162,42
Lubbock	579,508	287,019		362,687	190,726				1,419,94
Navarro County		480			5,355				5,83
Northeast Texas					45,060		160,625		205,68
Nueces County	253,084	232,174	163,623	121,881	172,376		28,140		971,27
Pecan Valley		1,040	108,177		78,164	8,192	256,011		451,58
Permian Basin			248,806	119,428	462,816	29,379			860,42
Sabine Valley	338,423	246,798	296,665	777,615	697,965				2,359,46
Southeast Texas		5,361		84,512			360,946		450,81
Tarrant County	2,897,157	39,409	102,258	300,825	293,665	311,715			3,945,02
Texas Panhandle		6,112		46,011	15,2149				67,34
Texoma	387,311	47,109	131,836	76,308	147,596	24,309			814,46
Tri County	788,599	65,619	195,879	571,752	192,199		1,962,040		3,776,08
Tropical Texas	567,890	418,560	206,351	657,074	380,803	65,433			2,296,11
Wichita Falls	531,169	80,291		46,796	76,473		65,744		800,47
Total	$12,026,359	$2,746,648	$4,539,437	$5,806,546	$8,098,531	$968,805	$4,601,622	$98,832	$38,886,78

Source: Audited and unaudited financial reports of the CMHMRCs (see Appendix 14.2).

Note: TDHS - Texas Department of Human Services
ICF-MR - Intermediate Care Facility for the Mentally Retarded
TRC - Texas Rehabilitation Commission
TDH - Texas Department of Health
TCADA- Texas Commission on Alcohol and Drug Abuse
TEA - Texas Education Agency
HWY - Texas Department of Highways and Public Transportation

Table 14.11. CMHMRC Mental Health Expenditures
for FY 1984 through 1988

Year	Federal MH Block Grant	State Taxes From TDMHMR	Local Taxes	Other Locally Generated Fees	Total
84	$ 6,741,831	$ 45,709,068	$ 9,101,200	$ 25,553,901	$ 87,106,000
85	$ 7,246,118	$ 53,934,582	$ 10,855,560	$ 24,825,740	$ 96,862,000
86	$ 7,393,869	$ 56,633,379	$ 13,028,990	$ 31,431,762	$108,488,000
87	$ 7,643,453	$ 59,805,710	$ 14,598,600	$ 36,291,237	$118,339,000
88	$ 8,690,253	$ 70,985,587	$ 13,509,600	$ 41,603,560	$134,789,000
Totals	$37,715,524	$287,068,326	$ 61,093,950	$159,093,950	$545,584,000
Percentage	6.9	52.6	11.2	29.3	100

Sources: Audited and unaudited financial statements of the CMHMRCs (see Appendix 14.2).

What is striking is the extreme variation between centers. The MHMRA of Harris County, with a population of over three million people, received less that 40 percent of the amount Tri County MHMR got from other agencies. The area that Tri County serves has one-tenth the population of Harris County. Many of the differences arise from the fact that TCADA, TRC, TEA, and other agencies contract with CMHMRCs in some locales and with other local service providers in other cities. However, some of this variation is due to the aggressiveness of CMHMRCs in obtaining contracts for service provision from other state agencies.

MENTAL HEALTH REVENUES

Mental health revenues at the community level have risen from $87.1 million in 1984 to $134.8 million in 1988. This increase of $47.7 million in additional funds has resulted in a 56.7 percent growth rate over the last five years. Funding for these expenditures came from the sources listed in Table 14.11.

The other locally generated revenues which account for 29.3 percent of the mental health funds came from the following sources:

1. Patient fees
2. Insurance reimbursements
3. Reimbursements for services provided for state agencies
4. Other miscellaneous revenues

As previously noted, the level of state funding for community centers through TDMHMR has ranged from $45 million in 1984 to almost $71 million in 1988. Community centers received funds from the state in the form of "staff to patient amounts" and "contracted services." Staff-to-patient funds are earned via formula and have increased from $7.4 million in 1985 to $16.3 million in 1988. Contracted services between TDMHMR and the community centers have ranged from $45.7 million in 1984 to $54.7 million in 1988 (Appendix 14.1).

FINANCIAL CONDITION OF THE COMMUNITY CENTERS

To obtain an overview of the financial condition of the community centers as of August 31, 1988, selected information was compiled from the centers' audited financial reports. This information is summarized in Table 14.12. The balance sheet information for Austin-Travis County MHMR Center and for the MHMR Authority of Harris County was obtained from their 1987 audited financial reports as the 1988 audit reports were not available. The expenditure amounts for these two centers were obtained from TDMHMR budget figures. Historically, actual expenditures have been almost identical to the amounts budgeted.

Table 14.12. Overall Liquidity of the CMHMRCs

Current Assets	$ 48,054,152
Fund Balance excluding Fixed Assets	$ 31,121,431
Expenditures in 1988	$ 249,838,958

Sources: Audited and unaudited financial statements of the CMHMRCs (see Appendix 14.2).

272

In looking at the financial condition of the centers, three areas were targeted for consideration. These areas included liquidity, long-term debt, and amounts invested in fixed assets. Fixed assets were defined to include land, buildings, and equipment.

Liquidity

The ability of the community centers to pay their day-to-day bills is critical in terms of continuing to provide services. The problems associated with cash-flow difficulties are evident in some centers. The overall liquidity of the CMHMRCs is listed in Table 14.13.

Current assets include cash, receivables, supplies, and inventories. Fund balance is the amount left over after subtracting bills from current assets. Although the $48 million in assets or the $31 million in fund balance available to fund future operations may seem large, these amounts represent only 19.2 percent and 12.5 percent respectively of annual expenditures. Another way of looking at this is that by examining the fund balance divided by expenditures multiplied by 365 days. Noting this column in Table 14.13 it can be seen that if all funding had ceased on August 31, 1988, the number of days that a center could operate range from a low of 6 days to a high of 188. The centers on an average would have been able to operate only for 45 days. It is obvious that the community centers are very dependent upon state and local tax dollars to fund their day-to-day operations. The reserves or fund balances accumulated by the community centers do not appear excessive as they could only operate for another 45 days without additional funds. As previously noted, the 45-day figure is the average for all centers.

Debt

The community centers had a combined total of notes and bonds payable outstanding at August 31, 1988, of $20,783,939. This amount is probably on the low side considering that some of the centers are renting space from affiliated entities that have their own debt outstanding. The $20 million amount does not appear excessive when considering that fund balance is $31 million. Also debt outstanding is only about 8 percent of total center expenditures. Although debt is currently at a reasonable level, there are indications that community centers are looking at additional debt as a possible way to reduce rent expenses. Increased debt does have the impact of committing future revenues for interest and debt service and thereby reducing monies available for services.

Investments in Fixed Assets

Through August 31, 1988, the community centers had invested a total of $72,577,855 in land, buildings, and equipment. This amount appears to be low in comparison with what other governmental entities typically expend for fixed assets. As many of the centers rent rather than own buildings, it does appear logical that fixed assets would be considerably less than the amount expended annually for operations (i.e., $249,838,958). In looking for trends it does appear that the amount expended annually for fixed assets will increase, especially as additional bond (debt) money becomes available.

CONCLUSIONS

Community centers are the key to community-based care of the chronically mentally ill. They are a hybrid of a local agency with a local board and local responsibilities. While they are primarily state funded, in the mental health area they have increasingly become responsible for community-based care of persons who were

273

Table 14.13. CMHMRC Financial Condition as of August 31, 1988

CMHMRC	Current Assets	(Debt) Notes Payable	Fund Balance	Investment in Fixed Assets	Expenditures	Fund Balance/ Expenditures x 365	Debt/ Expenditures Percentage
Abiline	$ 539,643	$ 540,464	$ 466,669	$ 1,295,617	$ 5,350,926	32	0.10
Austin-Travis	2,378,284	1,445,960	865,507	4,120,207	12,525,786	25	0.12
Bexar County	977,491	397,582	255,408	1,647,736	14,907,474	6	0.03
Brazos Valley	981,528	218,707	710,664	1,050,935	3,622,554	72	0.06
Central Cos.	1,277,597	327,042	1,028,841	2,016,511	6,364,305	59	0.05
Central Plains	884,226	93,749	729,401	1,733,751	3,386,015	79	0.03
Central Texas	586,368	0	230,149	895,764	3,461,496	24	0.00
Collin County	531,410	180,000	390,096	560,726	2,325,042	61	0.08
Concho Valley	472,217	41,810	325,190	582,994	2,741,776	43	0.02
Dallas County	3,834,860	1,223,766	1,424,030	4,940,456	23,120,650	22	0.05
Deep East Texas	2,778,586	504,184	1,008,569	3,152,291	10,492,624	35	0.05
Denton County	989,662	74,864	685,199	474,911	2,793,785	90	0.03
East Texas	3,252,157	0	2,562,386	965,488	8,027,985	117	0.00
Gulf Bend	365,858	0	91,269	794,474	3,170,584	11	0.00
Gulf Coast	1,293,744	137,422	889,590	1,677,183	7,332,068	44	0.02
Harris County	2,042,162	7,974,917	1,480,947	14,609,982	41,184,601	13	0.19
Heart of Texas	1,464,338	302,342	886,540	2,857,125	5,483,665	59	0.06
Hunt County	325,424	32,976	217,006	201,970	2,133,138	37	0.02
Johnson County	378,872	0	268,549	67,756	1,656,736	59	0.00
Life Management	2,263,277	1,418,327	1,341,182	3,235,417	8,019,544	61	0.18
Lubbock	940,500	970,725	671,722	3,440,900	7,194,458	34	0.13
Navarro County	253,093	0	236,548	16,339	568,549	152	0.00
Northeast Texas	629,506	0	544,154	391,731	1,715,540	116	0.00
Nueces County	1,553,948	1,013,140	1,537,434	2,759,859	5,552,080	101	0.18
Pecan Valley	1,061,670	0	775,253	654,555	3,482,175	81	0.00
Permian Basin	2,150,902	0	2,002,800	1,626,948	4,559,218	160	0.00
Sabine Valley	1,715,002	165,002	1,673,555	1,218,665	8,249,286	74	0.02
Southeast Texas	1,874,786	6,365	1,513,390	4,022,853	5,349,349	103	0.00
Tarrant County	4,279,784	395,820	2,202,157	2,001,563	16,843,543	48	0.02
Texas Panhandle	632,297	0	399,757	152,172	3,494,761	42	0.00
Texoma	1,608,471	0	1,299,901	955,657	3,634,810	131	0.00
Tri County	1,035,310	2,062,197	367,965	2,833,949	9,009,644	15	0.23
Tropical Texas	817,340	658,709	242,402	4,565,391	8,586,834	10	0.08
Wichita Falls	1,893,839	597,483	1,797,201	1,055,979	3,497,954	188	0.17
Total	$48,054,152	$20,783,939	$31,121,431	$72,577,855	$249,838,958	45	0.08

Source: 1988 audited financial reports for the individual CMHMRCs (Appendix 14.2) except for Austin-Travis County and Harris County. For these two centers the 1987 financial reports were used and budgeted amounts were used for expenditure figures (Appendix 14.2).

formally nearly permanent residents in the state hospitals. To a certain extent, some centers appear to have used this ambivalent status to avoid accountability. To the state they represent themselves as local organizations trying to do the best they can with limited funding, while local groups may be told that state funds and state priorities are pertinent.

In fact, funds have been inadequate and accountability systems have been very limited. Although the concept that funds follow the client is quite sound, it falls apart if no one is following the client and making sure that appropriate services are being provided. Alternative approaches to funding community-based care include arrangements such as those in Wisconsin, where the county is the funding authority and care at the state hospital is purchased by the mental health authority. Different approaches to capitation of the CMI are being developed whereby the responsible local authority receives a capitation payment for each mentally ill client assigned to it and in return must provide full services to all such clients assigned. In either case the responsibility is firmly in the hands of the local mental health authority.

At best, the current arrangement in Texas can be characterized as transitional. The legislature is recognizing that increased funds need to be appropriated for care at the community mental health centers. But the accountability systems with regard to monitoring care are quite limited. And equitable treatment of centers is difficult when some centers have much more serious problems with homeless persons and unsupervised board and care homes than do other states.

Appendix 14.1. Explanation of the Derivation of Financial Data[*]

For the community centers the first step was to see what existing data were available. TDMHMR had very little financial data about the centers in a logical and organized manner. The 34 individual audited financial reports of the community centers for FY 1988 were obtained from TDMHMR. The Austin and Harris County CMHMRCs did not have their audited reports ready for FY 1988, so FY 1987 was used. The most useful data obtained had been prepared by Austin-Travis County MHMR Center in the form of the Summary Data Books. This resource contained a significant amount of information about revenues and expenditures of all centers for FY 1984 though 1987.

Using the audited financial statements and the Summary Data Books, our next step was to analyze the data. Spreadsheets were built to compile significant revenue, expenditure, and financial condition data for FY 1988. These included information about operations (i.e., revenues by source and expenditures for assorted categories). The FY 1988 data were then merged with data from FY 1984 through 1987 to paint a five-year trend picture. This was the source of information for most of the tables in Chapter 14.

After we had compiled this five-year trend for community centers of their revenues and expenditures, the obvious question that remained unanswered was what ending balances to use. The financial condition of the centers was then analyzed by looking at the assets, liabilities, and remaining balances. The results of this analysis appear at the end of Chapter 14.

Financial information available for TDMHMR was obtained from the combined audited financial statements for the years 1984, 1985, and 1986. For 1987 the unaudited financial reports of the 28 hospitals, schools, and centers were combined. A copy of the combined unaudited financial report was used to analyze data from 1988.

In analyzing these data two things became clear. First, the consistency and classification of financial information was not good and, second, the financial condition of TDMHMR is not pertinent as it spends all of its appropriation each year and is allowed to carry any balances forward from year to year. A great deal of effort was expended to insure that the numbers were consistent. The spreadsheets in this appendix further illustrate the process whereby numbers were arrived at for the various tables in chapters 13 and 14.

---

[*]This appendix was prepared by Ronnie Jung.

276

Spreadsheet 14.1. TDMHMR Total Expenditures by Object, FY 1984 through 1988

	1984	1985	1986	1987	1988	Total	Average
Total Department Expenditures	$578,496,623	$609,273,346	$627,378,787	$661,534,019	$724,283,247	$3,200,966,022	$640,193,204
Pass - Through to State	15,034,575	13,017,420	11,748,646	10,995,482	10,628,510	61,424,633	12,284,927
Pass - Through to Other	8,879,018	7,613,525	8,840,354	0	8,853,724	34,186,621	6,837,324
Indirect Expenditures -							
Retirement Contribution and Related Costs	30,168,711	31,920,181	29,581,558	28,199,638	29,024,085	118,725,462	23,745,092
Social Security Contributions	45,694,849	49,124,189	50,554,037	32,385,142	0	132,063,368	26,412,674
State Contributions for Group Insurance	24,936,788	30,227,358	28,900,387	28,032,490	36,112,392	123,272,627	24,654,525
Unemployment Compensation Benefits	780,862	814,137	804,427	1,163,309	769,254	3,551,127	710,225
Worker's Compensation Benefits	6,466,690	7,655,787	8,927,418	11,046,153	15,225,982	42,855,340	8,571,068
Total Operations	$710,458,116	$749,645,943	$766,735,614	$773,356,233	$824,897,194	$3,825,093,100	$765,018,620
General Fund -							
Central Office	$17,427,248	$17,650,212	$40,800,055	$66,867,495	$86,617,074	$229,362,084	$45,872,417
Centralized Food Purchase Fund	335,942	(657,837)	13,007,001	10,692,005	2,188,181	25,565,292	5,113,058
Contract Treatment Services and							
State Grants-in-Aid	76,181,780	77,557,174	77,196,324	78,133,325	176,913,335	485,981,938	97,196,388
Houston Psychiatric Hospital	0	0	5,000,000	13,090,000	0	18,090,000	3,618,000
Improving Staff Ratios -							
Mental Health	0	7,400,278	0	0	0	7,400,278	1,480,056
Mental Retardation	0	1,812,156	0	0	0	1,812,156	362,431
State Centers	24,419,866	25,285,057	26,427,300	32,719,419	26,405,664	135,257,306	27,051,461
State Hospitals and Centers	169,225,667	178,173,056	181,765,527	181,663,431	170,240,267	881,067,948	176,213,590
State Schools	229,943,062	240,550,921	247,037,962	258,291,724	260,281,177	1,236,104,846	247,220,969
TRIMS	14,677,576	14,421,834	5,635,053	4,375,493	0	39,109,956	7,821,991
Other	170,643	187,790	1,504,964	128,241	0	1,991,638	398,328
Special Revenue Funds	12,000,605	11,973,695	11,158,445	0	0	35,132,745	7,026,549
Capital Project Funds	13,250,026	9,512,965	10,596,720	6,404,981	0	39,764,692	7,952,938
Expendable Trust Funds	669,855	747,007	680,301	10,640	0	2,107,803	421,561
Fringes -							
Retirement Contribution and Related Costs	30,168,711	31,920,181	29,581,558	28,199,638	29,024,085	148,894,173	29,778,835
Social Security Contributions	45,694,849	49,124,189	50,554,037	32,385,142	0	177,758,217	35,551,643
State Contributions for Group Insurance	24,936,788	30,227,358	28,900,387	28,032,490	36,112,392	148,209,415	29,641,883
Unemployment Compensation Benefits	780,862	814,137	804,427	1,163,309	769,254	4,331,989	866,398
Worker's Compensation Benefits	6,466,690	7,655,787	8,927,418	11,046,153	15,225,982	49,322,030	9,864,406
TOTAL	$666,350,170	$704,355,960	$739,577,479	$753,203,486	$803,777,411	$3,667,264,506	$733,452,901

277

Spreadsheet 14.2. TDMHMR Total Revenues, FY 1984 through 1988

	1984	1985	1986	1987	1988	Total	Average
General Revenue Fund -							
Regular Legislative Appropriations	$563,065,786	$556,753,579	$588,705,628	$616,322,288	$655,691,741	$2,980,539,022	$596,107,804
Additional Appropriations	1,179,000	1,923,342	3,425,362		21,653,138	28,180,842	5,636,168
OASI	45,694,849	49,124,189	50,554,037	32,385,142	56,883,551	234,641,768	46,928,354
Fringes -							
Retirement Contribution and Related Costs	30,168,711	31,920,181	29,581,558	28,199,638	29,024,085	118,725,462	23,745,092
State Contributions for Group Insurance	24,936,788	30,227,358	28,900,387	28,032,490	36,112,392	123,272,627	24,654,525
Unemployment Compensation Benefits	780,862	814,137	804,427	1,163,309	769,254	3,551,127	710,225
Worker's Compensation Benefits	6,466,690	7,655,787	8,927,418	11,046,153	15,225,982	42,855,340	8,571,068
Federal Funds -							
Federal Assistance Programs	6,736,823	6,236,709	5,335,456	26,086,252	7,526,865	51,922,105	10,384,421
Pass-Through to State	15,034,575	13,017,420	11,748,646	10,995,482	10,628,510	61,424,633	12,284,927
Pass-Through to Other	8,879,018	7,613,525	8,844,140		8,853,724	34,190,407	6,838,081
Other Revenue -	18,073,080	22,892,981	17,925,919	14,875,537	14,406,366	88,173,883	17,634,777
TOTAL REVENUE	$721,016,182	$728,179,208	$754,752,978	$769,106,291	$856,775,608	$3,829,830,267	$765,966,053
RECAP OF GENERAL REVENUE FUND:							
Total General Revenue Fund	$672,292,686	$678,418,573	$710,898,817	$717,149,020	$815,360,143	$3,594,119,239	$718,823,848
Less: Unappropriated Deposits to General Revenue Fund		259,241,768	287,915,937	191,955,709	237,824,275	976,937,689	195,387,538
Net Cost to General Revenue Fund	$672,292,686	$419,176,805	$422,982,880	$525,193,311	$577,535,868	$2,617,181,550	$523,436,310

Spreadsheet 14.3. TDMHMR Total Expenditures of State General Revenue Funds, FY 1984 through 1988

	1984	1985	1986	1987	1988
Central Office	$66,422,326	$67,707,802	$54,077,260	$27,481,801	$44,534,355
Contracted Services	76,181,780	77,557,174	77,196,324	77,419,991	91,134,902
Houston Psychiatric Hospital	0	0	5,000,000	13,090,000	15,702,973
Tarrant County Psy Hospital				713,333	2,651,876
Staff to Patient - MH	0	7,400,278	10,315,585	13,353,715	16,304,646
Staff to Client - MR	0	1,812,156	10,211,146	21,007,916	26,620,627
State Centers	29,622,290	31,001,080	32,752,492	34,672,312	35,652,408
State Hospitals	209,544,456	222,472,235	230,785,763	233,970,578	235,040,979
State Schools	290,096,094	306,642,438	320,172,992	330,055,827	353,475,167
TRIMS	14,677,576	14,421,834	5,635,053	2,145,000	0
Pass-through funds	23,913,593	20,630,945	20,592,786	19,445,733	19,482,234
TOTAL	$710,458,115	$749,645,942	$766,739,401	$773,356,206	$840,600,167

Note: Fringe benefits and food costs were allocated as follows:

State Schools	55.5%
State Hospitals	37.2%
State Centers	4.8%
Central Office	2.5%

These percentages represent the FY87 fringe benefit amounts per entity.

Spreadsheet 14.4. TDMHMR Expenditures from State General Revenue, FY 1984 through FY 1988

	1984	1985	1986	1987	1988
TDMHMR Central Office - Unallocat	28,755,740	29,798,998	23,362,127	11,795,079	18,745,239
State Hospitals	209,544,456	222,472,235	230,785,763	233,970,578	235,040,979
Houston Psychiatric Hospital	0	0	5,000,000	13,090,000	15,702,973
Tarrant County Psy Hospital				713,333	2,651,876
TRIMS	14,677,576	14,421,834	5,635,053	2,145,000	0
State Centers	8,886,687	9,300,324	9,825,748	10,401,694	10,695,722
Sub-Total	261,864,459	275,993,391	274,608,691	272,115,684	282,836,789
Community Centers -					
Contracted Services	45,709,068	46,534,304	46,317,794	46,451,995	54,680,941
Staff to Patient - MH	0	7,400,278	10,315,585	13,353,715	16,304,646
TOTAL	307,573,527	329,927,973	331,242,070	331,921,394	353,822,376

280

Spreadsheet 14.5. TDMHMR Total Mental Health Expenditures
In Texas, FY 1984 through FY 1988

Year	State Funds	Local Funds	Total
1984	307,573,527	41,396,932	348,970,459
1985	329,927,973	42,927,418	372,855,391
1986	331,242,070	51,854,621	383,096,691
1987	331,921,393	58,533,290	390,454,683
1988	353,822,377	63,803,413	417,625,790
Total	1,654,487,340	258,515,674	1,913,003,014

Note: Local funds include all monies received by CMHMRCs
except for state funds received from TDMHMR.

Spreadsheet 14.6. TDMHMR Total Expenditures: State General Revenue Funds by Object

	1984	1985	1986	1987	1988
Central Office	$66,422,326	$67,707,802	$54,077,260	$27,481,801	$44,534,355
Contracted Services	76,181,780	77,557,174	77,196,324	77,419,991	91,134,902
Houston Psychiatric Hospital	0	0	5,000,000	13,090,000	15,702,973
Tarrant County Psy Hospital				713,333	2,651,876
Staff to Patient - MH	0	7,400,278	10,315,585	13,353,715	16,304,646
Staff to Client - MR	0	1,812,156	10,211,146	21,007,916	26,620,627
State Centers	29,622,290	31,001,080	32,752,492	34,672,312	35,652,408
State Hospitals	209,544,456	222,472,235	230,785,763	233,970,578	235,040,979
State Schools	290,096,094	306,642,438	320,172,992	330,055,827	353,475,167
TRIMS	14,677,576	14,421,834	5,635,053	2,145,000	0
Pass-through funds	23,913,593	20,630,945	20,592,786	19,445,733	19,482,234
TOTAL	$710,458,115	$749,645,942	$766,739,401	$773,356,206	$840,600,167
Mental Health Expenditures					
Houston Psychiatric Hospital	0	0	5,000,000	13,090,000	15,702,973
Tarrant County Psy Hospital				713,333	2,651,876
Contracted Services - 60%	45,709,068	46,534,304	46,317,794	46,451,995	54,680,941
Staff to Patient - MH	0	7,400,278	10,315,585	13,353,715	16,304,646
State Hospitals	209,544,456	222,472,235	230,785,763	233,970,578	235,040,979
TRIMS	14,677,576	14,421,834	5,635,053	2,145,000	0
State Center at 30%	8,886,687	9,300,324	9,825,748	10,401,694	10,695,722
Sub-Total	278,817,787	300,128,975	307,879,943	320,126,314	335,077,138
Central Office Allocation Formula d33\(d21-d9)*d9	28,755,740	29,798,998	23,362,127	11,795,079	18,745,239
TOTAL	307,573,527	329,927,973	331,242,070	331,921,393	353,822,377

Spreadsheet 14.7. TDMHMR Total Expenditures by Object, FY 1984 through FY 1988

	1984	1985	1986	1987	1988	Total
Total Department Expenditures	$578,496,623	$609,273,346	$627,378,787	$653,083,753	$724,283,247	$3,192,515,756
Pass - Through to State	15,034,575	13,017,420	11,748,646	10,995,482	10,628,510	61,424,633
Pass - Through to Other	8,879,018	7,613,525	8,844,140	8,450,252	8,853,724	42,640,659
UT-Harris Co. Psy. Center					15,702,973	
Salary related fringe benefits	108,047,900	119,741,652	118,767,827	100,826,718	81,131,713	420,467,910
Total Operations	$710,458,116	$749,645,943	$766,739,400	$773,356,205	$840,600,167	$3,840,799,831
Central Office	$63,712,730	$64,730,707	$50,782,889	$24,693,833	$40,885,151	$244,805,310
Centralized Food Purchases	335,942	(657,837)	13,007,001	10,692,004	11,852,578	35,229,688
Salary related fringe benefits	108,047,900	119,741,652	118,767,827	100,826,718	134,115,593	
Contracted Services	76,181,780	77,557,174	77,196,324	77,419,991	91,134,902	399,490,171
Houston Psychiatric Hospital	0	0	5,000,000	13,090,000	15,702,973	33,792,973
Tarrant County Psy Hospital				713,333	2,651,876	3,365,209
Staff to Patient - MH	0	7,400,278	10,315,585	13,353,715	16,304,646	47,374,224
Staff to Client - MR	0	1,812,156	10,211,146	21,007,916	26,620,627	59,651,845
State Centers	24,419,866	25,285,057	26,427,300	29,319,413	28,645,936	134,097,572
State Hospitals	169,225,667	178,173,056	181,765,527	192,485,613	180,740,819	902,390,682
State Schools	229,943,062	240,550,921	247,037,962	268,162,936	272,462,832	1,258,157,713
TRIMS	14,677,576	14,421,834	5,635,053	2,145,000	0	36,879,463
Pass-through funds	23,913,593	20,630,945	20,592,786	19,445,733	19,482,234	
TOTAL	$710,458,116	$749,645,943	$766,739,400	$773,356,205	$840,600,167	$3,840,799,831
Allocation of Food and Fringes						
Hospitals	40,318,789	44,299,179	49,020,236	41,484,965	54,300,160	13,105,444
Center	5,202,424	5,716,023	6,325,192	5,352,899	7,006,472	1,691,025
Schools - 55.5%	60,153,032	66,091,517	73,135,030	61,892,891	81,012,335	19,552,477
Central Office - 2.5%	2,709,596	2,977,095	3,294,371	2,787,968	3,649,204	880,742

283

Spreadsheet 14.8. TDMHMR Total Expenditures, FY 1984 through 1988

	1984	1985	1986	1987	1988	Total	Average
Total Department Expenditures	$578,496,623	$609,273,346	$627,378,787	$661,534,019	$724,283,247	$3,200,966,022	$640,193,204
Pass - Through to State	15,034,575	13,017,420	11,748,646	10,995,482	10,628,510	61,424,633	12,284,927
Pass - Through to Other	8,879,018	7,613,525	8,840,354	0	8,853,724	34,186,621	6,837,324
Indirect Expenditures -							
Retirement Contribution and Related Costs	30,168,711	31,920,181	29,581,558	28,199,638	29,024,085	118,725,462	23,745,092
Social Security Contributions	45,694,849	49,124,189	50,554,037	32,385,142	0	132,063,368	26,412,674
State Contributions for Group Insurance	24,936,788	30,227,358	28,900,387	28,032,490	36,112,392	123,272,627	24,654,525
Unemployment Compensation Benefits	780,862	814,137	804,427	1,163,309	769,254	3,551,127	710,225
Worker's Compensation Benefits	6,466,690	7,655,787	8,927,418	11,046,153	15,225,982	42,855,340	8,571,068
Total Operations	$710,458,116	$749,645,943	$766,735,614	$773,356,233	$824,897,194	$3,825,093,100	$765,018,620
General Fund -							
Central Office	$17,438,334	$17,629,819	$41,706,643	$68,000,848	$86,879,656	$231,655,300	$46,331,060
Contract Treatment Services and State Grants-in-Aid	76,229,820	77,466,392	78,911,947	79,437,750	177,449,439	489,495,348	97,899,070
Houston Psychiatric Hospital	0	0	5,110,560	13,303,840		18,414,400	3,682,880
Improving Staff Ratios -							
Mental Health	0	7,391,726	0	0	0	7,391,726	1,478,345
Mental Retardation	0	1,810,182	0	0	0	1,810,182	362,036
State Centers	24,435,319	25,255,454	27,013,916	33,275,403	26,486,627	136,466,719	27,293,344
State Hospitals and Centers	169,332,497	177,965,180	185,804,201	184,721,344	170,758,866	888,582,088	177,716,418
State Schools	230,088,189	240,270,025	252,526,916	262,643,370	261,071,110	1,246,599,610	249,319,922
TRIMS	14,686,982	14,404,730	5,759,920	4,439,645	0	39,291,277	7,858,255
Other	170,643	187,133	1,540,083	138,933	0	2,036,792	407,358
Special Revenue Funds	12,000,605	11,973,695	11,158,445	0	0	35,132,745	7,026,549
Capital Project Funds	13,250,026	9,512,965	10,596,720	6,404,981	0	39,764,692	7,952,938
Expendable Trust Funds	669,855	747,007	680,301	10,640	0	2,107,803	421,561
Fringes -							
Retirement Contribution and Related Costs	30,168,711	31,920,181	29,581,558	28,199,638	29,024,085	148,894,173	29,778,835
Social Security Contributions	45,694,849	49,124,189	50,554,037	32,385,142	0	177,758,217	35,551,643
State Contributions for Group Insurance	24,936,788	30,227,358	28,900,387	28,032,490	36,112,392	148,209,415	29,641,883
Unemployment Compensation Benefits	780,862	814,137	804,427	1,163,309	769,254	4,331,989	866,398
Worker's Compensation Benefits	6,466,690	7,655,787	8,927,418	11,046,153	15,225,982	49,322,030	9,864,406
TOTAL	$666,350,170	$704,355,960	$739,577,479	$753,203,486	$803,777,411	$3,667,264,506	$733,452,901

Appendix 14.2. List of Audited Financial Reports of the CMHMRCs and TDMHMR, and Unaudited Reports of TDMHMR-Operated Facilities Used in the Compilation of Financial Data

Audited Financial Reports of the CMHMRCs

In alphabetical order by center name (see Table 14.2).

Arthur Young. 1988. General Purpose Financial Statements and Additional Information: Abilene Regional Mental Health-Mental Retardation Center. Abilene, Texas.

BDO Seidman. 1987. Financial Statements for Austin-Travis County Mental Health-Mental Retardation Center. Austin, Texas.

KPMG Peat Marwick. 1988. Financial Statements and Supplementary Information for the Bexar County Mental Health Mental Retardation Center. San Antonio, Texas.

John T. Reynolds & Associates. 1988. Report of Examination of the Mental Health Mental Retardation Authority of Brazos Valley. Bryan, Texas.

Simpson and Byrom. 1988. Comprehensive Annual Financial Report of the Central Counties Center For MHMR Services. Temple, Texas.

Williams, Adair, Rogers & Co., P.C. 1988. Financial Statements With Accompanying Information of the Central Plains Comprehensive Community Mental Health-Mental Retardation Center. Plainview, Texas.

Fred L. Bradley. 1988. Report on Examination of Financial Statements of Central Texas Mental Health Mental Retardation Center. Brownwood, Texas.

Pingleton & Associates, P.C. 1988. Financial Statements of Collin County Mental Health Mental Retardation Center, Inc. McKinney, Texas.

Jones, Hay, Sanders & Company. 1988. General Purpose Financial Statements for Concho Valley Center For Human Advancement. San Angelo, Texas.

Ernst & Whinney. 1988. General Purpose and Combining Financial Statements and Supplementary Schedules of the Dallas County Mental Health and Mental Retardation Center. Dallas, Texas.

Alexander Lankford & Hiers, Inc. 1988. Audited Financial Statements for Deep East Texas Regional Mental Health Mental Retardation Services. Lufkin, Texas.

Schalk and Smith. 1988. Financial and Compliance Report for Denton County MHMR Center. Denton, Texas

Bland & Johnson, P.C. 1988. Annual Financial and Compliance Report for the Mental Health Mental Retardation Regional Center of East Texas. Tyler, Texas.

Roloff, Hnatek and Co. 1988. Auditor's Report for Gulf Bend Mental Health Mental Retardation Center. Victoria, Texas.

Cook and Cook. 1988. Examination of Financial Statements for Gulf Coast Regional Mental Health-Mental Retardation Center. Galveston, Texas.

Ernst & Whinney. 1987. Comprehensive Annual Financial Report for the Mental Health and Mental Retardation Authority of Harris County, Texas. Houston, Texas.

KPMG Peat Marwick. 1988. Financial Statements and Schedules for Heart of Texas Regional Mental Health-Mental Retardation Center. Waco, Texas.

Scott, Singleton, Fincher and Company, PC. 1988. Annual Financial and Compliance Report for Hunt County Family Services Center, Inc. Greenville, Texas.

Pitcher & Company, Inc. 1988. Audit Report for Johnson County Mental Health Retardation Center. Cleburne, Texas.

Lauterbach, Borschow & Company. 1988. Financial Statements & Auditor's Report for the Life Management Center. El Paso, Texas.

Bolinger, Segars, Gilbert & Moss. 1988. Financial Statements with Accompanying Information for the Lubbock Regional Mental Health and Mental Retardation Center. Lubbock, Texas.

Pattillo, Brown, Hill & Anderson. 1988. Annual Financial and Compliance Report for Navarro County Mental Health Mental Retardation Center. Corsicana, Texas.

Williams and McDonnell. 1988. Annual Financial Report for the Northeast Texas Mental Health Mental Retardation Center. Texarkana, Texas.

Collier, Johnson & Woods. 1988. Comprehensive Audited Financial Report for Nueces County Mental Health and Mental Retardation Community Center. Corpus Christi, Texas.

Boucher, Morgan & Young. 1988. Annual Financial and Compliance Report for the Pecan Valley Mental Health Mental Retardation Region. Stephenville, Texas.

Elms, Faris & Company. 1988. Financial Statements With Supplementary Information and Auditor's Report for Permian Basin Community Centers For Mental Health And Mental Retardation. Midland, Texas.

(Riceland Regional MHMR Authority was established at the beginning of FY 1989).

John A. Jetter, P.C. 1988. Financial Statements for the Sabine Valley Center. Longview, Texas.

Juncker, McMillain & Bennett. 1988. Audit Report for MHMR of Southeast Texas. Beaumont, Texas.

Ernst & Whinney. 1988. General Purpose, Combining and Individual Fund Financial Statements, and Supplemental Financial Information for Tarrant County Mental Health Mental Retardation Services. Fort Worth, Texas.

H. V. Robertson & Co. 1988. Financial Statements and Auditor's Report for the Texas Panhandle Mental Health Authority. Amarillo, Texas.

Snyder & Floyd. 1988. Audited Financial Statements for the Mental Health Mental Retardation Services of Texoma. Denison, Texas.

Kenneth C. Davis. 1988. Audited Financial Statements for Tri-County Mental Health Mental Retardation Services. Conroe, Texas.

Arturo Z. Flores. 1988. <u>Audited Financial Statements of the Tropical Texas Center For Mental Health and Mental Retardation</u>. Edinburg, Texas.

Niles & Company. 1988. <u>Financial Statements for Wichita Falls Community Mental Health Mental Retardation Center</u>. Wichita Falls, Texas.

Audited Financial Reports of TDMHMR

Office of the Texas State Auditor. 1984. <u>Audit Report for the Texas Department of Mental Health and Mental Retardation</u>. Austin, Texas.

Office of the Texas State Auditor. 1985. <u>Audit Report for the Texas Department of Mental Health and Mental Retardation</u>. Austin, Texas.

Office of the Texas State Auditor. 1986. <u>Audit Report for the Texas Department of Mental Health and Mental Retardation</u>. Austin, Texas.

Unaudited Financial Reports of TDMHMR-Operated Facilities

(Listed alphabetically by facility type.)

Central Office

Texas Department of Mental Health and Mental Retardation. 1988. <u>Annual Report</u>. Austin, Texas.

Texas Department of Mental Health and Mental Retardation Central Office. 1987. <u>Annual Report</u>. Austin, Texas.

State Schools

Abilene State School. 1987. <u>Annual Report</u>. Abilene, Texas.

Austin State School. 1987. <u>Annual Report</u>. Austin, Texas.

Brenham State School. 1987. <u>Annual Report</u>. Brenham, Texas.

Corpus Christi State School. 1987. <u>Annual Report</u>. Corpus Christi, Texas.

Denton State School. 1987. <u>Annual Report</u>. Denton, Texas.

Fort Worth State School. 1987. <u>Annual Report</u>. Fort Worth, Texas.

Lubbock State School. 1987. <u>Annual Report</u>. Lubbock, Texas.

Lufkin State School. 1987. <u>Annual Report</u>. Lufkin, Texas.

Mexia State School. 1987. <u>Annual Report</u>. Mexia, Texas.

Richmond State School. 1987. <u>Annual Report</u>. Richmond, Texas.

San Angelo State School. 1987. <u>Annual Report</u>. San Angelo, Texas.

San Antonio State School. 1987. <u>Annual Report</u>. San Antonio, Texas.

Travis State School. 1987. <u>Annual Report</u>. Austin, Texas.

State Centers

Amarillo State Center. 1987. <u>Annual Report</u>. Amarillo, Texas.

Beaumont State Center. 1987. <u>Annual Report</u>. Beaumont, Texas.

El Paso State Center. 1987. <u>Annual Report</u>. El Paso, Texas.

Laredo State Center. 1987. <u>Annual Report</u>. Laredo, Texas.

Rio Grande State Center. 1987. <u>Annual Report</u>. Brownsville, Texas.

State Hospitals

Waco Center For Youth. 1987. <u>Annual Report</u>. Waco, Texas.

Austin State Hospital. 1987. <u>Annual Report</u>. Austin, Texas.

Big Spring State Hospital. 1987. <u>Annual Report</u>. Big Spring, Texas.

Rusk State Hospital. 1987. <u>Annual Report</u>. Rusk, Texas.

San Antonio State Hospital. 1987. <u>Annual Report</u>. San Antonio, Texas.

Terrell State Hospital. 1987. <u>Annual Report</u>. Terrell, Texas.

Vernon State Hospital. 1987. <u>Annual Report</u>. Vernon, Texas.

Wichita Falls State Hospital. 1987. <u>Annual Report</u>. Wichita Falls, Texas.

Kerrville State Hospital. 1987. <u>Annual Report</u>. Kerrville, Texas.

References

Austin-Travis County MHMR Center (ATCMHMRC). 1984. <u>Summary Data Book</u>. Austin, Texas.

_____. 1985. <u>Summary Data Book</u>. Austin, Texas.

_____. 1986. <u>Summary Data Book</u>. Austin, Texas.

_____. 1987. <u>Summary Data Book</u>. Austin, Texas.

Laritz, Michael. 1989. Director of Contracting, Texas Department of Mental Health and Mental Retardation, Austin, Texas. Interview by Joellen M. Harper, March 30.

_____. 1989. Interview by Joellen M. Harper, April 13.

Legislative Budget Board (LBB). 1989. <u>Performance Report to the 71st Legislature</u>. Austin, Texas. (January 10.)

Pettit, William L. 1989. Letter to the Honorable William P. Clements, Jr., Govenor of the State of Texas. Austin, Texas. (January 6.)

Roberts, Charles. 1989. Analyst, Management Analysis and Reporting Unit, Texas Department of Mental Health and Mental Retardation, Austin, Texas. Interview by Joellen M. Harper, April 13.

Texas Department of Mental Health and Mental Retardation (TDMHMR). 1988. "Request for Legislative Appropriations, Fiscal Year 1990-1991." Austin, Texas.

_____. 1989. <u>1989 Directory of Services</u>. Austin, Texas.

Texas Senate Bill 1. 70st Legislature, Regular Session (1987).

Texas Senate Bill 222. 71st Legislature, Regular Session (1989).

<u>Vernon's Annotated Texas Civil Statutes</u> (VATCS). 1988. Article 5547-201 and 5547-203.

Chapter 15. Federal Revenue Sources[*]

The federal government currently provides about 10 percent of the funds for community-based mental health care in Texas. While the numbers are not large, the importance of the federal government as a current and potential source of funds for mental health care cannot be overstated. This chapter will review the most significant sources of federal funds and will discuss the potential use of Medicaid to expand the federal role in financing care for the CMI.

FEDERAL BLOCK GRANTS

Alcohol Drug Abuse and Mental Health Block Grant

The Alcohol Drug Abuse and Mental Health Block Grant (ADMBG) funds make up a small but not insignificant amount of the funds allocated for community mental health delivery in Texas. In FY 1989 the mental health portion of ADMBG was $10,106,961. This makes up 70 percent of the federal funds coming into Texas for community mental health care and 5.4 percent of all funds for this purpose (TDMHMR, 1989a, pp. 94-110). ADMBG is designed to "support treatment and prevention programs for alcohol and drug abusers, outpatient treatment for the severely mentally disabled, and community treatment and rehabilitation programs of community mental health clinics" (TDMHMR, 1989a, p. 97).

This block grant compels states to target specific populations, the most important of which are severely mentally disabled adults, severely emotionally disturbed children and adolescents, and mentally ill elderly persons. States are supposed to find what resources are needed and to formulate a plan of action for a community-based system of care for these specified groups (U.S. Congress, Senate, 1988 p. 5).

Agencies Involved in ADMBG. The ADMBG is administered at the federal level by the Department of Health and Human Services (USDHHS). The funds are shared by two state entities in Texas: the Texas Department of Mental Health and Mental Retardation (TDMHMR) and the Texas Commission on Alcohol and Drug Abuse (TCADA). Through FY 1989 TDMHMR was directed to distribute 52.6 percent of ADMBG to TCADA and to retain 47.3 percent to be distributed to the community mental health and mental retardation centers (CMHMRCs) and other entities with which it contracts. TCADA also contracts with many CMHMRCs to provide drug and alcohol abuse treatment. As will be explained later in this section, TCADA now receives over two thirds of the ADMBG for Texas (England, Interview, April 6, 1989).

The state is allowed to use 1.5 percent of the grant for administrative purposes. TDMHMR receives an additional .15 percent from TCADA as reimbursement for administrative services. For FY 1989 the ADMBG for Texas was $21,268,283. The allocation to TDMHMR was $10,106,961 (TDMHMR, 1989b).

History of Block Grants. Grants to the states for mental health services go back to the early sixties. President Kennedy believed that the federal government should become more involved in the mental health care system. As pointed out in the Congressional Quarterly at the inception of the ADMBG:

Congress in 1963 first provided funding to community centers designed to treat mental illness primarily on an outpatient basis. Since the program's inception, the

---

[*]This chapter was written by Nicholas L. Hoover.

number of institutionalized persons has dropped from 500,000 to 148,000. In contrast, more than 2.4 million persons received some type of service from mental health centers in 1980. Under the program more than 750 local mental health centers were established; as of 1980, 20 percent of these were no longer receiving Federal support. (Congressional Quarterly 1981 Almanac, 1982, p. 483)

The community mental health center categorical grants, staffing grants, and constructions grants appropriated federal funds directly to the CMHMRCs for the establishment of community mental health centers throughout the country. Money was provided for initial operations, consultation and education, financial distress, and staffing. These categorical grants were replaced by the ADMBG with passage of the Omnibus Budget Reconciliation Act of 1981. The Reagan administration sought to streamline the grant process by combining different categorical grants into single block grants. ADMBG was made up of three categorical grants: Mental Health, Alcohol Abuse, and Drug Abuse. This move dramatically changed the manner in which federal funds were distributed and the level of funding (Peterson, 1986, p. 95).

The move to block grants was made to save money by simplifying the grant process, lessening the regulations, and reducing the aggregate level of funding. Before the era of block grants, money was sent directly to the more than 750 community mental health centers. Now the entire amount for a state is sent to a single entity within the state which divides up the funds to the individual CMHMRCs. States are now given more latitude in how the money is to be spent. The move to block grants also meant an approximately 20 percent reduction in funding for health services (Congressional Quarterly 1981 Almanac, 1982, p. 483). There are five basic differences between categorical grants and block grants:

1. Recipients of block grant monies have much more discretion in deciding what specific projects or purposes will be funded and whether in a broad program or functional area.

2. Planning, reporting, auditing, and other "red tape" aspects are considerably reduced in block grants with the intent of reducing grantor supervision and control.

3. Block grant funds are dispersed on the basis of a demographically based formula so that the intended recipient units will be more knowledgeable and certain of the aid amounts and the national administrative agency will not have discretion to decide the amount of funds allocated to a local unit.

4. Eligibility provisions are fairly precise for block grants. They tend to favor units of general government rather than special districts and favor state/local generalists over program specialists.

5. Financing provisions in block grants usually require very low or no state/local matching funds. (Peterson, 1986, p. 4)

ADMBG does get the federal government directly out of the CMHMRC business. It gives the federal level a less direct line of control over the direction of community mental health delivery.

Use of ADMBG Funds in Texas. Texas has received ADMBG funds since FY 1982. These funds are directed to be used in fairly specific ways. The individual

CMHMRCs do have some leeway in how this money is spent. Some activities performed by the CMHMRCs using these funds are as follows:

1. Outpatient, day care, and other partial hospitalization services, and 24-hour emergency services;

2. Programs of specialized services for the mental health of children and the elderly, including a full range of diagnostic, treatment, liaison, and follow-up services;

3. Screening services for individuals being considered for referral to a state mental health facility and provision, where appropriate, of treatment for such individuals;

4. Consultation and education services for individuals and entities involved with mental health services;

5. Follow-up care, including case management, for residents discharged from a mental health facility;

6. Community-based residential services for those discharged from a mental health facility or those who would otherwise require inpatient care in the absence of such a facility (as required by PL 98-509);

7. New mental health services for severely disturbed children and adolescents; and

8. New comprehensive mental health programs for unserved areas and underserved populations. (TDMHMR, 1987b, p. 3)

Public Law 98-509 required 10 percent of each fiscal year's award to be used to initiate and provide new mental health services for severely disturbed children and adolescents and for new mental health services. These funds are used to set up new CMHMRCs or start new programs in existing CMHMRCs (U.S. Congress, Senate, 1988). ADMBG funds cannot totally fund all of these programs. However, they are an important supplement to state and local funds used for these purposes.

One of the most important uses of ADMBG funds in Texas is to start up new CMHMRCs and programs during the interim between legislative sessions. The Texas legislature is not eager to appropriate funds for nonexistent facilities and services. By using ADMBG funds for these purposes, TDMHMR can present to the legislature programs and facilities that have a documented level of performance (England, Interview, March 14, 1989).

Distribution of ADMBG Funds to the CMHMRCs. The mental health portion of the ADMBG allocated and used has remained fairly constant throughout this decade. For FY 1982, the original grant of $6,548,482 for mental health services was given to 20 CMHMRCs. Not all ADMBG funds are expended throughout the year, and the remaining funds are rolled over to be used the next year. Grants have ranged from $6.6 million for FY 1982 to $11.5 million for FY 1987.

For FY 1983 through 1988 the totals are listed in Table 15.1. The variation in funding for each center is due to a formula used by TDMHMR to allocate funds. This formula is based upon the local financing capabilities of the CMHMRCs. Those with better local financing receive fewer ADMBG funds. While on one level this makes sense,

Table 15.1. ADMBG Mental Health Allocations for FY 1983 through FY 1988

Recipient	FY 1983	FY 1984	FY 1985	FY 1986	FY 1987	FY 1988
CMHMRC						
Abiline	$ 0	$ 20,312	$ 18,302	$ 10,856	$ 32,122	$ 29,746
Austin-Travis	419,795	287,824	239,975	235,967	236,274	
Bexar County	1,283,758	114,501	104,480	87,769	184,877	170,722
Brazos Valley		125,622	123,406	104,943	146,117	108,251
Central Cos.	574,562	634,984	577,937	516,620	518,827	515,180
Central Plains		16,254	14,641	8,025	30,273	27,236
Central Texas	494,125	516,604	458,706	414,261	409,173	407,776
Collin County					394,589	344,541
Concho Valley		15,127	13,617	8,282	22,482	20,801
Dallas County	307,113	238,418	465,141	287,438	366,780	388,164
Deep East Texas	522,900	602,862	517,806	462,508	465,070	461,673
Denton County					325,271	300,456
East Texas	317,468	11,471	5,672	(436)	52,399	48,523
Gulf Bend					28,920	73,813
Gulf Coast		34,429			68,309	65,894
Harris County		519,170	529,499	1,110,336	1,191,267	1,165,488
Heart of Texas	318,764	365,690	329,363	289,693	298,609	586,439
Hunt County					338,189	313,331
Johnson County			14,589	174,998	175,002	175,121
Life Management		148,874	77,638	156,328	177,361	171,721
Lubbock		30,974	25,846	18,554	50,591	50,626
Navarro County					7,520	7,525
North Central Texas	1,102,918	1,176,724	1,074,209	924,075		
Northeast Texas		35,614	13,955	10,542	23,676	21,300
Nueces County	421,269	284,680	248,693	65,125	85,231	78,925
Pecan Valley	793,874	816,855	737,850	669,564	601,769	673,226
Permian Basin	307,492	97,900	88,455	70.195	84,914	78,890
Riceland MHMR						13,943
Sabine Valley	733,334	849,616	735,074	664,741	655,146	634,582
Southeast Texas		115,201	41,889	84,132	98,297	93,764
Tarrant County		213,778	209,015	262,116	414,785	415,073
Texas Panhandle	84,865	59,267	47,057	82,722	97,170	89,982
Texoma	595,834	703,387	633,656	569,567	561,544	559,852
Tri County			11,864	136,189	139,617	138,022
Tropical Texas	1,442,982	992,831	860,940	674,295	745,173	739,053
Wichita Falls		18,941	17,061	9,885	31,579	37,926
Total CMHMRCs	$9,723,053	$9,047,940	$8,236,336	$8,108,647	9,066,616	8,943,886
Contracted Services						
Laredo State Center		52,942	9,642			
Rio Grande State Center		5,824				
Children's Heart Institute				149,406	150,000	
Houston Independent School District				617,938		
Total Contracted Services		58,766	9,642	767,344	150,000	
Total All ADMBG Recipients	9,723,053	9,106,706	8,245,978	8,875,991	9,216,616	8,943,886
Administrative Cost	196,239	328,156	391,217	441,927	462,040	946,324
Program Evaluation						68,630
Case Management						148,121
Total ADMBG Mental Health Portion Used	9,919,292	9,434,862	8,637,195	9,317,918	9,678,656	10,106,961
Total ADMBG Mental Health Portion	9,11,505	7,498,366	8,457,123	8,934,493	11,426,118	10,021,676
From TCADA for Administrative Services		16,009	37,178	28,062	37,072	25,202
Carried Forward to Next FY	$ 2,440,505	$ 520,021	$ 645,475	$ 290,112	$ 2,074,646	$ 2,014,563

Source: TDMHMR, 1983; 1984; 1985b; 1985c; 1986; 1987b, 1989b.

it also is a disincentive to the generation of local funds. There is competition among the CMHMRCs for funds above the basic funding amounts. The use of this formula means that CMHMRCs will not necessarily get the same amount from year to year. There are some dramatic changes from year to year due to consolidation of CMHMRCs and the setting up of new CMHMRCs in the areas of older ones (England, Interview, May 15, 1989).

The federal government uses a formula weighted on several factors in order to distribute ADMBG funds to the states. It is based on several demographic features of the state including poverty rate, median income, ethnic makeup, population, and others. The state bases the allocation of ADMBG funds through a process that forces the CMHMRCs to compete against each other for existing funds. The CMHMRCs do not specifically ask for ADMBG funds. Proposals are made for the state/federal funds by the CMHMRCs as part of their budget requests. A combination of state/federal funds are given to the CMHMRCs when their proposals are approved and the amounts settled upon.

Some of the CMHMRCs contract with TCADA to do alcohol and substance abuse prevention, intervention, and treatment. The CMHMRCs that did receive alcohol and drug abuse portions of the ADMBG funds during FY 1988 are shown in Table 15.2. While the CMHMRCs do not necessarily use all of these funds for the CMI, many dual-diagnosed CMI do benefit from the TCADA portion of these funds.

ADMBG 1988. In November of 1988 Congress passed the Comprehensive Alcohol Abuse, Drug Abuse and Mental Health Amendments of 1988. The changes to the administration of ADMBG included in these amendments are changing the nature of this block grant. These amendments included several "set-asides" which require that certain percentages of ADMBG funds be spent for specific purposes. While still having some of the advantages of a block grant, the restrictions on their use are making the grant more of a categorical grant. TDMHMR staff now refer to ADMBG as a "blockagorical" grant (England, Interview, March 14, 1989). Some of these "set-asides" include the following:

1.   Of the amount allotted to a State in any fiscal year . . . the State shall use not less that 5 percent of such amount to provide alcohol and drug abuse services designed specially for women.

2.   Not less than 35 percent of the amount will be made available for such activities relating to alcoholism and alcohol abuse. Not less than 35 percent of the amount to be made available for such activities shall be used for programs and activities relating to drug abuse.

3.   The State agrees to use not less than 10 percent of such amount to provide services and programs for seriously emotionally disturbed children and adolescents. The State shall use not less than 50 percent of the amount set aside in the preceding sentence by the end of FY 1990 to provide new or expanded services and programs not available prior to 10/1/88, which shall apply to the requirement above. (U.S. Congress, Senate, 1988, p. 108)

For FY 1990 Texas was given over $40 million in ADMBG funds, a 100 percent increase in funding. Because of the set-asides listed above, the mental health portion of this block grant will only increase to about $12 million, a 20 percent increase (England, Interview, May 15, 1989). The result is that much of the flexibility of the block grant is being diminished. Congressmen in the current budgetary climate can have some impact by setting aside funds for their pet projects. If this trend continues, most of the advantages of the block grant will be taken away.

Table 15.2. CMHMRCs Receiving TCADA Portions of ADMBG During FY 1988

CMHMRC	TCADA Grant Amount
Abilene Regional MHMR Center	$ 110,394
Austin-Travis County MHMR Center	423,972
Bexar County Board of Trustees for MHMR Services	866,619
MHMR of Brazos Valley	41,880
Central Counties Center for MHMR Services	54,878
Central Plains MHMR Center	124,480
Collin County MHMR Center	140,368
Denton County MHMR Center	255,122
MHMR Center of East Texas	74,075
Gulf Bend MHMR Center	21,859
Gulf Coast MHMR Center	70,000
Heart of Texas Region MHMR Center	33,315
Life Management Center	145,503
Lubbock Regional MHMR Center	362,687
Nueces County MHMR Center	121,881
Permian Basin Center MHMR	119,428
MHMR of Southeast Texas	84,512
Sabine Valley MHMR	777,615
Tarrant County MHMR	300,825
Texas Panhandle MH Authority	46,011
MHMR Services of Texoma	76,308
Tri-County MHMR Services	571,752
Tropical Texas Center for MHMR	657,074
Wichita Falls Community MHMR Center	46,796
Total	$ 5,806,546

Source: TDMHMR, 1989b, Attachment I.

Because the ADMBG is not a large percentage of the Texas mental health budget, its impact is not that great. It does allow the federal government to have some impact and regulatory say in the operations of state programs. It also allows the federal government to mandate programs in areas such as services to youth where the state mental health authorities have been notably slow to take the initiative. This limits somewhat the dramatic inconsistencies between the states in their delivery of community mental health services.

One important result in receiving the ADMBG is that states are being required to put together a comprehensive three-year plan for delivery of mental health services to the community. PL 99-660 compels the states to put together this plan or risk losing their portion of the ADMBG spent for administration. In Texas this amount is approximately $500,000 (England, Interview, March 14, 1989). Having the states take a closer look at what can be done to improve community mental health delivery, beyond what has already been done, is an important step in the right direction. If the trend toward putting further restrictions on the ADMBG continues, the states will be less and less able to mold a mental health delivery system that is distinct for that state.

Since the beginning of ADMBG Texas has not received its fair share of the funds. Governor Clements complained in 1981 that " . . . the 1982 allocation to the states is far from equitable. For example, Texas is the nation's second largest state in square miles, third in population, and is experiencing one of the greatest rates of population increase in the United States, yet it ranks <u>ninth</u> in percentage of the 1982 allocation" (Clements, Letter, November 30, 1981). For the FY 1989 proposed allocations Texas ranks sixth in magnitude of award.

Stewart B. McKinney Homeless Assistance Act Block Grant

The Stewart B. McKinney Homeless Assistance Act is a minor source of revenue for care of the CMI in Texas. In July of 1987 President Reagan signed into law PL 100-77. This act made federal funds available for a wide range of needs, including food, shelter, housing, health care (including mental health and substance abuse), education, and job training. The act also makes adjustments to the Food Stamp Program to ease access for homeless people, and extends the Veterans' Job Training program. Each category listed above is administered by a different federal agency, and each has different requirements in terms of local match and use restrictions (TDMHMR, 1989d, p. 7). Specifics of what the McKinney Act funds were used for are discussed in greater detail in Chapter 11.

During FY 1988 and 1989, TDMHMR was given $2.8 million for the mental health portion of this grant. Eleven sites were chosen to receive McKinney Act funds. Those that automatically received funds were the seven largest cities in Texas and four other sites that were chosen on the basis of a competitive review. The sites receiving McKinney Act funds are shown below in Table 15.3.

The amount for the FY 1990 McKinney Act funding is significantly lower and the amounts projected for FY 1991 are even lower. Many programs that were founded with McKinney Act funds will soon be disbanded for lack of funds (TDMHMR, 1989d). While programs such as the McKinney Act are important, they cannot be depended upon during this era of cutback budgeting.

Table 15.3. Sites Receiving McKinney Act Funds: Amount Allocated and Local Match for FY 1988 and 1989

Site	Federal	Local Match	Total
Houston	$ 759,093	$253,031	$ 1,012,124
Dallas	440,087	146,696	586,783
San Antonio	402,831	134,277	537,108
El Paso	216,552	72,184	288,736
Austin	204,909	68,303	273,212
Fort Worth	188,608	62,869	251,477
Corpus Christi	116,425	38,808	155,233
Sites Chosen by Competitive Review			
Laredo	110,129	36,710	146,839
Amarillo	110,129	36,710	146,839
Lubbock	110,129	36,710	146,839
Sabine Valley	110,129	36,710	146,839
Total	$2,769,021	$923,008	$3,692,029

Source: TDMHMR, 1989d.

MEDICAID EXPANSION: IMPLICATION FOR THE CMI IN TEXAS

Medicaid, authorized under Title XIX of the Social Security Act, is a federally aided, state-administered medical assistance program for low-income people. Generally, those receiving cash assistance under Aid for Families with Dependent Children (AFDC) or Supplemental Security Income (SSI) programs are eligible for Medicaid assistance. Additionally, each state has the option of providing Medicaid benefits to certain persons who cannot afford needed health care but have income above the maximum allowable for public assistance.

Medicaid coverage of mental health services is available through a variety of mandatory and optional services financed under Title XIX of the Social Security Act. Services for the mentally ill must be available to recipients on the same basis as for recipients of all other Title XIX services. Title XIX, however, specifically excludes federal reimbursement for the care of the mentally ill aged 22 to 64 in institutions for mental diseases (IMDs). IMDs are defined as institutions where more than 50 percent of the inpatient population has a primary diagnosis of mental illness. Each state has the option of providing coverage for institutional care of the mentally ill who are under 22 or over 64 years of age. At this time Texas does not use this option.

Each state is allowed to set use and dollar limitations on the amount, duration, and scope of Medicaid coverage. Each state also has the option of covering or not covering certain mental health services. As a result, each state has considerable flexibility in establishing the nature and extent of mental health services available to Medicaid recipients.

The U.S. Department of Health and Human Services (USDHHS) has overall responsibility at the federal level for administering Medicaid. Within USDHHS, the Health Care Financing Administration (HCFA) is responsible for developing program policies, setting standards, and ensuring compliance with federal Medicaid legislation and regulations. Depending on a state's per capita income, the federal share of a state's

Medicaid costs for health services in FY 1987 ranged from 50 to 78.5 percent. In Texas the federal portion of the match in 1989 is 59.04 percent. Because of the declining relative income in Texas, the federal match will be close to 65 percent by 1991 (McCormack, 1989, p. 3).

Medicaid in Texas is available for the treatment of mental diseases, but this coverage is extremely limited. The Texas Medicaid plan currently provides some mental health services through existing programs. Services provided through the psychiatric units of general hospitals are eligible for Medicaid payment. Under the Purchased Health Services Program, Medicaid coverage extends to those eligible with psychiatric diagnosis for acute and general care inpatient hospital services ordinarily furnished by a Title XIX hospital under the direction of a physician when medically necessary. In general terms, these services are bed and board in semiprivate accommodations and ancillaries. Inpatient services extend up to 30 days per spell of illness, and each spell of illness must be separated by 60 consecutive days that the recipient has not been an inpatient in a hospital (TDMHMR, 1985a, p. 2). Since January of 1989 there has been an annual cap per beneficiary of $200,000 per recipient per benefit year (TDHS, 1989b, p. 205).

Outpatient psychiatric services under this program are available but limited. The maximum amount is 62.5 percent of the charges up to $312.50 per year (TDMHMR, 1985a). Long-term institutional care services are reimbursed as long as the institution is not an IMD and the primary diagnosis is not mental illness (USDHHS/HCFA, January 1988, p. 154).

Expansion Options for Texas

There are four ways that Medicaid can be expanded to cover more mental health services. The first is to more fully use portions of the current Medicaid plan (such as the Vendor Drug Program, billing opportunities under physicians' services). The second way is to use the various waivers that have been passed by Congress since 1981. The third way is to amend the state Medicaid plan to cover services that are available, but optional, under current Medicaid regulations. The last way to expand coverage of Medicaid is for Texas to supplement SSI payments. The latter method would enable all those whose income is at or below the SSI eligibility level plus the state supplement level to become eligible for Medicaid. All or a portion of these alternatives could be used to help pay for the cost of mental health services in Texas.

Many services that are funded 100 percent by state and local appropriations could be eligible for Medicaid reimbursement. By using the "soft-match" approach to Federal Fund Participation, these funds would be reallocated from the existing, fully funded state/local program and used as match funds for this new Medicaid option. Most states using this approach have reallocated funds for services that are similar (or identical) to the new or expanded Medicaid services (NASMHPD, January 1987, p. 33).

Many states have been active and successful in increasing the federal contribution to the delivery of mental health services. The National Mental Health Association has identified the Medicaid outpatient and inpatient options contained in each state's plan (Table 15.4). Every state has a different mixture of services available. Of the services listed in Table 15.4, Texas covers only psychologists' services (under the supervision of an M.D.) and drugs; during the spring of 1990 the targeted case management for the mentally ill was added and the rehabilitation option was still pending. Texas provides fewer mental health services through Medicaid than any of the other ten most populous states.

Table 15.4. Medicaid Outpatient Options by State

State	Case Mgmt	Rehab	Out-Patient Therapy	Clinic Partial Hospitalization	Gen Hosp Day Treat	Hospital Psych Hosp: Outpatient	Limits on Psych Services	Psychologist Services	Social Worker Services	EPSDT Expanded Services	MH Personal Care	MH Home Health Care	Ho Co Wa
Alabama										X			
Alaska					X								
Arizona													
Arkansas		X	X	X	X					X			
California			X	X		X	X	X					
Colorado	X		X	X	X	X		X	X			X	X
Connecticut				X	X	X	X	X	X	X		X	
Delaware			X	X						X			
D.C.			X		X	X		X		X	X	X	
Florida		X	X			X				X			
Georgia	X		X	X	X			X				X	
Hawaii			X					X			X		
Idaho		X	X				X	X					
Illinois			X	X	X			X	X				
Indiana			X			X	X	X				X	
Iowa			X					X	X			X	
Kansas			X	X			X	X		X	X	X	
Kentucky			X	X			X	X	X	X	X	X	
Louisiana			X	X	X							X	
Maine		X			X	X		X	X		X	X	
Maryland			X	X	X	X	X			X	X	X	
Massachusetts			X	X	X	X		X	X				
Michigan			X	X	X	X					X		
Minnesota			X		X	X		X			X	X	
Mississippi			X		X		X						
Missouri			X	X		X							
Montana			X	X				X	X				
Nebraska			X	X		X							
Nevada			X	X				X					
New Hampshire	X	X	X	X			X	X					

(Continued Next Page)

Table 15.4 (Continued). Medicaid Outpatient Options by State

tate	Case Mgmt	Rehab	Clinic Out-Patient Therapy	Clinic Partial Hospit-alization	Gen Hosp Day Treat	Psych Hosp: Outpatient	Limits on Psych Services	Psychol-ogist Services	Social Worker Services	EPSDT Expanded Services	MH Per-sonal Care	MH Home Health Care	Home & Com. Waiver
ew Jersey			X		X	X	X	X		X	X		
ew Mexico			X					X					
ew York		X	X	X	X	X		X		X	X	X	
rth Carolina		X	X	X	X	X	X						
rth Dakota			X	X	X	X						X	
io	X	X	X	X	X	X	X	X				X	
lahoma			X	X	X	X	X	X					
egon		X	X		X	X			X				X
nnsylvania			X	X	X	X				X			
ode Island	X	X			X	X					X	X	X
uth Carolina	X	X	X	X		X				X	X		
uth Dakota		X	X	X	X	X		X		X	X	X	
nnessee			X	X		X	X			X			
xas	X	Pending					X	X					
ah			X	X			X	X		X	X	X	
rmont	X	X	X	X		X		X				X	X
rginia			X				X	X	X	X		X	
shington	X		X	X	X	X	X						
st Virginia	X		X	X		X	X				X		
sconsin		X	X			X			X	X	X		
oming			X										

urce: Koyanagi, 1988, pp. 91-92.

Texas covers none of the inpatient mental health options. Table 15.5 shows which states had inpatient mental health services in their state Medicaid plans as of August of 1987. Coverage for IMDs for those 21 and under was identified in 35 states. Coverage of IMDs for those 65 and older was found in 41 states, while psychiatric nursing facilities for the same population was found in 24 states.

The State of Texas has not been aggressive in its pursuit of federal funds for services to the mentally ill. Several options have been added to the legislation dealing with Medicaid. Only recently have the Texas Department of Human Services (TDHS) and TDMHMR acted to receive a greater share of federal dollars. This situation is due to the hesitation of the Texas legislature to spend more state dollars in this time of fiscal stress. All the options to be discussed have the potential of costing the state additional monies. If more options are made available, it is plausible that providers of services in the private sector could take advantage of them and greatly increase the state's Medicaid bill.

This lack of funding is also the legacy of many years of not placing a high priority on the funding of care for the mentally ill. One of the positive results of the R. A. J. and the Lelsz lawsuits is that they are forcing Texas legislators to pay greater attention to the needs of mentally ill Texans.

Areas of Possible Expansion

Medicaid offers several optional services of which Texas has not taken advantage. Inclusion of these options would greatly enhance the delivery of mental health services to the Medicaid-eligible persons in Texas. These optional services include

1.   Services Available under the Current State Medicaid Plan
           Physician Services for the Mentally Ill
           Vendor Drug Program
           Community Care Services
2.   Waiver Program
           Home and Community-Based Waiver (2176)
3.   Amendment of State Medicaid Plan
           Diagnostic, Screening, and Rehabilitative Services
           Case Management Services
           Institutes for Mental Diseases for Patients over Age 65
           Inpatient Psychiatric Facilities for Patients under Age 22

Increased Use of Services Available in the Current State Plan. According to the analysis of Touche Ross and Company (contracted by TDMHMR to aid in analyzing plans for increasing Medicaid monies to Texas), there are three areas of potential billing under the current state plan. The first is to pursue additional billing opportunities for physicians' services. Physician services to recipients with psychiatric diagnoses in the inpatient hospital setting are limited only by medical necessity. Generally, medical necessity requires a primary diagnosis and care requirement other than mental illness. All that would be required would be to obtain individual physician numbers for psychiatrists within the mental health delivery system of Texas. The estimated recovery to the state would be about $500,000 to $1,000,000 under Medicare and Medicaid (Touche Ross and Company, April 1987).

The second option immediately available is the Vendor Drug Program. The Vendor Drug Program provides up to three drugs prescribed by a physician per month for Medicaid recipients living at home or in a nursing home. A broad formulary is covered, including antipsychotic drugs. In FY 1984 there were 285,071 claims for

Table 15.5. Medicaid Mental Health Inpatient Options by State

State	Psychiatric Hospital for Age 21 and Under	Psychiatric Hospital for Age 65 and Older	Nursing Facility Service
Alabama	X		X
Alaska	X	X	
Arizona			
Arkansas	X	X	X
California	X	X	X
Colorado	X	X	X
Connecticut	X	X	
Delaware		X	
District of Columbia	X	X	X
Florida		X	
Georgia			
Hawaii			
Idaho			
Illinois	X	X	X
Indiana	X	X	
Iowa	X	X	
Kansas	X	X	X
Kentucky	X	X	
Louisiana	X	X	X
Maine		X	X
Maryland	X	X	X
Massachusetts	X	X	X
Michigan	X	X	X
Minnesota	X		X
Mississippi		X	
Missouri	X	X	
Montana	X	X	X
Nebraska	X	X	X
Nevada		X	X
New Hampshire		X	X
New Jersey	X	X	X
New Mexico			
New York	X	X	

(Continued Next Page)

Table 15.5 (Continued). Medicaid Mental Health Inpatient Options by State

State	Psychiatric Hospital for Age 21 and Under	Psychiatric Hospital for Age 65 and Older	Nursing Facility Service
North Carolina	X	X	
North Dakota	X	X	
Ohio	X	X	X
Oklahoma	X	X	
Oregon	X	X	
Pennsylvania	X	X	X
Rhode Island		X	
South Carolina	X	X	
South Dakota		X	X
Tennessee	X	X	X
Texas	-	-	-
Utah	X	X	X
Vermont	X	X	
Virginia		X	
Washington	X	X	X
West Virginia	X		
Wisconsin	X	X	
Wyoming			

Source: Koyanagi, 1988, pp. 93-94.

antipsychotic drugs with a total drug cost of $5,047,496. An estimated 58 percent of this cost was for aged recipients, 30 percent was for the disabled, and 12 percent for AFDC and blind recipients (TDMHMR, 1985a). If the CMHMRCs and TDMHMR were to obtain a contract with this program as licensed pharmacies, the providers could recover an estimated $100,000 to $200,000 if contracts for all eligible pharmacies are successfully obtained (Touche Ross and Company, April 1987).

The final opportunity for more efficient use of the current plan is to pursue billing for day activities for Medicaid-eligible clients. Community Care Services are currently provided with a combination of Titles XIX and XX, along with pure state funds for the aged and adult disabled who meet eligibility requirements. Some mentally ill clients "qualify for these services even though they are not primarily designed to serve this population" (TDMHMR, 1989c, p. 4). The state would need to obtain licenses from the Texas Department of Health and Medicaid certification as a provider of these types of services. The potential recovery is estimated to be about $100,000 to $200,00 if all identified Day Care Programs are licensed and certified (TDMHMR, 1989c, p. 4).

Medicaid Waivers for Mental Health Services. Significant changes to the Medicaid program were approved by Congress in 1981 as part of the Omnibus Budget Reconciliation Act. The legislation included a number of amendments designed to give states increased flexibility in implementing their Medicaid plans. Among other things, the measure authorized the Secretary of USDHHS to grant waivers for the states to provide, under certain conditions, a broad range of home and community services to persons who would otherwise require care in an institutional facility. These were known as 2176 waivers or home and community-based service waivers. USDHHS was also authorized to grant 2175 waivers which allowed states to restrict the practitioner or providers from whom a Medicaid recipient can receive services.

The idea behind 2176 waivers was to promote community-based services in place of nursing home care in targeted populations. This was to be done without increasing overall Medicaid expenditures. As Toff and Scallett point out in their study, "although states were permitted to cover some home and community-based services before the new waiver was enacted the measure expanded both the scope of services States could provide and their freedom to target services to specific populations who would otherwise require institutional care" (Toff and Scallett, April 1986, p. 1).

After several years of interim regulations, HCFA issued its final regulations in 1985. The various waivers offered under this act proved to be increasingly restrictive, difficult to administer, and ineffective. Most states have found the final regulations to be so restrictive the waivers were not cost-effective. The Touche Ross and Company analysis of the potential of using waivers in Texas found that "HCFA rulings and the reported experiences of other states suggest that the waiver application process could be a lengthy one with no guarantees for success. Currently only three states have been approved for home and community based waivers for the mentally ill population" (Touche Ross and Company, April 1987, p. 8). Only four states were ever granted 2176 waivers for the CMI population: Colorado, Oregon, Rhode Island, and Vermont. By the end of 1989 only Vermont retained this waiver for the CMI (Fox, March 1989, p. 44).

Because the waivers are not supposed to increase the aggregate Medicaid expenditures (i.e., be revenue neutral), waivers may not be the most appropriate vehicle for expanding coverage to the mentally ill population in Texas. Because this is a population that is not now receiving extensive Medicaid benefits for mental health services, they would be new beneficiaries to the system. Waivers are designed to help get people out of nursing homes and hospitals and back into the community. Since Texas has not used the options for coverage in IMDs, this waiver would not meet the revenue neutrality requirement. Because Texas does not use Medicaid funds to pay for stays in state hospitals, it cannot show that it would be cheaper for Medicaid to help pay for community-based care through this option.

Amendments to the State Medicaid Plan. There are several alternatives to amending the state Medicaid plan. One way to deliver services to the CMI that has been used by 50 of the 56 jurisdictions covered by Medicaid is the "Clinic Option." (Note "Selected Optional Services" on Table 15.5 for the numbers and types of programs used by other states.) Texas does not participate in this option. This option permits states to set up a "range of ambulatory care such as outpatient and partial hospital treatment services. Currently, there are major variations among states as to the service elements that can be provided" (Toff and Scallett, 1986, p. 16).

The main complaint with this option is that services are limited to those that can be provided within the confines of a clinic. This option cannot cover needed services such as home visits and emergency outreach, which can be used to "reduce the crisis usage of acute inpatient services" (Toff and Scallett, 1986, p. 16). While the clinic option would improve services to the mentally ill, it limits the coverable forms of treatment that are needed for the CMI to cope with life in the community.

Proposals to Amend the Texas State Medicaid Plan

There have been four proposals to amend the Texas State Medicaid Plan to cover more services for the mentally ill. The first is to adopt the "Rehabilitation Option" currently available under Medicaid regulations. The second option is targeted case management, and the third and fourth are the coverage of those over 64 and under 22 in institutes for mental diseases.

Rehabilitation Option. TDMHMR has requested an amendment to the Texas State Medicaid Plan to cover Diagnostic, Screening, and Rehabilitation Services, informally known as the rehabilitation option. Services currently provided in the TDMHMR system that would be covered under this option include "client evaluations and assessments, psychotherapy, medication management, and partial hospitalization . . . Coverage of these services under Medicaid could bring federal revenues to CMHMRCs of $25 to $35 million" (TDMHMR, 1987a, p. 18). An increase of this magnitude would be a 25 percent jump in the funding services in Texas with no corresponding rise in state appropriations.

The services that Texas is requesting to be covered under this option for the mentally ill and mentally retarded population are as follows:

1. Client Treatment Planning Services: Services provided by or under the supervision of a qualified professional related to the development, coordination, review, documentation, and monitoring of individual treatment plans and client responses to treatment plan implementation. All services delineated in the individual treatment plan must be approved by signature of the treating physician.

2. Diagnostic and Functional Assessment/Evaluation Services: Assessments/evaluations performed by qualified professionals for the purpose of establishing a medical diagnosis, psychological profile, or assessment of current functioning compared to functioning required to achieve a specific goal. Assessments and evaluations serve as the basis for identifying service needs and development of written treatment plans. This service includes psychiatric evaluations of mental status

by a psychiatrist or other physician functioning as a psychiatrist; intake evaluations; commitment evaluation and testimony; social evaluations; psychological interviews with or without testing; special child and family evaluations; evaluation of skills and support needed to achieve a specific goal; and evaluations of clients who cannot be tested at that time. All reports resulting from the assessment/evaluation are considered part of the service and their preparation is included in the billing rate.

3. Emergency/Crisis Services: Services provided by qualified professionals to reduce or resolve acute emotional dysfunction/crisis situations and to assure appropriate follow-up treatment and services.

4. Medication Services: Face-to-face contact to assess or monitor a person's status in relation to treatment with medication, or to administer prescribed medications.

5. Treatment/Training Services: Specific treatment/training services provided by, or under the supervision of, a qualified professional. Services are intended to assist clients to improve skills; maintain/improve health status; gain understanding and insight; reduce stress; improve decision making; alter maladaptive behaviors; and improve life adjustment. Specific methodology and anticipated outcomes are defined in the client's individual treatment plan.

6. Treatment/Training Programs: Structured programs provided by qualified professionals or other direct service staff working under the supervision of qualified professionals. Programs utilize a range of ongoing, scheduled therapeutic modalities to provide support; assist clients to develop adaptive coping skills; acquire insight, cognitive and behavioral change; and improve daily living skills.

7. Support/Ancillary Services: Services of a supportive nature necessary to client's participation in a treatment/training program. (TDMHMR, 1989e)

As of October of 1990 negotiations between TDMHMR and HCFA are ongoing to have this option put into place for mental health services. It is hoped that the Rehabilitation Option will be in place sometime during FY 1991.

Targeted Case Management Services. The Consolidated Omnibus Budget Reconciliation Act of 1985 and Omnibus Budget Reconciliation Act of 1986 added optional targeted case management services to the list of services that could be eligible for Medicaid payments. Texas was very active during 1989 and 1990 in getting targeted case management services approved for Medicaid payment. As of June of 1989 the state Medicaid plan amendment for targeted case management of the mentally retarded had been approved by HCFA (TDMHMR, 1989e), and the plan for mentally ill patients was approved in March of 1990 (Dittmar, Interview, May 14, 1990).

Case management services are provided to Medicaid-eligible CMI clients who are at risk of long-term institutionalization. Case management attempts to help those individuals who, without community-based support services, would require long-term hospitalization.

The case management services option has the potential of bringing several million federal dollars into Texas for the care of the CMI. A more detailed discussion of this option is found in Chapter 7.

<u>Institutes for Mental Disease for Those over 64 and under 22</u>. Options to cover the costs of adolescent and aged mentally ill patients in IMDs have been available since the late sixties. The Texas Medicaid program at one time covered inpatient hospital care for eligible individuals age 65 or older in state IMDs beginning September 1, 1967. This coverage was eliminated August 31, 1975, because of the inability to limit coverage to the public sector (TDMHMR, 1985a, p. 1).

The proposals to expand coverage for the population under 22 and over 64 years of age in IMDs have been considered recently by TDMHMR personnel. Providing coverage for persons age 65 and over receiving inpatient services from a state hospital or eligible private psychiatric facilities would include "room and board, medical care, psychotherapy, medication, lab, x-ray, and other habilitative hospital services. Controls would need to be developed that would limit growth of new inpatient hospitals and new beds in existing hospitals and to control utilization of services per patient" (TDMHMR, 1987a, p. 19).

The following is an estimate of the amount of extra monies that could be received from Medicaid from this expansion. Currently 18 percent of all patients treated in the state hospital inpatient units are age 65 or older. In 1987, TDMHMR spent a total of almost $185 million for state hospitals. Addition of this option could mean an additional $33.3 million in funds to the state. Services provided that would be eligible for federal matching funds would include room and board, medical care, evaluation/assessments, and psychotherapy (TDMHMR, 1987a, p. 20).

Coverage of those 21 years of age and younger in IMDs would have a similar impact on revenues to TDMHMR. Approximately 10 percent of state hospital patients are under age 22. Under this Medicaid option, virtually all of the residential and treatment and rehabilitation services at the state hospital would be eligible for reimbursement. In addition, some expenses related to facility administration and support services would also be eligible for federal matching funds (TDMHMR, 1987a, p. 21).

State Medicaid Plan Amendment Process

If the state wishes to include these options in its Medicaid plan, a state Medicaid plan amendment must be submitted to the HCFA for approval. Only after the plan is approved by HCFA can this optional service can be covered by Medicaid. For example, a state plan amendment to cover rehabilitation services must include information on the following topics:

1.   <u>Statewide availability.</u> A state must indicate whether Rehabilitation services will be made available to all members of the target group, statewide, or alternatively, if such services will be offered on less that a statewide basis. If the latter option is selected, the state must invoke Section 1915(g)(1) of the Act and specify the geographic areas or political jurisdictions in which such services will be available.

2. Freedom of choice. States must give assurances that Rehabilitation services will be provided in accordance with the requirements of section 1902(a)(23) of the Act, which specifies that no restrictions may be placed on the recipient's free choice of providers. In order to meet this statutory requirement, the state must give HCFA assurance that: (a) no Medicaid recipient will be forced to receive Rehabilitation services; (b) each recipient will be free to receive Rehabilitation services from any qualified provider (e.g. a recipient may not be limited to services provided by a given county agency or clinic, even if he or she receives all other services through the same provider); (c) any individual or entity meeting state standards for the provision of Rehabilitation services will be given the opportunity to qualify as a Medicaid provider of such services; and (d) Rehabilitation services will not be used to restrict any individual's access to other state plan services.

3. Provider qualifications. A state must specify the minimum standard it will use to govern the provision of Rehabilitation services. Provider qualifications must be " . . . reasonably related to the Rehabilitation function that a provider would be expected to perform." Providers may not be " . . . arbitrarily limited . . . to state or other public agencies"; instead, any person or entity that meets the qualification standards must be permitted to act as a provider of Rehabilitation services. In addition, a " . . . client may not be prohibited from receiving Rehabilitation services from a qualified provider in a locality other than that in which he or she resides."

4. Nonduplication of payments. "Payments for Rehabilitation services under Section 1915(g) may not duplicate payments made to public agencies or private entities under other program authorities for the same purpose." In addition, "separate payment cannot be made for Rehabilitation-type services which are an integral and inseparable part of another Medicaid covered service." A state, therefore, must "differentiate Rehabilitation services . . . from other Medicaid services and from Rehabilitation activities which are necessary for the proper and efficient administration of the State plan.

5. Administrative activities. Activities associated with administering the State Medicaid plan may not be treated as Rehabilitation costs, including costs related to: (a) determination/redetermination of Medicaid eligibility; (b) Medicaid intake services; (c) Medicaid preadmission screening; (d) prior authorization for Medicaid services; (e) Medicaid utilization review; (f) EPSDT administration; and (g) activities in connection with "lock-in" provisions under Section 1915(a) of the Act.

6. Payment methodology. States must specify the methodology it will use to establish Rehabilitation services payment rates.

7. Documentation of claims. States must be prepared to fully document all claims for Rehabilitation reimbursement at the FMAP rate. Unless the state pays for such services under a capitation or prepaid health plan arrangement, it must be able to document: (a) the date of services; (b) the name of the recipient; (c) the name of the provider agency and person providing the services; (d) the nature, extent or units of services provided; (e) the place of service.

States may document Rehabilitation claims at the administrative rate through the use of time studies, random motion studies, cost allocation plans, etc., when such services are performed as part of administration of the state plan; but this type of documentation will not be considered sufficient support of Rehabilitation claims under Section 1919(g) or 1905(a)(19) of the Act. (NASMHPD, January 1987)

Control of Private-Sector Participation

The studies that Touche Ross and Company did for TDMHMR do not recommend these options because of the potential for burgeoning state expenditures. TDMHMR would have to be extremely restrictive in who could be a provider of this service. Federal regulations prevent explicit exclusion of the private sector. Regulations do, however, allow requirements of the private sector to be equal to those of the public sector. The private sector may object to many standards as being exclusionary, but HCFA has upheld, in some cases, the validity of such standards recently (Touche Ross and Company, 1988). Table 15.6 gives examples of controls that other states have used in limiting private use in optional Medicaid programs.

Table 15.6 Examples of Controls on the Optional Medicaid Programs in Other States

Control	State
Provider Eligibility/Certification	
Providers must contract with state and receive state funds or subcontract with community mental health board.	Washington, Ohio, Pennsylvania, Colorado Michigan
Providers required to submit long-range/short-range goals/ growth expectation and expected Medicaid utilization.	Pennsylvania, Ohio
Employee standards set by state mental health agency.	Ohio, California
Private-sector providers required to submit same reports/docu- mentation as public-sector providers.	Ohio
Local funding required as part of state match.	Colorado, Ohio, Pennsylvania
Community mental health clinics must be JCAH certified.	Ohio

(Continued Next Page)

Table 15.6 (Continued). Examples of Controls on the Optional Medicaid Programs in Other States

Control	State
Allowable Setting	
Rehabilitation services are only authorized in community mental health centers and day centers.	Alabama, Florida
Services are limited to state-approved outpatient community mental health clinics that receive grants.	Nevada, Ohio, Colorado
Requirements imposed on eligible providers to be open a minimum number of hours per week.	Massachusetts
Physical therapy services limited to certain sites.	Ohio
Eligible providers must provide full continuum of mental health services.	Michigan, Colorado
Populations	
Define target populations and provide block funding for their care only.	Colorado
Provider cannot refuse service on the basis of ability to pay.	Colorado
Reimbursement	
Maximum allowable fees are imposed for psychological assessments and evaluations.	Massachusetts
Maximum allowable rates are imposed for adult care day services.	Massachusetts

Source: Touche Ross and Company, 1988.

Texas is pursuing a strategy whereby it can expand services to its mentally disabled citizens without additional expenditure of state funds. Because of the "Freedom of Choice" clauses in Title XIX, a state cannot limit Medicaid providers to those in the public sector. If a private provider meets the specifications set forth by the state to be a provider of a Medicaid-payable service, the state must match the federal payment for those services (Russell, Interview, May 18, 1989).

In the case of IMDs for those under 22 and over 65 the potential for private use is very clear. Private mental health care is currently a major growth field. Between 1980 and 1985 the number of available beds has virtually doubled (from 23 hospitals with 2,247 beds in March 1980, to 47 providers with 4,464 beds in March of 1985). In 1989 there were over 3,700 private adult psychiatric beds in Texas. Approximately 30 percent of these beds were vacant at any given time (Russell, Interview, May 18, 1989). Private bed growth may accelerate if additional reimbursement is available through Medicaid and if private providers find the level of reimbursement attractive. The state has limited options to control the growth of the private sector (TDMHMR, 1985a).

Texas is attempting to design a controlled approach using some of these Medicaid options. By expanding Medicaid to cover services, at present funded completely by state and local funds, the state could use these funds as matching funds, increasing Medicaid coverage without impacting state expenditures.

If the restrictions on who can be a provider are strict enough, then this will not be a problem. The state Medicaid plan amendments can define a provider of services as having to fulfill the same requirements as any CMHMRC or state hospital. The requirements of having the Medicaid agency do quarterly or monthly audits, not denying services regardless of ability to pay, and limiting the reimbursement levels below what would be profitable for a private provider are some of the strategies that could be used to limit the number of nonpublic providers of Medicaid services. While this can be done, HCFA has been increasingly reluctant to approve plans that are so transparent in their intent to bar private providers. However, other states have been successful in limiting private providers and there is no reason to believe that Texas could not do the same. Though this might cause some outcry from the private providers and their legislators, the state could not limit all private providers. It appears that it can keep private participation to a level that would not significantly impact state appropriations. If effective controls can be made to limit private-sector participation in these two options, then they could have a positive effect on delivery of services in the public IMDs in Texas. The extra $18 million these options could bring in would be very helpful in improving staffing ratios and conditions in IMDs. This would aid the state in further complying with the requirements of the R. A. J. lawsuit.

Potential Problems if Amendments Are Approved

Certain parts of the rehabilitation option have already been approved by TDHS and sent for HCFA for approval. Targeted case management for the mentally ill for Texas was approved by HCFA in April of 1990. The state has been allowed to bill back to July of 1989 when the application was first submitted (Dittmar, Interview, May 14, 1990). If the other portions of this option are approved, the providers (CMHMRCs, TDMHMR) of these services could be receiving nearly $63 million in additional federal funds (TDMHMR, 1987a). This would represent a rise in the proportion of Medicaid revenues coming into the state of Texas for mental health services from 1.06 percent of the state mental health budget to approximately 8.6 percent.

This would a positive shot in the arm for mental health care delivery in Texas. However, in these times of fiscal stress for Texas or at any other time, there is the possibility that the legislature could use the increase in federal funds as an excuse to cut the budget for mental health services. This was mentioned as a possibility by Legislative Budget Board personnel. If ways can be found to safeguard funds for services, it would be a great improvement for the traditionally underfunded mental health delivery system in this state.

Other problems may come from the federal level. If the rehabilitation option is taken up by too many states and the cost of this option proves too high, Congress may instruct USDHHS to restrict the use of this option. If this program is overutilized by the states, it could face severe cutbacks in scope and promise. Moreover, the increased emphasis on deficit reduction that may be an important part of the 101st and 102nd Congress does not bode well for continued reliance on federal funds for these services.

CONCLUSIONS

Those services provided that can be billed for under the current state Medicaid plan need to be implemented as soon as possible. While the net return on these services is not overwhelming, the addition of $1.4 million per year would help. TDMHMR is looking into the Vendor Drug Program.

The 2176 waiver program is too restrictive and should not be pursued. Although the waiver does allow for a wide variety of services, it is really not designed for the mentally ill. The revenue neutrality of these waivers has also caused problems for the states using them when it came time to renew them. Furthermore, it is unlikely that HCFA will approve additional 2176 mental health waivers.

By requiring that those providers who wish to participate in the rehabilitation option fulfill the same requirements as the CMHMRCs, the state could adequately discourage private providers from becoming participants in the program. If providers are required to render all of the core and noncore services, to furnish periodic performance and financial audits, and to perform most other duties of a CMHMRC, then this option could be effective in bringing more funds to the CMHMRCs and TDMHMR without increasing expenditures.

Texas needs to be more aggressive in its pursuit of federal dollars for care of the mentally ill. If there is to be an effective move toward increased community-based care for the CMI, there has to be greater involvement of federal funds. Although Texas cannot rely on the federal government for permanent funding of these services, it is ridiculous that so many other states are able to draw down so much more federal money for this population while Texas remains idle.

All of the federal programs discussed in this chapter are very important for financing care for the CMI. The federal government needs to develop systems for financing care of the mentally ill which are actually designed for aiding the mentally ill. The current federal system for dealing with the mentally ill are extrapolations of those systems put together for physical illness. Medicaid and Medicare are systems that were not designed for treatment of mental illness; SSI and SSDI were not designed to support the mentally ill. The federal system, like many state systems, has been put together to achieve short-term goals to deal with the mentally ill.

For those programs administered by USDHHS, one important step would be to have a special category for the chronically mentally ill. A separate CMI classification would insure SSI and Medicaid payments for all those CMI meeting income and resource requirements. The specific prohibition in Title XIX of the Social Security Act against Medicaid payments for treatment in IMDs for those between 21 and 65 has a negative impact on the state's attempt the treat the mentally ill. The other inadequacy of the federal effort is the low portion of the ADMBG that makes up the states' mental health budgets. While every little bit helps, a little bit more aid in this area would be of great use to Texas.

References

Clements, William. 1981. Letter to Secretary of the United States Department of Health and Human Services, November 30.

Congressional Quarterly 1981 Almanac. 1982. "25 Percent Cut in Health Spending." (January 31.)

Dittmar, Nancy. 1990. Director, Special Projects, Texas Department of Mental Health and Mental Retardation, Austin, Texas. Telephone interview with Nicholas Hoover, May 14.

England, G. F. 1989, Chief, Resource Development, Texas Department of Mental Health and Mental Retardation, Austin, Texas. Interview by Nicholas Hoover, March 14.

_____. 1989. Chief, Resource Development, Texas Department of Mental Health and Mental Retardation, Austin, Texas. Interview by Nicholas Hoover, April 6.

_____. 1989. Chief, Resource Development, Texas Department of Mental Health and Mental Retardation, Austin, Texas. Interview by Nicholas Hoover, May 15.

Fox, Harriette B. March 1989. An Addendum to: An Explanation of Medicaid and Its Role in Financing Treatment for Severely Emotionally Disturbed Children and Adolescents -- A Technical Report. Washington, D.C.: Georgetown University Child Development Center, CASSP Technical Assistance Center. Fox Health Policy Consultants.

Koyanagi, Chris. 1988. Operation Help: A Mental Health Advocate's Guide to Medicaid. Alexandria, Virginia: National Mental Health Association.

McCormack, Maureen P. 1989. "Comparison of Health Care Programs for the Indigent in Texas and California." Professional Report. Lyndon B. Johnson School of Public Affairs, University of Texas at Austin.

National Association of State Mental Health Program Directors (NASMHPD). January 1987. "Utilization of Medicaid Reimbursement for Community-Based Mental Health Services: Proceedings from a State-of-the-Art Symposium Held September 30 and October 1, 1986 in Crystal City, VA." Arlington, Virginia.

Peterson, George E. 1986. The Reagan Block Grants: What Have We Learned. Washington, D.C.: The Urban Institute Press.

Russell, Rush. 1989. Revenue Officer, Texas Department of Mental Health and Mental Retardation, Austin, Texas. Interview by Nicholas Hoover, May 18.

Texas Department of Mental Health and Mental Retardation (TDMHMR). 1983. "Texas Alcohol Drug Abuse and Mental Health Services Annual Report to USDHHS." Austin, Texas. (April 29.)

_____. 1984. "Texas Alcohol Drug Abuse and Mental Health Services Annual Report to USDHHS." Austin, Texas. (March 22.)

_____. 1985a. "Extending Medicaid to Cover Mental Health Services: A Report to the Lieutenant Governor." Austin, Texas. (March 15.)

314

_____. 1985b. "Texas Alcohol Drug Abuse and Mental Health Services Annual Report to USDHHS." Austin, Texas. (April 1.)

_____. 1985c. "Texas Alcohol Drug Abuse and Mental Health Services Annual Report to USDHHS." Austin, Texas. (December 30.)

_____. 1986. "Texas Alcohol Drug Abuse and Mental Health Services Annual Report to USDHHS." Austin, Texas. (December 23.)

_____. 1987a. "Federal Funding Issues." Austin, Texas.

_____. 1987b. "Texas Alcohol Drug Abuse and Mental Health Services Annual Report to USDHHS." Austin, Texas. (December 29.)

_____. 1989a. "Future Directions for Texas Comprehensive Community-Based Mental Health Services." Austin, Texas: Working Draft. (January 9.)

_____. 1989b. "Texas Alcohol Drug Abuse and Mental Health Services Annual Report to USDHHS." Austin, Texas. (March 29.)

_____. 1989c. "Service Definitions-Medicaid Rehabilitation Option-Draft May 10, 1989." Austin, Texas. (May 10.)

_____. 1989d. "Assurances and Intended Use of Block Grant Funds for Community Mental Health Services for the Homeless Available under the Stewart B. McKinney Homeless Assistance Act." Austin, Texas. (May 22.)

_____. 1989e. "Qualification of Providers-Draft May 18, 1989." Austin, Texas. (May 18.)

Toff, Gail E., and Leslie J. Scallett. April 1986. "RIP: Report on Issues of Policy: The Medicaid Waiver and Its Use in Financing Mental Health and Related Services in the Community." Washington, D.C.: National Institute for Mental Health, USDHHS, Division of Education and Service Systems Liaison and Intergovernmental Affairs and Public Liaison Branch of Policy Analysis and Coordination.

Touche Ross and Company. April 1987. "Final Report on Review of Opportunities for Prospective Medicaid Funding for Mental Health and Mental Retardation Services in Texas." Austin, Texas: Texas Department of Mental Health and Mental Retardation.

Touche Ross and Company. 1988. "Federal Participation in Community Support and Case Management Services." National Association of State Mental Health Commissioners Community Support Program Directors. Austin, Texas. (October 26.)

U.S. Department of Health and Human Services, Health Care Financing Administration (USDHHS/HCFA). January 1988. State Medicaid Manual - Part 4 - Services. HCFA Publication #45-4. Washington, D.C.: U.S. Government Printing Office.

U.S. Congress, Senate. 1988. Comprehensive Alcohol Abuse, Drug Abuse and Mental Health Amendments of 1988. 100th Congress, 2nd Session. S. 1943.

Chapter 16. The Role of Voluntary Organizations in Financing Care for the Chronically Mentally Ill[*]

Voluntary organizations make significant contributions in aiding the mentally ill in Texas, through a wide variety of activities ranging from the provision of direct services to funding research on mental illness. The role of volunteerism in Texas extends much beyond the actual funds allocated for direct services. Other aspects of volunteer contributions include self-help, advocacy, and the benefits received through donations of volunteer time.

It should be noted at the outset that several problems exist in attempting to quantify the actual dollar figures coming from voluntary organizations for the CMI. This problem arises particularly from the lack of specific categories for the CMI in allocations reports and from the overlap of CMI in other program areas like homelessness. The importance of voluntary organizations lies not just in the actual dollars given for services and research.

A study on voluntary agencies by Ralph M. Kramer illustrates this point that a voluntary organization provides more that just services. Kramer identifies four roles of voluntary agencies:

1. as a <u>vanguard</u>, their purpose is to innovate, pioneer, experiment, and demonstrate programs, some of which may eventually be taken over by government;

2. as <u>improvers</u> or <u>advocates</u>, voluntary agencies are expected to serve as critics, watchdogs, or gadflies, pressuring government to extend, improve, or establish needed services;

3. as <u>value guardians</u> of voluntaristic, particularistic, and sectarian values, voluntary agencies are expected to promote citizen participation, develop leadership, and protect the special interests of social, religious, cultural, or other minority groups; and

4. as <u>services providers</u>, voluntary agencies deliver those services they have selected, some of which may be a public responsibility that government is unable or unwilling to assume directly or fully. (Kramer, 1987, p. 242)

While many of the functions provided by voluntary agencies are not quantifiable, they are extremely important to the CMI. This chapter will attempt to identify some of the major contributors in this area. It will also identify gaps and problems in data collection that contribute to the lack of accurate aggregate data on the contributions of these voluntary organizations.

DIRECT VOLUNTEERISM

Specifically and directly related to the CMI in Texas is the number of volunteer hours provided at the Texas state hospitals. Table 16.1 lists numbers of volunteers, volunteer hours during 1987 through 1988, and dollar figures associated with those hours

---

[*]This chapter was written by Kathleen A. Fahey, Minh Ly Griffin, and Rudolfo R. Vega.

at state hospitals in Texas at the rate of $10.06 per hour.[1] This volunteer time represents a significant contribution (in terms of time and saving of state money) to the CMI in Texas.

**Table 16.1. Volunteer Hours and Dollars Contributed
to Texas State Hospitals in 1987 and 1988**

Hospital	Volunteers (per month)	Volunteer Hours (per year)	Value of Vol. Time (Vol. Hrs x 10.06)*
Austin	275	25,062	$ 252,123
Big Spring	401	20,769	$ 208,936
Kerrville	727	129,000	$ 1,297,740
Rusk	493	25,578	$ 257,314
San Antonio	673	47,980	$ 482,678
Terrell	841	78,529	$ 90,001
Wichita Falls	787	60,379	$ 607,412

Source: Austin State Hospital, December 1988.

Note: *The average hourly wage for nonagricultural workers in 1987 as published by the Economic Report of the President, increased by 12 percent to estimate fringe benefits.

Direct volunteerism to the state hospitals is not the only area that has value for the CMI. There are foundations, organizations such as the Mental Health Association (MHA) and the Texas Alliance for the Mentally Ill (TEXAMI), churches, groups associated with local CMHMRCs, and other agencies that provide direct and indirect services to the CMI in Texas. Most voluntary agencies have small budgets; however, the small funding numbers underrepresent the true value of these voluntary efforts.

MAJOR VOLUNTARY ORGANIZATIONS

This section discusses a targeted sample of the funding and activities of selected major voluntary agencies providing support to the CMI in Texas. The 1988 Foundation Grants Index lists awards to entities and foundations concerned with mental health which have some impact on the lives of the CMI. Table 16.2 identifies several major awards noted in the index.

---

[1]This figure is the hourly average wage plus benefits per American worker during 1987.

Table 16.2. Selected Foundation Grants to Texas Mental Health Agencies, 1988

Foundation	Year	Amount	Recipient
Brown Foundation	1986	$19,300	Mental Health Assoc., Dallas
Brown Foundation	1986	$20,000	TX Inst. of Family Psychiatry
Houston Endowment	1986	$25,000	Fayette Co. MHMR Authority
R. J. and H. C. Kleberg Foundation	1987	$55,000	Rio Grande Good Samaritan Counseling Center
Kleberg	1987	$62,000	Turtle Creek Manor

Source: Kovacs, 1988.

The program at Turtle Creek Manor, funded in part by a grant from the Kleberg Foundation, offers a good example of how donations like those listed in the table contribute to the CMI. Turtle Creek Manor is an aftercare residential facility which offers a rehabilitation program for individuals leaving long-term care facilities. This transitional program helps individuals to gain coping and living skills and to make a successful shift out of the hospital and into the community (Turtle Creek Manor, Inc., 1988). The significance of the money contributed to programs such as Turtle Creek Manor is that not only are individuals receiving supervised care in the community, they are also prevented from suffering further traumas and relapses. This is critical as a funding issue because these programs eventually save state money by helping to keep individuals out of primary care hospitals.

National Foundations: The Robert Wood Johnson Foundation

Major national foundations also contribute to programs for the CMI by being able to offer larger sums of money to agencies than smaller, regional foundations can. The Robert Wood Johnson Foundation is one large contributor to the CMI throughout the country as well as in Texas. The foundation's Program for Chronic Mental Illness is designed "to strengthen the potential of [the CMI] to live independently" by establishing a comprehensive care and rehabilitation system and enhancing housing options at the community level by working with the U.S. Department of Housing and Urban Development to provide Section 8 housing and the Social Security Administration in obtaining eligibility for entitlement programs. The foundation is providing approximately $28 million in grants and low-interest loans to eight of the nation's 60 largest urban centers. Grants will support community-wide projects aimed at consolidating and expanding services for the CMI. These community-wide systems of care will offer a broad range of health, mental health, social services, and housing options to help the CMI function more effectively in their everyday lives and avoid inappropriate institutionalization (RWJF, 1988, p. 3).

Two major grants have been awarded to Texas agencies. The Austin-Travis County Mental Health and Mental Retardation Center (ATCMHMRC) received $2.5 million over a five-year period beginning in 1987, as well as a $1 million low-interest loan through the foundation's program for the CMI. And Tropical Texas CMHMRC in Edinburg received $600,000 for a community-based program to address inappropriate

319

institutionalization from the foundation's Mental Health Services Development Program (RWJF, 1988). The total expenditures for the grant for ATCMHMRC during the five-year period are shown in Table 16.3.

Table 16.3. Robert Wood Johnson Foundation Funding for ATCMHMRC

Fiscal Year	Amount
1987	$ 195,331
1988	$ 599,995
1989	$ 546,494
1990	$ 554,591
1991	$ 603,589

Source: Salvation Army, 1987.

The impact of the Robert Wood Johnson Foundation grant on the ATCMHMRC has been tremendous. This large grant gave a great deal of money to the center to implement community-based programs for its clients. In particular, the center established the following:

1. Client-Operated Drop-In Center, which serves as a gathering place, safe "hangout," and program center run by and for the clients.

2. Cornerstone, a partial hospitalization program to provide structure and support services for individuals on the verge of needing psychiatric hospitalization (to keep them from needing the hospitalization).

3. Mobile Outreach Team located at the Austin Salvation Army, which identifies and attempts to find services for the mentally ill homeless.

4. Options, a housing program (in its beginning stages), whereby the center plans to use the low-interest loan to purchase small apartment complexes and make desperately needed housing available to the mentally ill.

5. Peer Companion Program, whereby higher functioning mentally ill clients are trained and paid and/or provided housing to help lower functioning clients develop coping and living skills in the community. (Ferris, Interview, December 19, 1988)

The significance of the Robert Wood Johnson Foundation grant is much more than the large amount of money contributed in this one grant. It has led to more contributions from other foundations. One example is the Hogg Foundation for Mental Health, which provided a matching grant as well as a monitoring system for the programs that its grant money helped implement.

The Robert Wood Johnson Foundation grant and other grants help to enhance quality services by encouraging alternative and innovative programs. The programs discussed above facilitate and go beyond the requirements of the seven core services that ATCMHMRC must provide to clients based on state law and TDMHMR regulations. The grants help provide additional and essential care that enhance the skills of the clients and keep them from reentering the state hospitals while saving the state money in the process. These contributions are difficult to quantify, but they certainly exceed the initial $2.5 million figure of the Robert Wood Johnson Foundation.

Hogg Foundation for Mental Health

Smaller, regional foundations contribute less in actual dollar figures, but they do contribute significantly to the CMI. The Hogg Foundation for Mental Health is one example of such an organization. The Hogg Foundation offers grants in a wide range of mental health issues in order to provide a broad mental health program for bringing greater awareness of mental health issues to the people of Texas. The Hogg and other foundations contribute beyond actual grant monies through program innovations for the CMI (Hogg Foundation for Mental Health, 1987). Table 16.4 gives a list of 1986-1987 grants to agencies providing services to the CMI in Texas.

Table 16.4. Hogg Foundation Grants to CMI-Related Projects, 1986 and 1987

Recipient	Grant Award
Austin-Travis County MHMRC	$ 64,506
Central Counties Center for MH and MR Services	$ 9,980
The Gathering Place	$ 22,000
Mental Health Association, Austin Area	$ 9,825
Mental Health Association, Dallas County	$ 3,125
Mental Health Association, Houston/Harris Co.	$ 40,330
Mental Health Association in Texas	$ 7,804
Mental Health Association in Texas	$ 29,851
TDMHMR	$ 36,500
U.T. Health Science Center, Dept of Psychiatry	$ 30,234
U.T. Medical Branch, Dept. of Psychiatry	$ 22,800

Source: Hogg Foundation for Mental Health, 1987.

The United Way

United Way agencies are a major source of funding for numerous programs throughout Texas, including programs for the seriously mentally ill. According to its mission statement, the United Way of Texas "seeks to provide the means by which a cross section of citizens, governmental and voluntary human service agencies and organizations join in a statewide effort to improve the efficiency and effectiveness of human service programs and work toward the development of comprehensive, coordinated community human service delivery systems within the State" (United Way of Texas, 1988a, p. 1). In Texas, 183 local United Way agencies raise and allocate funds according to the priorities established in each community. Based on these community priorities, the local United Way agencies provide funding to various service areas for the community. The United Way of Texas documents sources of funding and allocations of local United Way funds to specific agencies and to general program areas. The sources of giving for the United Way of Texas are listed in Table 16.5.

Table 16.5. United Way of Texas Sources of Giving

Funding Source	FY 86	FY 87
Corporate/Corporate Foundations	22.15%	23.80%
Employees-Corporate/Business	48.98%	48.80%
Employees-Government/Nonprofit	15.98%	16.20%
Small Business Gifts	3.26%	1.70%
Professionals	1.92%	2.00%
Non-Corporate Foundations	1.26%	1.20%
All Other	6.45%	6.20%

Source: United Way of Texas, 1988b.

The funding data provided by the United Way of Texas indicate several key problems in documenting the funding to CMI services by voluntary organizations. In particular, the lack of specific CMI funding categories (i.e., general categories like "mental health" which cover many services, some CMI-related and some not) and lack of data reported make it difficult to assess true dollar figures to funding. However, based on the information available, areas to which the United Way agencies contribute that impact the CMI are the program areas of mental health and information and referral, as well as two specific agencies, the Mental Health Association and the Salvation Army. Table 16.6 shows the trend in funding to these areas by the local United Way agencies in Texas.

Table 16.6. United Way Funding Areas to CMI in Texas: Five-Year Trend

Area	FY 84	FY 85*	FY 86	FY 87	FY 88
Mental Health	$1,379,222	1,173,127	2,336,107	2,404,985	2,344,550
Information & Referral Hotline	N/A	496,189	559,388	314,941	794,713
Mental Health Association of Dallas	N/A	N/A	751,042	794,114	820,611
Salvation Army	5,651,471	3,760,773	5,404,619	6,485,716	6,444,254
Information & Referral Hotline+	N/A	N/A	1,169,708	796,817	N/A

Source: United Way of Texas, 1988b.

Notes: *UW of San Antonio did not report its allocations.
    +provided specifically by the United Way

These data illustrate problems typical in tracking the funding of foundations and other voluntary organizations: broad program categories and inaccurate data. The local United Way agencies, for example, do not always report their funding to United Way of Texas, which skews that data, as indicated in the table by the figures for 1985. Moreover, the funding in the table includes allocations to agencies that provide programs for individuals beyond the CMI. This problem can also lead to a misinterpretation of the data. Unfortunately, no further detailed information is available at the state level.

The budgets of local United Way agencies provide more insight into the function of this organization in Texas. These data indicate a wide range of funding based on the priorities and sizes of each community. The United Way of Austin, for example, in calendar year 1988 provided the Salvation Army with $364,466 and the information and referral hotline at the ATCMHMRC with $14,955 (Berliner, Interview, November 18, 1988). The United Way of El Paso in 1988 provided the Salvation Army $205,000; MHA $6,000; Memorial Park Day Treatment Center for Adults (for Mental Health and Mental Retardation) $47,580; and Casa Blanca Halfway House $70,000 (United Way of El Paso, 1988). The United Way of Metropolitan Dallas in 1987 allocated $1,413,813 to the Salvation Army and $267,289 to the MHA of Dallas County (United Way of Metropolitan Dallas, 1988). Because the El Paso and especially the Dallas United Ways are much larger, these organizations are able to contribute a much more significant amount of funding for programs that affect the CMI.

The Mental Health Association

The Mental Health Association in Texas (MHAT) is another type of voluntary agency that helps the CMI. The MHAT defines its purpose as promoting "mental health; to work for improved prevention, research, detection and diagnosis of mental illnesses; and to improve care and treatment of persons with mental illnesses" (MHAT, 1988, p. 1). The LMHAs achieve this purpose mainly through advocacy and mutual support groups rather than through direct funding of services. For 1987, the total income for the MHAT was $673,125. The majority of this income came from special fund-raising events (47 percent), chapter assessments (22 percent), foundation grants (11 percent), and reimbursements on contracts (9 percent). The remainder came from the United Way and other contributions and interest payments (Hale, Interview, October 18, 1988).

Total expenditures for the MHAT for 1987 were $679,539. The program areas to which these funds were allocated are Community Services (30 percent), Public Affairs (42 percent), Organization Development (20 percent), Fund-raising Expenses (5 percent), and Management (3 percent) (Hale, Interview, October 18, 1988). These data include funding for many areas of mental health and are not strictly for the CMI. However, while the program areas listed above may not relate directly to the CMI, these areas (including organization development) are critical to the agency and provide services indirectly to the CMI; therefore, they should be included in funding assessments for the CMI in Texas.

There are 17 local MHAT chapters throughout the state. Like the United Way agencies, the amount of funds for these local chapters varies according to the size of the agency. For example, the budget for the Austin area MHA is quite small. According to its executive director, Wayne Ewen, the agency has received a small grant (approximately $9,000) from the Hogg Foundation to investigate the issue of boarding homes for the mentally ill in the Austin area. The MHA in Austin has worked to facilitate communication between boarding home providers and the ATCMHMRC to, hopefully, lead to the provision of shelter to more mentally ill individuals in the Austin area (Ewen, Interview, November 18, 1988).

The MHA in Greater San Antonio has a much larger budget of $386,863 (for 1986), and its allocation to support programs for 1986 was $365,210. These figures represent the funding input of the LMHAs, which affects the CMI more through advocacy than through direct services (Mental Health Association of Greater San Antonio, 1988).

The Texas Alliance for the Mentally Ill

The Texas Alliance for the Mentally Ill (TEXAMI) is another major voluntary organization for the CMI in Texas. TEXAMI is a nonprofit volunteer service organization affiliated with the National Alliance for the Mentally Ill. TEXAMI currently has 24 chapters in the state and a membership of approximately 3,000 families (Peterson, Interview, November 18, 1988; Hearon, Interview, November 18, 1988).

TEXAMI's purpose is fourfold. First, agency members serve as advocates for the mentally ill and their families. The members work to eradicate the stigma associated with mental illness through active community awareness programs. They also seek to educate legislators concerning needed systems of care to be provided by family advocates to help those who suffer severe and disabling mental illness.

Second, the members provide support service for the families and relatives of the mentally ill. With this service, TEXAMI serves as a mutual help group. Family members and friends of the family are able to speak about the stress and stigma of having a mentally ill family member.

Third, TEXAMI works to secure support for research on issues related to the mentally ill. Such research includes areas of rehabilitation and the delivery of efficient and effective services for the seriously mentally ill. The agency also attempts to improve the quality of diagnosis and the responsible use of medication.

Finally, TEXAMI serves an educational purpose. The agency works to educate family members of the mentally ill, as well as the general public, about the nature of mental illness and ways to cope with it. Through these numerous activities, TEXAMI aims to serve the mentally ill, family members of the mentally ill, and the general public in regard to mental health issues (Peterson, Interview, November 18, 1988; Hearon, Interview, November 18, 1988).

For 1988, the entire budget for TEXAMI was $47,000. This budget is broken down into several categories: administration (main office, telephone expenses, postage, contract employees); affiliate relations (newsletter); affiliate training (training manuals, workshops, startup funds for new affiliates); conventions (annual TEXAMI statewide convention); advocacy (contacts with the legislature); and miscellaneous expenses (Peterson, Interview, November 18, 1988; Hearon, Interview, November 18, 1988).

These dollar figures are very small in comparison with funds provided by agencies like the Robert Wood Johnson Foundation, and especially the TDMHMR budget. However, it is critical to recognize that many activities of these voluntary organizations go beyond provision of direct services. The advocacy work of agencies like TEXAMI and MHA often leads to legislation which significantly impacts TDMHMR and the furnishing of services to the CMI, but is not truly identifiable in the budgets of an MHAT or any other group.

The Salvation Army

The Salvation Army is another type of service organization that provides help, directly and indirectly, to the CMI in Texas. The Salvation Army was founded in 1865 as an international religious and charitable organization. This organization sees its role as "expressed by a spiritual ministry, the purposes of which are to preach the Gospel, disseminate Christian truths, supply basic human necessities, provide personal counseling and undertake the spiritual and moral regeneration and physical rehabilitation of all persons in need who come within its sphere of influence regardless of race, color, creed, sex or age" (Salvation Army, 1987, p. 2).

Social services provided to residents and the homeless include food, utilities, clothing, rent, medicine, and transportation. In larger cities, additional services are provided such as live-in programs with child care, counseling, employment services, budget training, and parenting. Tables 16.7 and 16.8 list service information regarding all the Salvation Armies throughout Texas.

Table 16.7. Salvation Army Services Provided in Texas in 1987

Resident individuals served	459,022
Transient individuals served	140,396
Individuals served at Christmas	402,226
Persons visited in nursing homes	253,754
Pre-release parolees from prisons aided	2,798
Inmates in prisons assisted	6,961
Alcoholics given lodgings	44,709
Campers in summer camp program	3,480
Number of camp days	16,172
Elderly served in Senior Citizen programs	10,714
Total number of persons served in 1987	931,837
Total number of volunteers	37,660
Number of volunteer hours	309,361

Source: Salvation Army, 1987.

Table 16.8. Salvation Army Service Unit Welfare Programs for 1987

Service	Individuals Served
Grocery orders given	15,966
Utilities paid	5,581
Rent paid	948
Garments and shoes provided	1,357
Transportation provided	970
Gas and oil orders given	5,752
Medical aid	1,665
Boys sent to camp	1,134
Christmas dinner provided	3,782
Children given toys	1,531
Miscellaneous aid	2,339
Services to the homeless	
Lodgings provided	3,425
Grocery orders and/or meals	4,157
Transportation provided	1,380
Gas and oil orders given	4,207
Miscellaneous aid	1,284
Total cases served	49,031

Source: Salvation Army, 1987.

Across the state of Texas, over $45,000,000 was spent in these care and welfare programs (Salvation Army, 1987). The Salvation Army also has five Adult Rehabilitation Centers (ARC) located in Austin, Dallas, Fort Worth, Houston, and San Antonio. In these centers, client-residents take calls and pick up items from people who want to donate furniture, clothing, and other household items. The residents collect, refurbish, and organize the donated pieces for sale in the Salvation Army Thrift Stores, and the money earned from the sales is used to pay for the ARC program.

Residents arrive at the centers daily, suffering from social, physical, spiritual, personal, family, or substance abuse problems. A resident works and lives at the center for at least 90 days or until both the resident and the counselor feel that he or she is able to go out into the world again. Meanwhile, the resident is expected to participate in group therapy, Alcoholics Anonymous, and other programs, and may choose to make use of the religious ministry available. In 1987, 2,448 men received rehabilitation care through the ARC program (Salvation Army, 1987).

Each of the services and programs provided by the Salvation Army represents a significant contribution to indigent members of society and in particular, the homeless. Many studies indicate that the CMI constitute between 25 percent and 50 percent of the homeless population (Levine and Stockdill, 1986, p. 5). Therefore, a large portion of the services and funds provided by agencies like the Salvation Army is contributed directly and indirectly to the CMI.

One service provided through the Salvation Army that directly affects the CMI is the Mobile Outreach Program. This program was established by the ATCMHMRC through a grant from the Robert Wood Johnson Foundation to respond to the needs of those who do not seek out help or who do not comply with treatment medications. The two MHMR caseworkers at the Salvation Army travel to the scenes of incidents to assist persons demonstrating signs of mental illness. This team conducts aggressive outreach across the county to identify those who do not seek, but who are identified as appropriate candidates for, the Mobile Outreach Program. The team supplies the clients with immediate necessities such as food, shelter, and clothing, and facilitates access to both medical and psychiatric care. When the client is provided with these necessities, the MHMR caseworkers can focus on moving the client into a stable environment with appropriate, ongoing mental health services. Once the client is linked with a treatment center unit, the caseworkers maintain contact to assure that the client is following through with necessary treatment (Kingsbury, Interview, December 14, 1988). This program is one of several in which the Salvation Army is involved in providing services to the CMI in Texas.

The Disciple Outreach for the Mentally Ill

Church organizations are another major source of provisions for society's indigent, particularly the CMI. The Disciple Outreach for the Mentally Ill (DOMI) is one such program. In 1982, the organizational board of the Disciples of Christ developed the goal of providing ministry for those suffering from long-term mental illness. These individuals were targeted and defined as people with a history of state hospitalization, whose ages usually range from the 20s to early 30s (Coleman, Interview, November 17, 1988).

DOMI is a tax-exempt organization supported by the Disciples of Christ, in association with Texas Christian University and Jarvis Christian College. Some affiliates of DOMI include Central Christian Church, Hyde Park Baptist Church, Shepherd of the Hills Christian Church, and Bluebonnet Hills Christian Church. The major focus of the program is in Austin because many of the organization's board members are located in Austin.

DOMI joined efforts with the ATCMHMRC and received a grant from the Hogg Foundation of $250,000 for a five-year period to pay for staff training. After it partnered with ATCMHMRC, DOMI purchased a house for $32,000 from Soroptomist International and the Texas Commission for the Blind in 1987. The ATCMHMRC moved its Fairweather Lodge training program and now serves an oversight role in staffing the program. The Travis County Commissioner's Court contributed $43,000 ($20,000 for renovations and $23,000 for furnishings). DOMI added $20,000 more for renovations. The Texas Rehabilitation Commission contributed approximately $15,000 for equipment and supplies to train the residents. The equipment and supplies, including buffers, mops, and miscellaneous cleaning equipment, give the residents the needed tools to set up as work groups with jobs in the community and to learn the necessary social skills to become independent. The house is now referred to as Harbor House.

Funding for DOMI comes from fund-raising through the congregations of participating churches. Its budget for 1988 was approximately $6,000-$8,000. These funds go toward the program through mailings and services like emergency services, food, etc. The money for staffing is contributed by the ATCMHMRC. The start-up costs were also funded by ATCMHMRC. These costs are minimal because the MHMR center pays for utilities and food only for a short period, as each group begins paying its own bills soon after it is established in the community (Coleman, Interview, November 17, 1988).

These church organizations provide direct services (such as clothing, food, and shelter), as well as less quantifiable but extremely vital services such as helping set up the CMI in the community. The role of these and other religious organizations, despite small funding, must be considered when estimating the services provided to the CMI in Texas.

CONCLUSIONS

This chapter gives only a partial account of the actual money involved in serving the CMI. For example, many of the smaller foundations which offer grants that help the mentally ill are not listed, nor is the role of volunteer/charity hospitals addressed in this chapter. Therefore, much further research, including data regarding all grant funding in Texas and more detailed information on the local chapters of organizations like the United Way, the Salvation Army, and the MHA, as well as information addressing the double-counting of funding dollars, is needed for a further assessment of voluntary agencies. More accurate information, including the direct and indirect services provided, the actual budgets of agencies, and the number of volunteer hours dedicated at all levels (federal, state, local, and nonprofit agencies) in Texas, is necessary to identify and quantify the true value of voluntary agencies and volunteers in providing care for the CMI in Texas.

The League of Women Voters of Texas conducted a survey of consumers and community leaders in Texas MHMR center areas which identified many problems where voluntary organizations could have significant impact. Among the community leaders interviewed it was felt that the greatest need in their communities was to increase awareness of issues relating to mental illness, more education, and more involvement and advocacy on these issues (Texas League of Women Voters, 1989, p. 20). These are places where voluntary organizations can have a great deal of influence when the fiscal hands of government agencies are tied. Voluntary organizations fill in the gaps that government cannot. These organizations fulfill a very important role that is more than the number of dollars expended or the number of hours of volunteer time donated.

References

Austin State Hospital. December 1988. <u>Annual Report - Volunteer Services</u>. Austin, Texas.

Berliner, Susan. 1988. Director, United Way of Austin, Austin, Texas. Telephone interview by Katherine Fahey, November 18.

Coleman, Rod. 1988. Director, Disciples Outreach for the Mentally Ill, Austin, Texas. Interview with Katherine Fahey, November 17.

Ewen, Wayne. 1988. Executive Director, Mental Health Association in Austin, Austin, Texas. Telephone interview by Katherine Fahey, November 18.

Ferris, Paul. 1988. Program Director, Robert Wood Johnson Grant, Austin-Travis County Mental Health and Mental Retardation Center, Austin, Texas. Telephone interview by Katherine Fahey, December 19.

Hale, Karen. 1988. Associate Director, Mental Health Association in Texas, Austin, Texas. Telephone interview by Katherine Fahey, October 18.

Hearon, Genevieve. 1988. Associate Director, Texas Alliance for the Mentally Ill, Austin, Texas. Interview by Rudolfo Vega, November 18.

Hogg Foundation for Mental Health. 1987. <u>Annual Report, 1986-1987.</u> Austin, Texas.

Kovacs, Ruth, ed. 1988. <u>The Foundation Grants Index</u>. 17th ed. New York, New York: The Foundation Center.

Kramer, Ralph M. 1987. "Voluntary Agencies and the Personal Social Services." In <u>The Non-Profit Sector: A Research Handbook</u>, ed. Walter W. Powell. New Haven, Connecticut: Yale University Press.

Kingsbury, Ron. 1988. Salvation Army Mobile Outreach Team, Austin, Texas. Interview by Norma Rodriguez, December 14.

Levine, Irene S., and James W. Stockdill. 1986. "Mentally Ill and the Homeless: A National Problem." In <u>Treating the Homeless: Urban Psychiatry's Challenge</u>, ed. Billy E. Jones. Washington, D.C.: American Psychiatric Association Press, Inc.

Mental Health Association of Greater San Antonio. 1987. <u>Annual Report 1986-1987</u>. San Antonio, Texas.

Mental Health Association in Texas (MHAT). 1988. <u>Annual Report 1987</u>. Austin, Texas.

Peterson, George. 1988. Associate Director, Texas Alliance for the Mentally Ill, Austin, Texas. Interview by Rudolfo Vega, November 18.

Robert Wood Johnson Foundation (RWJF). 1988. <u>Program for Chronic Mental Illness</u>. Boston, Mass.

Salvation Army. 1987. <u>Annual Report to Governor Clements</u>. Austin, Texas.

Texas League of Women Voters. 1989. "Perceptions of Community-Services for People with Serious Mental Illness in Texas: A Survey of Consumers and Community Leaders in Texas Mental Health and Mental Retardation Center Areas." LWVT Education Fund, Austin, Texas.

Turtle Creek Manor, Inc. 1988. "Turtle Creek Manor." Dallas, Texas. (Pamphlet.)

United Way of El Paso. 1988. "Budget Data." El Paso, Texas.

United Way of Houston. 1988. Annual Report of 1987-1988. Houston, Texas.

United Way of Metropolitan Dallas. 1987. Annual Report 1987. Dallas, Texas.

United Way of San Antonio. 1988. Annual Report 1987-1988. San Antonio, Texas.

United Way of Texas. 1988a. Mission Statement. Austin, Texas.

_____. 1988b. "Budget Data." Austin, Texas.

United Way of Texas. 1988c. "Volunteer Statistics: Texas United Ways and Associates - Estimated, 1988." Austin, Texas.

Chapter 17. Conclusions and Recommendations[*]

The preceding chapters have attempted to piece together the intricacies of the public mental health system in Texas. This examination has revealed a very complex system with complex problems that defy simple solutions. However, this volume is unique in that all of the components of this state's public mental health system have never before been described in as comprehensive a fashion. This chapter will draw on the evidence presented above and offer conclusions about and recommendations for the future of public mental health in Texas.

Our examination of the client population provided a very detailed picture of TDMHMR's case load. One important point that this discussion does show is the need for greater coordination between the state hospitals and the CMHMRCs. Of all individuals admitted to the state hospitals from FY 1984 through 1988, only 56.3 percent have a recorded community assignment. Equally important is the finding that only 11.3 percent of the total number have been assigned to case management services. Somewhere between the state hospitals and the CMHMRCs, 43.7 percent of the people admitted disappear before they can receive services in the community. This may be due simply to failure to record a person on the CARE system. This would appear to show that there is not only need for greater coordination, but also incentives for the CMHMRCs to locate and treat these clients and to record them.

The chapter on the minority populations in Texas showed that there needs to be increasing attention paid to cultural relevance in mental health service delivery. The demographic makeup in this state will change significantly in this generation. It is estimated that by 1995, no racial or ethnic group will represent a majority of the population in the public schools. By the first quarter of the next century there will be no racial or ethnic group which will represent a majority of the under 65 population (Hogg Foundation for Mental Health, 1990, p. 16). There is a shortage of mental health professionals who are members of these minority populations or who speak any language other than English. TDMHMR and the CMHMRCs need to provide training programs for all staff members to acquaint them with other cultures and traditions which have bearing on mental health and mental illness (Hogg Foundation for Mental Health, 1990, p. 17).

Our discussion regarding the care and treatment of the mentally impaired offender documents the importance of developing programs for law enforcement officers so that they can deal sympathetically and effectively with this population. Although there are model programs in Texas, they need to be expanded.

The provision of services to the mentally ill through the CMHMRCs was thoroughly detailed in Section Two of this volume. The provision of community-based services, while vastly improved during the past decade, is still in great need of improvement. Probably the greatest need lies in residential services for TDMHMR's client population. Until recently the only residential services that were provided for the mentally ill were in state hospitals. However, in this era of deinstitutionalization, persons with severe and persistent mental illness find it difficult to obtain adequate, safe, and affordable housing in a competitive market (Hogg Foundation for Mental Health, 1990, p. 14). Often, these persons find themselves dealing with the stresses of living on the street and increased odds of further readmissions to the state hospital.

---

[*]This chapter was written by Joellen M. Harper, Nicholas L. Hoover, Ronnie G. Jung, and Janice Rienstra.

The need for improved housing services for the chronically mentally ill was emphasized by a recent report published by the Hogg Foundation for Mental Health entitled "Texans With Severe Mental Illness: Recommendations for Action." That report pointed out that "the housing needs of Texas with severe and persistent mental illness are not being met. The mental health system's approach has been to provide residential treatment options that are severely limited, difficult to access, and based on the expectation that consumers will improve in 90 days or less and go on to independent living. A major difficulty with this assumption is that many people do not make the expected clinical improvement within this unrealistic time limit" (Hogg Foundation for Mental Health, 1990, p. 15). Often, the only housing available is unregistered board and care homes which cannot provide the services or support this population needs.

There needs to be greater emphasis placed on shifting the state's focus from institutional housing and treatment to community-based residential housing support. The limited funds that are available could be spent effectively on real housing assistance such as rent subsidies or household startup costs and support programs to aid clients in keeping housing once they get settled. To accompany this shift in focus, there should be legislative action to make provision of residential alternatives and supported housing a "core service" to be provided by all CMHMRCs. This designation would show the importance given this service at the state and local levels and would encourage more funding to flow to these much needed services (Hogg Foundation for Mental Health, 1990, p. 15).

The provision of adequate housing in the community can be the first step toward independent living. However, other services are needed by clients in the community in order to make a successful transition to the community. Case management services should be in place for clients to help identify and coordinate needed services and opportunities. Case management is a core service as defined by the Texas legislature. In spite of this, only 7 percent of individuals receiving services at community centers are involved in case management programs (Hogg Foundation for Mental Health, 1990, p. 16).

There must be community resources cultivated to serve this population, for the case management system can only be as effective as the local services that are available for the case managers to employ. The number of individuals served by case management must also be increased with a corresponding decrease in the number of people on waiting lists for services. But there must also be a decrease in the case load of individual case managers. More case managers will have to be hired. The recent expansion of Medicaid to cover case management services will help in this effort, but there will have to be increased state support for improvement of case management services.

Section Three attempted to pull together relevant financial information about financing for the chronically mentally ill. The five-year summary information of Texas Department of Mental Health and Mental Retardation operations and for the community mental health and mental retardation centers has not previously been compiled and made available for analysis and review. This information is critical in analyzing any trends or patterns in mental health funding in Texas.

Although the total funding picture for mental health services is complex and involves many players, it is obvious that the key in Texas for the mentally ill is in the hands of the Texas Department of Mental Health and Mental Retardation and the community mental health and mental retardation centers. Significant progress has been made in moving patients to the community as the center for providing mental health services. Current legislative appropriations have reaffirmed the state's commitment to provide additional funding at the local community level. With this increased funding comes a continued need to be accountable for the quality and quantity of services at the community level. Currently state hospitals are under scrutiny by the courts as part of a federal lawsuit to ensure a certain level of service. The quality of services at the community level has not received the same level of scrutiny as the state hospitals. Services at the community level may be the next area of litigation in the continuing saga of dealing with the federal courts.

Section Three also presents a detailed discussion of financing alternatives for expanding Medicaid benefits for the mentally ill. These options deserve serious consideration in attempting to provide the maximum benefits available to the chronically mentally ill. The recent inclusion of targeted case management for the mentally ill into the state Medicaid plan and the forthcoming addition of the rehabilitative services option will go very far in increasing the amount of federal Medicaid funds for mental health services. However, the state's aversion to the addition of the options for institutes for mental diseases for those under 22 and over 64 allows tens of millions of dollars in Medicaid eligible funds to go unmatched. While the potential for private-sector participation in this option could possibly be significant, there is great potential for the state to provide these inpatient services at a 61 percent discount.

The tremendous economic burden imposed by chronic mental illness is the driving force behind the need for reshaping the system of financing the care of persons with chronic mental illness (Goldman, 1987, p. 581). Strategies should be developed for changing the way components of the mental health and related human services system actually work. One problem in such strategies is deciding what sort of changes are desirable and what kinds of incentives, penalties, or other devices are likely to bring them about (Rivlin, 1977, p. 383). Five major recommendations for the improvement of the system are discussed below. These are (1) increase funding from federal, state, and local governments; (2) focus state policy on long-term community-based care; (3) organize the system to provide long-term community-based services; (4) design financing mechanism to support long-term community care; and (5) develop system-wide accountability standards and performance incentives.

INCREASE FUNDING

The major problem in the financial structure of Texas mental health services is the overall low level of funds from all sources, which has a fairly even, across-the-board impact on the entire system of inpatient and community-based services. Many persons with serious mental illness receive inadequate services; many others in need receive no services at all.

Texas' basic financing structure for mental health services remains much the same as it was in the 19th century, when the state assumed complete responsibility for care of persons with mental illness. In FY 1988, TDMHMR reported its revenues by source for mental health services as 94.6 percent state, 4.0 percent federal, and 1.4 percent other (TDMHMR, 1989, p. 17).

The costs of public mental health care are too great for the state to bear alone. Significant efforts should be made to expand the degree of financial participation by federal and local governments, in addition to efforts to increase the level of state appropriations and augment other resources available to mental health clients through improved state agency coordination.

If Texas increases the federal proportion of its mental health resources to the average of other states, it could add between $81 and $264 million each year to its mental health budget (Hoover, 1990, p. 88). Under the Medicaid program, there are eight amendments which could fund outpatient mental health services and two amendments which could benefit outpatient mental health services. In 1986, Texas was the only state of the ten largest that did not participate in any of these Medicaid plan amendments. The clinic option and the rehabilitative services option are the most widely used options for outpatient mental health services. By moving appropriate clients from the state hospitals to community settings, and by using the associated state hospital funds as Medicaid match for those eligible, up to one-half the cost of community-based treatment could be funded by the federal government (Craig and Kissell, 1987, p. 17).

The Texas legislature is not likely to appropriate significant amounts of additional funds for public mental health services. However, there are at least two strategies that TDMHMR could pursue which might assist its efforts to increase its state appropriations at a higher incremental rate than it has received in the past. The first strategy is to improve the quality of the information used to support its legislative budget requests. The budget requests for the last two biennia contain little supporting information to justify the continuation of dollars requested or to demonstrate how the new dollars requested would be used (TDMHMR, 1988; TDMHMR, 1987).

The second strategy, since public mental heath services in Texas operate in a political arena, is for TDMHMR to take steps which would help unite the efforts of its constituent consumer, advocate, professional, and provider groups and the general public. A collective effort to inform legislators of the inadequacy of existing services, the great size of the unmet need, and the resultant indirect cost to the public for jail, hospital, public health, welfare, and other services used by persons with mental illness may help to increase the level of direct state appropriations for public mental health services.

TDMHMR should exert a much greater effort to coordinate services for persons with mental illness with other large state human service agencies, including the Texas Department of Human Resources, the Texas Commission on Alcohol and Drug Abuse, the Texas Department of Health, and the Texas Rehabilitation Commission. Clients of community-based mental health services often need services from these agencies; the lack of coordination of policies and procedures at the state level seriously hampers the accessibility of necessary services at the community level. Agency boundaries become service barriers. Effective coordination and elimination of services barriers could serve to enhance the necessary supportive resources available to mentally ill persons in the community without requiring a substantial expenditure of new funds.

Most city and county governments in Texas contribute little to the payment for public mental health care. In Texas, local tax funds averaged less than 15 percent of all the CMHMRCs' total FY 1989 mental health budgets. This proportion is greatly below that contributed by local governments in some other states. In Ohio, counties contributed 39.9 percent of the total budget of that state's 53 community mental health boards in FY 1988 (ODMH, 1988). Several states (e.g., Colorado, Illinois, Ohio) have passed legislation authorizing counties to levy a mill tax to be used for funding local mental health services (National Conference of State Legislatures, 1986).

The potential for increasing the financial participation of local governments for care of persons with mental illness seems promising in light of apparently evolving beliefs about the respective roles of various levels of government for public mental health care. The current local match requirements under the CMHMRC performance contracts do not appear to serve as an incentive to local governments to contribute funds. Local match from those local governments served by state-operated outreach clinics is not required by TDMHMR, although it is required by statute. Normally, there is little or no funding that these communities can spare to provide mental health services. The only local match often comes from in-kind support. For example, communities often provide free furniture, supplies, and office space to the clinics (LBJ School of Public Affairs, 1990, p. 179).

Although few local governments contribute funds directly to public mental health services, many inadvertently fund a considerable portion of the indirect costs incurred as a result of inadequate mental health services. A recent study estimated that, over a 30-month period, the city and county governments in Bexar County paid for an estimated $550,000 in local jail, hospital, and public shelter costs for a group of 21 mentally ill persons (Diamond and Schnee, 1990).

Perhaps local governments could be persuaded to contribute funds directly to local community mental health services if it could be demonstrated that their costs for indirect services for mentally ill persons would be reduced as a result. A portion of the state's funds for community services should be structured as a state-local match designed to provide a state-funded base and encourage the participation of local governments. The state share should be based on indicators of needs and fiscal capacity and the match requirement should be based upon indicators of fiscal capacity.

LONG-TERM COMMUNITY-BASED CARE

The present state policies and practices for the definitions of its priority population and its mental health services emphasize acute care in state inpatient facilities. The definitions for the priority population and mental health services should be revised to reflect the long-term community-based service needs of persons with serious mental illness.

A major operational problem with both the statutory and administrative eligibility criteria is that they define persons in the priority population primarily in terms of their actual or potential presence in a state hospital, and not in terms of the presence of long-term functional disabilities characteristic of severe mental illness.

Mental health experts nearly unanimously agree that persons with serious and chronic mental illness are an extremely heterogeneous group, as identified by various degrees of disability along a number of dimensions (Vischi, 1988, p. 18). The salient point, for purposes of designing cost-effective services for this group, is that the chief distinguishing characteristic of chronic mental illness has been found to be prolonged functional disability caused or aggravated by severe mental disorders, not former hospitalization (Goldman, Gattozi, and Taube, 1981, p. 23).

Texas policy and practice for the definition of its priority population should be revised to emphasize the long-term community-based care needs, as well as the acute care needs, of this group. Eligibility for services should not be dependent on whether a person is, has been, or might be in a state hospital. An accurate and well-tracked assessment should be made of who and where these persons are and what their respective service needs are. This information leads to an effective operational definition of the priority population, to which state funds can be targeted and monitored for the entire system of mental health services, and not just the CMHMRCs.

ORGANIZE THE SYSTEM TO PROVIDE LONG-TERM COMMUNITY-BASED SERVICES

The current Texas system is really three systems of care; the state inpatient facilities are the *de facto* core of the system. The two public community-based mental health services systems, operated through the CMHMRCs and the state-funded hospital-outreach clinics, are administered and funded differentially. Moving the core of the system from an inpatient focus to a community-based focus will require a system-wide approach to organizational structure, as well as system-wide mechanisms for performance and accountability. This cannot be achieved with sole emphasis on the CMHMRCs.

The two existing separate, and unequal, systems of public community mental health services should be unified if system-wide goals are to be achieved. This implies equal resources as well as equal expectations. One possible answer is to move the administration of the state-operated outreach clinics from the state hospitals to a central state administrative unit, which would work actively with local governments to encourage the creation of CMHMRCs in those areas. The strengths of the CMHMRC structure, with local board direction, support of local governments, and their ability to leverage state funds with a variety of other funding sources, should be used to help change the focus and increase the financial resources of the system.

FINANCING MECHANISM TO SUPPORT LONG-TERM COMMUNITY CARE

Traditionally in Texas, there has been a system of "dollars follow the client" because the state hospitals received all of the funding and provided all of the care. Since deinstitutionalization, however, Texas has had a system of "clients follow the dollars" (ATCMHMRC, 1985, p. 3). Because community programs are not funded adequately to provide needed services, mental health clients must be admitted to state hospitals where a majority of the mental health funding continues to be spent.

More and more states (Washington, California, Arizona, Michigan, Wisconsin, Ohio) are choosing a system of mental health care financing in which the mental health dollars follow the clients to where they are receiving care. Texas has attempted to do this with the $35.50 program (discussed in Chapter 13). However, the $35.50 program represents a small percentage of the mental health funding and does not fully pay for services in the community or in the hospital, and it is not tied to specific clients. The most common way of structuring such a financing philosophy seems to be through establishment of county boards to act as the responsible entities. These boards receive all or most of the mental health dollars and take full responsibility for providing or contracting for the provision of all outpatient and inpatient mental health care, whether that care is given in a hospital or in the community.

Switching to a system like this in Texas would involve major changes in authority and financing. Currently, the state mental health authority--TDMHMR--receives most of the funding, which it distributes for provision of community services. A system modeled after the successful Wisconsin or Ohio systems would provide the majority of the funds to the responsible authorities in the community. Funding would be for specific clients, rather than for maintaining state hospitals that are underutilized, as in Texas.

Several issues must be addressed before implementing such a system. Local authorities, which would have financial, clinical, and administrative responsibility for the public mental health clients, must be established. TDMHMR must develop a binding contract for services with an effective monitoring system in place. Finally, TDMHMR must make a decision about the role of the state hospitals. Under some "dollars follow the client" systems, most mental health funding is sent to the local mental health authorities, which contract for inpatient care where they choose. Such a proposal would change radically the funding and the focus of the state hospitals. Current attempts to develop regionalization of spending still fall considerably short of putting most of the funding at the local level.

Texas' partial capitation financing through the $35.50 program is in a sense a backwards capitation program; the difference is that local mental health authorities are paid based on what they do not do (use bed-days) rather than for what they do (provide community-based mental health services) (Hale, Interview, March 15, 1989). A capitation system of financing public mental health care has many variables. First, there are many different levels of functioning of mental health clients; which clients receive care under the system depends upon the priorities within the state for serving the mentally ill population. Second, it must be decided which mental health services fall under the capitated price. The range includes basic medical care, full outpatient services, or comprehensive care, including inpatient services. Finally, the capitated price must be chosen. The price, while linked to the types of clients and services, must also include considerations of variations in population growth, availability of housing, and cost of living across the state.

A system of capitation could be implemented in Texas. The first step in implementing a capitation financing system is to define the population to be served. For Texas, the current priority population could be used; nevertheless, policy on who to serve must be clearly established. The services offered could also remain the same: the core services required by law, in addition to any other services that the local mental health authorities (LMHA) choose to provide, such as housing, substance abuse counseling, etc. However, since the service providers agree to supply a range of services, a unit cost accounting system must be established and used. Such a system would ensure that a comparable range of services is available statewide to all mental health clients. Third, access to services must be guaranteed. Currently, although programs and services exist, access is extremely limited. Finally, once again TDMHMR must decide upon the role of the state hospital. Under a capitation system of financing, the most appropriate role for the state hospital may be as the provider of long-term care. If that is the case, it is unlikely that there would be a need for the maintenance of eight facilities as they are currently used.

As noted above, choice of the capitated price must be based on consideration of a variety of factors. It is important to acknowledge that under this scheme the chosen price would not in fact cover the full cost of all the services provided to the clients, because the scheme does not assume that the capitated per person price is the only source of funds available to the LMHA for the provision of services. Federal, local, and third-party funds are purposely excluded in an attempt to closely parallel the proposal with the current system. One issue in particular that should be considered is whether to establish different capitated prices for different types of clients. For example, client characteristics that could be considered are diagnosis, prior hospitalizations, functional status, perceived health, coexisting physical problems, and coexisting social disadvantages (Lehman, 1987, p. 34). As is evident from the discussion above, implementation of a capitation system in Texas would involve major changes, but a capitation system would go far in adjusting the Texas system to one that ensures that appropriate services are provided to all clients who need them.

In 1984, there were many patients in the state hospitals who could be more appropriately placed in the community. That is not the situation in 1990. Continued reduction in the use of the state hospitals for acute care is desirable and could be achieved by requiring the LMHAs to pay for use of acute bed days. If the hospitals have a role to play in the delivery of mental health services, possibly in the provision of long-term care, that role should be acknowledged and incorporated into a financing system with a goal of appropriate care in the appropriate settings for all who need it.

The R. A. J. court case, and a companion case dealing with the mentally retarded, have established the priorities of Texas' mental health system by requiring the limited dollars to be used to reach specific goals. While these goals are desirable, unfortunately they allow Texas to ignore other segments of the population, such as children's mental health services and preventative services for the nonpriority population. A systematic view of the Texas system must be considered in setting goals and allocating limited mental health funds.

Every evaluation of the Texas mental health care system concludes that additional funding is needed. Expending funds for mental health services without a rational financing framework may not be terribly effective. Several options for new financing arrangements are included here. Unfortunately, while a successful financing system does much to improve the delivery of mental health services, it cannot do so indefinitely without adequate funding (Torrey, Wolfe, and Flynn, 1988, p. 50).

TDMHMR has made progress in developing its relationship with the CMHMRCs, particularly through the use of performance contracts. Unfortunately, no such progress has occurred with respect to the state-operated LMHAs. As a result, those areas served by state facility outreach programs continue to be underfunded and underserved. The department must clarify its relationship with all of the LMHAs, both state- and community-operated, in order to ensure sufficient and appropriate mental health care across the state.

Currently, the costs of mental health services vary substantially across the state, even allowing for differing economic conditions. TDMHMR must develop a system of accounting so that mental health services are priced with a unit cost. Such a system will allow better comparison of the costs and types of mental health services available in Texas and identification of areas lacking them.

TDMHMR has pursued the goal of equalization for three years. There are changes that must be made to the equalization formula to make it fair and rational. TDMHMR has acted to remove the $35.50 funds from the equalization formula and should be applauded for doing so. The inclusion of those performance funds in the budgeted formula reduced the incentive for centers below the CMHMRC average per capita level of state funding. The concentration of mentally ill in an area should be considered, given that some urban areas may have a large proportion of mentally ill. In addition, the population figures currently used by TDMHMR are projections made in 1986 that certainly don't represent the actual population of the state. Finally, state-operated community programs should be included in the equalization process. They are much less well funded than the CMHMRCs. Their omission in the equalization process perpetuates the inequalities in Texas.

SYSTEM-WIDE ACCOUNTABILITY STANDARDS AND PERFORMANCE INCENTIVES

To date, requirements for workload and performance measures have been limited to the CMHMRCs. In an interdependent system such as mental health services, improvements in accountability and performance cannot be achieved by one part of the system alone.

Administration of the CMHMRC performance contracts wholly lacks a systems approach. Requirements for the CMHMRCs must be matched with equivalent negotiations, requirements, and enforcement of standards with state inpatient facilities and a state-operated network of community mental health services. The goal should be to uniformly require that all components in the system work together to ensure provision of quality services to identified clients.

So long as the state hospital and CMHMRCs dealt with different populations, there was no clinical need to integrate their purposes. But when they serve the same patient, there are certain problems, such as continuity of care, entry and exit from each program, and the need for simultaneous services from several different agencies (Kraft,

1981, p. 361). Operationally, continuity of care exists to the extent that there are no obstacles to a client's either remaining in or moving from any of the direct treatment services needed and that administrative mechanisms exist to enable this (Barton and Sanborn, 1975, p. 131).

System-wide performance measures, if properly defined, would serve as a measure of how well the system components are working together. Performance measures have been defined as "operational specifications of how well an organization is functional along one or more dimensions that represent agreed-upon goals or values of the program" (Windle, 1986, p. 1). Performance measures should be quantitative, objective, and calibrated against some standard(s) that allow comparisons both within organizations over time and among different participating organizations (Windle, 1986, p. 1)

Standards for accountability and performance are only as good as their enforcement. Most of the service data which are currently self-reported by the CMHMRCs and the state-operated services should be monitored routinely and frequently. Clients who are eligible for state-supported services should be so certified by the state. The quality and adequacy of community-based services should be judged by the state's assessment of the welfare of the clients served, while local providers determine the service mix appropriate for each client.

Even if good system-wide performance measures are developed, the low level of overall system funding mitigates against true cooperation within the system. Demands for increased accountability from the mental health system are legitimate and should be met. However, without adequate funding, system accountability by itself cannot rectify the basic inequities in Texas's public mental health services.

Changes are necessary if further progress in mental health in Texas is to be made. Continued program evaluation is necessary to determine the correct course for Texas. The need for further research cannot be used as an excuse to delay action. Purposeful steps must be taken now to prevent Texas from slipping any further in the provision of mental health care.

References

Austin-Travis County Mental Health-Mental Retardation Center (ATCMHMRC). 1985. "The Dollar Follows the Patient." Austin, Texas.

Barton, W. E., and C. J. Sanborn, eds. 1975. An Assessment of the Community Mental Health Movement. Lexington, Mass.: Lexington Books.

Craig, Rebecca T., and M. Kissell. 1987. "1986--1987 Mental Health Issues and Select State Responses." Denver, Colo.: National Conference of State Legislatures.

Diamond, Pamela M., and Stephen Schnee. 1990. "Patterns of Multiple System Use Among 'Revolving Door' Clients." Paper presented to the 36th Annual Convention of the Southwestern Psychological Association. Dallas, Texas. (April 14.)

Goldman, H. H. 1987. "Financing the Mental Health System." Psychiatric Annals, vol. 17, no. 9 (September).

_____, A. Gattozi, and A. Taube. 1981. "Defining and Counting the Chronically Mentally Ill." Hospital and Community Psychiatry, vol. 32, no. 1 (January).

Hale, Karen. 1989. Associate Director, Mental Health Association in Texas, Austin, Texas. Interview by Joellen Harper, March 15.

Harper, Joellen M. 1990. "Financing Mental Health Care in Texas: Issues and Alternatives." Public Affairs Comment, vol. 36, no. 2 (Spring).

Hogg Foundation for Mental Health. 1990. "Texans With Severe Mental Illness: Recommendations for Action." A Report of the Commission on Community Care of the Mentally Ill. Austin, Texas.

Hoover, Nicholas L. 1990. The Expansion of Medicaid to Cover Mental Health Services in Texas. Professional report, Lyndon B. Johnson School of Public Affairs, Austin, Texas.

Kraft, A. M. 1981. "Systems for the Chronically Mentally Ill." In The Chronic Mentally Ill: Treatment, Programs, Systems, ed. J. A. Talbott. New York, New York: Human Sciences Press.

Lehman, Anthony F. 1987. "Capitation Payment and Mental Health Care: A Review of the Opportunities and Risks." Hospital and Community Psychiatry, vol. 38, no. 1 (January).

Lyndon B. Johnson (LBJ) School of Public Affairs. 1990. Community Mental Health in Texas: Four Case Studies. Special Project Report, LBJ School of Public Affairs/Hogg Foundation for Mental Health, Austin, Texas.

National Conference of State Legislatures. 1986. "Selected Legislation, Proposed and Enacted, Relating to Mental Health Services Funding." Denver, Colo.

Ohio Department of Mental Health (ODMH). 1988. Annual Report for Fiscal Year 1988. Columbus, Ohio.

Rienstra, Janice Virginia Briggs. 1990. Financing Community Mental Health Services in Texas. Professional report, Lyndon B. Johnson School of Public Affairs, Austin, Texas.

Rivlin, A. M. 1977. "Social Policy: Alternate Strategies for the Federal Government." In *Public Expenditure and Policy Analysis*, 2nd ed., ed. R. H. Haverman and J. Margolis. Chicago, Ill.: Rand McNally.

Texas Department of Mental Health and Mental Retardation (TDMHMR). 1987. "FY 1988-1989 Legislative Appropriations Request, Second Submittal." Austin, Texas.

_____. 1988. "FY 1990-1991 Legislative Appropriations Request, Second Submittal." Austin, Texas.

_____. 1989. "FY 1989 Operating Budget." Austin, Texas.

Torrey, E. Fuller, Sidney M. Wolfe, and Laurie M. Flynn. 1988. *Care of the Seriously Mentally Ill: A Rating of State Programs*, 2nd ed. Washington, D.C.: Public Citizen Health Research Group and the National Alliance for the Mentally Ill.

Vischi, T. R. 1988. *Financing Community Services for Person with Severe and Disabling Mental Illness: A Technical Assistance Manual*. Rockville, Maryland: National Institute for Mental Health.

Windle, C. 1986. "An Orientation to Performance Measurement." In National Institute for Mental Health. *Mental Health Program Performance Measurement*. Series BN No. 7. USDHHS Pub. No. (ADM)86-1441. Washington, D.C.